The Giant Book of
Murder

The Giant Book of Murder

Edited by Roger Wilkes

Magpie Books, London

Constable & Robinson Ltd
3 The Lanchesters
162 Fulham Palace Road
London W6 9ER
www.constablerobinson.com

First published in the UK as
The Mammoth Book of Murder and Science by Robinson,
an imprint of Constable & Robinson Ltd 2000

This edition published by Magpie Books,
an imprint of Constable & Robinson Ltd 2006

A copy of the British Library Cataloguing in
Publication Data is available from the British Library

ISBN-10: 1-84529-204-9
ISBN-13: 978-1-84529-204-1

Printed and bound in the EU

1 3 5 7 9 10 8 6 4 2

CONTENTS

VI CONTENTS

INTRODUCTION

In the 1930s, when the mass-circulation Sunday newspapers still savoured faintly of brown stout and chitterlings, a headline in the old *Empire News* proclaimed: TWO HAIRS HANGED THIS MAN! The story beneath was a startling example of how modern forensic science was finally getting the better of criminals like William Podmore, hanged (it seemed) on the evidence of two tiny hairs. Like most murderers, Podmore was a stupid and unattractive man who mistakenly believed he could get away with it. He had tried to swindle a man called Vivian Messiter, who'd given him a job not knowing his history as a fraudster. When Messiter realized he was being duped, he confronted Podmore who seized a heavy hammer and smashed it down on Messiter's face, killing him. Not two hairs but one, a single wiry hair from Messiter's eyebrow, was later found on the hammer, but what landed Podmore on the hangman's trap was not a hair at all but a stubby, grubby pencil. A receipt book was also recovered containing records of Podmore's fraudulent dealings with Messiter. The top copies had been torn out, but the pencil used to write up these transactions had left tell-tale indentations on the pages beneath. The appliance of science came when the police photographed these indented pages using special lighting. The wretched Podmore was hanged, not on the strength of microscopic hairs but by the ghosts of a few hastily-jotted names, dates and places. What helped to propel the case to public notice was the appearance at Podmore's trial of the celebrated pathologist

Sir Bernard Spilsbury. Ever since his spectacular debut at the Crippen trial in 1910, Spilsbury's name had made news. Revered by Bench and Bar, lionised by the public, Spilsbury had earned a reputation for infallibility. His evidence, low-key and matter-of-fact, had helped convict the likes of the poisonous Major Armstrong, Patrick Mahon – the Crumbles murderer, and Norman Thorne, the chicken-run killer. Although Spilsbury played only a small part in the case against Podmore, his appearance in the witness box sowed the seed of the legend about a man hanged on the strength of two hairs. "The revealing lens," confided the *Empire News*, "had focused on two tiny hairs on the weapon. Sir Bernard made up his mind very quickly. Hair . . . human . . . male . . . eyebrow . . . These two hairs pointed the killer to the police." The story had a fine Holmesian ring to it, but nothing else. As Spilsbury's biographers pointed out: "There was one hair, not two, on the hammer, and since it was Messiter's, not Podmore's and the hammer was never traced to Podmore, a whole scalp would not have pointed the killer to the police". And while it was the kind of story that appealed to a sensation-loving public, to the dour Spilsbury it was an irritating folderol. He detested personal publicity, and when he saw his carefully-weighed testimony reduced to a Sunday newspaper sideshow he was angry and ashamed. Shortly after the Podmore trial, Spilsbury got wind of a forthcoming book dealing with his career and cases. He was mortified and complained that it gave the impression of having been compiled from his personal case-notes. Spilsbury never understood the public fascination with the way in which science wages war on crime.

Criminals and scientists are old adversaries. For centuries, men of science peered through a glass darkly at the debris of murder. In the mid-eighteenth century, long before the modern tests devised by Marsh, Reinsch and Gutzeit, the detection of arsenic was a mightily inexact science. "Why do you believe it to be white arsenic?" Dr Anthony Addington was asked at the trial of Mary Blandy in 1752. Addington held aloft a parcel of powder, described it as milky white, like arsenic, gritty and almost insipid, and explained that although part of it floated on cold water, most sank to the bottom undissolved, again like arsenic. "This thrown on red-hot iron," Dr Addington added, "does not flame, but rises entirely in thick white fumes . . . white arsenic does the same." It was another hundred years before investigators in cases of suspected arsenic poisoning discarded their red-hot irons, for the mid-point of the Victorian age marked the dawn of the Age of Detection. With a backward glance to the Blandy case (the first recorded case of murder in which scientific evidence was adduced), this is the starting point for our exploration of the story of murder and science.

The cases collected here spin a scarlet thread running from the Age of Reason to our own computer age on the rim of the twenty-first century. Many tell of tremendous forensic triumphs, but others serve as a warning against trusting blindly to science.

The ancient Romans knew a surprising amount about crime and medicine. The physician Antistius examined the assassinated Julius Caesar and concluded that of the twenty-three stab wounds, only the chest wound had been mortal. The French surgeon Ambroise Paré (c.1510–90), the father of modern surgery, studied the effects of violence on the vital human organs. In Palermo, Fortunato Fidelis discovered how to tell an accidental drowning from one caused deliberately. In Rome Paolo Zacchia studied bullet wounds, cuts and stab wounds, stranglings and infanticide, and understood how to tell suicide from murder. In the late seventeenth century, the Italian anatomist Morgagni compared changes in the organs of the dead with the symptoms of the diseases that had killed them, so laying the foundations of the science of pathology. The microscope, invented around this time, enjoyed a forensic flowering in the nineteenth century, although the medical establishment took a sceptical view of such pioneers as Johann Ludwig Casper who produced his practical handbook of forensic medicine in 1856. Yet despite huge strides in the progress of Victorian medicine, the profession itself seemed dogged by taint. The public, marvelling at such achievements as the steam engine and electric telegraph, was impatient for similar life enhancements from the men of medicine. By mid-century, the doctors had yet to produce any. Their ranking in public esteem declined. To make matters worse, a celebrated few featured in notorious murder cases of the day, either as defendants or "expert" witnesses. At the trial of Dr Smethurst, the judge ticked off Crown counsel for baffling the jury with detailed medical evidence. The distinguished medical expert recruited by the Crown made such a hash of his tests for arsenic that he had to admit that none was present in the body of Smethurst's late lamented wife. Public confidence vanished. Professional reforms ensued.

Towards the century's end, a young assistant in the French Sureté, Alphonse Bertillon, developed a system of identification that classified various characteristics – size of head, fingers and so on – and codified them in an accessible way. His anthropometric system became known as Bertillonage and although it was widely adopted in Europe, the authorities in England, particularly Scotland Yard, remained sceptical. They pointed out that Bertillon's system was far from infallible because it failed to produce a unique set of data for each individual criminal. Something was needed that defined such an individual absolutely and uniquely. The answer was the fingerprint.

The ancient Chinese had recognized the potential of fingerprints, sealing their documents with thumbprints by way of a "signature". An English naturalist, Thomas Bewick, used wood-block engravings of his own fingerprints as an imprint on the books he published. In the early nineteenth century, a Czech physiologist called Purkinje set out a description of the nature of fingerprints and classified various kinds. But it wasn't until 1880 that an expatriate Scottish physician, Dr Henry Faulds, living in Japan, first recognized their forensic potential, suggesting that fingerprints found at the scene of a crime could lead to the conclusive identification of the culprit. His idea led to the publication in 1892 of the scientific exploration of fingerprints by Dr (later Sir) Francis Galton. This in turn prompted Edward Henry (later head of Scotland Yard) and an Argentinian researcher Juan Vucetich to develop more sophisticated classification systems for fingerprints. By the early 1900s, fingerprinting had become a front-line weapon in the fight against crime. In London in 1905 two brothers were convicted of murder on fingerprint evidence. How they earned their unique place in criminal annals is related here. So is the case of Emile Gourbin. He was caught out thanks to a break-through accomplished in 1910 by the French criminologist Edmond Locard of the University of Lyon who formulated his famous principle of interchange. This held that every criminal leaves something at a crime scene that wasn't there before and takes away something that he didn't have when he arrived. Locard's theory laid the cornerstone of modern criminal investigation, and became the basis of the "clue" in crime stories. It was applied with dramatic results as early as 1912 in the Gourbin case. Gourbin had murdered his mistress. Her face powder was analyzed under a microscope that by today's standards would seem clumsy and crude. Modern electron microscopes can magnify up to 150,000 times, making it possible to analyze the tiniest fragments of debris such as paint flakes, fibres, hairs, wood and paper and use them as evidence. Such technology, harnessed to revolutionary changes in police methods, has dramatically shortened the odds in their favour. In almost every country of the world, police forces have become more effective during the course of the twentieth century because they have come to terms with science and are ready and equipped to use it in the fight against crime. The discovery of DNA fingerprinting in the 1980s placed an awesome weapon at the disposal of crime investigators. With the Pitchfork case in the English Midlands, the new technique achieved early success (as the American writer Joseph Wambaugh recounts in these pages), but the full potential of genetic typing for crime fighters is still imperfectly understood.

This selection of cases – some famous, a few infamous and one or two, perhaps, less well-known – represents a series of milestones on the long haul from the forensic dark ages to the dawn of the new millennium. With only a few exceptions, I have chosen accounts by established writers in the true-crime field. The cases have all been written for the general reader, and no specialist or technical knowledge is needed to understand in each case how science proved decisive in the outcome. We meet murderers like the American, Professor Webster, whose furnace consumed almost (but not quite) enough of Dr Parkman to earn him the distinction of becoming the first of his countrymen to be convicted of murder without his victim's body being wholly present. Mark the similarities with the British case (exactly a century later) of the acid-bath monster Haigh. Both men reckoned without the enduring properties of false teeth, fragments of which, when sieved, raked and tweezed out of the murderous residuum, bit back from beyond the grave. For in death, nothing outlasts teeth, especially synthetic ones, and this durability makes them ideal as a means of identification. There are the riddles, written in scarlet, of Dr Sam Sheppard and Jeremy Bamber, both convicted on blood evidence, and the mystery, wrapped in an enigma, of the Australian dingo baby case, where blood and bite-marks combine. The great forensic breakthroughs of the twentieth century are charted, with landmark cases such as those of Dr Crippen (whose wife was identified because he'd unwittingly preserved the poison that had killed her) and another deadly doctor, Buck Ruxton (whose victims were identified by the superimposition of photographs). Also included are cases in which forensic science has been less footsure, as the Lindbergh baby kidnap case (the great American *cause celebre* of the 1930s) and the saga of the Birmingham Six, whose conviction and imprisonment for murderous IRA atrocities in the mid-1970s was shown to be demonstrably unsafe when, some twenty years later, the original forensic evidence was discredited.

An early American case involving questioned documents, cases in which dentists were able to identify murder victims from surgery records, and others in which the time of death – often a vital factor in assigning guilt – was fixed by examining stomach contents and even the pupation cycle of maggots: the stories that follow range across the entire spectrum of forensic science. Ballistics and bacteria, blood, teeth and hair all leave their traces on these pages. As the frontiers of forensic knowledge and expertise are pushed ever outwards, this is the kaleidoscopic story of how science and scientists have tried to meet the changing demands of crime investigators in their unending crusade against the complexities of murder.

WHO KILLED BAMBI?

(Jeremy Bamber, UK 1985)

Jim Shelley

Jeremy Bamber was convicted of murdering five of his own family in cold blood. At first detectives believed him when he blamed the killings on his deranged sister. But Bamber's jilted girlfriend denounced him to the police, and he was arrested a few weeks later. At his trial, the judge told Bamber that his conduct had been "evil beyond belief" and that for all his glamorous image and playboy lifestyle, the young farmer's son had "a warped, callous and evil mind." Bamber himself has always maintained his innocence. He says that when the killer rampaged through White House Farm on that dreadful harvest night, he was several miles away at home, in bed, alone, asleep. He insists it was his drug-fuelled sister Sheila who shot her sleeping twin sons and gunned down her adoptive parents before turning the gun on herself. The complex forensic evidence in this case principally concerned blood found in the silencer fitted to the murder weapon. Bamber and his lawyers challenge this evidence. The facts are examined here by the journalist Jim Shelley (b.1963) who wrote for The Guardian *for ten years. He now freelances and contributes a weekly TV column to* The Guardian Guide.*

This is a story about a silencer, a telephone call, an ex-girlfriend and a schizophrenic. It's a story about mass murder and the massive uncertainties surrounding it, involving two potential culprits but offering no obvious explanation. One of the suspects,

Sheila Caffell, is dead. The other, Jeremy Bamber, is serving five life sentences for something he says he didn't do. Bamber was found guilty in 1986 of killing his adoptive father and mother, his step-sister and her twin sons. The jury which convicted him had been divided, and after nine and a half hours of deliberation still couldn't reach a unanimous verdict. The judge eventually settled for a majority verdict of 10:2. So it's not surprising that every scenario that can be thrown up by the crime remains so clouded by inconclusive or questionable evidence. The press and the public, however, were in no doubt that Bamber was guilty.

In the early hours of Wednesday 7 August 1985, the bodies of Nevill and June Bamber, their adopted daughter Sheila "Bambi" Caffell and her two young children Daniel and Nicholas were found dead from multiple gunshot wounds at their home in Essex. In the mire of possibilities surrounding the events that night, one thing, at least, is certain: the killer was either Jeremy Bamber or his schizophrenic step-sister Sheila Caffell. The Bambers' son, Jeremy, had alerted police at about 3.30 a.m. and told them his father had just phoned him saying: "Please come over . . . Your sister has gone crazy and has got a gun."

This phone call ensured that the possibility of the perpetrator being some sort of deranged drifter or burglar or jealous ex-lover could be discounted, and fixed the possibility that Bamber himself was responsible for the killings at precisely 50 per cent. Either he was telling the truth, and "Bambi" had shot her family before turning the gun on herself, or he was lying in which case he was almost certainly responsible for the slaughter himself.

The bodies were found at the Bambers' farm in Tolleshunt D'Arcy, Essex, five miles from Jeremy Bamber's cottage, from where he phoned the police. Between them, the five victims had been shot twenty-five times by a .22 Anschutz semi-automatic rifle, mostly at extremely close range.

Sheila's six-year-old twins were found in their beds and were probably shot first in their sleep. Daniel had been shot five times through the back of the head and was found curled up in a foetal position, sucking his thumb. Nicholas had been shot three times, through the nose, cheek and eyebrow. Nevill and June were also shot in bed but had not died instantaneously. June had crawled across the bedroom, but died having been shot seven times, in the ear, neck, arm, chest, the right knee and, point blank, between the eyes.

Despite being shot twice in the bedroom, Nevill Bamber made it to the kitchen where, after what looked like a violent struggle, he was found dead slumped on a stool having received a further six shots to the head and neck. The kitchen phone was found off the hook. Finally, Sheila Caffell was found dead by her parents' bed from two gunshot wounds to her chin and throat. Her right hand was lying across the butt of a .22 rifle, which was across her chest, pointed upwards towards her head.

That Thursday's *Daily Mail* was in no doubt – "Drugs Probe After Massacre By Mother of Twins" – and certainly Sheila's wounds, together with Bamber's phone call, led police to treat the case as if only she could have committed the murders and had then committed suicide. The police were so certain at this stage about the case that shortly afterwards, many items from the crime scene, including bloodstained bedding and carpets, were destroyed.

But the 50 per cent chance that Bamber was the killer endured. There were two sets of fingerprints on the gun – Sheila's and Jeremy's. As the days passed, police suspicions changed. Fifty-three days after the bodies were found, Jeremy Bamber was charged with murder. He pleaded not guilty but a year later, on 28 October 1986, he was convicted of all five murders.

Sentencing him to life imprisonment, Mr Justice Drake described him as having "a warped, callous and evil mind . . ." and condemned his conduct as "evil beyond belief". But the uncertainties about the entire series of events on the murder night and the three days that followed remained. Bamber has always protested his innocence and in September 1993 made a second application for his case to be referred back to the Court of Appeal, an application that supporters of the campaign for his eventual release were confident he would win.

The campaign has raised serious doubts about the validity of his conviction, focusing on questionable forensic evidence, the judge's guidance to the jury, police incompetence and even possible fabrication of evidence.

Such are the circumstances of this case that neither Jeremy Bamber's guilt or his innocence has ever really been certain. Nevertheless the announcement that Bamber's solicitors had asked the Home Secretary to refer his case back to the Court of Appeal was greeted with a certain amount of disbelief: Jeremy Bamber was one of the most reviled criminals of the 1980s. The murders, if he committed them, were planned, pre-meditated and callous. And his motives seemed obvious.

Bamber was said to have actively disliked his adoptive family, and he stood to inherit an estate of 300 acres and over £430,000 from his parents' wills. He had already admitted stealing £980 in cash from the family's caravan site five months before the murders, offering the court a blunt explanation for the theft: "greed". But it was Bamber's conduct before and after the killings that really turned the tide of public opinion against him.

In the press and in court, Bamber was portrayed as appallingly arrogant and pompous. In an early exchange with the prosecution, when the QC accused him of not telling the truth, Bamber loftily replied: "That is what you have got to establish." It emerged in court that Bamber often complained to the family about not being made a company director and evidently aspired to a more glamorous lifestyle than his £100 a week farming job afforded him. He had celebrated the caravan burglary by drinking pink champagne and was generally portrayed as someone who longed for the good life. Much was made of his sun bed and his plan to buy a kit car.

It was said Bamber detested his parents because, having adopted him and Sheila as babies, they had then sent them to boarding school. It was alleged that he disliked Sheila and resented her success in London as a model, and the allowances made for her illnesses while he was stuck working on a farm in the sticks.

Even though Bamber was photographed weeping at the family's funeral, in the days immediately following the discovery of the bodies, relatives reported that he had showed little distress and seemed interested only in his parents' financial assets.

During the fifty-three days between the massacre and being charged, he was said to have spent freely and generally enjoyed himself, even travelling to Amsterdam. Immediately after the funeral he went on holiday to the south of France.

"He wanted to sell everything," said his ex-girlfriend. Through Sotheby's, he sold an antique clock, three paintings and some of the silver bequeathed to him, claiming later that he wanted to pay death duties without breaking up the farm. It was reported that before the funeral, he bought a Hugo Boss suit and a Rolex watch. His relative David Boutflour, who was involved in the discovery of the silencer which eventually helped convict Bamber, said he noticed Bamber looking at his watch at the funeral and remarking: "Come on, let's get out of here. Time's up."

The tabloids crucified him, particularly with the story that he had approached them with soft porn pictures of "Bambi" from her modelling days for which he wanted £100,000. In court, although the police doctor described how, when told of the deaths, Bamber broke down and cried and then vomited, other officers described him as "unusually cool" and "very calm", and even that he had told them he was "starving" and cooked himself breakfast.

But other than this emotive testimony, the evidence was slim. Bamber's fingerprints had been found on the murder weapon. But so had Sheila Caffell's. So, incidentally, had the prints of the police officer who picked up the gun with his bare hands. Bamber had explained how his prints had come to be on the murder weapon, telling police that on the day before the murders, he had taken the gun out to shoot rabbits.

The prosecution provided no other forensic evidence against Bamber from the scene, from his clothes or his person – no hairs, blood or bruising, no incriminating fibres and no gunshot residues – partly because police procedure had been so inadequate. (The police had destroyed the bedding and carpets from the bedrooms at Bamber's request – he said they were too upsetting – and left other examinations too late to be meaningful.) After an inquiry by the Chief Inspector of Constabulary in March 1989, the then Home Secretary, Douglas Hurd, endorsed eighteen recommendations to all police forces for future investigations. But a nineteen month inquiry by the Police Complaints Authority decided that no action was to be taken against officers, despite twenty-six specific complaints by Bamber – including thirteen allegations of tampering with evidence and perjury.

After the trial, Essex's deputy chief constable, Ronald Stone, admitted: "We were duped by a very clever young man". However, the prosecution's case had rested on three pieces of bizarre circumstantial evidence, all of which had been needlessly provided by the "very clever young man" himself.

According to the prosecution, the phone call that Bamber claimed to have received from his father had clearly been intended to establish Bamber's whereabouts at the time of the crime, placing him away from the scene and also placing the blame firmly with Sheila. Yet if it was intended as an alibi, the phone call – besides narrowing possible guilt to either himself or Sheila – actually left Bamber open to several difficult questions.

If Sheila had indeed gone berserk with a gun, wounding Nevill and June Bamber in bed, why had Nevill Bamber left his wife alone, at Sheila Caffell's mercy, to go to the kitchen and telephone Jeremy? And why, having made it downstairs to the phone, would he call Jeremy instead of dialling 999? It was suggested that Nevill Bamber would not have wanted to involve the police with the family's problems, though this might seem unlikely, especially as Jeremy was not close enough to Sheila to be the best person to pacify her.

Furthermore, Jeremy Bamber told the police that his father's call had ended abruptly ("the line went dead") and that when he phoned his father back "it was engaged each time". Would it technically have been possible for Jeremy Bamber to dial out and call the police if his phone was still connected to his father's line? And, if the telephone was, as Bamber said, engaged, who else did his father phone?

According to a police statement, the British Telecom telephonist on duty that night said that when she was asked by the police to check the line, she could "tell that the receiver was off the hook . . . I could hear a dog barking."

Shortly before police entered the house, the telephonist was asked to check again. "The line was still open. The only thing I could hear was a very slight moving sound." In order for this statement to be true, Nevill Bamber must have abuptly ended his call to his son, and called someone else, who never came forward. If he simply dropped the receiver while talking to his son, Bamber would not have been able to get a line and phone the police.

But simply because Bamber could not explain his father's actions, it did not necessarily follow that he had not received that call. The prosecution could not prove that he had not.

The most vital piece of evidence against Bamber was a silencer found in the Bambers' farmhouse several days after the murders.

It was discovered in the gun cupboard on 10 August by relatives of the deceased – June Bamber's niece, Christine Ann Eaton, and her brother, David Boutflour – who had gone to the farm to secure and remove the remaining firearms. They admitted they were "looking for clues", but emphasized "it was quite a surprise for us to find such particular essential pieces of gun lying in the cupboard".

Various members of the family saw it, and in their statements reported seeing a grey hair, traces of red paint, a large scratch and a dot of blood the size of a match-head.

According to Bamber's campaigners, of the thirty or forty police officers who had searched the farmhouse, at least three had searched the gun cupboard, even removing items (such as ammunition) from the very box that contained the silencer. Yet none of them came across it. The relatives took the silencer to Ann Eaton's house, but it was not collected by police until the evening of 12 August five days after the killings. It was examined on 13 August at the Home Office's forensic science laboratory at Huntingdon, and returned to Essex police the same day.

Thirty-six days after the killings, forensic scientist John Hayward examined the *inside* of the silencer and found blood that, he concluded, was of the same type as Sheila Caffell's, in an example of what is known as "backspatter". If the blood in the silencer *was* Sheila Caffell's, she plainly had not committed suicide. First, with the silencer attached, the gun would have become too long for her to have shot herself in the chin with it. Second, she could not, of course, have returned it to the gun cupboard after using it.

The prosecution's logic dictated that if Sheila Caffell could not have committed suicide, then she was murdered. If she was murdered, then Jeremy Bamber's story about the phone call was a lie. And if Jeremy Bamber was lying, then it could only have been for one reason. He was guilty.

Like the police with the gun, the Boutflours and the Eatons had omitted to wear gloves when handling the silencer, even though they had realized its importance. And they had kept it at their house from Saturday until Monday evening, before it was collected by the police for examination.

At the trial the family's version of events surrounding the silencer did not entirely tally, perhaps not surprisingly, as a year had passed since its discovery.

Some of them asserted that they had seen a grey hair on the silencer (similar to Nevill Bamber's), something the Judge brought up later (telling the jury that Hayward "was then asked about the grey hair that had been seen") even though this grey hair had never been produced in court. (It was said to have been lost by the police in transit.) David Boutflour was asked if the silencer was in the same box as "an ABU carrier bag". "I do not recall," he replied. "It may well have been in the second box."

Ann Eaton could not remember who had contacted the police ("probably me") and who had moved it: "I could have taken it upstairs, or my husband . . ." But, as she pointed out: "I never knew we were going to be put through all this."

In the end, it was a remarkable coincidence that the family's discovery proved so important, and that Bamber the adoptive son, was thus prevented from claiming the family inheritance.

Apart from the traces of blood, there was nothing to indicate that the silencer had been used. Malcolm Fletcher, a firearms expert for the prosecution, said: "I have been unable to establish whether any of these bullets or bullet fragments have been fired through a sound moderator [silencer]."

He admitted under cross-examination that a .22 calibre weapon was "the least likely" weapon to produce "backspatter", and that a silencer made it less likely still.

The jury were clearly troubled by the silencer, and even sent out a question to the judge during their deliberations, asking:

"What was the chance of the blood group being Mr and Mrs Bamber's?"

Smears of blood were found all over the rifle, particularly on the broken butt used to beat Nevill Bamber, but forensic scientists were not able to identify any of it, not even to group it. Yet the prosecution forensic expert, John Hayward, *was* able to state that blood found *inside* the silencer was group A,1 and conclude that it was Sheila Caffell's. Bamber's campaign says that Hayward now accepts that the blood could be a mixture of Nevill Bamber's (O,1) and/or June Bamber's blood (A, 2–1). In his statement of 13 October, Hayward also noted that the blood group of prosecution witness Robert Boutflour, who was at the farmhouse when his son, David, found the silencer, was identical to Sheila Caffell's.

Forensics and ballistics experts, including a senior lecturer at London Medical College, support the campaign's view that "the possibility remains that there was blood from more than one source inside the silencer" and that "the way the blood tests were carried out could have resulted in an error in interpretation".

At the trial, the judge emphasized to the jury how, from experience, Hayward could judge the possibility of a mixture by appearance. Hayward had said the opposite and, in fact, under cross-examination, admitted he had never in all his experience seen "backspatter" before.

The campaign says he now admitted the judge "did not direct the jury accurately regarding his evidence." In his summing up, Mr Justice Drake said: "The sound moderator is clearly of very great importance and the evidence relating to the sound moderator could, on its own, lead you to the conclusion that the defendant is guilty."

He also floated two possibilities about the sequence of deaths that not even the prosecution had sought to prove: that June Bamber had been shot first, and also that Sheila Caffell had died before June Bamber. June Bamber's bloodtrails (which were under the body of Sheila Caffell) showed this was the one thing that had not happened.

Freddie Mead, an expert in forensic ballistics and a specialist in the investigation of accidents involving firearms for the army, says: "The speculation in the learned judge's summing-up is totally wrong." Mead's conclusion is that "there aren't any grounds to believe a silencer was involved, apart from that the silencer was found."

According to the police and the prosecution, Jeremy Bamber's carefully devised plan to murder his family and fake Sheila Caffell's suicide was undone largely by one minor detail: he had told his girlfriend about it. He not only told her about it; after he had murdered them, he dumped her. And thirty-one days after the murders she went to the police.

According to Julie Mugford, Bamber had been talking about "the perfect murder" the previous summer. He had talked of sedating his parents and burning the farm down, but had then learnt that the insurance on the house and some of the antiques (including, interestingly, the clock) wasn't high enough. She claimed Bamber had been "killing rats with his bare hands" to steel himself for the attack. Bamber denied this.

She also said he had bragged about hiring a mercenary to kill them for £2,000. In court, she testified that hours before the murder, Jeremy Bamber had called her and said: "It's tonight or never." She claimed she told him not to be a fool, and he hung up. She did not phone the Bambers to warn them. Later that night (around the same time he called the police), Bamber called her again. "He said: 'Everything is going well. Don't worry, something is wrong at the farm. I love you lots.'" When Mugford arrived at the scene, she said that she and Bamber "went into the dining room for a cuddle and he said to me: 'I should have been an actor', and just laughed."

Mugford claimed that hours after the bodies were discovered, with the house still full of police, he had told her a man called Matthew had carried out the killings, and that Matthew had instructed Sheila Caffell to shoot herself.

The jury (presumably) believed her, but didn't believe Bamber's story about the hitman. (In court a Mr Matthew MacDonald denied that he was a hitman, or that he had been offered £2,000, saying that he was "a plumber". No charges were ever brought against him, and police did not pursue this line of inquiry.) And yet a month after the murders, Julie Mugford had still done nothing. She escorted Bamber to, and comforted him at, the family funeral.

"I was scared to believe it," she testified. "He said that if I said anything that I could be implicated in the crime as well because I knew about it."

Although some of her testimony was detailed enough to be convincing, it was mostly uncorroborated – virtually hearsay. Julie Mugford was openly besotted with Bamber, and only went to the police after she discovered he had cheated on her, and finished their relationship. Bamber said in evidence that he attributed her testimony to jealousy, bitterness, and believing what the tabloids had been writing about him. He said: "There are two people I think who are lying; Julie – she is the main one who is making up stories – and Robert Boutflour (Bamber's uncle and a witness for the prosecution), who could not have been mistaken."

Most of the crucial questions at the heart of this case revolve, not around Jeremy Bamber, but around one of the victims, Sheila Caffell. Several people who knew Sheila testified that she did not have the necessary expertise to have fired twenty-three shots, killing four people, without any "wasted" bullets.

June Bamber's niece, Ann Eaton, said that as soon as she heard the weapon had been reloaded, she realized Sheila could not possibly have done it. "She would not know one end of the barrel of a gun to another." Peter Eaton told the police: "Sheila, I would have said, was definitely frightened of guns. I had never seen Sheila hold a gun or fire one."

David Boutflour said: "I do not think I can recall seeing her with a gun." He added, "though I have seen a photograph of her holding a gun . . ."

However, nothing from Sheila Caffell's actual person supported the possibility that she had perpetrated this violent and bloody massacre. Her nightdress revealed no traces of cartridge oil or blood from the other victims, and it had no pockets, posing doubts about how she would have reloaded. (A box of cartridges for a .22 was found on the kitchen sideboard and Sheila could, arguably, have carried the box around with her.) What's more, Sheila's fingernails were described as "long and painted with red

varnish", and not at all damaged by having (inexpertly) fired and
re-loaded a .22 rifle.

As "a mere slip of a girl", doubts were also expressed that she
could not possibly have been involved in the fight with Nevill
Bamber, a fight in which stools were upturned, crockery broken,
and in which he received lacerations and bruising to his nose,
forehead, cheekbones, temples, wrists, forearms and chest, having been battered with the butt of a rifle. And yet Sheila showed
no sign of a struggle at all.

The judge felt compelled to rémark that these things pointed
to it "being very, very unlikely indeed that she fought and
overcame that tough farmer . . ." In fact, the palms of Sheila's
hands and the soles of her feet were clean; no blood, no sugar
(spilt during the fight with Nevill Bamber), no incriminating
substances of any kind. Added to this, Sheila's psychiatrist, Dr
Hugh Ferguson, stated that he "did not see Sheila as a violent
person, and certainly not as a patient who would have committed suicide."

From the tracks of the bullets, and the entry wounds, a post-
mortem concluded that Sheila was shot at point-blank range
"from right under the throat, pointing up". The tracks of the
wounds had gone "upwards and backwards" through the chin
and throat and the blood had run "down her face in a vertical
direction", suggesting that she was seated when she was shot. But
could she have shot herself twice?

Although the post-mortem said the first wound would have
caused "substantial" haemorrhaging, it also reported that Sheila
could have been "stunned" and "not necessarily rapidly lose
consciousness", thus making the second shot, which was fatal
"virtually instantaneously", quite feasible.

However, the possibility remained that this was exactly what
Jeremy Bamber had intended, and that he had murdered Sheila
Caffell and made it look like suicide. The problem was how? How
did Bamber get close enough to shoot her, and to shoot her from
that angle, with Sheila showing no signs of struggle or resistance?

Certainly the coroner, influénced by the police at the scene,
believed that Sheila Caffell had committed suicide. Exactly a
week after the killings, at the inquest, the coroner gave permis-

sion for the family to bury her body, and returned it to the authority of Jeremy Bamber, who decided to have it cremated.

David Boutflour had said in court that when police suggested Sheila had been the culprit, he told them: "Let's see the forensics." He said: "I wanted them to show me her fingerprints on the cartridges."

He could have made the same demands in Bamber's case. No blood or dust or incriminating fibres were ever found. Bamber's clothing was not taken for forensic tests until after he came back from holiday, nor was he examined for bruising or cartridge residues until a month after the event. As for the question of how Jeremy Bamber had managed to murder Sheila Caffell and fake her suicide, be it by lying on the floor below her, drugging her or threatening her, the prosecution never offered any explanation. It is true that traces of the tranquilliser drug, Halo-peridol (used to treat schizophrenia) were found in Sheila's blood, and Sheila's psychiatrist, Hugh Ferguson, told the court that if Sheila had been over-sedated, "it is quite possible she would have slept quite soundly and deeply". In fact, her own doctor, Dr Angeloglou, had requested her dosage be reduced for this reason.

A statement by one of Bamber's relatives suggested Sheila was on medication, and that Bamber told him (correctly) that even if Sheila had taken the drugs a considerable time before, they would still be detected. But then Sheila had been on medication for years.

Just as Julie Mugford told the court that Jeremy Bamber had threatened to kill his family, so, according to other witnesses, had Sheila Caffell.

When she got divorced from her husband, Colin Caffell, the twins had been put into his custody because of her mental instability. Her cousin testified that Sheila had asked her whether she ever had thoughts of killing herself; and that she had contemplated suicide on more than one occasion. It was said she had "expressed morbid thoughts about killing herself or the boys".

Sheila's doctor, Hugh Ferguson, from St Andrew's Hospital, Northampton, told the court that Sheila had "bizarre delusions about possession by the devil". She had told him she hated her mother and, in the past, she had seen herself as both Joan of Arc and the Virgin Mary.

Sheila had been discharged as recently as 29 March 1985 (four months before the murders), and Dr Ferguson wrote he "was not happy about her leaving so soon."

We get a glimpse of the extent of Sheila's illness from a letter she had written to Ann Eaton. "The reason I'm here . . . I asked God into my life so that I can understand mum's moods more and became completely high on his love, so much so that I wanted to join CND, thinking I had a calling from God to sort the world's problems out myself. Then I got a thing about the CIA following me. I finally thought a friend saw the devil, so I went through a tough time of unreality . . . I'm missing the boys. Love Sheila."

According to Jeremy and June Bamber's sister, on the night of the murders, Nevill and June Bamber had talked to Sheila about putting her children in foster homes. Bamber said Sheila had become upset. Ferguson had confirmed in court: "She had complex ideas about having sex with her twin sons. She thought her sons would seduce her and saw evil in both of them. In particular, she thought Nicholas was a woman-hater and a potential murderer."

Although her husband Colin Caffell said that "over the years I have known Sheila, she has never used or had any involvement with guns", he also said that if she had used firearms, he would have been "concerned, bearing in mind her violent outbursts".

He justified this by saying "her outbursts have always been towards property rather than people – pots and pans etc. Apart from the odd occasion when she struck me in temper, she has, to my knowledge, never struck anyone."

In his report for the defence, Major Mead points out: "The actual facts of the shooting make accuracy an irrelevancy . . . the distances were so close as to make the question of hitting academic." He goes on to add: "A degree of familiarity would be needed." But, as Jim Stephenson maintains: "She'd been on farms, and around shoots, all her life – twenty-seven years. She couldn't have done that without knowing something about shotguns."

The prosecution argued that the fight with Nevill Bamber pointed to someone other than Sheila, but the opposite could also be true. As Nevill Bamber was badly wounded from the shots he had received in bed (probably to the arm and lower jaw), it is quite possible that it was Sheila, not Jeremy, who had followed, him downstairs and battered him with the butt of the rifle before shooting him a further six times.

As for an explanation as to why Sheila's hands or feet bore no forensic evidence. Home Office pathologist and Professor of Forensic Pathology at the University of Wales, Professor Bernard Knight, testified that it was quite normal and common for suicide victims to wash themselves. A religious fanatic such as Sheila could well have done this. Suicide victims, said Professor Knight, performed all sorts of "mundane" and "ritualistic tasks". Sheila could have put the silencer away in the gun cupboard before shooting herself. Knight also testified that "women almost never commit suicide by shooting", especially in this manner (to the neck; the mouth being more common). At the same time he also expressed the opinion that "for a third party to do this seems rather extraordinary . . . I think it would be difficult for someone else to do this without her objecting." As the post-mortem said: "One cannot say with any degree of certainty whether the injuries were produced by another party."

And that uncertainty remains. The new evidence collected by Bamber's campaigners does not resolve the crucial question: Who killed Bambi? If the blood in the silencer could indeed be Nevill or June Bamber's, as expert witnesses now claim, it remains feasible that either Bamber or Caffell could have killed their family. So although this evidence throws considerable doubt over the prosecution's case, it does not establish Bamber's innocence either. If it were possible that Bamber's conviction had left a killer at large, the Home Secretary would be compelled to look more carefully at Bamber's grounds for appeal. There can be little doubt that the case needs to be very seriously looked at again. But whether any Home Secretary will take the chance or whether the Court of Appeal would recommend a new trial is another matter. Whether a new trial would find Jeremy Bamber innocent or guilty remains the final question of all.

THE MEDEA OF KEW GARDENS HILLS

(Alice Crimmins, USA 1965)

Albert Borowitz

Stomach contents often enable murder investigators to fix the time at which a victim died. In the case of the raunchy American housewife Alice Crimmins, time of death proved critical. Mrs Crimmins' two children had been the subject of a tug-of-love contest between their mother and her estranged husband. The children were reported missing, and found strangled. Mrs Crimmins claimed they'd been abducted, and described making them a meal of manicotti (noodles) and beans at about 7.30 p.m. on the night she said they'd been taken. She put them to bed at 9 p.m. and last saw them alive at midnight when she looked in on them. But her daughter's stomach contained that last meal virtually undigested, indicating that the child died within two hours of eating it. "It was evident to me," declared Milton Helpern, who was present at the autopsy, "that somebody was lying." Albert Borowitz (b.1930) is a retired Cleveland attorney and the author of several true-crime books.

On the morning of 14 July 1965, Eddie Crimmins received a telephone call from his estranged wife Alice, accusing him of having taken the children. When she had opened their bedroom door, which she kept locked by a hook-and-eye on the outside, she had seen that the beds had been slept in but Eddie Jr, aged five, and his four-year-old sister Alice (nicknamed Missy) were gone. The casement window was cranked open about 75 degrees; Alice remembered having closed it the night before because there was a hole in the screen and she wanted to keep the bugs out. The screen was later found outside, leaning against the wall beneath the window, and nearby was a "porter's stroller" – a converted baby-carriage with a box on it.

Alice's husband, an aeroplane mechanic who worked nights, protested that he knew nothing of the children's whereabouts and, alarmed by the message, said he would come right over to see her. Alice and the children lived in a dispiriting redbrick apartment complex flatteringly named Regal Gardens, located near the campus of Queens College in the Kew Gardens Hills section of the New York City borough of Queens. Shortly after joining his wife, Eddie called the police, and the first contingent of patrolmen were on the scene in a matter of minutes. By 11 a.m. precinct cars were parked all around the grassy mall adjoining Alice's apartment building at 150–22 72nd Drive.

Jerry Piering, who was the first detective to arrive, quickly made the case his own. Hoping for a promotion to second grade on the Queens' detective command, he immediately sensed that he had stepped into an important investigation. It took only one glance at Alice for him to decide that she did not look the picture of the anxious mother, this striking redhead in her twenties, with thick make-up, hip-hugging toreador slacks, flowered blouse and white high-heeled shoes. Patrolman Michael Clifford had already filled Piering in on the background – the Crimminses were separated and in the middle of a custody fight, but the role that the vanished children might have played in their skirmishing was still obscure.

The first fruits of Piering's look around the premises confirmed the unfavourable impression Alice had made. In the garbage cans there were about a dozen empty liquor bottles that Alice later attributed to good housekeeping rather than over-indulgence, explaining that she had been cleaning the apartment in anticipation of an inspection visit from a city agency in connection with the custody suit. Still more revealing to Piering was a proverbial "little black book" that Alice had dropped

outside; the men listed outnumbered women four to one. While
Piering was making his rounds, Detective George Martin found
trophies of Alice's active social life in a pastel-coloured overnight
bag stowed under her bed. The greetings and dinner programmes
that filled the bag documented her relationship with Anthony
(Tony) Grace, a fifty-two-year-old highway contractor with ties
to important Democratic politicians. Alice's souvenirs showed
that Tony Grace had introduced her to such party stalwarts as
Mayor Robert Wagner and Senator Robert Kennedy; messages
from Grace and important city officials addressed her as
"Rusty".

Piering took Alice into her bedroom and questioned her about
her activities on 13 July. Between 2.30 and 4.30 in the afternoon
she and the children had picnicked in Kissena Park, six blocks
from the apartment. They came home after stopping to pick up
some food for dinner; at Sever's delicatessen in the neighbourhood she had bought a package of frozen veal, a can of string
beans and a bottle of soda. When she arrived home she called her
attorney, Michael LaPenna (recommended to her by Grace), to
discuss the custody case which was scheduled for a hearing in a
week. She was concerned about a former maid, Evelyn Linder
Atkins, who claimed that Alice owed her $600 and, according to
Alice, had hinted that if she were paid she would not testify
against her in the proceedings. Evelyn had a worrisome story to
tell the judge if she decided to do so, for Alice had without
warning abandoned the children one weekend while she took a
boat trip to the Bahamas with Tony Grace and his friends. Alice
told Piering that it was not her fault; she had thought she was
aboard only for a *bon voyage* party but the men had playfully
locked her and a girlfriend in a washroom and carried them off to
sea. Perhaps LaPenna shared her concern about the maid, because the lawyer did not seem as optimistic about her chances of
retaining custody as he usually did.

After dinner, Alice took the children for a ride in the direction
of Main Street, wanting to find out the location of a furnished
apartment to which her husband had recently moved. Knowing
that Eddie had planted a crude "bug" on her telephone, she was
hoping to retaliate by finding him to be living with a woman. She

drove around for more than an hour until it was almost dark and then gave up the search.

Upon returning home, Alice prepared the children for bed about 9 p.m. (Theresa Costello, aged fourteen, Alice's former babysitter, later told the police that it was at this very moment that, passing below the bedroom window on her way to a babysitting job, she heard the Crimmins children saying their prayers.) Alice brought a replacement screen from her room to the children's bedroom but noticed that it had been fouled by her dog, Brandy. She therefore reset the children's punctured screen in the window without bothering to bolt it into place. Mindful of the coming agency visit, she disposed of wine and liquor bottles and made a pile of old clothing; by 10.30 p.m. she was tired, and collapsed on the living-room couch to watch *The Defenders* on TV. The programme did not make her forget that Tony Grace had not returned the call she had made earlier in the day. She reached him at a Bronx bar and to her jealous questions he responded that he was alone. After she hung up, Alice received a call from a man Grace had apparently replaced in her favour, a house renovator named Joe Rorech. Alice had met Rorech in January 1964 when she was working as a cocktail waitress at the Bourbon House in Syosset, Long Island. After Eddie had moved out of the Crimmins apartment, another Bourbon House waitress, Anita ("Tiger") Ellis, had come to live with Alice. For a while they had shared the favours of Joe Rorech, but "Tiger" had soon moved on to new attachments. In their conversation last night, Joe Rorech asked Alice to join him at a bar in Huntington, Long Island, but she evaded the invitation, pleading the unavailability of a babysitter.

After talking to Joe, Alice returned to her television set. At midnight she took little Eddie to the bathroom but could not wake Missy; she thought she had re-latched the bedroom door. (The door was kept locked, she explained, to keep Eddie from raiding the refrigerator.) Afterwards, Alice took the dog Brandy for a walk, then sat on the front stoop for a while. She told Piering that she may not have bolted the front door at the time. When at last she was getting ready for bed, her husband called and angered her by repeating the maid's claim that Alice owed her money.

Alice calmed down by taking the dog out again and, after a bath, went to sleep between 3.30 and 4 a.m.

Alice and Eddie, childhood sweethearts, had been married seven years. They were reasonably happy for a while but, soon after the birth of their son, they quarrelled frequently about Eddie's staying out late working or drinking with friends. After Missy was born, Alice decided to have no more children and Eddie, brought up a good Catholic (as was she) never forgave her after he found birth control devices in her purse. Their relationship went from bad to worse until, on 22 June 1965, he went to the Family Court to seek custody of the two children. By then, the couple were already separated, the children living on with Alice at the Regal Gardens. The custody petition charged that, immediately after the separation, Alice "began to indulge herself openly and brazenly in sex as she had done furtively before the separation". It was further detailed in the petition that Alice "entertains, one at a time, a stream of men sharing herself and her bedroom, until she and her paramour of the evening are completely spent. The following morning, the children awake to see a strange man in the house."

Combining a high degree of jealousy with a flair for the technology of snooping, Eddie had devoted many of his leisure hours to surveillance of her relations with men. He had much to observe, for when Alice gave up her secretarial work to become a waitress at a series of Long Island restaurants and bars, her opportunities for male acquaintance multiplied. To keep his compulsive watch, Eddie bugged her telephone and installed a microphone in her bedroom which he could monitor from a listening-post he had established in the basement below. Once he had burst in on Alice and a usually overdressed waiter named Carl Andrade, who had fled naked out of the window to his car.

Eddie liked to think that the purpose of his spying was to gather evidence for the custody case, but he ultimately admitted that he had often invaded Alice's apartment when she was out just to be near her "personal things". During their separation, so Alice said, Eddie told her that he had exposed himself to little girls in a park, but Alice disbelieved him, thinking that he was trying to play on her sympathy for his loneliness and distress.

Eddie's preoccupation with his wife's love life dominated his activities on 13 July, as he recounted them to the police. At 7 a.m. he had played a poor round of golf at a public course at Bethpage in Nassau County. Afterwards he drank three beers in the clubhouse with a friend and watched the New York Mets baseball game on television, leaving around 2 p.m. before the game ended. He then drove to Huntington to see whether Alice was visiting Joe Rorech but was disappointed to find no sign of her four-year-old Mercury convertible there. He arrived home at 5 p.m. and spent the evening watching television. Then, about 11 p.m., he drove along Union Turnpike to a small fast food stand near St John's University, bought a pizza and a large bottle of Pepsi Cola, and returned home. Alice, though, was still very much on his mind. After driving back to the Union Turnpike and drinking gin and tonic at a bar until 2.45 a.m., he drove into the parking lot behind his wife's bedroom window; he thought he saw a light there and in her living-room. He went home and called up Alice to talk about the maid. When Alice hung up, he watched a movie on television, read briefly and fell asleep by 4 a.m. A detective who checked out Eddie's story found that the movie he claimed to have seen on the CBS channel had actually been on much earlier.

In addition to questioning Alice, Jerry Piering, a fledgling in his job, directed the police inspection and photographing of the apartment, apparently with more enthusiasm than expertise. Piering later claimed that when he first came into the children's room, he observed a thin layer of dust on the bureau-top, which in his mind eliminated the possibility that the children had left the room through the window since they would have had to cross over the bureau. However, technicians had covered the top of the bureau with powder for detecting fingerprints before the bureau could be photographed in its original condition. It was Piering's further recollection that when he had moved a lamp on the bureau, it had left a circle in the layer of dust. This story was later disputed by Alice's brother, John Burke, and others, who agreed that the lamp on the bureau had tripod legs. Also, many people had come into the room before Piering arrived; Eddie Crimmins had leaned out of the window to look for the missing children, and, of course, Alice on the previous evening had removed and replaced the screen; it seemed unlikely that Piering's dust-film would have remained undisturbed amid all this activity. In any event, neither the layer of dust nor the impression left by the lamp base was noted in Piering's first reports.

In the early afternoon of 14 July 1965, the Crimmins case was transformed from mysterious disappearance into homicide. A nine-year-old boy, Jay Silverman, found Missy's body in an open lot on 162nd Street, about eight blocks from the Regal Gardens. A pyjama-top, knotted into two ligatures, was loosely tied around her bruised neck. An autopsy, performed with the participation of Dr Milton Helpern, New York City's distinguished Chief Medical Examiner, found no evidence of sexual assault; haemorrhages in the mucous membrances in the throat and vocal cords confirmed that Missy had been asphyxiated. The contents of the stomach were sent to an expert, who reported finding, among other things, a macaroni-like substance. This discovery rang a bell with Detective Piering, who recalled that on the morning of 14 July he had seen in Alice's trash can a package that had held frozen manicotti and had also noticed a plate of leftover manicotti in her refrigerator. However, none of this evidence had been preserved – nor had Piering's discoveries been referred to in his contemporaneous reports.

Following the discovery of Missy's body, the search for young Eddie intensified. A false alarm was raised in Cunningham Park when what looked like a blond-headed body turned out to be a discarded doll. On Monday morning, 19 July, Vernon Warnecke and his son, walking together to look at a treehouse used by the children in the neighbourhood, found Eddie Crimmins on an embankment overlooking the Van Wyck Expressway. The boy's body was eaten away by rats and insects and in an advanced state of decay. The site was about a mile from Alice Crimmins' apartment and close to the grounds of the New York World's Fair that was then in progress.

After the children were buried, Alice and her husband, re-united by their tragedy, faced a relentless police investigation which explored many trails, always only to return to Alice. Detectives pursued reports of strange intruders in the Crimmins' neighbourhood, including a so-called "pants burglar" who broke into homes only to steal men's trousers. A closer look was taken at the boyfriends whose names filled Alice's black book. Anthony Grace admitted in a second interview that he had lied when he told the police he had never left the Bronx on the night of 13/14 July. He now stated that he had driven over the Whitestone Bridge to a restaurant called Ripples on the Water with a group of "bowling girls", young married women who partied around town under the pretext that they were going bowling. Grace maintained that he had stayed away from Alice during the period of the custody battle and had not seen her much recently. She had called him several times on 13 July but he was preoccupied with business and had taken his wife to dinner without remembering to call Alice back. At 11 p.m. she phoned him again at the Capri Bar, telling him that she wanted to join him for a drink. He had put her off by telling her that he was about to leave and had denied her well-founded suspicion that he was with the bowling girls.

Joe Rorech told Detective Phil Brady that he had called Alice twice on the night of the disappearance, first after 10 p.m., when she declined his invitation to the Bourbon House bar, and then at 2 a.m., when there had been no answer. Rorech had been drinking all night and admitted he might have misdialled the number. On 6 December 1965 the police administered the first of two sodium pentothal "truth tests" to Rorech. Satisfied with the results, and finding Rorech's self-confidence weakened by business reverses, they conscripted him as a spy. Joe took Alice to motel rooms where recorders had been planted, but their conversations contained nothing of interest.

At first Eddie Crimmins had been more inclined to co-operate with the police than Alice. He submitted to a session with the lie detector, and persuaded Alice to take the test. However, after she agreed and the preliminary questions were completed, she refused to continue. With the exception of Detective Brady, the police now decided to forget about Eddie and concentrate on Alice. Before the Crimminses moved into a new three-room apartment in Queens to avoid the eyes of their unwanted public, the police, succeeding to the role long played by Alice's jealous husband, planted ultrasensitive microphones and tapped the telephone wires. Detectives monitored the apartment around the clock from the third floor pharmacy of a neighbouring hospital, but could not pick up a single incriminating statement. Their failure was not remarkable since Alice seemed well aware of the police presence, beginning many of her conversations, "Drop dead, you guys!" Unable to overhear a confession, the secret listeners were tuned into the sounds of Alice's sexual encounters, which resumed shortly after she took up her new residence. As their high-tech recording devices picked up Alice's cries of physical need, her pursuers became more certain of her guilt, convinced as they were that grief for the dead children would demand an adjournment of the flesh.

According to reporter Kenneth Gross, who has written the principal account of the case, police investigators vented their hostility against Alice by interfering with the love affairs that they were recording so assiduously. When the tireless eavesdroppers overheard Joe Rorech and Alice making love, they informed Eddie Crimmins, who promptly called and was assured by Alice that she was alone. The police, hoping for a confrontation between lover and outraged husband, flattened Rorech's tyres, but he managed to have his car towed safely out of the neighbourhood before Eddie got home. When Alice moved out of the apartment to live with an Atlanta man for whom she was working as a secretary, the police thoughtfully advised the man's wife, and when she came to New York, helped her destroy Alice's clothing. Undaunted by this harassment, Alice reappeared in her familiar nightspots, now as a customer instead of cocktail waitress.

The investigation dragged on for a year and a half without result, and meanwhile there was a growing public clamour for action. At this point New York politics intervened to step up the pace of events: Nat Hentel, an interim Republican appointment as Queens District Attorney, was soundly defeated for re-election and decided to convene a grand jury before his term of office expired. The grand jury failed to return an indictment, and a second grand jury impanelled under Hentel's Democratic successor "Tough Tommy" Mackell also disbanded without indictment in May of the following year. Then, on 1 September 1967, Assistant District Attorney James Mosley went before still another grand jury to present the testimony of a "mystery witness", who was soon identified as Sophie Earomirski.

Sophie's original entrance into the case had been anonymous. On 30 November 1966, she had written to then District Attorney Hentel telling him how happy she was to read that he was bringing the Crimmins case to a grand jury. She reported an "incident" she had witnessed while looking out of her living-room window on the early morning of 14 July 1965. Shortly after 2 a.m., a man and woman came walking down the street towards 72nd Road in Queens. The woman, who was lagging about five feet behind the man, was holding what appeared to be a bundle of blankets shining white under her left arm, and with her right hand led a little boy walking at her side. The man shouted at her to hurry up and she told him "to be quiet or someone will see us". The man took the blanket-like white bundle and heaved it onto the back seat of the nondescript automobile. The woman picked up the little boy and sat with him on the back seat; she had dark hair, and her companion was tall, not heavy, with dark hair and a large nose. Sophie apologised for signing merely as "A Reader".

Shortly after he was entrusted with the Crimmins case by Mackell, Mosley came across Sophie's letter, and the hunt for her began. The police obtained samples of the handwriting of tenants living in garden apartments from which the scene described in the letter could have been viewed, and they identified Sophie, who recognized Alice's photograph as resembling the woman she had seen. Sophie's testimony before the third grand jury was decisive, and Queens County finally had its long-coveted indictment, charging Alice Crimmins with the murder of Missy. The prosecution had persuaded the grand jury that there was reasonable cause to believe that the bundle of blankets Sophie had seen contained the little girl's dead body.

On 9 May 1968, the trial began in the ground floor courtroom of the Queens County Criminal Court Building amid widely varying perceptions of the defendant. To the sensationalist press, Alice was a "modern-day Medea" who had sacrificed her children to a deadly hatred for her husband, and the pulp magazine *Front Page Detective*, invoking another witch from antiquity, called her an "erring wife, a Circe, an amoral woman whose many affairs appeared symptomatic of America's Sex Revolution". A group of radical feminists offered to identify Alice's cause with their own, but she declined their help. Between these two wings of public opinion there was a dominant vision of Alice as a manhunting cocktail waitress, and her longer years as housewife, mother and secretary receded into the background.

The prosecution case was presented for the most part by James Mosley's aspiring young assistant, Anthony Lombardino, but Mosley himself scored the first important point while questioning Dr Milton Helpern. The forensic expert testified that the discovery of as much food as was found in Missy's stomach was consistent with a post-ingestion period of less than two hours. If Helpern was right, then assuming that Alice had been the last to feed the children, she could not have seen them alive at midnight, as she claimed.

Lombardino insisted that the prize job of examining the prosecution's star witness was his – his alone. Since the police had first enlisted Joe Rorech's aid, Joe's difficulties had continued to mount; his marriage was in trouble and he had been upset by a brief period of arrest as a material witness. In his testimony he made it plain that he had lost any vestige of loyalty to his former mistress.

The defence, led by Harold Harrison, was unmoved when Rorech indirectly quoted Alice, "She did not want Eddie to have the children. She would rather see the children dead than Eddie have them." Harrison had not heard this before, but he did not regard the statement as damaging; surely the jury would understand that it was just the kind of thing that a divorcing spouse was likely to say in the heat of a custody battle. Rorech, though, had something more to disclose that would change the course of the trial. Though the police had learned nothing incriminating from electronic eavesdropping, Joe testified to a long conversation with Alice at a motel in Nassau County. After weeping inconsolably, she had said again and again that the children "will understand, they know it was for the best". At last she had added, "Joseph, please forgive me, I killed her."

Stung by the witness's words, Alice jumped out of her chair and banged her fists on the defence table, crying, "Joseph! How

could you do this? This is not true! Joseph . . . you, of all people!
Oh, my God!" Harrison was unable to follow Alice's outburst
with telling cross-examination for he had no effective means of
rebutting Rorech's quotes. In fact, he may have been preoccupied
by a dilemma of his own: the next morning he went before Judge
Peter Farrell and unsuccessfully sought to withdraw from the
case on the grounds that prior to the trial he had represented Joe
Rorech as well as Alice, to whom Joe had introduced him.

After Rorech's damning testimony, the appearance of Sophie
Earomirski, The Woman in the Window, came as an anticlimax.
Sophie elaborated the scene she had recalled in her anonymous
letter by adding a pregnant dog. She told the jury that the woman
had responded to her male companion's order to hurry by
explaining that she was waiting for the dog. She had said,
"The dog is pregnant," and the man had grumbled, "Did you
have to bring it?" In fact, Brandy *was* pregnant that night, but
several witnesses swore that nobody had recognized the pregnancy – that when the dog produced a single puppy the week after
the killing, Alice and the neighbours were surprised.

The defence tried to destroy Sophie's credibility, but the scope
of the attack was narrowly limited by Judge Farrell. The judge
excluded an affidavit of Dr Louis Berg to the effect that a head
injury suffered by Mrs Earomirski at the World's Fair had
resulted in "permanent brain damage". Defence lawyer Marty
Baron questioned her about two suicide attempts, but to no avail:
the courtroom spectators cheered her recital that she had placed
her head in an oven to see how dinner was coming along. A press
photograph records Sophie's exit from the courthouse, her hand
raised in triumph like a triumphant boxer, still champion, on
whom the challenger could not lay a glove.

The principal strategy of the defence was to put Alice on the
stand to deny the murder charge and to show that she was not
made of granite, as portrayed by certain sections of the media.
When Baron's questioning turned to the children, Alice began to
tremble and whispered to Judge Farrell that she could not
continue. Farrell declared a recess. When the trial resumed,
Alice concluded her testimony with a strong denial of Rorech's
account of her confession.

The decision to permit Alice to testify gave prosecutor Lombardino the opportunity he had been waiting for: to question her closely about her love life. All the most titillating incidents were brought out: the night Eddie had caught her in bed with the amorous waiter Carl Andrade, an afternoon tryst with a buyer at the World's Fair, a 1964 cruise with Tony Grace to the Democratic National Convention in Atlantic City, and nude swimming at Joe Rorech's home when, Lombardino was careful to stress, the children were dead. To reporter Kenneth Gross it seemed that Lombardino had torn away the last shred of Alice's dignity when he enquired whether she remembered making love with her children's barber in the back of a car behind the barbershop; Alice admitted having had ten dates with the barber, but, straining at a gnat, couldn't recall the incident in the car. Lombardino continued the catalogue of Alice's conquests with obvious relish until the judge ordered him to conclude.

The trial ended after thirteen days on Monday 27 May, and early the next morning the jury returned a verdict of guilty of manslaughter in the first degree; one of the jurors said that a large majority had voted for conviction on the first ballot, but that he had doubts about the proof and did not regard her as a danger to society. At her sentencing hearing, Alice protested her innocence and angrily told Judge Farrell, "You don't care who killed my children, you want to close your books. You don't give a damn who killed my kids." The judge sentenced her to be confined in the New York State prison for women at Westfield State Farms, Bedford Hills, New York, for a term of not less than five nor more than twenty years.

Alice's conviction was far from the last chapter of the case. In December 1969 the Appellate Division of the New York Supreme Court, an intermediate appeals court, ordered a new trial because three of the jurors had secretly visited the scene of Sophie Earomirski's identification of Alice. One of the jurors had made his visit alone at about two in the morning, hoping to verify what Sophie could have seen at that hour. The court reasoned that "the net effect of the jurors' visits was that they made themselves secret, untested witnesses not subject to any cross-examination". The State's highest court, the Court of Appeals, agreed, ruling in

April 1970 that the unauthorized visits were inherently prejudicial to the defendant, and adding, in a significant aside, that the evidence of guilt "was not so overwhelming that we can say, as a matter of law, that the error could not have influenced the verdict". The Court noted that only two witnesses, Sophie Earomirski and Joe Rorech, had directly implicated Alice, and that Rorech's testimony "was seriously challenged, and the witness was subjected to searching cross-examination".

When the case was retried in 1971, a change in counsel and the presiding judge and the cooling of community passions resulted in a more restrained courtroom atmosphere. Gone from the prosecution team was Tony Lombardino, replaced by Thomas Demakos, the experienced chief of the District Attorney's trial bureau. The judge to whom the second trial was assigned, George Balbach, planted court attendants in the courtroom and adjacent corridors to assure better order. Perhaps the most significant change was at the defence table, where Herbert Lyon, a leader of the Queens trial bar, now sat in the first chair. Lyon had devised a more conservative defence plan, intended to place greater stress on Alice's grief and loss, and to keep her off the witness stand so that the prejudicial parade of her love affairs could not be repeated.

The stakes had been raised in the second trial, which began on Monday, 15 March 1971. As Alice's first jury had found her guilty of manslaughter in the death of Missy, principles of double jeopardy prohibited her from being charged with a greater offence against her daughter, but the prosecution had compensated for that limitation by obtaining an additional indictment for the murder of young Eddie. Though the state of his remains ruled out proof of cause of death, Demakos offered the evidence of Dr Milton Helpern that murder could be "inferred" because of the circumstances of his sister's death. Joe Rorech, obliging as ever, adapted his testimony to the new prosecution design; according to his revised story, Alice had told him that she had killed Missy and "consented" to the murder of her son.

The presentation of defence evidence was already in progress when Demakos, over vigorous objection by Lyon, was permitted to bring a surprise witness to the stand. Mrs Tina DeVita, a

resident of the Kew Gardens Hills development at the time of the
crime, testified that on the night of 13/14 July, while driving
home with her husband, she had looked out of the driver's
window from the passenger's side and seen "people walking, a
man carrying a bundle, a woman, a dog, and a boy". The angry
Lyon could not shake Mrs DeVita's story but did much to
neutralize its impact by introducing an unheralded witness of
his own, Marvin Weinstein, a young salesman from Massapequa,
Long Island. Weinstein swore that on the morning of 14 July he,
together with his wife, son and daughter, had passed below
Sophie Earomirski's window on the way to his car; he had carried
his daughter under his arm "like a sack" and they were accompanied by their dog – who might well have looked pregnant for
she had long ago lost her figure. As a final jab at the State's case,
Lyon called Vincent Colabella, a jailed gangster who had report-
edly admitted to a fellow prisoner that he had been Eddie's
executioner, only to deny that report when questioned by the
police. On the stand Colabella chuckled as he disowned any
knowledge of the crime; he said that he had never seen Alice
Crimmins before.

In his closing argument, Lyon cited Sophie Earomirski's
testimony that she had been led to tell her story by the voices
of the children crying from the grave; if they were crying, Alice's
defence lawyer suggested, they were saying, "Let my mother go;
you have had her long enough!" Demakos had harsher words,
reminding the jury of Alice's failure to take the stand, "She
doesn't have the courage to stand up here and tell the world she
killed her daughter." Alice interrupted to protest, "Because I
didn't!" but the prosecutor went on without being put off his
stroke, "And the shame and pity of it is that this little boy had to
die too."

The jury deliberations began after lunch on Thursday 23 April
and ended at 5.45 p.m. on the following day. Alice was found
guilty of murder in the first degree in the death of her son and of
manslaughter in the strangling of Missy.

On 13 May 1971 Alice Crimmins was remanded to Bedford
Hills prison, and there she stayed for two years while her lawyers
continued the battle for her freedom in the appellate courts. In

May 1973 the Appellate Division ruled for a second time in her favour. The court threw out the murder conviction on the grounds that the State had not proved beyond reasonable doubt that young Eddie's death had resulted from a criminal act. With respect to the manslaughter count relating to Missy, the court ordered a new trial on the basis of a number of errors and improprieties, including the prosecutor's comment that Alice lacked the courage to admit the killing of Missy: this argument amounted to an improper assertion that the prosecutor knew her to be guilty and, in addition, was an improper attack on her refusal to testify. Alice was freed from prison following this ruling, but the rejoicing in her camp was premature. The tortuous path of the judicial proceedings had two more dangerous corners.

The first setback was suffered when the Court of Appeals in February 1975 announced its final decision in the appeals relating to the verdicts in the second trial. The court sustained the decision of the Appellate Division only in part: it agreed with the dismissal of the murder charge but reversed the grant of a new trial in the manslaughter conviction for the killing of Missy, returning that issue to the Appellate Division for reconsideration. Explaining the latter ruling, the Court of Appeals conceded that Demakos's comment on Alice's refusal to testify violated her constitutional privilege against self-incrimination. However, in seeming contradiction of its sceptical view of the prosecution case in the first trial, the court decided that the constitutional error was harmless in view of the weighty evidence of Alice's guilt.

The Appellate Division confirmed the manslaughter conviction in May 1975, and Alice was once again sent back to prison to continue serving her sentence of from five to twenty years. Persevering in his efforts for her vindication, Lyon still had one card to play, an appeal from the denial of his motion for retrial, based on newly discovered evidence. A would-be witness, an electronics scientist named F. Sutherland Macklem, had given the defence an affidavit to the effect that, shortly after one o'clock on the morning of 14 July 1965, he had picked up two small children, a boy and a girl, hitchhiking in Queens County. The boy had told him he knew where his home was, and Macklem had let them out, safe and sound, at the corner of 162nd Street and 71st Avenue. The affiant did not learn the children's names, but stated that the boy could well have identified his companion as "Missy" instead of "my sister", as he had first thought. He admitted that he had identified his passengers as the Crimmins children only after reading newspaper accounts of the first trial, three years after the incident.

On 22 December 1975, the New York Court of Appeals affirmed the trial court's rejection of this defence initiative. The court was influenced by the affiant's seven year delay in coming forward, and commented scathingly that the affidavit "offers an imaginative alternative hypothetical explanation [of the crime], worthy of concoction by an A. Conan Doyle".

In January 1976 Alice Crimmins became eligible for a work-release programme and was permitted to leave prison on week days to work as a secretary. In August 1977 the New York *Post* reported that Alice had spent the previous Sunday "as she has spent many balmy summer Sundays of her prison-term – on a luxury cruiser at City Island". (Under the work-release programme, participants were allowed every other weekend at liberty.) In July 1977, Alice married the proprietor of the luxury cruiser, her contractor boyfriend, Anthony Grace. The *Post* was indignant over the nuptials, furnishing telephoto shots of Alice in a bikini and T-shirt, and headlining a follow-up story with a comment of the Queens District Attorney, "Alice should be behind bars!"

On 7 September 1977, Alice Crimmins was granted parole, after thirty months in prison and nine months in the work-release programme. When a new petition for retrial was denied in November, she slipped into what must have been welcome obscurity; she had become that stalest of all commodities, old news.

The Crimmins case remains an intractable puzzle. In his opening argument in the second trial, Herbert Lyon invited the jury to regard the case as a troubling mystery that had not been solved. It is always difficult to persuade the community to live at ease with an unknown murderer, but never more so than when a child or spouse has been killed and the evidence suggests that the household was the scene of the crime or of the victim's disappearance. As in the Lindbergh kidnapping or the murder of Julia Wallace, there is a strong tendency to suspect an "inside job". Alice Crimmins, who slept close by but claimed to have heard nothing out of the ordinary during the murder night, naturally came under suspicion. She was a mother (perhaps harbouring the nameless daily hostilities familiar to the annals of family murder) and the only adult living in the Kew Gardens Hills apartment, and she had the opportunity to commit the crime – but can anything more be said to justify the certainty the investigators showed from the start that she was guilty? If we reject the equation that the State of New York made between sexuality and murderousness, it appears that Alice displayed only one suspicious trait: despite her avowed grief over her lost children, she does not seem to have shown much interest in helping the authorities to identify the killer. Even this curious passivity may have been due to the defensive posture into which she was immediately thrust by police antagonism and surveillance, and she may also have genuinely believed that the murderer was not to be found in her circle of acquaintances, however wide and casual.

The prosecution never attributed a plausible motive to Alice. The presence of Missy and young Eddie in the apartment does not seem to have inhibited Alice's amorous adventures, but if she found the children to be under foot, she could easily have surrendered custody to her husband. It was rumoured that she had never liked Missy much, that she had killed her in anger and then called for underworld help to dispose of her son as an inconvenient witness. Under those circumstances it is hard to visualize the boy going willingly to his doom, a docile figure in the peaceful domestic procession belatedly recalled by Sophie Earomirski in which the murderers and their future victim were accompanied by a pregnant dog. If the theory of sudden anger did not sell, the police investigators were likely to fall back on Alice's own words, that she would rather see her children dead than lose them to Eddie in the pending custody battle. Alice enjoyed a tactical advantage as a mother in possession of the children, and there is no reason to conclude that, despite the lessened optimism

she detected in her lawyer's voice during their conversation
before the children's disappearance, the prospect was hopeless
or that she thought so. If the uncertainty of the divorce court's
ruling provided a viable motive, the police had as good a reason to
charge Eddie with the crime, but they never took him seriously as
a suspect.

In the mind of Joe Rorech, the theory of underworld involvement in the murder of Alice's son took on an even more sinister
tone. After the second trial he told New York *Post* reporter
George Carpozi Jr that Alice "had to have those children out
of the way to avoid the custody proceedings" that were to have
been held on 21 July 1965. He spelled out his belief that Alice had
arranged for three of her girlfriends to sleep with a prominent
New York politician, who was afraid that the details of his
indiscretion would come out at the custody hearing. Therefore,
the man, who was "deeply involved in New York politics and
relied almost solely on the Democratic organisation for his bread
and butter", had called on his gangland connections to eliminate
the children, thereby averting the hearing. Rorech had no satisfactory answer when Carpozi asked him why the same objective
could not have been accomplished with less pain to Alice by the
murder of her estranged husband. Rorech's theory also fails to
explain why the politician's scandal was deemed more likely to be
publicised in a custody hearing than in the course of a murder
investigation that was bound to focus on Alice Crimmins and her
florid love life.

If Alice was in fact guilty, the reason for her crime must,
despite the best surmises of the police and Joe Rorech, remain
wrapped in mystery. Even more puzzling, though, is the autopsy
evidence regarding Missy's last meal, which raises doubts concerning the time and place of the child's murder. This strange
facet of the case was prominently featured in the dissenting
opinion rendered by Justice Fuchsberg when the New York
State Court of Appeals rejected Alice's motion for a new trial
in 1975. Justice Fuchsberg noted that the testimony of the
Queens medical examiner, Dr Richard Grimes, indicated that
Missy had died shortly after ingesting a meal including a macaroni-like substance that differed substantially from the last dinner

that Alice had told the police she served the children. This evidence suggested to the judge that "the child might have had another meal at some unknown time and unknown place considerably after the one taken at home".

Could Alice Crimmins have been so cunning a criminal planner as to have created this enigma by lying to the police about the food she had served on the night of the crime? Apart from the difficulty of finding traits of calculation and foresight in her character, many circumstances militate against the inference that the veal dinner was a fabrication intended by Alice to mislead the investigation. When she first mentioned the purchase of the frozen veal to Detective Piering, neither of the children's bodies had been found. If she was the murderer and had hidden the corpses, she had reason to hope that they would long remain undiscovered. Even if she feared the worst – that the victims would soon be found – it seems doubtful that she was so familiar with the capabilities of forensic medicine that she decided to turn to her own account the possibility that an autopsy might be performed in time to analyses the contents of the last meal.

There would have been a powerful deterrent to Alice's lying about the veal dinner. She told Piering that she had purchased the veal on the afternoon of 13 July in a neighbourhood delicatessen; she was presumably well known there, and the grocer who had waited on her could very likely have contradicted her story. As events turned out, the grocer did not remember what she had purchased, but she could not have counted on that in advance.

If the Crimmins case is viewed with the hindsight of the 1980s – when a young mother with a strong sexual appetite is less likely to be pronounced a Medea – it seems that Alice is entitled to the benefit of the Scottish verdict: Not Proven.

THE LOVE PHILTRE

(Mary Blandy, UK 1752)

Horace Bleackley

The trial of Mary Blandy in 1752 for the murder of her father is the first on record to feature convincing scientific proof of poisoning. Francis Blandy, a well-to-do attorney, doted on Mary, his only daughter. According to the prosecution at her trial, Mr Blandy put it about that he intended to settle a massive £10,000 on her to encourage "neighbouring gentlemen" in the marriage stakes. But it was a hoax. "This pious fraud," counsel explained, "which was intended for her promotion, proved his death and her destruction." Captain Cranstoun, hearing she was to have £10,000, fell in love, not with Mary but with her fortune, concealing from her the fact that he was already married. Cranstoun began sending Mary packets of white powder to put in her father's food. The result was that Mr Blandy become violently ill, and died with symptoms suggestive of arsenical poisoning.

The scientific evidence at Mary Blandy's trial was given by Dr Anthony Addington, who had attended the poisoned man, examined the body and tested the white powder sent by Captain Cranstoun. Addington stated that this was arsenic, and that he found the same poison in Mr Blandy's gruel. Asked in cross-examination why he believed it to be white arsenic, Dr Addington described the different tests he had applied to the powder and to a sample of pure white arsenic that he had bought. He showed how the same results were obtained in each case, concluding with the remark: "I never saw any two things in nature more alike than the decoction made with the powder found in Mr Blandy's gruel and that made with white arsenic." Although the case dates back some 250 years, at least one modern scientist has hailed the scientific evidence in the Blandy case as a model of what such evidence should be.

Horace Bleackley (1868–1931) was a writer on crime history and something of an eccentric, living latterly in a villa at Cannes and listing his recreation as "baiting Bolshies". Bleackley's ornate, almost operatic, style is exemplified in this decorative Edwardian essay.

> "Who hath not heard of Blandy's fatal fame,
> Deplored her fate, and sorrowed o'er her shame?"
>   *–Henley,* a poem, 1827

During the reign of George II – when the gallant Young Pretender was leading Jenny Cameron toward Derby, and flabby, gin-besotted England, dismayed by a rabble of half-famished Highlanders, was ready to take its thrashing lying-down – a prosperous attorney, named Francis Blandy, was living at Henley-upon-Thames. For nine years he had held the post of town clerk, and was reckoned a person of skill in his profession. A dour, needle-witted man of law, whose social position was more considerable than his means or his lineage, old Mr Blandy, like others wiser than himself, had a foible. His pride was just great enough to make him a tuft-hunter. In those times, a solicitor in a country town had many chances of meeting his betters on equal terms, and when the attorney of Henley pretended that he had saved the large sum of ten thousand pounds, county society esteemed him at his supposed value. There lived with him – in an old-world home surrounded by gardens and close to the bridge on the London road – his wife and daughter, an only child, who at this period was twenty-five years of age.

Mrs Blandy, as consequential an old dame as ever flaunted *sacque* or nodded her little bugle over a dish of tea, seems to have spent a weary existence in wringing from her tight-fisted lord the funds to support the small frivolities which her social ambition deemed essential to their prestige. A feminine mind seldom appreciates the reputation without the utility of wealth, and the lawyer's wife had strong opinions with regard to the propriety of living up to their ten-thousand-pound celebrity. While he was content with the barren honour that came to him by reason of the reputed *dot* which his daughter one day must enjoy – pluming himself, no doubt, that his Molly had as good a chance of winning a coronet as the penniless daughter of an Irish squireen – his lady, with more worldly wisdom, knew the value of an occasional jaunt to town, and was fully alive to the chances of rout or assembly hard-by at Reading. Thus in the pretty little home near the beautiful reach of river, domestic storms – sad object-lesson to an only child – raged frequently over the parental truck and barter at the booths of Vanity Fair.

Though not a beauty – for the smallpox, that stole the bloom from the cheeks of many a sparkling belle in hoop and brocade, had set its seal upon her face – the portrait of Mary Blandy shows that she was comely. Still, it is a picture in which there is a full contrast between the light and shadows. Those fine glistening black eyes of hers – like the beam of sunshine that illumines a sombre chamber – made one forget the absence of winsome charm in her features; yet their radiance appeared to come through dark unfathomable depths rather than as the reflection of an unclouded soul. With warmth all blood may glow, with softness every heart can beat, but some, like hers, must be compelled by reciprocal power. Such, in her empty home, was not possible. Even the love and devotion of her parents gave merely a portion of their own essence. From a greedy father she acquired the sacred lust, and learnt from infancy to dream, with morbid longing, of her future dower; while her mother encouraged a hunger for vain and giddy pleasure, teaching unwittingly that these must be bought at the expense of peace, or by the sacrifice of truth. To a girl of wit and intelligence in whose heart nature had not sown the seeds of kindness, these lessons came as a crop of tares upon a fruitful soil. But, as in the case of all women, there was one hope of salvation. Indeed, since the passion of her soul cried out with imperious command that she should fulfil the destiny of her sex, the love of husband and children would have found her a strong but pliable material that could be fashioned into more gentle form. Without such influence she was one of those to whom womanhood was insufferable – a mortal shape where lay encaged one of the fiercest demons of discontent.

Molly Blandy did not lack admirers. Being pleasant and vivacious – while her powers of attraction were enhanced by the rumour of her fortune – not a few of the beaux in the fashionable world of Bath, and county society at Reading, gave homage and made her their toast. In the eyes of her parents it was imperative that a suitor should be able to offer to their daughter a station of life befitting an heiress. On this account two worthy swains, who were agreeable to the maiden but could not provide the expected dower, received a quick dismissal. Although there was nothing exorbitant in the ambition of the attorney and his dame, it is clear that the girl learnt an evil lesson from these mercenary transactions. Still, her crosses in love do not seem to have sunk very deeply into her heart, but henceforth her conduct lost a little of its maidenly reserve. The freedom of the coquette took the place of the earnestness and sincerity that had been the mark of her ardent nature, and her conduct towards the officers of the regiment stationed at Henley was deemed too forward. However, the father, whose reception into military circles no doubt made the desired impression upon his mayor and aldermen, was well satisfied that his daughter should be on familiar terms with her soldier friends. Even when she became betrothed to a captain of no great fortune, he offered small objection, on account of the position of the young man. Yet, although the prospect of a son-in-law who held the king's commission had satisfied his vanity, the old lawyer, who foolishly had allowed the world to believe him richer than he was, could not, or (as he pretended) would not, provide a sufficient dowry. Thus the engagement promised to be a long one. Fate, however, decided otherwise. Very soon her suitor was ordered abroad on active service, and the hope of marriage faded away for the third time.

In the summer of 1746, while no doubt she was sighing for her soldier across the seas, the man destined to work the tragic mischief of her life appeared on the scene. William Henry Cranstoun, a younger son of the fifth Lord Cranstoun, a Scottish baron, was a lieutenant of marines, who, since his regiment had

suffered severely during the late Jacobite rebellion, had come to
Henley on a recruiting expedition. At first his attentions to Miss
Blandy bore no fruit, but he returned the following summer, and
while staying with his grand-uncle, General Lord Mark Kerr,
who was an acquaintance of the lawyer and his family, he found
that Mary was off with the old love and willing to welcome him as
the new. All were amazed that the fastidious girl should forsake
her gallant captain for this little sprig from North Britain – an
undersized spindleshanks, built after Beau Diddapper pattern –
in whose weak eyes and pock-fretten features love must vainly
seek her mirror. Still greater was the astonishment when ten-
thousand-pound Blandy, swollen with importance, began to
babble of "my Lord of Crailing," and the little bugle cap of
his dame quivered with pride as she told her gossips of "my Lady
Cranstoun, my daughter's new mamma." For it was common
knowledge that the small Scot was the fifth son of a needy house,
with little more than his pay to support his many vicious and
extravagant habits. Such details seem to have been overlooked by
the vain parents in their delight at the honour and glory of an
alliance with a family of title. In the late autumn of 1747 they
invited their prospective son-in-law to their home, where, as no
one was fonder of free quarters, he remained for six months. But
the cruel fate that presided over the destinies of the unfortunate
Mary intervened once more. Honest Lord Mark Kerr (whose
prowess as a duellist is chronicled in many a page), perceiving the
intentions of his unscrupulous relative, made haste to give his
lawyer friend the startling news that Cranstoun was a married
man.

This information was correct. Yet, although wedded since the
year before the rebellion, the vicious little Scot was seeking to put
away the charming lady who was his wife and the mother of his
child. Plain enough were the motives. A visit to England had
taught him that the title which courtesy permitted him to bear
was a commercial asset that, south of the Tweed, would enable
him to sell himself in a better market. As one of his biographers
tells us, "he saw young sparklers every day running off with rich
prizes," for the chapels of Wilkinson and Keith were always
ready to assist the abductor of an heiress. Indeed, before his

arrival at Henley, he had almost succeeded in capturing the daughter of a Leicestershire squire, when the father, who suddenly learnt his past history, sent him about his business. Still, he persisted in his attempts to get the Scotch marriage annulled, and his chances seemed favourable. Most of the relatives of his wife, who had espoused the losing side in the late rebellion, were fled in exile to France or Flanders. Moreover, she belonged to the Catholic Church, which at that time in stern Presbyterian Scotland had fallen upon evil days. Believing that she was alone and friendless, and relying, no doubt, upon the sectarian prejudices of the law courts, he set forth the base lie that he had promised to marry her only on condition she became Protestant. His explanation to the Blandys, in answer to Lord Mark's imputation, was the same as his defence before the Scottish Commissaries. The lady was his mistress, not his wife!

Miss Blandy took the same view of the case that Sophy Western did under similar circumstances. Human nature was little different in those days, but men wore their hearts on their sleeve instead of exhibiting them only in the Courts, and women preferred to be deemed complacent rather than stupid. Doubtless old lawyer Blandy grunted many Saxon sarcasms at the expense of Scotch jurisprudence, and trembled lest son-in-law Diddapper had been entangled beyond redemption. Still, father, mother, and daughter believed the word of their guest, waiting anxiously for the result of the litigation that was to make him a free man. During the year 1748 the Commissaries at Edinburgh decided that Captain Cranstoun and the ill-used Miss Murray were man and wife. Then the latter, being aware of the flirtation at Henley, wrote to warn Miss Blandy, and provided her with a copy of the Court's decree. Great was the consternation at the house on the London road. Visions of tea-gossip over the best set of china in the long parlour at Crailing with my Lady Cranstoun vanished from the old mother's eyes, while the town clerk forgot his dreams of the baby whose two grandfathers were himself and a live lord. Nevertheless, the young Scotsman protested that the marriage was invalid, declared that he would appeal to the highest tribunal, and swore eternal fidelity to his Mary. Alas, she trusted him! Within the sombre depths of her soul there dwelt a fierce resolve to make this man her own. In her sight he was no graceless creature from the barrack-room, but with a great impersonal love she sought in him merely the fulfilment of her destiny.

> "In her first passion, woman loves her lover:
> In all the others, all she loves is love."

At this time Cranstoun's fortunes were in a parlous state. More than half of his slender patrimony had been sequestered for the maintenance of his wife and child, and shortly after the peace of Aix-la-Chapelle, his regiment being disbanded, he was left on half-pay. Still, he did not waver in his purpose to win the heiress of Henley.

On the 30th of September 1749, the poor frivolous old head, which has sported its cap so bravely amidst the worries of pretentious poverty, lay still upon the pillow, and Mary Blandy looked upon the face of her dead mother. It was the turning-point in her career. While his wife was alive, the old lawyer had never lost all faith in his would-be son-in-law during the two years that he had been affianced to his daughter, in spite of the rude shocks which had staggered his credulity. Cranstoun had been allowed to sponge on him for another six months in the previous summer, and had pursued his womenfolk when they paid a visit to Mary's uncle, Serjeant Stevens, of Doctors' Commons. However, soon after the death of his wife the patience of Mr Blandy, who must have perceived that the case of the pretender was hopeless, seems to have become worn out. All idea of the baron's grandchild faded from his mind; the blear-eyed lover was forbidden the house, and for nearly twelve months did not meet his trusting sweetheart.

Although a woman of her intelligence must have perceived that, but for some untoward event, her relationship with her betrothed could never be one of honour, her fidelity remained unshaken. Having passed her thirtieth birthday, the dreadful stigma of spinster-hood was fast falling upon her. If the methods of analogy are of any avail, it is clear that she had become a creature of lust – not the lust of sensuality, but that far more insatiable greed, the craving for conquest, possession, the attainment of the unattainable, calling forth not one but all the emotions of body and soul. A sacrifice of honour – a paltry thing in the face of such mighty passion – would have been no victory, for such in itself was powerless to accomplish the essential metamorphosis of her life. In mutual existence with a lover and slave the destiny of this rare woman alone could be achieved. Thus came the harvest of the tempest. It was not the criminal negligence of the father in encouraging for nearly three years the pretensions of a suitor, who – so a trustworthy gentleman had told him – was a married man, that had planted the seeds of storm. Nor did the filial love of the daughter begin to fade and wither because she had been taught that the affections, like anything which has a price, should be subject to barter and exchange. Deeper far lay the roots of the malignant disease – growing as a portion of her being – a part and principle of life itself. Environment and education merely had inclined into its stunted form the twig, which could never bear fruit unless grafted upon a new stalk! And while the sombre girl brooded over her strange impersonal passion, there rang in her ears the voice of demon-conscience, unceasingly – a taunting, frightful whisper, "When the old man is in his grave you shall be happy."

The esteem of posterity for the eighteenth century, to which belong so many noble lives and great minds, has been influenced by the well-deserved censure bestowed upon a particular epoch. The year 1750 marks a period of transition when all the worst characteristics of the Georgian era were predominant. For nearly a quarter of a century the scornful glance that the boorish little king threw at any book had been reflected in the national taste for literature. Art had hobbled along bravely on the crutches of caricature, tolerated on account of its deformity, and not for its worth. The drama, which had drifted to the lowest ebb in the days of Rich and Heidegger, was just rising from its mudbank, under the leadership of Garrick, with the turn of the tide. Religion, outside the pale of Methodism, was as dead as the influence of the Church of England and its plurality divines. The prostitution of the marriage laws in the Fleet and Savoy had grown to be a menace to the social fabric. London reeked of gin; and although the business of Jack Ketch has been seldom more flourishing, property, until magistrate Fielding came forward, was never less secure from the thief and highwayman. Our second George, who flaunted his mistresses before the public gaze, was a worthy leader of a coarse and vicious society. Female dress took its form from the vulgarity of the times, and was never uglier and more indecent simultaneously. Not only was the "modern fine lady," who wept when a handsome thief was hung, a common type, but the Boobys and Bellastons were fashionable women of the day, quite as much alive as Elizabeth Chudleigh or Caroline Fitzroy. Such was the age of Miss Blandy, and she proved a worthy daughter of it.

In the late summer of 1750 the fickle attorney, who had become weary of opposition, consented to withdraw the sentence of banishment he had pronounced against his daughter's lover. Possibly he fancied that there was a chance, after all, of the Scotch lieutenant's success in the curious law-courts of the North, and perhaps a present of salmon, received from Lady Cranstoun, appeared to him as a favourable augury. Consequently the needy fortune-hunter, who was only too ready to return to his free quarters, paid another lengthy visit to Henley. As the weeks passed, it was evident that the temper of the host and father, whose senile humours were swayed by gravel and heartburn, could not support the new ménage. Fearful lest the devotion of his Molly had caused her to lose all regard for her fair fame, wroth that the clumsy little soldier should have disturbed the peace of his household, the old man received every mention of "the tiresome affair in Scotland" with sneers and gibes. Vanished was the flunkey-optimism that had led him to welcome once more the pertinacious slip of Scottish baronage. Naught would have appeased him but prompt evidence that the suitor was free to lead his daughter to the altar. Nothing could be plainer than that the querulous widower had lost all confidence in his unwelcome guest.

The faithful lovers were filled with dismay. A few strokes of the pen might rob them for ever of their ten thousand pounds. Their wishes were the same, their minds worked as one. A deep, cruel soul-blot, transmitted perhaps by some cut-throat borderer through the blood of generations, would have led William Cranstoun to commit, without scruple, the vilest of crimes. Those base attempts to put away his wife, and to cast the stigma of bastardy upon his child, added to his endeavour to entrap one heiress after another into a bigamous marriage, make him guilty of offences less only than murder. In his present position he had cause for desperation. Yet, although utterly broken in fortune, there was a rich treasure at his hand if he dared to seize it. Were her father dead, Molly Blandy, whether as wife or mistress, would be his – body, soul, and wealth. Within the veins of the woman a like heart-stain spread its poison. All the lawless passion of her nature cried out against her parent's rule, which to her mind, was seeking to banish what had become more precious than her life. Knowing that her own fierce will had its mate in his, she believed that his obduracy could not be conquered, and she lived in dread lest she should be disinherited. And all this time, day after day, the demon-tempter whispered, "When the old man is in his grave you shall be happy."

Which of the guilty pair was the first to suggest the heartless crime it is impossible to ascertain, but there is evidence, apart from Miss Blandy's statement, that Cranstoun was the leading spirit. Possibly, nay probably, the deed was never mentioned in brutal plainness in so many words. The history of crime affords many indications that the blackest criminals are obliged to soothe a neurotic conscience with the anodyne of make-belief. It is quite credible that the two spoke of the projected murder from the first (as indeed Miss Blandy explained it later) as an attempt to conciliate the old lawyer by administering a supernatural love philtre, having magical qualities like Oberon's flower in *A Midsummer Night's Dream*, which would make him consent to their marriage. Presently a reign of mystic terror seemed to invade the little house in the London road. With fear ever present in her eyes, the figure of the sombre woman glided from room to room, whispering to the frightened servants ghostly tales of things supernatural – of unearthly music that she had heard during the misty autumn nights, of noises that had awakened her from sleep, of the ghastly apparitions that had appeared to her lover. And to all these stories she had but one dismal interpretation – saying it had come to her from a wizard-woman in Scotland – they were signs and tokens that her father would die within a

year! Those who heard her listened and trembled, and the words
sank deep into their memory. So the winter crept on; but while all
slunk through the house with bated breath, shrinking at each
mysterious sound, the old man, doomed by the sorceress, remained unsuspicious of what was going on around him.

Not long before Christmas, to the great relief of his churlish
host, the little Scotsman's clumsy legs passed through the front
door for the last time, and he set out for his brother's seat at
Crailing in the shire of Roxburgh. Yet, though his lengthy visit
had come to an end, his spirit remained to rule the brain of the
woman who loved him. Early in the year 1751 she received a box,
containing a present from Cranstoun, a set of table linen, and
some "Scotch pebbles." Lawyer Blandy viewed the stones with
suspicious eyes, for he hated all things beyond the Cheviot Hills,
but did not make any comment. The relationship between father
and daughter had become cold and distant. Quarrels were constant in the unhappy home. Often in the midst of her passion she
was heard to mutter deep curses against the old man. Indeed, so
banished was her love that she talked without emotion to the
servants of the likelihood of his death, in fulfilment of the witch's
prophecy.

Some weeks later, when another consignment of the mysterious "Scotch pebbles" had arrived for Miss Blandy, it was
noticed that her conduct became still more dark and strange.
Slinking through the house with slow and stealthy tread, she
appeared to shun all eyes, as though bent upon some hidden
purpose. A glance within the box from the North would have
revealed the secret. When the crafty accomplice found that she
was unable to procure the means of taking her father's life, he had
been forced to supply her with the weapons. During the spring,
the health of the old lawyer, who suffered more or less from
chronic ailments, began to grow more feeble. His garments hung
loosely upon his shrunken limbs, while the teeth dropped from
his palsied jaws. The old witch's curse seemed to have fallen upon
the home, and, to those who looked with apprehension for every
sign and portent, it was fulfilled in many direful ways. Early in
June, Ann Emmet, an old charwoman employed about the house,
was seized with a violent illness after drinking from a half-

emptied cup left at Mr Blandy's breakfast. A little later, Susan Gunnel, one of the maid-servants, was affected in a similar way through taking some tea prepared for her master. One August morning, in the secrecy of her own chamber, trembling at every footfall beyond the locked door, Mary Blandy gazed with eager, awestruck eyes upon a message sent by her lover.

"I am sorry there are such occasions to clean your pebbles," wrote the murderous little Scotsman. "You must make use of the powder to them, by putting it into anything of substance, wherein it will not swim a-top of the water, of which I wrote to you in one of my last. I am afraid it will be too weak to take off their rust, or at least it will take too long a time."

From the language of metaphor it is easy to translate the ghastly meaning. She must have told Cranstoun that the white arsenic, which he had sent to her under the pseudonym of "powder to clean the pebbles," remained floating on the surface of the tea. Possibly her father had noticed this phenomenon, and, not caring to drink the liquid, had escaped the painful sickness which had attacked the less cautious servants. But now she had found a remedy – "anything of substance!" – a safe and sure vehicle that could not fail. Louder still in the ears of the lost woman rang the mocking words, "When the old man is dead you shall be happy."

During the forenoon of Monday, the 5th of August, Susan Gunnel, the maid, met her young mistress coming from the pantry.

"Oh, Susan," she exclaimed, "I have been stirring my papa's water gruel"; and then, perceiving other servants through the half-open door of the laundry, she added gaily, "If I was ever to take to eating anything in particular it would be oatmeal."

No response came from the discreet Susan, but she marvelled, calling to mind that Miss Blandy had said to her some time previously, noticing that she appeared unwell:

"Have you been eating any water gruel? for I am told that water gruel hurts me, and it may hurt you."

Later in the day, her wonder was increased when she saw her mistress stirring the gruel in a half-pint mug, putting her fingers into the spoon, and then rubbing them together. In the evening the same mug was taken as usual to the old man's bedroom. On Tuesday night Miss Blandy sent down in haste to order gruel for her father, who had been indisposed all day, and such was her solicitude that she met the footman on the stairs, and taking the basin from his hands, carried it herself into the parlour. Early the next morning, while Ann Emmet, the old charwoman, was busy at her wash-tub, Susan Gunnel came from upstairs.

"Dame," she observed, "you used to be fond of water gruel. Here is a very fine mess my master left last night, and I believe it will do you good."

Sitting down upon a bench, this most unfortunate old lady proceeded to consume the contents of the basin, and for a second time was seized with a strange and violent illness. Soon afterwards Miss Blandy came into the kitchen.

"Susan, as your master has taken physic, he may want some more water gruel," said she. "As there is some in the house you need not make fresh, for you are ironing."

"Madam, it will be stale," replied the servant. "It will not hinder me much to make fresh."

A little later, while tasting the stuff, Susan noticed a white sediment at the bottom of the pan. Greatly excited, she ran to show Betty Binfield, the cook, who bore no good-will towards her young mistress.

"What oatmeal is this?" asked Betty, significantly. "It looks like flour."

"I have never seen oatmeal as white before," said the maid.

Carefully and thoroughly the suspicious servants examined the contents of the saucepan, taking it out of doors to view it in the light. And while they looked at the white gritty sediment they told each other in low whispers that this must be poison. Locking up the pan, they showed it next day to the local apothecary, who, as usual in those times, was the sick man's medical attendant.

Nothing occurred to alarm the guilty woman until Saturday. On that morning, in the homely fashion of middle-class manners, the lawyer, who wanted to shave, came into the kitchen, where hot water and a good fire were ready for him. Accustomed to his habits, the servants went about their work as usual. Some trouble seemed to be preying upon his mind.

"I was like to have been poisoned once," piped the feeble old man, turning his bloodshot eyes upon his daughter, who was in the room.

"It was on this same day, the tenth of August," he continued, in his weak, trembling voice, for his frame had become shattered during the last week. "It was at the coffee-house or at the Lyon, and two other gentlemen were like to have been poisoned by what they drank."

"Sir, I remember it very well," replied the imperturbable woman, and then fell to arguing with her querulous father at which tavern the adventure had taken place.

"One of the gentlemen died immediately," he resumed, looking at her with a long, reproachful glance. "The other is dead now, and I have survived them both. But" – his piteous gaze grew more intense – "it is my fortune to be poisoned at last."

A similar ordeal took place in a little while. At breakfast Mr Blandy seemed in great pain, making many complaints. As he sipped his tea, he declared that it had a gritty, bad taste, and would not drink it.

"Have you not put too much of the black stuff into it?" he demanded suddenly of his daughter, referring to the canister of Bohea.

This time she was unable to meet his searching eyes.

"It is as usual," she stammered in confusion.

A moment later she rose, trembling and distressed, and hurriedly left the room.

There was reason for the old man's suspicion. Before he had risen from his bed, the faithful Susan Gunnel told him of the discovery in the pan of water gruel, and both agreed that the mysterious powder had been sent by Cranstoun. Yet, beyond what he had said at breakfast, and in the kitchen, he questioned his daughter no more! Still, although no direct charge had been made, alarmed by her father's hints she hastened to destroy all evidence that could be used against her. During the afternoon, stealing into the kitchen under pretence of drying a letter before the fire, she crushed a paper among the coals. As soon as she was gone the watchful spies – servants Gunnel and Binfield – snatched it away before it had been destroyed by the flames.

This paper contained a white substance, and on it was written
"powder to clean the pebbles." Towards evening famous Dr
Addington arrived from Reading, summoned by Miss Blandy,
who was driven on account of her fears to show a great concern.
After seeing his patient the shrewd old leech had no doubt as to
the symptoms. With habitual directness he told the daughter that
her father had been poisoned.

"It is impossible," she replied.

On Sunday morning the doctor found the sick man a little
better, but ordered him to keep his bed. Startling proofs of the
accuracy of his diagnosis were forthcoming. One of the maids put
into his hands the packet of arsenic found in the fire, while
Norton the apothecary produced the powder from the pan of
gruel. Addington at once took the guilty woman to task.

"If your father dies," he told her sternly, "you will inevitably
be ruined."

Nevertheless she appears to have brazened the matter out, but
desired the doctor to come again the next day. When she was
alone, her first task was to scribble a note to Cranstoun, which she
gave to her father's clerk to "put into the post." Having heard
dark rumours whispered by the servants that Mr Blandy had
been poisoned by his daughter, the man had no hesitation in
opening the letter, which he handed over to the apothecary. It ran
as follows:—

"Dear Willy, – My father is so bad that I have only time to tell
you that if you do not hear from me soon again, don't be
frightened. I am better myself. Lest any accident should happen
to your letters be careful what you write.

"My sincere compliments. – I am ever, yours."

That evening Norton ordered Miss Blandy from her father's
room, telling Susan Gunnel to remain on the watch, and admit no
one. At last the heartless daughter must have seen that some other
defence was needed than blind denial. Still, the poor old sufferer
persisted that Cranstoun was the sole author of the mischief. On
Monday morning, although sick almost to death, he sent the maid
with a message to his daughter.

"Tell her," said he, "that I will forgive her if she will bring that villain to justice."

In answer to his words, Miss Blandy came to her father's bedroom in tears, and a suppliant. Susan Gunnel, who was present, thus reports the interview.

"Sir, how do you do?" said she.

"I am very ill," he replied.

Falling upon her knees, she said to him:

"Banish me or send me to any remote part of the world. As to Mr Cranstoun, I will never see him, speak to him, as long as I live, so as you will forgive me."

"I forgive thee, my dear," he answered. "And I hope God will forgive thee, but thee should have considered better than to have attempted anything against thy father. Thee shouldst have considered I was thy own father."

"Sir," she protested, "as to your illness I am entirely innocent."

"Madam," interrupted old Susan Gunnel, "I believe you must not say you are entirely innocent, for the powder that was taken out of the water gruel, and the paper of powder that was taken out of the fire, are now in such hands that they must be publicly produced. I believe I had one dose prepared for my master in a dish of tea about six weeks ago."

"I have put no powder into tea," replied Miss Blandy. "I have put powder into water gruel, and if you are injured," she assured her father, "I am entirely innocent, for it was given me with another intent."

The dying man did not wait for further explanation, but, turning in his bed, he cried:

"Oh, such a villain! To come to my house, eat of the best, drink of the best that my house could afford – to take away my life, and ruin my daughter! Oh, my dear," he continued, "thee must hate that man, thee must hate the ground he treads on. Thee canst not help it."

"Oh, sir, your tenderness towards me is like a sword to my heart," she answered. "Every word you say is like swords piercing my heart – much worse than if you were to be ever so angry. I must down on my knees and beg you will not curse me."

"I curse thee, my dear!" he replied. "How couldst thou think I could curse thee? I bless thee, and hope that God will bless thee and amend thy life. Go, my dear, go out of my room . . . Say no more, lest thou shouldst say anything to thy own prejudice . . . Go to thy uncle Stevens; take him for thy friend. Poor man, – I am sorry for him."

The memory of the old servant, who repeated the above conversation in her evidence at Miss Blandy's trial, would seem remarkable did we not bear in mind that she went through various rehearsals before the coroner and magistrates, and possibly with the lawyers for the prosecution. Some embellishments also must be credited to the taste and fancy of Mr Rivington's reporters. Still, the gist must be true, and certainly has much pathos. Yet the father's forgiveness of his daughter, when he must have known that her conduct was wilful, although piteous and noble, may not have been the result of pure altruism. Naturally, the wish that Cranstoun alone was guilty was parent to the thought. Whether the approach of eternity brought a softening influence upon him, and he saw his follies and errors in the light of repentance, or whether the ruling passion strong in death made the vain old man struggle to avert the black disgrace that threatened his good name, and the keen legal intellect, which could counsel his daughter so well, foresaw the coming escheatment of his small estate to the lord of the manor, are problems for the student of psychology.

During the course of the day brother leech Lewis of Oxford – a master-builder of pharmacopœia – was summoned by the sturdy begetter of statesmen, and there was much bobbing of learned wigs and nice conduct of medical canes. Addington asked the dying man whom he suspected to be the giver of the poison.

"A poor love-sick girl," murmured the old lawyer, smiling through his tears. "I forgive her – I always thought there was mischief in those cursed Scotch pebbles."

In the evening a drastic step was taken. Acting on the principle of "thorough," which made his son's occupancy of the Home Office so memorable at a later period, the stern doctor accused Miss Blandy of the crime, and secured her keys and papers. Conquered by fear, the stealthy woman for a while lost all self-possession. In an agony of shame and terror she sought to shield herself by the pretence of superstitious folly. Wringing her hands in a seeming agony of remorse, she declared that her lover had ruined her.

"I received the powder from Mr Cranstoun," she cried, "with a present of Scotch pebbles. He had wrote on the paper that held it, 'The powder to clean the pebbles with.' He assured me that it was harmless, and that if I would give my father some of it now and then, a little and a little at a time, in any liquid, it would make him kind to him and to me."

In a few scathing questions the worldly-wise Addington cast ridicule upon this weird story of a love philtre. Taking the law into his own resolute hands, with the consent of colleague Lewis he locked the wretched woman in her room and placed a guard over her. Little could be done to relieve the sufferings of poor ten-thousand-pound Blandy – who proved to be a mere four-thousand-pound attorney when it came to the test – and on Wednesday afternoon, the 14th of August, he closed his proud old eyes for ever. In her desperation the guilty daughter could think of naught but escape. On the evening of her father's death, impelled by an irresistible frenzy to flee from the scene of her butchery, she begged the footman in vain to assist her to get away. During Thursday morning – for it was not possible to keep her in custody without legal warrant – a little group of children saw a dishevelled figure coming swiftly along the High Street towards the river. At once there arose the cry of "Murderess!" and, surrounded by an angry mob, she was driven to take refuge in a neighbouring inn. It was vain to battle against fate. That same afternoon the coroner's inquest was held, and the verdict pronounced her a parricide. On the following Saturday, in charge of two constables, she was driven in her father's carriage to Oxford Castle. An enraged populace, thinking that she was trying again to escape, surrounded the vehicle, and sought to prevent her from leaving the town.

Owing to the social position of the accused, and the enormity of her offence, the eyes of the whole nation were turned to the tragedy at Henley. Gossips of the day, such as Horace Walpole and Tate Wilkinson, tell us that the story of Miss Blandy was upon every lip. In spite of the noble irony of "Drawcansir" Fielding, journalists and pamphleteers had no scruple in referring to the prisoner as a wicked murderess or a cruel parricide. Yet the case of Henry Coleman, who, during the August of this year, had been proved innocent of a crime for which he had suffered death, should have warned the public against hasty assumption. For six months the dark woman was waiting for her trial. Although it was the custom for a jailor to make an exhibition of his captive to anyone who would pay the entrance fee, nobody was allowed to see Miss Blandy without her consent. Two comfortable rooms were set apart for her in the keeper's house; she was free to take walks in the garden, and to have her own maid. At last, when stories of a premeditated escape were noised abroad, Secretary Newcastle, in a usual state of fuss, fearing that she might repeat the achievement of Queen Maud, gave orders that she must be put in irons. At first Thomas Newell, who had succeeded her father as town clerk of Henley four years previously, was employed in her defence, but he offended her by speaking of Cranstoun as "a mean-looking, little, ugly fellow," and so she dismissed him in favour of Mr Rives, a lawyer from Woodstock. Her old invincible courage had returned, and only once – when she learnt the paltry value of her father's fortune – did she lose self-possession. For a dismal echo must have come back in the mocking words, "When the old man is in his grave you shall be happy."

At last the magistrates – Lords Cadogan and "New-Style" Macclesfield, who had undertaken duties which in later days Mr Newton or Mr Montagu Williams would have shared with Scotland Yard – finish their much-praised detective work, and on Tuesday, the 3rd of March 1752, Mary Blandy is brought to the bar. The Court meets in the divinity school, since the town-hall is in the hands of the British workman, and because the University, so "Sir Alexander Drawcansir" tells his readers, will not allow the use of the Sheldonian Theatre. Why the most beautiful room in Oxford should be deemed a fitter place of desecration than the archbishop's monstrosity is not made clear. An accident delays the trial – this second "Great Oyer of Poisoning!" There is a small stone or other obstruction in the lock – can some sentimental, wry-brained undergraduate think to aid the gallows-heroine of his fancy? – and while it is being removed, Judges Legge and Smythe return to their lodgings.

At eight o'clock, Mary Blandy, calm and stately, stands beneath the graceful fretted ceiling, facing the tribunal. From wall to wall an eager crowd has filled the long chamber, surging through the doorway, flowing in at the open windows, jostling even against the prisoner. A chair is placed for her in case of fatigue, and her maid is by her side. A plain and neat dress befits her serene manner – a black bombazine short *sacque* (the garb of mourning), white linen kerchief, and a thick crape shade and hood. From the memory of those present her countenance can never fade. A broad high forehead, above which her thick jet hair is smoothed under a cap; a pair of fine black sparkling eyes; the colouring almost of a gipsy; cheeks with scarce a curve; mouth full, but showing no softness; nose large, straight, determined – it is the face of one of those rare women who command, not the love, but the obedience of mankind. Still it is intelligent, not unseductive, compelling; and yet, in spite of the deep, flashing eyes, without radiance of soul – the face of a sombre-hearted woman.

Black, indeed, is the indictment that Bathurst, a venerable young barrister who represents the Crown, unfolds against her, but only once during his burst of carefully-matured eloquence is there any change in her serenity. When the future Lord Chancellor declares that the base Cranstoun "had fallen in love, not with her, but with her fortune," the woman's instinct cannot tolerate the reflection upon her charms, and she darts a look of bitterest scorn upon the speaker. And only once does she show a trace of human softness. When her godmother, old Mrs Mountenay, is leaving the witness-box, she repeats the curtsey which the prisoner had previously disregarded, and then, in an impulse of pity, presses forward, and, seizing Miss Blandy's hand, exclaims, "God bless you!" At last, and for the first time, the tears gather in the accused woman's eyes.

Many abuses, handed down from a previous century, still render barbarous the procedure of criminal trials. The case is hurried over in one day; counsel for the prisoner can only examine witnesses, but not address the jury; the prosecution is accustomed to put forward evidence of which the defence has been kept in ignorance. Yet no injustice is done to Mary Blandy. Thirteen hours is enough to tear the veil from her sombre heart; the tongue of Nestor would fail to show her innocent; of all that her accusers can say of her she is well aware. Never for one moment is the issue in doubt. What can her scoffing, sceptic age, with its cold-blooded sentiment and tame romance, think of a credulity that employed a love-potion in the guise of affection but with the result of death! How is it possible to judge a daughter who persisted in her black art, although its dire effects were visible, not once, but many times! Her defence, when at last it comes, is spoken bravely, but better had been left unsaid.

"My lords," she begins, "it is morally impossible for me to lay down the hardships I have received. I have been aspersed in my character. In the first place, it has been said that I have spoke ill of my father; that I have cursed him and wished him at hell; which is extremely false. Sometimes little family affairs have happened, and he did not speak to me so kind as I could wish. I own I am passionate, my lords, and in those passions some hasty expressions might have dropt. But great care has been taken to recollect every word I have spoken at different times, and to apply them to such particular purposes as my enemies knew would do me the greatest injury. These are hardships, my lords, extreme hardships! – such as you yourselves must allow to be so. It was said, too, my lords, that I endeavoured to make my escape. Your lordships will judge from the difficulties I laboured under. I had lost my father – I was accused of being his murderer – I was not permitted to go near him – I was forsaken by my friends – affronted by the mob – insulted by my servants. Although I begged to have the liberty to listen at the door where he died, I was not allowed it. My keys were taken from me, my shoe-buckles and garters too – to prevent me from making away with myself, as though I was the most abandoned creature. What could I do, my lords? I verily believe I was out of my senses.

When I heard my father was dead and the door open, I ran out of the house, and over the bridge, and had nothing on but a half sack and petticoat, without a hoop, my petticoats hanging about me. The mob gathered about me. Was this a condition, my lords, to make my escape in? A good woman beyond the bridge, seeing me in this distress, desired me to walk in till the mob was dispersed. The town sergeant was there. I begged he would take me under his protection to have me home. The woman said it was not proper, the mob was very great, and that I had better stay a little. When I came home they said I used the constable ill. I was locked up for fifteen hours, with only an old servant of the family to attend me. I was not allowed a maid for the common decencies of my sex. I was sent to gaol, and was in hopes, there, at least, this usage would have ended, but was told it was reported I was frequently drunk – that I attempted to make my escape – that I never attended the chapel. A more abstemious woman, my lords, I believe, does not live.

Upon the report of my making my escape, the gentleman who was High Sheriff last year (not the present) came and told me, by order of the higher powers, he must put an iron on me. I submitted, as I always do to the higher powers. Some time after, he came again, and said he must put a heavier upon me, which I have worn, my lords, till I came hither. I asked the Sheriff why I was so ironed? He said he did it by command of some noble peer, on his hearing that I intended to make my escape. I told them I never had such a thought, and I would bear it with the other cruel usage I had received on my character. The Rev. Mr Swinton, the worthy clergyman who attended me in prison, can testify that I was very regular at the chapel when I was well. Sometimes I really was not able to come out, and then he attended me in my room. They likewise published papers and depositions which ought not to have been published, in order to represent me as the most abandoned of my sex, and to prejudice the world against me. I submit myself to your lordships, and to the worthy jury. I can assure your lordships, as I am to answer it before that Grand Tribunal

where I must appear, I am as innocent as the child unborn
of the death of my father. I would not endeavour to save my
life at the expense of truth. I really thought the powder an
innocent, inoffensive thing, and I gave it to procure his love.
It was mentioned, I should say, I was ruined. My lords,
when a young woman loses her character, is not that her
ruin? Why, then, should this expression be construed in so
wide a sense? Is it not ruining my character to have such a
thing laid to my charge? And whatever may be the event of
this trial, I am ruined most effectually.

A strange apology – amazing in its effrontery!

Gentle Heneage Legge speaks long and tenderly, while the
listeners shudder with horror as they hear the dismal history
unfolded in all entirely for the first time. No innocent heart could
have penned that last brief warning to her lover – none but an
accomplice would have received his cryptic message. Every word
in the testimony of the stern doctor seems to hail her parricide –
every action of her stealthy career has been noted by the watchful
eyes of her servants. And, as if in damning confirmation of her
guilt, there is the black record of her flight from the scene of
crime. Eight o'clock has sounded when the judge has finished.
For a few moments the jury converse in hurried whispers. It is
ominous that they make no attempt to leave the court, but merely
draw closer together. Then, after the space of five minutes they
turn, and the harsh tones of the clerk of arraigns sound through
the chamber.

"Mary Blandy, hold up thy hand . . . Gentlemen of the jury,
look upon the prisoner. How say you: Is Mary Blandy guilty of
the felony and murder whereof she stands indicted, or not
guilty?"

"Guilty!" comes the low, reluctant answer.

Never has more piteous drama been played within the cold fair
walls of the divinity school than that revealed by the guttering
candles on this chill March night. Amidst the long black shadows,
through which gleam countless rows of pallid faces, in the deep
silence, broken at intervals by hushed sobs, the invincible woman
stands with unruffled mien to receive her sentence. As the verdict

is declared, a smile seems to play upon her lips. While the judge, with tearful eyes and broken voice, pronounces her doom, she listens without a sign of fear. There is a brief, breathless pause, while all wait with fierce-beating hearts for her reply. No trace of terror impedes her utterance. Thanking the judge for his candour and impartiality, she turns to her counsel, among whom only Richard Aston rose to eminence, and, with a touch of pretty forethought, wishes them better success in their other causes. Then, and her voice grows more solemn, she begs for a little time to settle her affairs and to make her peace with God. To which his lordship replies with great emotion:

"To be sure, you shall have proper time allowed you."

When she is conducted from the court she steps into her coach with the air of a belle whose chair is to take her to a fashionable rout. The fatal news has reached the prison before her arrival. As she enters the keeper's house, which for so long has been her home, she finds the family overcome with grief and the children all in tears.

"Don't mind it," she cries, cheerfully. "What does it matter? I am very hungry. Pray let me have something for supper as soon as possible."

That sombre heart of hers is a brave one also.

All this time William Cranstoun, worthy brother in all respects of Simon Tappertit, had been in hiding – in Scotland perhaps, or, as some say, in Northumberland – watching with fearful quakings for the result of the trial. Shortly after the conviction of his accomplice he managed to take ship to the Continent, and luckily for his country he never polluted its soil again. There are several contemporary accounts of his adventures in France and in the Netherlands, to which the curious may refer. All agree that he confessed his share in the murder when he was safe from justice. With unaccustomed propriety, our Lady Fate soon hastened to snap the thread of his existence, and on the 3rd of December of this same year, at the little town of Furnes in Flanders, aged thirty-eight, he drew his last breath. A short time before, being seized with remorse for his sins, he had given the Catholic Church the honour of enrolling him a proselyte. Indeed the conversion of so great a ruffian was regarded as such a feather

in their cap that the good monks and friars advertised the event
by means of a sumptuous funeral.

Worthy Judge Legge fulfils his promise to the unhappy Miss
Blandy, and she is given six weeks in which to prepare herself for
death. Meek and more softened is the sombre woman, who, like a
devoted penitent, submits herself day after day to the vulgar gaze
of a hundred eyes, while she bows in all humility before the altar
of her God. Yet her busy brain is aware that those to whom she
looks for intercession are keeping a careful watch upon her
demeanour. For she has begged her godmother Mrs Mountenay
to ask one of the bishops to speak for her; she is said to entertain
the hope that the recently-bereaved Princess will endeavour to
obtain a reprieve. In the fierce war of pamphleteers, inevitable in
those days, she takes her share, playing with incomparable tact to
the folly of the credulous. Although the majority, perhaps,
believe her guilty, she knows that a considerable party is in
her favour. On the 20th of March is published "A Letter from
a Clergyman to Miss Blandy, with her Answer," in which she
tells the story of her share in the tragedy. During the remainder of
her imprisonment she extends this narrative into a long account
of the whole case – assisted, it is believed, by her spiritual adviser,
the Rev. John Swinton, who, afflicted possibly by one of his
famous fits of woolgathering, seems convinced of her innocence.
No human effort, however, is of any avail. Both the second and
third George, knowing their duty as public entertainers, seldom
cheated the gallows of a victim of distinction.

Originally the execution had been fixed for Saturday, the 4th of
April, but is postponed until the following Monday, because the
University authorities do not think it seemly that the sentence
shall be carried out during Holy Week. A great crowd collects in
the early morning outside the prison walls before the announcement of the short reprieve, and it speaks marvels for the discipline
of the gaol that Miss Blandy is allowed to go up into rooms facing
the Castle Green so that she can view the throng. Gazing upon
the assembly without a tremor, she says merely that she will not
balk their expectations much longer. On Sunday she takes sacra-
ment for the last time, and signs a declaration in which she denies
once more all knowledge that the powder was poisonous. In the

evening, hearing that the Sheriff has arrived in the town, she sends a request that she may not be disturbed until eight o'clock the next morning.

It was half-past the hour she had named when the dismal procession reached the door of her chamber. The Under-Sheriff was accompanied by the Rev. John Swinton, and by her friend Mr Rives, the lawyer. Although her courage did not falter, she appeared meek and repentant, and spoke with anxiety of her future state, in doubt whether she would obtain pardon for her sins. This penitent mood encouraged the clergyman to beg her declare the whole truth, to which she replied that she must persist in asserting her innocence to the end. No entreaty would induce her to retract the solemn avowal.

At nine o'clock she was conducted from her room, dressed in the same black gown that she had worn at the trial, with her hands and arms tied by strong black silk ribbons. A crowd of five thousand persons, hushed and expectant, was waiting on the Castle Green to witness her sufferings. Thirty yards from the door of the gaol, whence she was led into the open air, stood the gallows – a beam placed across the arms of two trees. Against it lay a step-ladder covered with black cloth. The horror of her crime must have been forgotten by all who gazed upon the calm and brave woman. For truly she died like a queen. Serene and fearless she walked to the fatal spot, and joined most fervently with the clergyman in prayer. After this was ended they told her that if she wished she might speak to the spectators.

"Good people," she cried, in a clear, audible voice, "give me leave to declare to you that I am perfectly innocent as to any intention to destroy or even hurt my dear father; that I did not know, or even suspect, that there was any poisonous quality in the fatal powder I gave him; though I can never be too much punished for being the innocent cause of his death. As to my mother's and Mrs Pocock's deaths, that have been unjustly laid to my charge, I am not even the innocent cause of them, nor did I in the least contribute to them. So help me, God, in these my last moments. And may I not meet with eternal salvation, nor be acquitted by Almighty God, in whose awful presence I am instantly to appear hereafter, if the whole of what is here asserted is not true. I from the bottom of my soul forgive all those concerned in my prosecution; and particularly the jury, notwithstanding their fatal verdict."

Then, having ascended five steps of the ladder, she turned to the officials. "Gentlemen," she requested, with a show of modesty, "do not hang me high." The humanity of those whose task it was to put her to death, forced them to ask her to go a little higher. Climbing two steps more, she then looked round, and trembling, said, "I am afraid I shall fall." Still, her invincible courage enabled her to address the crowd once again. "Good people," she said, "take warning by me to be on your guard against the sallies of any irregular passion, and pray for me that I may be accepted at the Throne of Grace." While the rope was being placed around her neck it touched her face, and she gave a deep sigh. Then with her own fingers she moved it to one side. A white handkerchief had been bound across her forehead, and she drew it over her features. As it did not come low enough, a woman, who had attended her and who had fixed the noose around her throat, stepped up and pulled it down. For a while she stood in prayer, and then gave the signal by thrusting out a little book which she held in her hand. The ladder was moved from under her feet, and in obedience to the laws of her country she was suspended in the air, swaying and convulsed, until the grip of the rope choked the breath from her body.

Horrible! Yet only in degree are our own methods different from those employed a hundred and fifty years ago.

During the whole of the sad tragedy, the crowd, unlike the howling mob at Tyburn, maintained an awestruck silence. There were few dry eyes, though the sufferer did not shed a tear, and hundreds of those who witnessed her death went away convinced of her innocence. An elegant young man named Edward Gibbon, with brain wrapped in the mists of theology, who for three days had been gentleman commoner at Magdalen, does not appear to have been attracted to the scene. Surely George Selwyn must be maligned, else he would have posted to Oxford to witness this spectacle. It would have been his only opportunity of seeing a gentlewoman in the hands of the executioner.

After hanging for half an hour with the feet, in consequence of her request, almost touching the ground, the body was carried upon the shoulders of one of the sheriff's men to a neighbouring house. At five o'clock in the afternoon the coffin containing her remains was taken in a hearse to Henley, where, in the dead of night, amidst a vast concourse, it was interred in the chancel of the parish church between the graves of her father and mother.

So died "the unfortunate Miss Blandy," in the thirty-second year of her age – with a grace and valour which no scene on the scaffold has ever excelled. If, as the authors of *The Beggar's Opera* and *The History of Jonathan Wild* have sought to show, in playful irony, the greatness of the criminal is comparable with the greatness of the statesman, then she must rank with Mary of Scotland and Catherine of Russia among the queens of crime. Hers was the soul of steel, theirs also the opportunity.

In every period the enormity of a sin can be estimated only by its relation to the spirit of the age; and in spite of cant and sophistry, the contemporaries of Miss Blandy made no legal distinction between the crimes of parricide and petty larceny. Nay, the same rope that strangled the brutal cut-throat in a few moments might prolong the agony of a poor thief for a quarter of an hour. Had the doctors succeeded in saving the life of the old attorney, the strange law which in later times put to death Elizabeth Fenning would have been powerless to demand the life of Mary Blandy for a similar offence. The protests of Johnson and Fielding against the iniquity of the criminal code fell on idle ears.

Thus we may not judge Mary Blandy from the standpoint of our own moral grandeur, for she is a being of another world – one of the vain, wilful, selfish – children to whom an early Guelph was king – merely one of the blackest sheep in a flock for the most part ill-favoured. As we gaze upon her portrait there comes a feeling that we do not know this sombre woman after all, for though the artist has produced a faithful resemblance, we perceive there is something lacking. We look into part, not into her whole soul. None but one of the immortals – Rembrandt, or his peer – could have shown this queen among criminals as she was: an iron-hearted, remorseless, demon-woman, her fair, cruel

visage raised mockingly amidst a chiaroscuro of crime and mur-
kiness unspeakable.

> "a narrow, foxy face,
> Heart-hiding smile, and gay persistent eye."

In our own country the women of gentle birth who have been
convicted of murder since the beginning of the eighteenth century may be counted on the fingers of one hand. Mary Blandy,
Constance Kent, Florence Maybrick – for that unsavoury person,
Elizabeth Jefferies, has no claim to be numbered in the roll, and
the verdict against beautiful Madeleine Smith was "Not proven"
– these names exhaust the list. And of them, the first alone paid
the penalty at the gallows. The annals of crime contain the
records of many parricides, some that have been premeditated
with devilish art, but scarce one that a daughter has wrought by
the most loathsome of coward's weapons. In comparison with the
murderess of Henley, even Frances Howard and Anne Turner
were guilty of a venial crime. Mary Blandy stands alone and
incomparable – pilloried to all ages among the basest of her sex.

Yet the world soon forgot her. "Since the two misses were
hanged," chats Horace Walpole on the 23rd of June, coupling
irreverently the names of Blandy and Jefferies with the beautiful
Gunnings – "since the two misses were hanged, and the two
misses were married, there is nothing at all talked of." Society,
however, soon found a new thrill in the adventures of the young
woman Elizabeth Canning.

PHYSICIANS, HEAL YOURSELVES

(Dr Thomas Smethurst, UK 1859)

Leslie Hale

The trial of Dr Smethurst was the bleakest hour in the history of nineteenth-century forensic medicine. Smethurst was accused of poisoning Miss Isabella Bankes, a woman to whom he was biga-mously married. A leading toxicologist, Dr Alfred Taylor, testified to the magistrates that he had found traces of arsenic in Miss Bankes's body. But at the trial he admitted that the arsenic came from a flaw in the apparatus used in his analysis. Furthermore, Dr Taylor and two other medical witnesses for the prosecution contra-dicted each other, in the words of the British Medical Journal, *"in matters where there could be no possibility of doubt." Nevertheless, Dr Smethurst was convicted of murder. The subsequent outcry led to the Home Secretary's historic decision to refer Smethurst's case to yet another medical authority. In the result, he was granted a free pardon. Forensic medicine, railed at by its detractors as "a beastly science", was humiliated. The* Dublin Medical Press *wrote of Dr Taylor that he had, "brought an amount of disrepute upon his branch of the profession that years will not remove." So it proved. Here, the writer's purpose is to illuminate the possibility of hanging an innocent man, but he covers the medical muddle too. This brief account appeared in 1961, when the campaign for the abolition of capital punishment was at its height. Leslie Hale (1902–85) was Labour MP for Oldham for many years, later becoming a life peer. A noted parliamentary wit: short, stout and bald, it was fitting that a man so*

passionately opposed to hanging should have earned himself a
reputation for speaking in debates at breakneck speed.

> "Who shall decide when doctors disagree
> And soundest casuists doubt, like you and me?"
>   Alexander Pope

"Have you heard the news?"
    "No."
    "She's dead."
    There was no need to say who. All Richmond knew that, on the
previous day, little Dr Smethurst, generally regarded as a quiet,
inoffensive, and rather ineffective man, had been charged at the
local court with administering poison to his wife. He had surprisingly been released on bail, but now that the lady was dead
the charge must be one of murder. This was sensational news
indeed and from that time the case was the subject of excited
conversation wherever two or three were gathered together.
There were more thrills to come. The famous toxicologist,
Professor A. S. Taylor, had been entrusted with the inquiry as
to cause of death. Then it became generally known that the
deceased lady was not the wife of Dr Smethurst, for at the time
of their wedding, in December of the previous year at Battersea
Church, his first wife was still living at Bayswater. The relatives
of the deceased had retained one of the most famous advocates of
the day, the great Serjeant Ballantine, to prosecute. He had even
condescended to appear in Richmond at the inquest and at the
police-court proceedings.
    On the first day of the hearing at the local Sessions House, on
11 May 1859, the proceedings were rather disappointing, the
evidence being largely formal; but on the resumed hearing nineteen days later a sensation soon came. Serjeant Ballantine rose to
make a second speech and announced that Professor Taylor was
now present. Among the bottles removed from the prisoner's
home was one containing chloride of potass, "a most destructive
salt of a highly inflammable nature . . . which taken internally

would . . . act upon the kidneys and produce nausea . . ." The bottle had originally contained quinine.

"On complete analysis Professor Taylor deduced this fearful result. He removed the chloride of potass by means of warm water and, this having been done, he was able to eliminate arsenic from that which was left. This mixture . . . would be pleasant to the taste, and appear similar to a saline mixture, but the effect would be to lodge the arsenic most certainly and fatally upon the coats of the stomach, and the poison would the more quickly become introduced into the system." The Serjeant added that Professor Taylor had not found any arsenic in the body but in view of the nature of the mixture he did not expect to.

In the witness-box the Professor fully confirmed this. He had used the Reinsch test. (The mixture is boiled with hydrochloric acid and copper gauze and any arsenic is precipitated on the copper in powder form). At his first test the noxious mixture had destroyed the gauze but he tried again, carefully draining off the chloride of potass, and this time arsenic was at once precipitated. He had no doubt that small doses of this mixture given from time to time would produce nausea, vomiting, pain, and later death. He had searched for arsenic and antimony and had found a clear trace of antimony in one of the kidneys. Death was certainly due to the slow administration of irritant poison.

After that there seemed no room for doubt. When it is remembered that evidence had already been given that the deceased lady had executed a will a day or two before her death, leaving all she possessed to the prisoner, the almost unanimous view that Dr Smethurst was guilty is readily understandable.

The facts which led up to this were very simple. Dr Smethurst, a small man with a reddish-brown moustache, who was fifty-four but said he was forty-eight, was a fully qualified medical practitioner, had practised without much success in various places, had studied hydropathy or "the water-cure" in Germany, and had ceased general practice six years previously. He had saved a little money and still made about £100 a year by treating a few friends. At the age of twenty-three he had married a woman twenty years his senior and since his retirement they had lived chiefly in boarding-houses. It was at such an establishment in Bayswater that Dr Smethurst met Miss Isabella Bankes. She was fair, fattish, forty-two, and distinctly bilious. She had about £2,000 of her own, and other charms, but the romance seems to have been founded upon the doctor's professional interest in her constant diarrhoea.

On 29 November 1858 Isabella left the boarding-house on the order of the landlady who complained of her familiarity with the doctor. The latter remained there with his wife until 12 December when he left for a "honeymoon" with Isabella whom he had "married" three days previously at Battersea. On 28 March 1859, when both were living at Old Palace Gardens, Richmond, Isabella became worse and on 3 April Dr Smethurst called in Dr Julius, one of the best-known physicians in Richmond. On 15 April the pair moved to 10 Alma Villas. Isabella was still ill, travelled by cab, and went straight to bed and remained under the care of Dr Julius. She had recently acquired, on the death of her father, a life interest in a sum of £5,000.

Dr Julius was very unhappy about the condition of Miss Bankes and, with the consent of Dr Smethurst, called in his partner Dr Bird on 18 April. A few days later Dr Smethurst suggested that Dr Todd, a distinguished London physician, should also be consulted. By this time both the local doctors suspected that it was a case of poisoning. Dr Todd confirmed this view and at the end of April a stool was taken for analysis and the arrest of Dr Smethurst soon followed.

Dr Smethurst's trial should have commenced in June when Lord Chief Justice Cockburn would have presided but, on the application of the Crown, opposed by the accused, it was postponed until July. The Lord Chief Baron of the Exchequer, the seventy-six-year-old Sir Frederick Pollock, took his seat on the bench and the prisoner at once objected to him on the ground that he was an intimate personal friend of Professor Taylor. In overruling this the judge said he had not seen Professor Taylor for a considerable time "until a few days ago at a party at his own house". One of the jurymen asked to be excused on the ground that "he entertained a strong prejudice against the accused". He was told that, having taken the oath, he must remain. The trial ended on the second day, when a juryman was taken seriously ill.

A new trial was opened on 15 August. Despite the fact that it was now the turn of the Chief Justice of the Common Pleas and despite the previous objection to himself, Pollock insisted on appearing again. This four-day trial was described by a barrister who was present as a sham and a mockery. "Spectators, witnesses, prisoner's counsel (Serjeant Parry), judge, jury, prosecuting counsel, one and all seemed weighed down, absolutely unable to escape from some mysterious weight hanging over their imaginations, which impelled them to believe in the prisoner's guilt."

This description of the proceedings is fair enough. There was immense hostility against Dr Smethurst and few doubted his guilt. The verdict seemed to have been reached before the trial started, but the weight of the evidence against him was immense. The case for the prosecution disclosed at, and publicized from, the police-court proceedings provided as strong a case of murder by poisoning as could well be imagined.

Dr Smethurst had committed bigamy, and had made clear to his first wife an intention, ultimately, to return to her. He had a substantial pecuniary interest in the death of Isabella Bankes as a result of a will he had procured her to make a day or two before she died. Three separate physicians had each independently arrived at the conclusion that her symptoms were consistent only with the deliberate administration of poison. There was nothing in her condition which could be accounted for by natural causes. She had died from poisoning and the greatest living toxicologist had conclusively established the presence of arsenic and antimony, and the deliberate administration of them during life. Reasonable doubt seemed far away.

One final piece of evidence had been volunteered by the doctor himself. He had been so constantly at Isabella's bedside and had nursed her so assiduously that, had poison been administered in the food, it must have been by him. Nor did he deny the bigamous second marriage. At his trial the question of motive was not contested in detail. The prosecution had to concede that an independent solicitor had been called in to make a will and that Miss Bankes had appeared fully to concur in its terms. The defence agreed that the doctor benefited to the extent of her capital but pointed out that he lost the joint use of her substantial life interest. The real defence, the only possible defence, was that death was due to natural causes.

At the trial itself, however, long before the defence witnesses were called, the prosecution had to make some staggering admissions. It was not true that the three medical men had formed their opinions independently of one another. Dr Julius, obviously bitterly hostile to the accused, continued to assert this.

Serjeant Parry (cross-examining): "And at that time [when Dr Bird was consulted] had you formed the opinion that the lady was in a very precarious state?"

Dr Julius: "Yes; and that my medicines were counteracted by some means or other."

Serjeant Parry: "Will you swear positively that you gave no intimation to Dr Bird of the unfavourable opinion you entertained, before he attended on the case?"

Dr Julius: "I will."

But later on Dr Bird went into the witness-box.

Serjeant Parry: "What opinion had you formed with regard to the illness of the deceased?"

Dr Bird: "I certainly formed the opinion that the deceased was the subject of slow arsenical poisoning, but Dr Julius first suggested the probability of this being the case."

Some independent medical observers were of the opinion that Miss Bankes's symptoms could be largely accounted for by the medicines which Dr Julius and his partner prescribed. The unfortunate woman, who had long shown dysenteric symptoms, had during her last illness absorbed medicine containing quinine, chalk mixture, catechu, compound tincture of camphor, grey powder, ether, gentian, dilute sulphuric acid, dilute prussic acid, ipecacuanha, sulphate of copper, opium, bismuth, and hydrate of magnesia. The grey powder contained minute, and normally harmless, quantities of arsenic and antimony and the bismuth also contained arsenic.

This theory was sharply reinforced when the post-mortem disclosed that the deceased was seven weeks' pregnant, something never suspected by the three physicians who attended her during life. She was forty-two years of age, this was her first pregnancy, and her serious symptoms had commenced with its onset. This alone could have accounted for many, if not all, of her symptoms. It was also clear that some of the medicines, if applied to a pregnant woman, would aggravate those symptoms.

Then came the final humiliating admission by the prosecution. The greatest living toxicologist had blundered. There was no arsenic in the medicine bottle and none in the stool submitted for analysis. Professor Taylor went into the witness-box to say, "It turned out that I was mistaken," and that the mixture did not contain either arsenic or antimony. The arsenic precipitated had come from the professor's own piece of copper gauze. Before the magistrates he had sworn that he had, previous to the experiment, carefully tested the gauze to make sure that it was pure.

The trial might surely have been permitted to end on this admission. Professor Taylor's new evidence (not quite so freely given as was suggested, for an article in the *Lancet* had called attention to the unreliability of the methods he had used) left the Crown in the position that they had failed to establish death from poison and also that they had failed to prove that the accused ever possessed either of the poisons. He was not in practice, he did no dispensing, he lived in lodgings which had been thoroughly searched, and every bottle in the house had been examined. It was true that as a qualified medical man he could have obtained them on his own prescription but there was no scrap of proof that at any material time he had ever done so.

Nevertheless the battle of the doctors continued. Dr Julius and his colleagues were still emphatic that death had been caused by administered poison.

For the defence seven qualified medical witnesses, including two experts in midwifery, and a police surgeon, all testified that death was due to natural causes. Death was due to dysentery aggravated by pregnancy. One said that fifteen thousand persons had died from dysentery in the six most recent recorded years. Another had conducted a careful series of experiments with chlorate of potass, which was very much in use as a mouthwash, and was satisfied that it was a harmless salt which had no effect on the elimination of poison from the system. Several were convinced that some of the prescribed medicines would aggravate the symptoms. The death of Charlotte Brontë was quoted as being from similar causes and producing the same appearances.

In his concluding speech for the Crown Serjeant Ballantine said, "It is not pretended to say positively that the death was occasioned either by antimony or by arsenic; all we say is that death was occasioned by some poison or other, but we are unable to say when and in what manner the poison was administered. If poison was administered at all it must have been administered by the accused; no one else could have done so and it was therefore unnecessary to say any more upon that point."

He could hardly have said less.

The summing up was one of the most venomous ever recorded:

"It may be that no arsenic, no poison, is traced to the possession of the accused, it may be that no poison is found in the body, and yet it may be the easiest thing in the world to put a case where no sensible man could doubt that the accused had possessed the poison, that he had used it, and that the deceased had died of it."

The Lord Chief Baron invited the jury to assume that the prisoner must have known that his "wife" was pregnant. He asked them to assume that the "marriage" had been procured by some trick on his part.

"However strange and unaccountable you may think the charge against the prisoner, it is a heavy one; all such charges must be assumed to be improbable. I do not think it is more improbable than that a woman of the age of forty-two, with an independent income, would consent to go with him and pass through a ceremony of marriage, while her own sister knew that there was a Mrs Smethurst living with him at the boarding-house, without some prospect, some view, some representation – it is more improbable than anyone can understand.

". . . what you are certainly asked to believe is that, with the knowledge that he was a married man, this lady went to that church, and through the marriage ceremony that was to make her a felon and a strumpet she was to commit with him the crime of bigamy . . .

"I own I cannot contemplate without emotion that scene of sorrow and privation when the poor suffering creature, whatever was the cause of it, had her relations excluded, and an attorney thrust upon her, and was allowed to pass into another world without one word of religious consolation, as if she were perishing an unbeliever in a heathen land."

After this striking demonstration of judicial impartiality the jury took only forty minutes to return a verdict of guilty. After Dr Smethurst had made a most able and detailed statement, the judge expressed full agreement with the verdict and passed sentence of death. The prisoner was ordered for execution in a fortnight.

Rarely has a verdict produced so immediate and decided a revulsion of feeling. The columns of the Press, today no longer open until after an appeal because of our new and peculiar laws of contempt of court, were filled with criticism and counter-argument. Thirty London medical practitioners signed a memorial declaring that the Crown entirely failed to establish the first fact necessary to convict, namely, that Isabella Bankes was ever poisoned at all. Twenty-eight members of the Bar submitted a petition to the Queen declaring that each had studied the evidence and that it did not warrant the verdict. The real Mrs Smethurst submitted a petition, presented by Henry Brinsley Sheridan MP., to the effect that she had lived happily with her husband for thirty years and had always received from him the tenderest kindness and affection. She added that Miss Bankes well knew that Dr Smethurst was married, that she made the first advances, and that until then her husband's moral conduct had been irreproachable.

There can be little question that the marriage took place in order to permit Miss Bankes to produce a document of respectability for the inspection of her family.

In face of this strong consensus of opinion the Home Secretary took an unprecedented and much-criticized step. He submitted the evidence to Sir Benjamin Brodie, reputedly the greatest living surgeon, for his report. The Lord Chief Baron bitterly protested.

Sir Benjamin replied that he had weighed the evidence on both sides, "that Dr Smethurst's moral character made him a just object of suspicion", but that there was no trustworthy evidence that Miss Bankes had ever taken arsenic and that many of the symptoms which arsenic normally produces were absent in her case. He added, "No one can doubt that the symptoms during life and the morbid changes of the body afterwards might have occurred as a result of disease," and concluded that there was not absolute and complete evidence of Dr Smethurst's guilt.

The Home Secretary granted a "free pardon" to the doctor who was promptly re-arrested on a charge of bigamy, convicted, and imprisoned.

The last, and most astonishing, word came from the Lord Chief Baron. In an informal letter of protest to the Home Secretary he complained that Sir Benjamin did not,

> in any degree notice the suggestion – that Smethurst's object (at any rate at *first*) was to procure abortion – perhaps that only. In my opinion the guilt of Smethurst in this last point of view is *demonstrable* using that term not as it is applied to the exact sciences but as applied to the subjects which occur practicably in the Courts of Justice and if the improper practice of suppressing evidence had not prevailed . . . I think Smethurst would have been hanged long ago . . . As to there not being absolute and complete evidence of his guilt I think that is no ground for a pardon – there is not absolute evidence in nine cases out of ten – there was not in Palmer's case – two of Smethurst's witnesses considered that Palmer did not die of strychnine.
>
> Faithfully yours,
> Fred Pollock

Dr Smethurst was a curious and unusual character, but clearly not the most curious and unusual personality who took part in the trial.

THE HILLDROP CRESCENT MYSTERY

(Hawley Harvey Crippen, UK 1910)

Philip Willcox

Everybody knows the Crippen case. Poisoned his wife, thinking hyoscine – a rare and deadly alkaloid – was undetectable. Chopped her up and hid her remains under the cellar. Fled with his mistress, but got caught by wireless. The very name Crippen is the epitome of the classic British murder (although not everyone realizes that Crippen himself was an American). The case was a landmark in the history of forensic medicine, and the first in a long series of sensational murder trials in which the great pathologist Bernard Spilsbury was to play a leading role. Indeed, it was Spilsbury's appearance that established his name with the general public. Spilsbury, at thirty-three, was the junior of the four pathologists who gave evidence for the Crown, but he made by far the biggest impact. But the case was important in the development of modern forensic science, which had lain largely in the doldrums following the fiasco of the Smethurst trial more than half a century before. Crippen's guilt turned almost entirely on the identification of a piece of skin which was found buried in the cellar of his house in Hilldrop Crescent, Camden Town. It was essential that the scientific witnesses at Crippen's trial were able to convince the jury that the flesh in question came from the body of Crippen's wife Cora. The responsibility for this vital aspect of the case rested with Richard Muir, the junior Crown counsel, and number two to the attorney-general, Sir Rufus Isaacs. Working under Muir's direction, Spilsbury – a man of

whom the public had hitherto never heard – conclusively demon-
strated that the human remains found in Crippen's cellar were those
of Cora Crippen and no one else. Crippen's own precautions proved
to be his downfall. He buried his wife's body in lime, hoping it would
be destroyed. Not only did this fail, but the lime actually preserved
the hyoscine Crippen used to kill her. Without the lime, it would have
been impossible to definitely fix the cause of Mrs Crippen's death. In
court, Dr (later Sir) William Willcox described how he had detected
the poison as being alkaloidal, first a mydriatic and then a vegetable
mydriatic alkaloid. Final tests showed the alkaloid to be hyoscine.
The Crippen case was a triumph for the science of toxicology, and
Willcox's son, Dr Philip Willcox (1910–2000) focuses on this aspect
in his reconstruction of the story using his father's unpublished case
notes and papers.

In the history of crime in Britain probably no other mystery has
attracted more profound fascination than the disappearance of
Mrs Cora Crippen on January 31st, 1910. This, and the events
which followed, notably the trial and conviction of Dr Crippen on
a charge of wife-murder, have provided useful and profitable
material for plays and articles in the press. Certainly no other
crime has been more frequently discussed or debated for so long a
period, and the name of Crippen has become almost a household
word. Even when the case was finished, the secret of the true
course of events surrounding his wife's death was never revealed
but died with Crippen at Pentonville. The police investigations,
and the inquiries at the inquest and at Bow Street and the Old
Bailey were headline news in the press for almost the whole
period from July until the end of that year.

In the trial of Crippen, so fully described in Filson Young's
book (*Notable English Trials*) written ten years later, the medical
evidence was of paramount importance; that of Willcox was
second only to that of Augustus Pepper in length and authority.
At no stage in his career did Willcox describe in any kind of detail
the role he played in the corroborative evidence of identification
of the remains, and the cause of death.

Hawley Harvey Crippen was born in Michigan in 1862. He was reasonably well educated and studied medicine at Cleveland Homoeopathic Hospital, becoming a doctor of medicine there in 1885. This qualification did not enable him to practise in this country on the medical register. He was interested in the ear, nose and throat speciality. He first married at the age of twenty-five, and had one son. After his wife died in 1891 his son was brought up by his grandmother. Dr Crippen worked in New York for a time and the following year married an attractive blonde Russian Pole, by whom he had no children. For a time they lived in St Louis, but came to London in 1900 when Crippen became manager of Munyon's advertising business for homoeopathic remedies, established in Shaftesbury Avenue. According to Crippen and other witnesses at the trial, Mrs Crippen had had an abdominal operation for the removal of an ovary. In 1902 Crippen returned to New York on business for his firm. During this period of six months, Mrs Crippen was said to have become friendly with Bruce Miller, but he had returned to America before Crippen's return to London and he never met Cora Crippen again. At this stage, according to Crippen, their marriage began to disintegrate and she became irritable, bad tempered and impossible to live with as a wife. In 1905 they took up residence at 39 Hilldrop Crescent off the Camden Road and near Holloway prison – a rented semi-detached house which was too large for them and gave them the opportunity to supplement his income by taking in paying guests. In 1909 Munyon's offices were in Albion House, New Oxford Street, but Crippen resigned his position in order to join a dental surgeon in a business known as the Yale Tooth Specialists in the same building as Munyon's. His position as medical adviser to several other firms dealing with drugs and an aural clinic ceased when they were shut down in 1909.

Mrs Crippen was apparently a vain, flamboyant and selfish woman who lost her affection for her husband several years before her mysterious "disappearance". She was also extravagant and resented her duties as a lodging-house keeper, fancying herself as an actress, with an ambition for operatic work. Styling herself Belle Elmore, she was scarcely a success even as a music hall actress with a moderately good singing voice, though she did acquire periodic engagements in this role. Mixing with the stage fraternity, she became treasurer of the Ladies' Music Hall Guild whose meetings were held at Albion House.

In 1909 Crippen's affections had drifted towards a young typist, Ethel Le Neve, who was in his employment. His finances were in a precarious state, maybe on account of his wife's extravagance rather than his own. At the time of Mrs Crippen's disappearance his current banking account was overdrawn.

Their friends Mr and Mrs Martinetti dined at Hilldrop Crescent on January 31st – "quite a nice evening" as Mrs Martinetti described it at the trial. But they had accepted the invitation under pressure from Crippen. They left the house at 1.30 a.m. Mrs Crippen was never seen alive again. Crippen's explanation of her disappearance, which he later confessed was false, was that she had been summoned to go immediately to America to care for a sick relative. The secretary of the Music Hall Guild received this news and notification of her resignation as treasurer in a letter written by hand, but not by Mrs Crippen's.

On February 9th Crippen pawned her brooch and rings for £115 and on the same day visited the Martinetti's to let them know that Cora had preferred to go to America herself rather than let him go. Had Crippen played his cards well he would probably have succeeded in evading undue suspicion. He had merely to play the part of a lonely husband awaiting the return of his wife, but like so many criminals he blundered on several occasions, no doubt losing his head.

On February 20th in company with Miss Le Neve wearing several pieces of his wife's jewellery, Crippen attended a dinner and ball of the Ladies' Music Hall Guild, meeting several of his wife's friends. By March 12th Ethel Le Neve was openly living at Hilldrop Crescent, and about this time he gave three months' notice to terminate the lease of his house. Before Easter he told the Martinetti's that Cora had developed pneumonia. Two days later he departed with Ethel to Dieppe for an Easter holiday but sent a telegram to the Martinetti's informing them of Cora's death at Los Angeles. Unfortunately for Crippen, it so happened that a Mr Nash, whose wife was one of Cora's friends, was on business in California in May. While visiting Los Angeles he had been unable to obtain any news of Cora's illness or any record of her death. Returning to England, he visited Scotland Yard without delay on June 30th, being dissatisfied with Crippen's explanation of his wife's disappearance and death.

Chief Inspector Dew was detailed to launch an inquiry into the disappearance of Mrs Crippen. When he visited Hilldrop Crescent on July 6th, he found Ethel Le Neve already running the house with the help of a French maid. Crippen gladly conducted him over the house, displaying his wife's furs, clothes, and the unpawned jewellery. But by then his nerve began to fail him. Confessing that his story of her death was a complete fabrication he explained that he had said this in order to cover up the "scandal" of her sudden departure to rejoin her ex-lover Bruce Miller; for all he knew his wife was still alive and well in America, but he did not know where. Crippen promised Dew that he would write a description of his wife to be published in the American press in order to solve the mystery of her disappearance – a step that was never fulfilled. When Dew returned the next day, he found that Crippen and Ethel Le Neve had gone. Crippen had notified Albion House of his resignation as assistant to his employer, the dental surgeon. Dew and his assistants then made a most exhaustive search of the house. Noticing several loose bricks on the floor of the coal cellar he explored further and found human remains caked with soil and lime, wrapped in a pyjama jacket corresponding in pattern to Crippen's pyjama trousers found in the bedroom. The police then circulated descriptions of the missing couple and issued a warrant for their arrest.

On Friday, July 29th, the missing couple became headline news when their identity by the captain of S.S. *Montrose* was first made known. Captain Randall had been given details of the missing couple. After the departure of his ship from Antwerp bound for Quebec on July 20th he kept his passengers under close observation. Being himself interested in crime, he used his powers of detection with unusual effect. He noticed that "Mr Robinson" and his son were an unusually devoted couple. Not only so, but "Master" Robinson was a girl disguised as a boy, wearing trousers with hair cut short. Two days after sailing, he

ordered his wireless operator to tap out a message to Scotland
Yard – the first time wireless telegraphy was used to assist in the
arrest of a criminal at sea.

Dew wasted no time. Leaving Liverpool the next day on the
Laurentic, which was a faster ship, they overtook the *Montrose* on
the St Lawrence River at Father Point on July 31st. The Ro-
binsons were arrested, taken into custody and, after extradition
formalities at Quebec, were brought back to England, arriving at
Liverpool on August 28th.

Pepper was the first scientific expert summoned by the police to
inspect the remains *in situ* in the excavated cellar. Piece by piece
he conveyed them to Islington mortuary for detailed inspection
on July 14th. It was on July 22nd at the end of the day's work that
Willcox himself received specimens at his laboratory at St Mary's
Hospital from the coroner's officer of Holloway. His extensive
examination and description was made on the following day, a
Saturday afternoon.

Five stoppered glass jars were properly sealed but not labelled
as usual, for Pepper had already told him the news. He first
labelled the jars and systematically examined the contents of each
in turn. The first jar contained the stomach, heart, one kidney
and part of the liver. No organ showed signs of disease, but there
was some putrefaction. The second contained a pair of combina-
tions coated with lime, blood-stained in places; the third, brown
human hair in a hair curler with the name of the maker inscribed,
a tattered handkerchief, a cotton camisole with six pearl buttons;
the fourth, the armpiece of a flannelette pyjama jacket with brown
and green stripes, caked with blood and lime; the fifth contained
another piece of the same bloodstained jacket labelled "Jones
Bros. Ltd. Holloway, Shirt Makers".

Willcox was eager to obtain as much as was possible of the
human remains from the grave, for analysis for poisons, in order
to be able to calculate as accurately as possible the amount of any
discoverable poison in the body as a whole. He requested further
supplies, preferably whole organs if possible. Further samples of
human hair varying from 2 ins. to 6 ins. in length, a hair curler
and another piece of liver were brought by the police surgeon, Dr

Marshall, on July 25th. On August 8th Pepper himself delivered the piece of skin which was to supply the chief evidence of identification at the trial in October. At the end of the portion of skin human hairs were growing, resembling pubic hair. After writing a careful description of it he put the skin in a special fluid designed to prevent further changes of putrefaction and handed it to Dr Bernard Spilsbury on the same day for pathological study.

On August 2nd Pepper informed Willcox that the police had discovered that Crippen had purchased five grains of hyoscine on January 1st, 1910, from a chemist in Oxford Street. By that time the analysis was well under way. On August 13th Pepper witnessed Willcox's experiments on the alkaloid extracted from the liver and stomach contents. The effect on the cat's eye of a few drops of the extract was to dilate the pupils widely, thus showing the presence of a mydriatic alkaloid, one of a group of drugs of which hyoscine was a member.

Further specimens were brought to him by Marshall on August 14th, another hair curler, the lungs, intestines, portions of muscle and more hair. Soil from the grave in a separate jar was found to contain traces of an alkaloid.

When Willcox visited Hilldrop Crescent on August 23rd with Inspector Cornish, his purpose was not merely idle curiosity. He wanted to satisfy himself that all possible contents were investigated, and also to take samples of soil. He took three separate specimens away. Not content with his discovery of a mydriatic alkaloid, he was intent on investigating for arsenic as well. But his analysis showed that the soil was free of all poison and could not have been the source of the alkaloid already found in the remains.

He next set out to identify the individual alkaloids by chemical tests and microscopical examination of the crystals, the brown spheres characteristic of hyoscine.

By the time-honoured method of extraction devised by Stas, the pure alkaloid obtained from all the organs amounted to .43 of a grain. But it must be remembered that the head, neck and limbs with their muscles were never recovered from the cellar. Willcox's calculation that there was probably half a grain in the whole body was perhaps an understatement clearly on the cautious side, as the content in the brain and muscles must have been considerable. In his final report of September 2nd he commented that the relatively large amount found in the stomach (1/30 grain) and intestines (1/7 grain) showed that the poison was taken by mouth. The liver (1/10 grain) and kidney (1/40 grain) content suggested that the deceased probably lived for an hour or more after the poison was taken.

Earlier the inquest had opened on July 18th at Holloway. But the unexpected death of Mr Danford Thomas, the coroner, rendered it invalid. It was accordingly re-opened by Mr (later Sir) Walter Schroder, on August 16th when formal evidence was submitted. On September 12th Willcox presented the results of his investigations and his opinion on the cause of death. The Crippen case was unusual in that the inquest proceedings terminated several days after the end of the Magistrates' Court inquiry at Bow Street, the former proceedings being held up by the prolonged police inquiries and the necessity to call many witnesses. The opinion of Pepper and Willcox was that the remains had been buried for a period between four and eight months. The jury returned a verdict of wilful murder against Crippen. But on the coroner's advice the jury made no reference to Miss Le Neve as an "accessory after the fact".

Crippen and Ethel Le Neve appeared before the magistrates on August 29th, the former charged with the wilful murder of his wife, and the latter with being an accessory after the fact. Presided over by Sir Albert de Rutzen the hearing was attended by many notable people connected with the stage, including Sir W. S. Gilbert and H. B. Irving on all six days. The court was fully packed.

Travers Humphreys appeared for the prosecution and Arthur Newton for the two prisoners. The evidence of Pepper lasted for most of the morning of the fourth day, and was supported by that of Spilsbury for a period of forty minutes on the fifth day. Their evidence was mainly concerned with the skin of the abdominal wall and the scars on it – the most important part of the remains used for identification.

Willcox was in the box for three hours. He agreed with the previous experts that the piece of skin was from the abdominal wall and that the scar was identifiable.

He had never before given evidence in a case of alleged murder by hyoscine, this being the first case of its kind in Britain. The isolation of a mydriatic alkaloid meant that it was either hyoscine, atropine or hyoscyamine, confirmed by Vitali's test. The differentiation by the bromine test and the nature of the residue – a gummy mass – pointed to hyoscine, the typical brown spheres being seen under the microscope. His evidence was of great technical interest as it illustrated the difficulty that faces the analyst working on contaminated specimens sent for analysis. He had been puzzled by finding traces of cresol in the stomach, and arsenic in the intestines and liver, but not in other organs. On inquiry, he found that the mortuary attendant had sprinkled liberal amounts of cresol on the specimens in the mortuary. The solution and powders at the mortuary were also analyzed and found to contain a small percentage of arsenic. The presence of arsenic in some organs, and none in others, indicated that it was due to contamination in this way, as he had informed Travers Humphreys three days earlier. He regarded a fatal dose of hyoscine to be half a grain, the medicinal dose being 1/100th of a grain or less. The poison could have been taken in a drink such as sweetened tea or coffee without altering the flavour. Putrefaction of the remains would be delayed by the presence of lime in the grave – but adipocere formation would be accelerated by it. The remains had been buried for less than a year; in that period some of the hyoscine would have been destroyed. In cross-examination he denied the possibility that alkaloids produced by the changes of putrefaction could have been confused with hyoscine.

At the trial, it was said that there were over four thousand applications for seats at the Old Bailey, so great was the interest attached to the case. Half-day tickets were accordingly issued. At Crippen's entry into a packed court on October 18th, a hushed silence suddenly prevailed. The case was tried before the Lord Chief Justice, Lord Alverstone, and lasted five days. Counsel for the Crown were Mr Richard Muir and Mr Travers Humphreys and Mr Ingleby Oddie, later well known as a London coroner. Appearing for Crippen were Mr A. Tobin, KC, Mr Huntly Jenkins and Mr H. D. Roome. Thirty-six witnesses gave evidence, two of whom came specially from America – Mr Bruce Miller who had been friendly with Mrs Crippen several years previously, and Mrs Hunn, Mrs Crippen's sister.

The evidence of the scientific experts occupied close on half the time taken up by all thirty-six witnesses; the testimony of Augustus Pepper lasted nearly twice as long as that of Willcox and was heard for the greater part of the second day.

The main scientific evidence expected from the experts concerned the identification of the remains, the approximate time of their burial and the cause of death. All were interrogated about the all important exhibit of skin and muscle, but for Pepper and his young colleague Spilsbury, then aged thirty-seven, this was the main object of their attention in their evidence concerning the identification of the remains. Willcox's main concern was the cause of death – poisoning by hyoscine, as he had already indicated at Bow Street.

Muir and Humphreys had been coached in the subject of the chemical and medical properties of hyoscine before they appeared at Bow Street; and Willcox had loaned them a well-known text book of toxicology.

When Willcox entered the box on October 20th, it was almost a repetition of his evidence at Bow Street, but the audience was a new one. By the Stas technique of extraction he had obtained a gummy substance, the mydriatic alkaloid which dilated the cat's pupil. Applying the bromine test he had found typical brown spheres of hyoscine under the microscope; the first occasion in which this drug had been used in alleged criminal poisoning. The well-established Vitali test yielded the typical change of colour to violet, thus confirming that it was a vegetable alkaloid distinct from certain alkaloids sometimes produced by bacteria in putrefaction of animal flesh.

Willcox had been disappointed to be unable to estimate the melting point of his alkaloid. It was a method which served to differentiate not only alkaloids from one another but the individual members of the mydriatic group, hyoscine, hyoscyamine and atropine. Cross-examined by Tobin, he explained that the melting point of hyoscine treated with gold chloride was 190°C, at least thirty degrees higher than the other two. In the Crippen case he had less than half a grain at his disposal, whereas he needed at least two grains to carry out this test along with the other investigations; and he had failed to find any further supplies in his personal search of the soil from the grave. Nevertheless, the fact remained that the method offered a new line of advance in the identification of alkaloids in courts of law.

Recent technical advances have now enabled scientists to estimate the melting point of alkaloids by micro-physical methods whereby minute amounts can be melted under the micro-scope while a special thermometer is read. Not only so, but many new techniques of analysis can now be used, such as paper chromatography and ultra-violet and infra-red spectroscopy. But the Stas process of extraction, though further elaborated, still remains in use today. Police inquiries revealed that Crippen had purchased five grains of hyoscine from an Oxford Street chemist on January 1st. It was perhaps unfortunate that Pepper communicated the information to Willcox about two weeks before the analysis was completed. Willcox was thus exposed to the suggestion by defence counsel that hyoscine was discovered as an afterthought – a cruel and unkind inference which was not used by Tobin in the later stages of the trial, to his own advantage in view of the fact that Willcox claimed a period of three weeks to complete extraction and analysis of the alkaloid.

Willcox's evidence was supported by that of A. P. Luff who had been junior Home Office analyst until succeeded by Willcox in 1904. Luff's experience of cadaveric alkaloids had been greater than his successor's, and his reliance on Vitali's test was equally firmly held.

The scientific experts for the Crown were all from St Mary's Hospital; Pepper supported by Spilsbury, and Willcox by Luff. It seemed that the case might lead to a battle between teams from two London hospitals, for the three experts for the defence were G. M. Turnbull (pathologist), R. C. Wall (physician and pathologist) and A. W. Blyth, all from the London Hospital. But try as they did, their evidence lent feeble support to the defence counsel. Turnbull and Wall had previously formed the opinion that the exhibited piece of skin had come from the thigh and that the supposed scar was merely a fold in the skin. But during their testimony in the box they were forced to change their minds and agree that it was more probably part of the abdominal wall. Blyth was equally unable to counter the firmly held view of Willcox and Luff about the nature of the alkaloid. He had to admit comparative ignorance of cadaveric alkaloids in putrefaction and was merely able to quote from an obscure Italian text-book which was critical of the value of the Vitali test.

The jury was left in little doubt that the Crown experts were right; death had been caused by hyoscine, the remains had been buried for a period between two and four months, and the exhibited skin with its scar of the old operation was in fact from the abdominal wall of Mrs Crippen.

Richard Muir enhanced his reputation by his masterly conduct of the case as prosecuting counsel.

After retiring for half an hour the jury found the prisoner guilty at 2.45 p.m. on the fifth day of the trial, after a strictly impartial summing-up by the Lord Chief Justice.

The trial of Ethel Le Neve at the Old Bailey on October 25th was completed in one day. The same three counsel appeared for the Crown. She was defended by F. E. Smith (later Lord Birkenhead), who had earlier refused the more difficult brief for the defence of Crippen, supported by Mr Barrington Ward. Only nine witnesses were called; Pepper and Willcox gave formal evidence each for only a few minutes. She was found not guilty and acquitted.

Crippen appealed against his verdict. The case came before the Court of Criminal Appeal on November 5th, before Mr Justice Darling, Mr Justice Channell and Mr Justice Pickford, but was unsuccessful. Crippen was executed at Pentonville on November 23rd, 1910.

As a criminal, Crippen was notable for his strangely attractive qualities of character, his courtesy and unselfishness, and the calmness with which he faced up to his succession of misfortunes. He certainly faced his trial and death with courage, and earned the sympathy of a wide circle of people who appreciated the horrors of a selfish, nagging and overbearing wife. Even Inspector Dew liked him, and enjoyed his company at lunch at the Holborn Restaurant after the first unproductive search of his house. None of the witnesses at the three court inquiries described him as other than a pleasant man; and one described him as one of the nicest men she had ever met. His affection for Ethel never wavered and in his last letters he did his best to protect her from any accusation of guilt.

For close on sixty years, the case has been the subject of frequent debate. Having poisoned his wife with hyoscine, why did Crippen need to dispose of her remains in the way he did? Why did he not call a doctor and claim that she had poisoned herself with the drug he had left lying about the house? Doubtless the ruse would have been successful and would have saved him the need for the hasty flight and the ghastly task of disposal. And how did he dispose of the head and limbs? Only Crippen knew the answers and the secrets died with him.

Willcox resented being referred to as "the man who hanged Crippen", and rightly so. He would have been far happier if it had been shown that Mrs Crippen had committed suicide. In spite of his acute sense of right and wrong, he felt sorrow and compassion for Crippen as did many people. Nevertheless, the case established certain records. It was the first case of alleged murder by hyoscine in British legal history and the first case in which wireless telegraphy was used to arrest a criminal on ship at sea.

Willcox alluded to the case in various lectures on toxicology in later years, and a quotation from his Harveian Lecture to the Harveian Society on March 15th, 1928, refers to Crippen's purchase of poison in relation to the Poisons Register:

"The numerous Acts and Regulations governing the sale of poisons in this country have served as a great protection to the public. In many noted trials the purchase of poison by the accused has been revealed by the record of the register of the sale kept by the vendors. This happened in the Crippen case, where the purchase of hyoscine had been recorded in the poison register of the chemist."

The liberal sprinkling of quicklime on the remains in the cellar was a fatal mistake referred to in a lecture to the Society of Dyers, and to the Literary and Philosophical Society of Manchester in 1924:

"Before the Crippen case it had been stated that hyoscine was a very decomposable alkaloid that no one could detect a few days or weeks after death . . . To make assurance doubly sure Crippen buried the viscera in quicklime which was just what the expert wanted, for it helped to preserve the viscera, and without it I doubt whether the hyoscine would ever have been discovered. Crippen possessed the little knowledge that is dangerous."

Willcox was asked by a barrister interested in forensic chemistry about the mode of action of quicklime as a preservative, as it had been understood that executed criminals had customarily been buried in quicklime to destroy the body rapidly. The answer lay in the rapid hydration of quicklime yielding calcium hydrate, a fairly efficient alkaline antiseptic, but in addition calcium hydrate combines with the fat of viscera to form a calcium soap called adipocere, which forms a protective covering round buried remains.

The cat used in his experiment at the laboratory was subsequently named "Crippen" and was cared for by one of the students. It lived for several years, produced a family of kittens. But the name of Crippen must have carried a curse, for it was later unfortunately killed by a dog.

Miss Ethel Le Neve escaped the publicity that often pursues acquitted prisoners by emigrating to Canada soon after the trial. There she married and had children. She returned to Britain after many years and lived to a ripe old age, dying in obscurity in 1965.

Postscript

There is a curious sequel. Nearly twenty years after Ethel's death, the author Jonathan Goodman was researching a book on the Crippen case and traced her two children, a son and a daughter, who were living in southern England. His letter seeking an interview was received with astonishment and some consternation, since it transpired that Ethel Smith (as she had become) had never told her children who she really was. In their mother's lifetime, neither knew that she had been Ethel Le Neve, Crippen's mistress, who in the autumn of 1910 had been the most infamous woman in England.

THE DINGO BABY CASE

(Lindy Chamberlain, Australia 1980)

Colin Wilson

"We are not treading in the ground of unequivocal, unchallenged scientific opinion," declared the judge in the Chamberlain case. "To the contrary, the scientific opinion on these vital issues is divided." But after a seven-week trial, the jury's verdict was unanimous: Lindy Chamberlain was guilty of murdering her baby daughter Azaria, and her pastor husband guilty of being an accessory after the fact. Mrs Chamberlain, thirty-four at the time of her trial and heavily pregnant with her fourth child, had claimed a dingo had carried Azaria into the Australian bush from the family tent. The child's clothing was recovered, and it was forensic evidence uncovered during exhaustive tests on the bloodstained jump-suit and singlet that eventually led to one of Australia's most sensational trials. According to the prosecution, this evidence showed that Lindy Chamberlain had murdered Azaria by slitting the baby's throat in the family car. Other forensic experts called by the defence said it was possible for a dingo to take a small child. Some of the forensic evidence, gathered more than a year after Azaria's disappearance, showed traces of blood in the car, inside the tent and in a camera bag. But pathologists disputed whether the traces were foetal blood. Moreover, dental and forensic experts gave conflicting evidence about the marks found in the dead child's clothing. Mrs Chamberlain's appeal failed, but the doubts in the case persisted and she was released from prison early in 1986, having served just over two years of her life sentence. One of Britain's most prolific chroniclers of crime, Colin Wilson (b. 1931) examines the evidence

and concludes that Lindy Chamberlain was the victim of a mis-carriage of justice.

It was 8 o'clock on a warm August evening, and most of the occupants of the camping site below Ayers Rock, the mammoth red-stone landmark that rises out of the desert of central Australia, were engaged in preparing supper. This included thirty-two-year-old Alice Lynne ("Lindy") Chamberlain and her thirty-six-year-old husband Michael, a minister in the Seventh Day Adventist Church. Their elder son, seven-year-old Aidan, was still awake; the other two children, Reagan, four, and Azaria ("Blessed of God"), nine weeks old, were already asleep in the tent.

It was Michael Chamberlain who asked, "Is that Bubby crying?", and Lindy Chamberlain returned to the tent. A moment later she shouted, "My God, the dingo's got my baby!" Michael rushed to the tent. The baby's blankets were scattered round the empty carrycot.

Within minutes most of the campers on the site were rushing into the darkness with torches. Lindy explained that, as she approached the tent, she had seen a dingo – a wild dog – walking away from it, with its rear towards her. It had been moving its head from side to side, although she had been unable to see whether it was carrying anything. The night was pitch black, without a breath of wind; although 300 searchers scoured through the scrub, they found nothing. Back in the camp, some women were praying. Lindy Chamberlain was trying to quieten Aidan, who was crying, "Don't let the dingo eat our baby." Frank Morris, the local police officer, arrived to organize the search. But he suspected that Azaria Chamberlain was already dead.

By dawn, it was obvious that he was right. Lindy Chamberlain had also come to accept it. Over the radio telephone she told her parents, "Our baby was killed by a dingo last night." Then she sobbed.

By mid-morning, the Chamberlains had another problem:

their story had caused a nationwide sensation – Baby Stolen by Dingo at Ayers Rock – and press and television reporters were beginning to arrive. Michael Chamberlain agreed to talk to them – a decision that was later to arouse some criticism. Meanwhile, Lindy told her story to the police: how her elder son had been in bed when he said he was still hungry. Instead of fetching him some food as he lay in bed, she made the fatal mistake of telling him to come with her; and, since he would be returning in a few minutes, she left the tent flap unzipped. Before the day was out, Michael Chamberlain had already noticed that some people were asking questions in an oddly suspicious way, as if they felt that the idea of a baby being stolen by a dingo was preposterous.

This was not the view of the police. The day after Azaria's disappearance, they began shooting dingos and wild dogs in the area of Ayers Rock, hoping to find the child's remains in the stomach of one of them. They shot several dingos but their search was unsuccessful. On Tuesday, the Chamberlains returned to their home in Mount Isa, Queensland. Their religious faith had given them the strength to accept the tragedy. But there were many people who felt they had accepted it a little too stoically.

In fact, they might have received far more sympathy if they had been less religious. As Seventh Day Adventists, they were regarded as a little "odd". Seventh Day Adventists have been described as "Fundamentalists of Fundamentalists". Like the Jehovah's Witnesses, they believe in the literal truth of every word of the Bible, and in an imminent return of Christ to earth. Their movement was founded in the first half of the nineteenth century by an American, William Miller, who announced that the end of the world would occur in 1843 or 1844. On 22 October 1844, twenty families sat out all night in Phoenixville, Pennsylvania, waiting for the end, and two children froze to death. That night was known as the Great Disappointment. But the Adventists declared that the Second Coming had been delayed by their failure to recognize Saturday as the Sabbath, and that it could be expected fairly soon. In spite of the Great Disappointment, the sect continued to prosper.

Modern Seventh Day Adventists disapprove of alcohol, gambling, jewelry, cosmetics, cinema and television, with the inevitable consequence that there is a tendency among the worldly to regard them as cranks and "killjoys". This helps explain why, instead of receiving universal sympathy and commiseration, the Chamberlains found themselves confronted by a curious hostility after the loss of their baby.

Eight days after Azaria's disappearance, a tourist on the west side of Ayers Rock noticed some clothing; it proved to be a bloodstained stretchsuit, napkin, singlet and booties. Yet there was not the slightest trace of flesh. It looked as if the dingo had removed the baby from the stretchsuit and taken it to its lair. Oddly enough, the singlet was inside out. How could a dingo do that? One local theory was that the dingo had dropped the baby, which had then been taken home by a camp dog, and that the owner of the camp dog, worried about being implicated, had removed the clothes and buried the body. But that still failed to explain why such a person had not simply buried the baby with her clothes on.

The Chamberlains were questioned several times by the police. A rumour began to circulate that she had fallen from a supermarket trolley and become spastic, and that her parents had decided to kill her for this reason. Another rumour was that Azaria meant "the sacrifice", and that she had been sacrificed on top of Ayers Rock in some gruesome ceremony.

Forensic evidence seemed to throw some doubt on the story about the dingo. A stuffed stretchsuit was dragged across the ground from the camp site to the base of Ayers Rock, then examined by botanists. There were fragments of charcoal in the experimental stretchsuit, as might have been expected, since there had been bush fires in the area. Yet there was no charcoal on Azaria's suit. Forensic tests seemed to indicate that Azaria's clothes had been rubbed in the dust at the base of the rock. A dead goat was put into baby clothes and thrown into the dingo pen at Adelaide Zoo. The dingo buried the carcass and clothes in various parts of the pen. Forensic experts concluded that the damage caused to the clothing – particularly the teeth-marks – was quite unlike the damage to Azaria's stretchsuit. Moreover, the blood that soaked the stretchsuit seemed to suggest that the baby had been in an upright position during the bleeding.

Michael Chamberlain, pursued by journalists who wanted to know what he thought about this suggestion that his baby had not been taken by a dingo, admitted that it was possible that a human being had carried Azaria off, "but he or she would have been a maniac". But where was the baby? It seemed unlikely that a dingo had eaten every morsel of a 9 lb baby.

The inquest opened in Alice Springs in December, and moved to Ayers Rock. By that time, the Chamberlains were living in an atmosphere of continual hostility – there were even death threats. Many people simply doubted that a small wild dog would steal a nine-week-old baby. And when the police forensic laboratory announced that the holes in the garment had been made with an instrument like a pair of scissors, the Australian public began to feel that there was more in this case than met the eye. On Wednesday, 18 February 1981 Coroner Barritt startled everyone by announcing that because of the widespread interest in the case, he had granted permission for television to film the findings of the inquest. But Australians who hoped for some sensational revelation, or accusation, were disappointed when the coroner found that Azaria Chamberlain had met her death through a wild dingo. He added that it was untrue that Azaria meant "sacrifice in the wilderness".

The debate continued. In September that year the police were ordered to reopen their investigations. In November, a supreme court judge ordered a new inquest. It opened on 14 December 1981. Just before the inquest, the police received a letter from an anonymous couple who claimed that they had seen a dingo carrying what they thought was a doll, and that when one of them threw a stone at the dog, it dropped its burden, which they found to be a badly mutilated child. The couple decided to bury the baby, so the parents would not see it in this condition; they undressed it, and later got rid of the clothes at Ayers Rock. But the writers could not be located.

At the inquest, Michael Chamberlain was asked whether he had cleaned blood out of the car. He agreed that he may have cleaned "some blood", but insisted that it was not much. Lindy was asked why she had sent a bloodstained tracksuit – which she had worn on the night of the baby's disappearance – to the cleaners. When a policeman told how he had unbolted the front seats of the car and found bloodstains on the cross section, the court sensed that this inquest was, in fact, a trial of the Chamberlains. This became even clearer when Joy Kuhl, a forensic biologist, told how she had discovered foetal bloodstains on a pair of nail scissors, and on the inside of a yellow container found in the car. But the most sensational evidence came from a British expert in legal medicine, Professor James Cameron. He had been sent the baby's clothing at the London Hospital Medical College, and his examination had led him to conclude that the blood on the stretchsuit suggested that it had flowed down from above. He also commented that the holes in the stretchsuit had been made with scissors, and that he had been surprised at the absence of teethmarks or of animal saliva around the neck of the suit. And when he added that ultra violet light had revealed a bloodstained handprint on the stretchsuit – a print too large to be a child's but too small for a man – it was obvious that the finger of guilt was now pointing at Lindy Chamberlain.

When the inquest resumed after Christmas 1981, Mr Desmond Sturgess, the barrister appointed to help the coroner, finally made the accusation that everyone was expecting. He believed that Azaria had been killed in the family car, and her body concealed in a camera bag. The coroner then committed Lindy Chamberlain for trial on a murder charge, and Michael Chamberlain was charged as an accessory after the fact.

The trial of Lindy Chamberlain began on 13 September 1982, and the prosecuting counsel, Ian Barker QC, announced that he would attempt to prove that Azaria Chamberlain died of a cut throat while Lindy Chamberlain was in the front passenger seat of the car. The prosecution case was that Lindy Chamberlain had taken the baby from the tent and into the front seat of the car, where she had cut Azaria's throat. The case depended largely on forensic evidence. It lacked one vitally important element – a reason why Lindy Chamberlain, mother of a happy family, should have murdered her own baby.

The defence called experts who disagreed that the stains found in the car were foetal haemoglobin, and a dental expert argued that the holes found in the stretchsuit were caused by an animal's teeth. Lindy Chamberlain's doctor testified that she was not suffering from post-natal depression after the birth of Azaria. A mother testified that a dingo had tried to grab her twelve-year-old child by the elbow at Ayers Rock on the evening before Azaria disappeared. A Geelong pathologist flatly denied that the blood-stains on the tracksuit could have been caused by a head injury or a cut to the throat. And he denied that there was a bloodstained handprint on the suit.

The one point that emerged very clearly from the trial was that the evidence of the various experts could not be accepted as scientifically unshakeable. The defence made the telling point that if Lindy Chamberlain had murdered her baby, surely she would have claimed that the child had been carried off in the dingo's mouth? From the beginning she had stuck to her story of only seeing the dingo moving away into the darkness.

The trial lasted for seven weeks. When the jury returned from six and a half hours of deliberation, the foreman announced that their verdict was unanimous: the Chamberlains were guilty as charged. Thereupon the judge, Mr Justice Muirhead, told Lindy Chamberlain, "There is only one sentence I can pass upon you – hard labour for life." She was taken away to Berrimah Jail where, within a few days, she would give birth to another daughter. Michael Chamberlain was sentenced to an eighteen-month sus-pended sentence.

When, in April 1983, the Federal Court rejected Lindy Cham-berlain's appeal, it seemed that the Dingo Baby Case was finally over. But soon Lindy Chamberlain support groups were formed all over the country. In February 1984 the High Court of Australia rejected Lindy Chamberlain's appeal. But soon after that a family described how, eight weeks before the disappearance of Azaria, a dingo at Ayers Rock had dragged their child from the car. The chief ranger from the Ayers Rock district, Derek Roff, wrote to the *National Times* saying he was convinced the dingoes might well attack a child. Thirty-one scientists signed an open letter protesting about the conclusions drawn from Joy Kuhl's evidence. A psychologist who had examined Lindy Chamberlain in prison stated on television that he was unable to account for criminal behaviour on her part; and affirmed his conviction that she was totally innocent.

Although these pleas had no effect on the authorities, Lindy Chamberlain was released from prison on 7 February 1986 on the grounds that she had paid her debt to society. She had served just over two years of her life sentence. After her release, she announced that she and her husband would continue the fight to establish their innocence. Part of that campaign was a long television interview with reporter Ray Martin, in which she spoke frankly about the charges against her, and of the reasons why so many had felt her to be guilty – her apparently cool demeanour during the inquests and in television appearances. She pointed out the obvious – that if a mother who has lost her baby is then faced with a campaign of rumour and innuendo, her reaction is bound to be one of anger, and she is not likely to look bereaved and miserable. During the course of the programme, one of the jurors who had been responsible for the guilty verdict announced that she had since become convinced that Lindy Chamberlain was innocent. She went on to admit that many of the other jurors had felt doubts but said that the forensic evidence had seemed conclusive.

In retrospect, it is difficult to see why Lindy Chamberlain was ever suspected of murder. No one disputed that the Chamberlains were a happy and affectionate family unit, and no one was ever able to allege any kind of motive. It seems fairly certain that the Lindy Chamberlain case will be regarded as Australia's most tragic miscarriage of justice.

DID THE EVIDENCE FIT THE CRIME?

(Bruno Hauptmann, USA 1936)

Tom Zito

The kidnap and murder of the Lindbergh baby in 1932 was among the first to earn the accolade "Crime of the Century". On the wild night of 1 March, a ramshackle ladder was placed up against the first-floor nursery window of the Lindbergh country home in New Jersey. Someone stole the sleeping child from his cot and left a ransom note demanding $50,000. Colonel Charles Lindbergh, whose solo transatlantic flight in 1927 had made him a world hero, was a wealthy man; the money in marked bills was delivered, by arrangement, to a cemetery in New York's Bronx. Waiting in his car, Colonel Lindbergh heard one of the kidnap gang shout just two words: "Hey, Doc" Six weeks later, the kidnapped baby was found dead, buried in a shallow grave. It was another two and a half years before the breakthrough in the case. One of the marked bills was traced to Bruno Hauptmann, an immigrant carpenter who lived in the Bronx. Hauptmann was tried for kidnap and murder. Evidence was lost, other evidence invented. A timesheet giving Hauptmann a perfect alibi for the day of the kidnapping went missing (it has never been found). Forensic evidence fuelled further controversy, particularly that of a detective and wood expert who, in order to link Hauptmann to the kidnapping, said that one of the rails of the ladder had come from the attic floor of Hauptmann's landlord. Hauptmann was convicted and sent to the electric chair, still protesting his innocence, in 1936. In the early 1980s, shortly after the Freedom *of Information Act became law in the United States, the journalist Tom Zito (b.1948) re-examined Hauptmann's case for Life magazine. He received a tip from someone at the FBI that there were reams of evidence vindicating Hauptmann sitting in its vaults. Although he has since quit journalism to run his own multi-million dollar software company, Zito vividly remembers the Lindbergh assignment. "Little did I know what a journey it would become," he wrote. "The eeriest part of the reporting was meeting with Wilentz, the prosecutor, who was still in legal practice fifty years later, still in New Jersey. His self-righteous attitude was that he had performed a public service to close a long national disgrace (namely having the murder be unsolved)."*

Just hours before he was scheduled for execution in the electric chair to atone for "the Crime of the Century" – kidnapping and murdering the son of Charles and Anne Morrow Lindbergh – Bruno Richard Hauptmann had scrawled a letter to New Jersey Governor Harold Hoffman and, indirectly, to the prosecutor in the case, New Jersey Attorney General David Wilentz. "My writing is not in fear of losing my life, this is in the hands of God, it is His will," Hauptmann wrote.

> I will go gladly, it means the end of my tremendous suffering. Only in thinking of my dear wife and my little boy, that is breaking my heart . . . Mr Wilentz, with my dying breath I swear by God that you convicted an innocent man. Once you will stand before the same Judge to whom I go in a few hours. You know you have done wrong on me . . . I beg you, Attorney General, believe at least a dying man. Please investigate because this case is not solved, it only adds another dead to the Lindbergh case.

Hauptmann's execution was in fact, delayed for three days because another man had confessed to the crime. But that man recanted, and notwithstanding a grand jury investigation into the matter, the execution went ahead. On the evening of April 3,

1936, with crowds ringing the New Jersey State Prison in Trenton shouting for his death, the thirty-six- year-old carpenter from Kamenz, Germany, was led to the electric chair and strapped into place. "Here was Hauptmann's chance to talk," wrote Edward Folliard for the next morning's *Washington Post*. "It was the moment when he was expected to talk – when reporters had their pencils poised to catch his words, words that would end forever the controversy as to whether he snatched that little child from his crib in the Sourland Mountains.

"No words came. There was only that dazed look – that look of the soldier about to get the bayonet and knowing that nothing could save him . . . There was now a steady whine in the death chamber, the death song of the dynamo. It continued for what seemed an eternity . . ."

A few minutes later, six physicians, one after the other, laid their stethoscopes to Hauptmann's chest and pronounced him dead.

When word reached Hauptmann's wife, Anna, in her hotel room across town, she threw her hands up to her face and cried, "Ach, Gott! Mein Richard!" The words were immediately scribbled by hordes of reporters who had broken down her door. When asked for his reaction, Lloyd Fisher, the Hauptmann defence attorney who had filed and lost the appeals, said to reporters in the warden's office, "This is the greatest tragedy in the history of New Jersey. Time will never wash it out."

Tragedy or not, time still has not washed out the questions in the Lindbergh case. A half century after the March 1, 1932, kidnapping, the mysteries have only grown. In 1977, under the Freedom of Information Act, San Francisco attorney Robert Bryan reviewed the FBI's voluminous files on the case. In the fall of 1981, Anna Hauptmann herself, with the help of Bryan, forced open the records of the New Jersey State Police. Armed with the federal documents, she filed a civil suit against the State of New Jersey, former Attorney General David Wilentz (still practising law in Woodbridge, NJ), the Hearst Corporation and others for "wrongfully, corruptly and unjustly" trying and executing Hauptmann.

The new evidence strongly suggests that witnesses were coached and even coerced, evidence was tampered with or suppressed and testimony by key witnesses was altered between the crime itself and the trial – a period of two years and 10 months – to fit the suspect. There is an excellent chance that a competent defense attorney, in possession of these documents and operating under today's more stringent legal proceedings, could have gotten Hauptmann off on technical grounds, arguing a mis-trial or "reasonable doubt." Far more disturbing, however, is another possibility these dusty files raise: that Bruno Richard Hauptmann might have been telling the truth.

Clearly that thought did not seriously occur to the eight men and four women who found Hauptmann guilty of murder in the first degree. And who could blame them? The outlines of the case, as presented by Wilentz in his brilliant prosecution, are remembered by millions of Americans, as well as by more recent readers of George Waller's best-selling book, *Kidnap*. The case seemed airtight. Indeed, one of the chief arguments of Hauptmann's defense attorney at the time was that Wilentz's case was "too perfect."

According to Wilentz, on the night of March 1, 1932, Bruno Richard Hauptmann, an illegal immigrant with a prison record back in Germany, placed a crudely built wood ladder against the wall of the Lindberghs' Hopewell, NJ, country home, pried open the nursery window and grabbed twenty-month-old Charles Lindbergh Jr in his sleep. He escaped the way he came, after leaving behind the ladder and a ransom note demanding $50,000. At some point during the kidnapping, the child had been killed and buried about five miles from his home under a pile of leaves. Before his body had been found, the ransom money had been turned over in St Raymond's Cemetery in the Bronx to a man called "John" – a man later identified by America's greatest living hero, Charles Lindbergh, as well as by his go-between, as Bruno Richard Hauptmann.

As presented during the trial, the case against Hauptmann seemed overwhelming. Over $14,000 of the $50,000 ransom money had been found hidden in his garage; eyewitnesses had placed the Bronx carpenter near the scene of the crime; a

Forestry Department expert had traced to Hauptmann's attic a board used in fashioning the kidnap ladder; handwriting experts had testified that Hauptmann had written all the ransom notes.

Wilentz's presentation of the evidence was so dramatic, so thorough, that at one point he suggested that the unusual geometric symbols used to sign the ransom notes spelled out Hauptmann's guilt. The blue intersecting circles, with a center filled with red and punched with three holes. Wilentz argued, spelled, "*b* in blue for Bruno; *r* in red for Hauptmann!"

The entire nation hungered for the verdict that the jury so swiftly rendered. On the streets near the Hunterdon County Courthouse in Flemington, where the trial was held, a crowd of 10,000 screamed, "Kill Hauptmann! Kill the German!!" Indeed, who better than the man who had faced the Allies from the wrong end of a machine gun in World War I, who had gone on to become a convicted thief and second-story man and who had arrived in America as a fugitive from justice? Hauptmann seemed to symbolize not only the once and future German menace abroad but also the larger "alien" threat back home. "What type of man would murder the child of Colonel Charles A. Lindbergh and Anne Morrow . . ." Wilentz asked rhetorically during his summation. "He wouldn't be an American. No American gangster . . . ever sank to the level of killing babies. Ah, no! An American gangster that did want to participate in a kidnapping wouldn't pick out Colonel Lindbergh." Just years before, in 1927, "Lucky Lindy," having made his historic solo fight across the Atlantic, had become, in Wilentz's words, "the most popular and the most glorious man in this world." His family was the true first family of the country, and his son was, according to a periodical of the time, "the most famous child on earth." The murder of that child had been more than a personal loss; it was a national tragedy.

President Herbert Hoover immediately announced, "We will move heaven and earth to find out who is this criminal that had the audacity to commit a crime like this." There ensued one of the greatest criminal investigations ever mounted, one that finally, on September 19, 1934, ensnared its first indictable suspect. The trial of Bruno Richard Hauptmann was, in the words of

H. L. Mencken, "the biggest story since the Resurrection," and its outcome a national catharsis. But even at the time, a few questions could be heard through the cries for revenge.

The trial judge, Thomas Trenchard, had admitted in his charge to the jury that "the evidence produced by the state is largely circumstantial in character." Said famed trial lawyer Clarence Darrow, "No man should be executed on such flimsy evidence." "The entire trial left me with a question in my mind," said Eleanor Roosevelt.

Far more substantive, however, was a confidential memo that came to rest on the desk of J. Edgar Hoover, the director of the FBI. Since kidnapping did not become a federal crime until after the passage of the so-called Lindbergh law, the FBI had not controlled the investigation but had nonetheless participated throughout, observing as a silent witness from the day of the kidnapping until after Hauptmann's arrest. This memo – one of thousands on the case sent by Hoover's agents – suggested that the investigative agencies were playing free and loose with the case against Hauptmann. Just days before the trial began, an FBI agent wrote that the "questionable tactics of all the other governmental agencies would probably come to light in a new trial." That memorandum, along with many other mitigating documents, remained sealed away in federal and state labyrinths until Anna Hauptmann sued to reopen the case.

"The questionable tactics," FBI memos make clear, extended to virtually every aspect of the state's case, including virtually every piece of evidence. Nowhere was that case more flawed than in the witnesses it produced to place Hauptmann, who lived a two-hour drive away, near the Lindbergh home in Hopewell, NJ. An October 1934 FBI memo stated that the New Jersey police "did not have one single reliable witness who could place Hauptmann in the vicinity of Hopewell prior to or on the date of the crime." Yet witness after witness did just that.

Millard Whited, for instance, testified at the trial that he had seen Hauptmann near the Lindbergh home on two occasions; yet state records of his initial interrogation shortly after the crime reveal that he saw no one suspicious. In a New Jersey State Police report of April 26, 1932, Whited is asked, "Is there any information that you can give us that would assist us in this investigation . . ." He answers, "No." Only after Hauptmann was arrested, and it was suggested that Whited might share in some of the bounty for capturing the Lindbergh kidnapper, did he change his testimony. (Whited eventually received $1,000 of the $25,000.) In another 1934 FBI memo, an agent reported: "Mr Wilentz . . . stated that he had run into a little difficulty over the witness, Millard Whited . . . Mr Wilentz stated that several neighbours of the Whiteds, as well as the brother of this witness, had given affidavits to the effect that he was a confirmed liar, and totally unreliable."

In court, witness Amandus Hochmuth placed Hauptmann in Hopewell on the very day of the crime and said that Hauptmann had glared "at me as if he saw a ghost." A Public Welfare record at the time, in fact, listed Hochmuth as "partly blind" and mentions his "failing eyesight due to cataracts." When Hochmuth was called into Governor Hoffman's office in 1937 in an effort to determine who should receive the reward money for Hauptmann's arrest, Hoffman asked Hochmuth to identify an object ten feet away – a file cabinet, topped by a silver cup filled with flowers. Hochmuth said it was a woman wearing a hat; when people in the room laughed, he changed his description to a bowl of fruit sitting on a piece of furniture.

Other identifications of Hauptmann also are suspect in light of these newly released documents. Joseph Perrone, a cab driver, testified during the trial that Hauptmann had handed him one of the ransom notes to deliver to go-between Dr John F. Condon. Yet just six weeks after the delivery, he had told police that he could not remember details of what the man who handed him the ransom note had looked like. After Hauptmann's arrest, Perrone's memory was refreshed by police, according to FBI documents, with "what might be termed a 'pep talk': 'Now, Joe, we've got the right man at last. There isn't a man in this room who isn't convinced that he is the man who kidnapped that baby . . . Now we're depending on you, Joe. Take a good look at him when we bring him in but don't say anything until I ask you if he is the man . . .'" Hauptmann, rather than being placed in a lineup as is customary, was flanked by only two men, one in a police uniform.

In a subsequent memo an FBI agent wrote, "I informed Mr Lanigan [New Jersey assistant attorney general] that several of us were present when Inspector Lyons practically coerced Joseph Perrone into identifying Hauptmann."

As important as anything at the trial was the courtroom identification of Hauptmann by the prosecution's two star witnesses, Charles Lindbergh himself and go-between Condon. Both Lindbergh and Dr Condon had gone to St Raymond's Cemetery to deliver the ransom money to the man who called himself John. Condon, who had spent considerable time talking face to face to "John" during the ransom negotiations, was positive that "John" was indeed Hauptmann. Lindbergh's identification, coupled with Condon's, proved decisive. Writing for the Hearst newspapers, Adela Rogers St Johns seemed to speak for the jurors, if not for the entire country, when she reported: "Watching Lindbergh today in this ordeal I cannot believe he would swear away the life of any man unless he was sure."

Yet just how sure was Lindbergh? An FBI agent wrote a memo before the trial, saying, "I am somewhat skeptical of some of the evidence now being produced in New Jersey, particularly some of the identifications and the testimony of Lindbergh relative to recognizing the voice, etc."

Several months before the trial, Lindbergh had testified before a Bronx grand jury that he could not positively identify the voice, which he had heard say only two words ("Hey, Doc") from more than 200 feet away over two and a half years earlier. Yet at the trial Lindbergh was positive. And the words he had heard were. "In a foreign accent: 'Hey, Doctor.'"

The identification by Dr John F. Condon was even more puzzling. A highly eccentric seventy-two-year-old retired schoolteacher, Condon had placed an advertisement in the Bronx *Home News* a week after the kidnapping, offering his services as an intermediary between the Lindberghs and the kidnappers. Condon had spent considerable time conversing with "John"; he told police and friends he "could pick him out of a thousand." When asked by Wilentz who "John" was during the trial, Condon had announced in a strong, deliberate voice, separating each syllable for dramatic effect: "John is Bru–no Rich–ard⋅ Haupt–mann!"

When first shown Hauptmann in a police lineup, however, Condon had acted very confused. He talked to Hauptmann; asked him to repeat something he, Condon, wrote on a piece of paper; looked for a growth he remembered on his right thumb. Said the FBI memo describing the meeting: "Finally, after a totally lapsed time of approximately 10 minutes, Inspector Lyons asked Dr Condon if Hauptmann was the man and Dr Condon replied, I would not say he was the man. I am not sure." Another memo says, "He [Condon] remarked on one occasion that Hauptmann is not the man because he appears to be much heavier, has different eyes, different hair, etc. . . ." When Hauptmann left the police lineup, reported an FBI agent, the following exchange took place: Q. "Have you seen him before, Doctor?" A. "No, he is not the man."

Before the trial, Condon went to visit Hauptmann in jail. Describing that visit, a recently discovered New Jersey State Police report quotes Condon saying to Hauptmann, "I believe you, but the evidence is against you." In fact, documents reveal that Condon not only was unsure about Hauptmann but also was unsure that the kidnapper was German. A much earlier New Jersey police file quotes Condon as saying, "I figure he [the kidnapper] was not a German, from the way he spoke to me."

If the testimony of "eyewitnesses" was suspect, the testimony of the so-called experts seems more so in retrospect. Wilentz's case rested heavily on the testimony of a handwriting expert and a wood expert. One of Wilentz's tasks in the courtroom was to establish that the kidnapper and the extortionist were one and the same. It had been considered highly possible during the investigation of the crime that the original note – left by the kidnapper – had been seen by so many people that it could have been copied, and subsequent notes could have been written by people totally unconnected with the kidnapping.

Such possibilities were dismissed authoritatively by Albert S. Osborn and his son Albert D. Osborn, two of the nation's best-known handwriting analysts. The Osborns and other handwriting experts brought in to testify against Hauptmann claimed that all the ransom notes were written by Hauptmann. There could be no doubt. Yet a 1934 FBI memo discovered only recently describes a conversation between the younger Osborn and Colonel

Schwarzkopf, who led the investigation for the New Jersey State Police. After talking to Osborn, Schwarzkopf hung up the phone, turned to the other officers present and said, " 'It doesn't look so good. He [Osborn] says that when he first looked at the specimens he thought they were the same, and that there were some striking similarities, but after examining them for a while he found a lot of dissimilarities, which outweighed the similarities, and is convinced he [Hauptmann] did not write the ransom notes.' " It was only after the ransom money was found in Hauptmann's garage that Osborn reversed his opinion. The same FBI memo reports: "Within an hour [of being informed that the money had been found] Mr Osborn called the Undercover Squad headquarters . . . and advised that he and his son had positively decided that Hauptmann wrote the ransom letters." The report concludes, "There was . . . laughing [among police officers present] as to the ability of handwriting experts, it being pointed out that the Osborns did not make the identification until after the money was found."

In a trial filled with high drama, there was perhaps no more dramatic testimony than that of Arthur Koehler, a scholarly Forestry Department wood expert who at one point clamped a vice on one end of the judge's bench and planed down a piece of ponderosa pine. Koehler testified that there was overwhelming proof that one of the boards used in the ladder had actually come from Hauptmann's attic. The ladder rail was almost the same length as a gap in the flooring on one side of the attic, and square nail holes in the board exactly fit the pattern of nail holes in the floor joist running below the gap. Even the most skeptical juror had to be impressed by the evidence. Lindbergh might have been wrong. Condon might have been wrong, but what were the odds that four square nail holes would line up perfectly with four other square nail holes – so perfectly that four square-cut nails could be tapped into place with a finger!

Yet here again the FBI had its doubts. Several FBI memos from the fall of 1934 note that there had been numerous searches of the attic and that no evidence had been found. No less than thirty-seven police officers – directed to look specifically for boards that might match a rail of the ladder – had conducted nine searches of the attic, to no avail. It was not until the FBI was denied access to the attic that the gap was found. The gap was discovered by New Jersey State Police Detective Lewis J. Bornmann on September 26, 1934 – seven days after Hauptmann's arrest. Bornmann had actually moved into the Hauptmann house after the arrest and had participated in several of the previous fruitless searches. And even on the 26th, Bornmann had filed this report: "This date detailed by Captain Lamb to continue the search on the above-captioned home. Meeting Detective Tobin, two police carpenters, and Supt. Wilson on the premises at 9 a.m., we immediately proceeded to make a thorough search of the attic. Nothing of value was found." Yet in another report bearing the same date, Bornmann disclosed his important discovery in the attic. The following day the FBI requested access to the Hauptmann house but were denied entry by the New Jersey State Police. Why?

The FBI's collective eyebrows, often raised during the Lindbergh kidnapping investigation, seemed particularly arched in respect to Koehler's testimony. A review of the FBI's own files, conducted a month after Hauptmann's execution, notes that Hauptmann's defence lawyers had been expected during the 1935 trial to subpoena FBI records to prove the ladder-rail identification was "fabricated by the joint efforts of the New Jersey State Police and the New Jersey prosecutor's office in co-operation with Arthur Koehler; however, this request was not received by the bureau from the defense attorneys."

The ladder was not the only physical piece of evidence that might have been tampered with by the police. In his book *Scapegoat*, author Anthony Scaduto makes a persuasive case that the police also may have tampered with the payroll books from Hauptmann's job at the Majestic Apartments in Manhattan – books that could have backed up his alibis for both the day of the kidnapping (March 1) and the day that the ransom money was passed by Dr Condon (April 2).

Hauptmann first told police that he had worked all day on March 1; and the supervisor from the Majestic Apartments gave an affidavit to that effect shortly after the hearings on Hauptmann's extradition from New York to New Jersey. Yet the

payroll books that would have proved the matter one way or
another were missing – missing, even though the New York City
police files bore receipts indicating that they had at one point
received them. Without those records, Hauptmann's supervisor
felt obliged to soften his own affidavit to "I am not positive . . . I
do not know," and Hauptmann had lost one of his best defences.

The payroll records covering April 2, the day of the ransom
pass, do exist, but they, too, may have been tampered with.
Where there should be a check opposite Hauptmann's name for
April 2, there is, instead, a large ink blob, a blob big enough to
cover the check mark that would have been there if Hauptmann
was telling the truth. All the other circles in the book that mark
someone's absence from work are neat and small.

If there was a smoking gun in the case, it was the ransom
money. Hauptmann had been arrested after cashing a $10 Lind-
bergh ransom bill at a Manhattan gas station two years and seven
months after the kidnapping. After many days of searching,
police found $14,600 more in ransom bills hidden in Haupt-
mann's garage. Almost as incriminating was the incredible tale
Hauptmann told to explain the money. A friend and business
partner, Hauptmann said, a man named Isidor Fisch, had left a
shoe box in his care before returning to Germany for a visit,
without telling him its contents. Hauptmann had stuck it on a
kitchen closet shelf and forgotten about it. Even after relatives
wrote from Germany that the tubercular Fisch had died, Hauptmann did not remember. Finally, a few weeks before his arrest, he
had poked the decomposing box accidently with a broom and
noticed the money (the closet had a leak, and the water had
partially destroyed the box). He had buried the money in his
garage, intending to spend the few thousand dollars Fisch owed
him and to keep the rest for Fisch's relatives who were coming to
the US to settle the estate.

A tall tale – or so Wilentz made it sound in court. He called it
Hauptmann's "Fisch story." But now, almost 50 years later,
documents suggest that the "Fisch story" was not so fishy after
all. Business ledgers confiscated by the police and never introduced in court established that Fisch and Hauptmann were
indeed business partners. Further supporting evidence could

have been supplied by police files – references to letters written by Isidor Fisch's friend and room-mate, Henry Uhlig, that were also confiscated by the police and never introduced in court. A rediscovered New Jersey State Police file refers to a letter Uhlig wrote to a friend in Germany the day *before* Hauptmann's arrest, in which he claims that Hauptmann had loaned Fisch $7,500 and states that Fisch "had been swindling people." After Uhlig learned of Hauptmann's arrest, according to another state police document, he wrote a letter stating that Fisch had "bought some hot money and gave it to Hauptmann." Uhlig added, "Now the poor man is going to have to pay."

Also unavailable for Hauptmann's defence was a letter written to the carpenter by Isidor's brother from Germany shortly after Isidor's death and later confiscated from Hauptmann's home by police. Pinkus Fisch wrote to Hauptmann of his brother's death: "I feel it is my duty to let you know about it in America as my brother has often talked about you and your business connections with him . . . In his last few hours he mentioned your name and I suppose he wanted to say something to us about you, or something for us to tell you, but he did not have the strength . . ."

Hauptmann well understood the importance of this letter as evidence to support his case. A New Jersey State Police report on the secret and illegal surveillance of Hauptmann in his jail cell has the prisoner saying to his wife, "If Isidor Fisch had not died in Germany, I would not be here behind bars. Have you the letter from Fisch's brother?" Anna Hauptmann responds that the police have taken it.

Other documents also support Hauptmann's contention that he had not known about the ransom money, let alone spent any, until shortly before his arrest. Lindbergh ransom bills discovered between 1932 and the summer of 1934 almost all shared similar characteristics. New York police files contain lab réports of all known ransom money passed in the city, showing that most of those bills bore traces of lipstick and mascara, not to mention microscopic traces of gold or brass particles. Moreover, the bills were folded repeatedly so as to fit into a small watch or vest pocket. The half dozen or so ransom bills known to be passed by Hauptmann bore no resemblance to bills passed earlier. No lipstick traces. No gold or brass particles. No folds of any kind. Furthermore, they all showed evidence of being waterlogged, consistent with his testimony of the saturated shoe box.

Perhaps even more interesting, a magazine report published shortly after Hauptmann's arrest refers to Lindbergh ransom money cashed in by Isidor Fisch to buy his boat ticket to Germany. In its December 31, 1934, issue, *Time* magazine, summarizing evidence that would be brought forward by the prosecution against Hauptmann in his trial, wrote, "Isidor Fisch, Hauptmann's partner in random business ventures, used ransom money to pay for his passage back to Germany, where Fisch died of tuberculosis in 1933." Yet this fact was never mentioned by the prosecution during the trial.

The reason: police evidently believed at the time that the $2,000 in Lindbergh bills cashed by Fisch was the same $2,000 that Hauptmann had told them he had loaned to Fisch the day he sailed for Germany. The money seemed to constitute important evidence against Hauptmann. Only later was it discovered that Fisch had cashed the ransom money several hours *before* Hauptmann withdrew $2,000 from his bank account to give to his friend. The implication is clear: either Hauptmann had been telling the truth, and it was Fisch, not Hauptmann, who had the ransom money in 1933, or they were partners in the crime as well as in stocks and furs.

From the very beginning of the Lindbergh case, police believed that more than one person was involved in the kidnapping and extortion. Even more important, they were very suspicious that at least someone in the kidnapping group had come from, or had friends inside, the Lindbergh household.

An FBI report, quoting state police, put it bluntly: "At least two persons perpetrated the kidnapping." According to state records, one of the first police officers to arrive at the Lindbergh home found two sets of footprints leading from the road near the house to the nursery and back. But the trooper, Joseph Wolf, was not called to testify. In his reports on his contacts with the kidnapper, Dr Condon mentioned other people – people he had heard over the telephone, speaking Italian in the background . . . a small, dark-skinned woman who had approached him at a charity bazaar in the Bronx to say that her accomplices were nervous but that she would be in touch. And both Condon and Lindbergh reported seeing a second man – a lookout – at their cemetery rendezvous with the kidnapper.

Yet Hauptmann was electrocuted on the theory that he was the "lone-wolf" kidnapper and murderer. What had happened in between to all the other suspected accomplices? What had happened to the story of Violet Sharpe?

A young serving maid, Violet Sharpe, who worked in the household of Anne Morrow Lindbergh's mother, had become a suspect shortly after the kidnapping when she gave vague and conflicting testimony about what she had done the night of the kidnapping. Under further questioning about a telephone call she had received the afternoon of the crime, Sharpe remembered that her mystery caller had been a man named Ernie, a petty thief whose business cards were found in Sharpe's room. Yes, she admitted, Ernie had called in time to have learned that the baby would remain in Hopewell that night. The following day, the police told Violet Sharpe to get ready to go to the police barracks for additional questioning. Highly distraught, she ran upstairs to her room, choked down the cyanide chloride she had stored in a tin can on her shelf, and was dead within minutes. Colonel Norman Schwarzkopf hastened to tell reporters that "the suicide of Violet Sharpe strongly tends to confirm the suspicions of the investigating authorities concerning her guilty knowledge of the crime against Charles Lindbergh Jr." Yet, when the trial finally took place, the prosecution not only forgot about Violet Sharpe but about the possibility of a conspiracy as well.

Of all the things that weighed against Hauptmann at his trial, few undermined him as much as the incompetence of his own chief defence lawyer. Once a brilliant criminal attorney in New York, Edward Reilly clearly was approaching the end of his career when he reached the Lindbergh trial; two years later he would have a nervous breakdown.

Reilly was hired to defend Hauptmann by none other than William Randolph Hearst, who was anxious in return to have exclusive access to the defendant and his wife for his newspapers.

Hearst passionately believed in Hauptmann's guilt. He told one reporter, "In this trial, I am sure we can produce a flame of nationwide indignation which will deter other criminals." Hearst's control over Reilly raised conflict of interest questions unknown to the jurors and never properly understood by the Hauptmanns themselves.

A heavy drinker, Reilly had little interest in talking to Hauptmann before the trial and revealed his own prejudices by having stationery down one side of which was printed a blood-red ladder, the prosecution's main piece of evidence. A recently discovered 1936 FBI memo notes that during the course of the trial, Reilly had told T.H. Sisk, the top FBI agent assigned to the Lindbergh case, that "he knew Hauptmann was guilty, didn't like him, and was anxious to see him get the chair."

Nowhere was Reilly's incompetence more apparent than in the matter of the *corpus delicti*. In order to convict Hauptmann for murder as well as extortion, it was essential to establish that Lindbergh's son was dead. The prosecution argued that of course he was, and that the proof was the body found about five miles from the Lindbergh home in the Sourland Mountains, a body that had been identified by the baby's governess as well as by his father. Reilly was all too happy to concede the point. Yet the body had been so horribly decomposed that its sex, let alone its identity, could not be firmly established. The pediatrician to Charles Lindbergh Jr summoned to the funeral home just before the corpse was cremated, was quoted as saying, "If you were to lay ten million dollars on that table and tell me it was mine if I said positively this was the Colonel's son, I'd have to refuse the money." When Reilly failed to challenge the body's identity, his assistant counsel, Lloyd Fisher, stalked out of the courtroom shouting, "You are conceding Hauptmann to the electric chair!"

In addition to being represented by such feeble counsel, Hauptmann was tried in a courtroom atmosphere as chaotic and biased as almost any in the history of American jurisprudence. The courtroom was not just crowded; it was jammed. On a particularly titillating day, some 20,000 people showed up in Flemington, NJ, to gain entrance. Spectators sneaked in on phone passes, even came through the windows. The jurors

themselves had to enter and exit the courthouse through pha-
lanxes of onlookers and journalists, all rendering their soapbox
judgments at will. Merchants peddling miniature 10-cent repli-
cas of the kidnap ladder could barely keep up with the demand;
many spectators entered the courtroom with their ladders pinned
on, literally wearing their verdicts on their lapels.

While Hauptmann was in jail awaiting trial, he was severely
beaten by the police – a fact established by FBI documents. His
treatment inside the courtroom was not much better. Judge
Thomas Whitaker Trenchard allowed prosecutor Wilentz to
shake his fist at Hauptmann, to shout at him without interruption, often calling him "a snake." "Since I am a foreigner and
besides an irregular immigrant," Hauptmann wrote to his mother
in Germany while on death row, "I was a person on whom they
could vent everything . . . The prosecutor addressed me [as] wild
animal, snake, tiger, lowest being on the animal kingdom. You
can hardly conceive how I felt . . ."

That Hauptmann felt anything would have come as a surprise to
most Americans, much less to the jury. Wilentz portrayed him not
only as a snake but also as a man with "ice water in his veins" – a
humourless, bloodless unreformed criminal capable of perpetrat-
ing any crime, however heinous. It was an image that Reilly himself
scarcely tried to counter. Yet there was evidence, in the form of
pictures and the testimony of friends, that might have been introduced to show a very different Hauptmann – a sometime musician, a
gregarious and curious traveller, an amateur photographer who
took warm and witty portraits of himself and his friends.

When Hauptmann first met Anna, his bride to be, he confessed
his life of crime back in Germany and said he had changed his
ways. And so it seemed. The New Jersey police never found so
much as a traffic violation against him in the nine years he had
lived in the United States.

In his cell immediately after hearing the verdict, Bruno Richard Hauptmann muttered. "Little men, little pieces of wood,
little scraps of paper." A guilty man cursing the various witnesses
and pieces of evidence that finally forced a harsh justice upon
him? Perhaps. However much the FBI's memorandums cast
doubt upon the case against Hauptmann, they never argue his

innocence, and the man who received them all, J. Edgar Hoover, claimed years later that he had never doubted Hauptmann's guilt. But it now seems at least possible that Hauptmann was innocent as claimed, and that he was ruminating on the brittleness of justice, hanging as it so often does on "little men, little pieces of wood, little scraps of paper."

When New Jersey Governor Harold Hoffman received word of Hauptmann's execution, he sat alone at his desk in the state house in Trenton and reread the impassioned letter Hauptmann had sent him just days before. Hoffman wondered anew, he wrote years later in his memoirs, "if the almost friendless alien who became the focal point of one of the world's bitterest controversies" had, in fact, been innocent "of the crime that for over two years baffled the high command and the brainiest sleuths in the country."

Certainly there is no doubt about his innocence in the mind of his widow. The wedding band that Richard Hauptmann gave Anna Hauptmann 56 years ago still remains on her hand, now gnarled by arthritis: on her coffee table once again rests the leather-bound album of pictures her husband had taken on their three-month trip across the United States in 1931, an album the police finally returned to her years after the trial, tattered, with many of the pictures missing. At eighty-three, Anna Hauptmann is still committed to carrying the case forward. "You ask me why I am so sharp and so agile?" she says. "I tell you that I had to stay like this so I can clear the good name of my husband."

Bruno Richard Hauptmann on death row in 1936:
"The poor child has been kidnapped and murdered, so somebody must die for it. For is the parent not the great flier? And if someone does not die for the death of the child, then always the police will be monkeys. So I am the one who is picked to die."

Former New Jersey Attorney General David Wilentz, in an interview with *The New York Times*, March 28, 1977:
"If you disbelieve Lindbergh, disbelieve the handwriting experts, the government expert on wood — if you believe District Attorney Foley suppressed evidence, and I suppressed evidence — then of course you have a different story."

THE MAN WHO COULD READ THOUGHTS

(Vernon Booher, Canada 1928)

Mike Gier

When conventional science fails, perhaps it's time to try the unconventional. This is the curious case of Vernon Booher, the first recorded murder case solved by psychic detection. A Viennese doctor claiming to have special powers led police to the weapon used to murder two members of the Booher family and two of their farmhands. The killings took place in a remote area of Edmonton, Alberta, and there were no surviving witnesses. Yet the little white-haired doctor was able to tell officers how the murder was committed, and by whom. Hitherto unsuspected, Vernon Booher was confronted, broke down and confessed. The Booher investigation was headed by police chief Mike Gier, who recalled the case some thirty years later in this short memoir.

To recognize a killer and know that you will never be able to put him where he belongs is infuriating enough, but to be faced with a murder whose very simplicity presages defeat . . . well, that is just humiliating.

As a matter of fact the Booher case involved the slaying of not one but four persons; the tracks led everywhere and nowhere, and since the department of which I was the head was under heavy fire from various quarters, I decided that the situation called for unorthodox measures.

I knew already what people were saying about police methods, and I could guess what some of my officers were thinking when I told them what I proposed to do. Particularly Detective Jim Leslie, who was to meet the train in at Edmonton and bring Dr Maximilian Langsner, late of Vienna, to my office.

Leslie was an astute investigator with a good record, but the Booher case had him foxed, and he had not been able to uncover a single lead that offered any hope of a solution. The slaying of four people appeared as mad and motiveless now as it did when the crime was discovered.

Let me say that I knew I might be leading with my chin in introducing Dr Langsner to the problem. He could be a mountebank rather than the marvel some people claimed him to be.

Nevertheless, I knew of his successes elsewhere. There was, for instance, the episode at Vancouver when he had walked into police headquarters and announced that he could put the finger on the missing jewels in a robbery case which was baffling the authorities, despite the fact that they had managed to pick up a suspect.

Dr Langsner undoubtedly had a way with him, for the police, at his suggestion, had allowed him to enter the cell of the suspect. He stood stiffly in a corner for half an hour without saying a word and then signalled to the jailer that he had finished.

To the detective in charge of the case Dr Langsner had said: "You'll find the stolen jewels hidden behind a picture in a room whose walls are yellow."

The description did not fit the suspect's apartment, but that of his girl friend, and the detective found the jewels exactly as Dr Langsner had depicted.

The Vancouver affair was one of three cases in which Dr Langsner had displayed his extraordinary powers. As far as I could understand it, he had the ability to read the thoughts of others and was demonstrating this long before studies in extrasensory perception were introduced at various universities. When asked to explain his ability to tune in to another's mind he said: "It is not easy to say what happens, but there are some people who can do it."

To get back to the Booher case, Detective Leslie was hopping mad as he waited at the railway station. I know all this, because he told me everything that happened that day – later, of course, and when he was calmer. In fact, Jim Leslie never forgot the little doctor from Vienna, and he had good reason not to, as you will see.

Dr Langsner got off the train with an umbrella and a battered piece of luggage. Leslie stepped forward, introduced himself, and said: "Welcome to Edmonton. I am happy to meet you, and all of us are looking forward to the help we know you can give us."

There was not much of Dr Langsner, and he appeared even smaller when he took off his hat and his hair popped out all over the place. He looked at Leslie for a moment, tapped his umbrella, and replied: "I don't believe a word you say. You would rather I hadn't come, and I know you are sure that I shall accomplish nothing. I hope, though, that we shall become friends and that I can help."

Leslie crimsoned, knowing that the doctor had read his mind. He was a good loser, though, and shrewd enough to realize at once that Dr Langsner was no ordinary person. He asked the doctor to talk about himself, and it was not just out of politeness.

Langsner smiled and said: "I was born and educated in Vienna, and it was my good fortune to study under Freud. During the First World War I saw a lot of shell-shocked cases, and, more than ever, became interested in the mind and its functioning. In 1926 I went to India and stayed longer than I intended. I found much that surprised me in the field of intuitive control of the mind.

"It was from this experience that I learned much of what I now know. People are sceptical about my powers, but it is not my wish to be a bloodhound. I help the police whenever they ask me, or when I have a strong pull, such as I felt in the Vancouver case."

Leslie asked Langsner what had brought him to Canada, and he explained that he wanted to study the minds of the Eskimos. The Melanesians and Polynesians of the South Pacific had become indoctrinated and corrupted by Western influences, but the intuitive abilities of the Eskimos had remained unimpaired. "They sense weather changes," said Dr Langsner with enthusiasm. "They are able to sense danger long before its

appearance and they have their minds, so to speak, at their
fingertips. I want to live with them and communicate with them
through the channels of thought."

When Detective Leslie walked into my office with our visitor
I could see that he had had a change of heart and mind. I had the
feeling that Langsner did not need briefing, but I had prepared
a report and began to read it and he listened without interrupt-
ing.

"On July 9th," I said, "the police at Mannville, eighty miles
from here, were notified by a Dr Heaslip that half the members of
the Booher ranch had been murdered. It was evening, but the
summer nights in the Arctic regions are bright and glowing and
Constable Olson drove over from Mannville and found Dr
Heaslip waiting for him at the ranch house, together with the
survivors, Henry Booher, his youngest son Vernon, and a neighbour, Charles Stevenson.

"Booher, middle-aged and still greatly shocked, led the way
into the house. In the kitchen the body of Mrs Booher was
slumped over the table. She had died from three bullets in the
back of the neck. In the next room Fred, another of the Booher
sons, was sprawled on the floor. He had been shot through the
mouth. A third victim was Gabriel Cromby, one of the hired
hands. He was an Austrian immigrant and his body was found in
the bunkhouse. Two shots had found their mark, one in the head
and the other in the chest.

"Olson was unaccustomed to dealing with this type of crime,
but he had the good sense to get everybody out on the porch for
questioning. Vernon Booher said he had found the bodies about
eight o'clock that evening. He had been working in the fields for a
couple of hours and heard the shots. They seemed to come from
the house, and he hurried over and found the body of his mother
first. He then saw his dead brother, and when he ran over to the
bunkhouse for help he discovered what had happened to Cromby. There was no telephone in the house and he got a neighbour
to call Dr Heaslip.

"The constable wanted to know if anything was missing, and
Henry Booher said he thought not. His wife had a diamond ring,
and it had not been taken. Vernon then remembered the other

cowhand, a man named Rosyk. He had not been seen and Vernon asked if he might not be the murderer.

"The little party began to search the outhouses, and in one of the barns they found the missing man . . . Rosyk was dead from a couple of bullets. Henry Booher was asked what he had been doing at the time and if he had not heard the shots. He said: 'No, I wish to God I had heard them, but I was working too far away. There is a lot of acreage to this farm and the sounds did not carry that far.' Stevenson, the neighbour, explained his presence. He had stopped at the house to look at a farming catalogue Henry Booher had told him about. They were thinking of buying a harvester together.

"Booher corroborated this, and when asked if he had any idea who might be responsible for the murders replied: 'No. As far as I can tell we have no enemies anywhere. Rose, my wife, was a well-loved woman among our community. She was always ready to help any of our neighbours.' "

I explained to Dr Langsner that when the crime was notified to Edmonton I had sent Detective Leslie and Inspector Longacre out to the farm. "Tell the doctor what you found," I said to Leslie.

He looked a bit uncomfortable and glanced at Langsner, who was sitting very upright in his chair and grasping his umbrella.

"We carried out a routine examination, but found no strange fingerprints; just those of the Booher family and hired help. The murder weapon was a .303 rifle, but we were unable to find it. There was a .22 rifle and an old shotgun in the house, but neither had been fired for some time. One thing that interested us was the absence of rifle shells. Whoever had done the killing had picked them up, except one, which we found in a pan of water.

"We organized a search of the countryside with the help of neighbours, but it was no good. The murder weapon is still missing, and at the moment we are stuck without a clue."

Dr Langsner nodded sympathetically. "I can see how difficult everything is. Perhaps I shall be able to help you a little."

The inquest took place that afternoon, and Dr Langsner occupied a seat at the Press table. Everyone wondered who he was. The inquiry did not yield much more than we knew already.

Mrs Booher was the first victim and she was killed at the table as she was preparing a dish of strawberries. Fred died next, Rosyk a little later and Cromby last of all – about two hours after the first murder.

The time factor was testified to by neighbours and other witnesses and the shots were heard between half-past six and eight o'clock in the evening. They did not arouse any concern, because around Mannville it is hunting country and almost everybody keeps a gun.

One important piece of evidence was that provided by Councilman Robert Scott, who said he had driven down the farm road about six-thirty and had stopped to talk with Vernon Booher. Rosyk put in an appearance and asked Vernon what remained to be done around the house. Vernon told him to feed the stock in the barn.

Vernon gave evidence and was asked how it was that he had not heard those shots which occurred earlier in the evening. He said that since thinking the events over he must have heard them, but had paid no attention. He knew there was a fox in the neighbourhood and that Charles Stevenson had told him that he meant bagging it.

Charles Stevenson, somewhat nervous, had not long been sworn when he was asked if he owned a gun.

"Yes, I do, but I haven't it at the moment," he said. "It has been troubling me and I want to tell you about it. My gun is a .303 and the same calibre as the murder weapon. It was in my closet, but it is not there now and I think somebody must have stolen it."

"Can you tell the court when the gun was stolen?"

"Yes. It was taken last Sunday during the time I left home to go to church. I know it was there before I left because I saw it."

"Why didn't you report the theft?"

"Aw, shucks, you know how it is round here. Neighbours just come over and borrow things if you don't happen to be around. If I wanted a gun I wouldn't think twice of taking one from the Boohers."

Henry Booher and Vernon, too, were at the church service and said that they knew nothing about the missing rifle.

Following the inquest we had a conference in my office to

decide our next step, but neither Detective Leslie nor Inspector Longacre looked very happy, and that was understandable, for we had not much to work on. Nobody seemed very talkative, so to get the ball rolling I said: "It seems to me that three people could have done these murders . . . Henry Booher or Vernon or Charles Stevenson. What puzzles me most is the motive, and maybe we shall find the killing was done by a lunatic. Our first and most important task is to find the gun. It may tell us all we want to know."

Dr Langsner was looking at me steadily and I must confess that I was half joking when I asked him: "You look as if you know something. Could it be the name of the killer?"

He was not in the mood for badinage, and like a professor addressing an inattentive class he said in a clipped voice: "The rifle is not important. There are no suspects in this case, only the murderer, and I have already recognized him."

Detective Leslie leaned forward, prepared to listen. I was not at all certain if the little doctor was not now paying me back in my own coin. Nevertheless, I asked him to name the person he thought was the killer. "Vernon Booher," he said quite simply.

"Have you any proof?" asked Inspector Longacre.

Dr Langsner was surprised by the question. "Of course I have no proof. How is that possible? I am sure, though, and yet I cannot tell you why I am sure. I can tell you, though, that I knew what one or two people were thinking about in court today."

"Do you mean to say you could read the minds of the witnesses as they were giving evidence?"

"I do not know if I was reading their minds, as you say, but I knew what they were thinking about."

Inspector Longacre looked very puzzled, and Dr Langsner began to develop his theory.

"When a man commits a crime, and it may not necessarily be murder, he knows he has offended against the social code. Nevertheless, he seeks for ways to protect himself and his mind plays with the details of the crime so that he can have an explanation prepared, should it be necessary to defend himself. The problem is much more acute, naturally, when he has killed somebody, and often the persistency of thought becomes too great to bear and the criminal confesses, because only by so doing can he find relief from an intolerable burden. For instance, I know that Vernon is terribly worried by something that may prove his guilt."

"You mean the discovery of the missing rifle?" I asked. "If you know where it is, why not say so?"

Dr Langsner sighed as if he somehow regretted our persistence. "Yes, I know where it is. When Mr Stevenson told the court of finding that it had been taken from his home, Vernon began to think intently about the weapon. I could see where he had put it."

"And I'll bet he could, too," said Leslie quietly.

We waited for Dr Langsner to continue. He closed his eyes and quietly said: "It is in a clump of prairie grass beyond the back of the house. It is to the west, because I can now see the sun in that direction."

Inspector Longacre gave him a hard look. He was by no means convinced that he was not a charlatan.

"I am willing to go out to the farm with you," continued Langsner. "But let us go tomorrow and I will find the rifle for you. I am very tired now."

By noon next day the four of us arrived at the Booher farm. It commanded a lot of land, and the house, timbered and two-storey, was well constructed with a large veranda which the family must have used on many a summer evening when they had visitors. Everything looked well kept and spruce, and the various farm buildings stood under the shadow of some great linden trees.

I glanced once more at Dr Langsner, and could hardly repress a chuckle. He was still carrying his umbrella on this hot day and wore the black suit he had arrived in. I was certain it was the only one he possessed. His bangs of white hair were imprisoned by his black hat, except, of course, the thick fringe that lay on the back of his neck. The Booher farm had never seen a stranger figure than Dr Langsner.

Despite the heat of the day and his unsuitable clothes, he appeared quite cool and composed, and we followed him as he walked slowly to the back of the house. He reminded me of the old water-diviners who used a hazel twig to discover a hidden well, except that he had nothing in his hand.

For twenty minutes or so he quartered the ground and then, apparently, got the scent and hurried ahead. We followed, and he stopped somewhere between the bunkhouse and one of the linden trees. His eyes were closed and he drew his hand over his brow.

"*Ja, ja! Ach Gott!*" he exclaimed. "I have it now. If you will take about ten big steps forward."

Leslie was the nearest to him and began to count the steps. At the ninth he stumbled and bent down. We hurried over, and there was the rifle lying in the grass.

"Oh no," said Inspector Longacre as if he could not believe what he saw. It was the murder weapon right enough, and it was lifted and wrapped very carefully. When we got back to Edmonton it would be examined for finger-prints.

"You will not find any," warned Dr Langsner. "Vernon wiped the rifle very carefully and kept thinking of what he had done."

And so it turned out. In the meantime, though, I booked Vernon, not on suspicion of murder, but as a material witness, and he was placed in the jail at Edmonton, "for his own protection."

"Would it be impertinent for me to tell you what I think should now be done?" asked Dr Langsner.

We were only too willing to hear his opinion. It certainly appeared as if Vernon was the murderer, but we had to prove it, and at the moment we had not the semblance of a case against him. It would need much more conclusive evidence than Dr Langsner's ability to read thoughts to convince any jury.

The little doctor then outlined his plan, and to meet his wishes we placed a chair outside Vernon's cell and saw to it that there was no unnecessary noise or interruption.

Dr Langsner seated himself and then leaned forward to stare at Vernon through the bars. At first the young man appeared quite pleasant and tried to make conversation, but later he became angry and turned his back on the doctor. Dr Langsner just sat there and stared. He was there for about an hour and then got up and said "Goodbye" to Vernon, but got no reply.

We were waiting for him in my office, and he said: "Vernon is

guilty, there is not a shadow of a doubt about it. He killed his
mother because he had come to hate her. I don't know the reason,
but he has no regret. He walked into the kitchen to kill her, and
she spoke to him without turning round. In his fury he fired three
shots, and Fred, his brother, heard them. Vernon knew he had to
kill him, although he did not want to, and he is sorry for it.

"When he ran out to hide the gun, he saw Rosyk and Cromby
in the fields; he was sure Rosyk had seen him, and killed him
when he had the chance. Two hours later he decided that it was
unsafe to allow Cromby to live. He felt he had to eliminate every
possible witness."

I told the doctor that I thought his reconstruction of the
murders was correct. "How can we prove it?" I asked.

"Find the woman," he said quickly, and when he saw he had us
puzzled he explained:

"I do not know her name. Vernon stole the gun on the Sunday
that Stevenson missed his weapon. He sneaked out of church,
took it away and then returned. The woman who saw him leave
was wearing a poke-bonnet. She has small eyes and a long jaw and
she was sitting at the back of the church, to the left of the aisle.
She saw him leave and watched to see if he would return."

"Find her," I said to Leslie, and he got up and went out
immediately.

At noon the following day Leslie brought Erma Higgins to
police headquarters. She was exactly as Langsner had described
her and looked like an ancient pixie. She was a spinster and very
much alert to what was going on around her, especially the
flirtations between young people. Yes, she had seen Vernon leave
and return later.

Now was the time to put the pressure on Vernon, but before he
was brought into my room we set up the "scene." I sat at my desk
and I had Erma Higgins and Dr Langsner placed in the centre of
the room facing the door, on either side of which stood Detective
Leslie and Inspector Longacre. A chair was so placed that
Vernon would face Miss Higgins and the doctor.

As soon as Vernon came in and sat down Miss Higgins said to
him as she had been instructed: "Vernon, I saw you leave the
church the day Charlie's rifle was stolen."

Vernon looked at her and then stared at the doctor.

"I know you did," he said heavily, "I know you did."

I heard the clock on the wall tick away the lost seconds and began to watch the gentle swing of the brass pendulum. Then Vernon turned a desperate face towards me and said pleadingly: "Let me confess. I killed them. Let me confess to you."

He began to sob, and his story was a broken account of a quartet of killings that had happened in the way Langsner had said. The motive was his rage against his mother. She was a woman of good deeds, but she ruled the home and she ruled Vernon, who was her favourite son. He had brought a girl to the house, the daughter of a farm worker, one Sunday whom Mrs Booher had ordered out. Vernon believed he loved the girl and not only did his mother ridicule the attachment but she wounded him even more cruelly by telling him what she thought of his choice. He began to hate his mother, and when his talk of an elopement made no impression on her his resentment became murderous.

On April 26th, 1929, Vernon Booher was hanged for his fourfold murders.

Some months before, however, Detective Leslie and I drove Dr Langsner to the station. He was leaving Edmonton and going north to Eskimo territory. I think he realized how grateful we were to him, even though we expressed our thanks so clumsily. Against his wishes he had accepted a small cheque, which, as I told him, was only a token tribute to his invaluable help.

As he left us he said with a rueful smile: "It is fine to make friends, but rather sad to leave them."

We shook hands and that was the last we saw of him. Time went by and then one day Detective Leslie laid a news clipping on my desk. It read:

Maximilian Langsner, PhD. (University of Calcutta), was found dead yesterday in a small hut on the outskirts of Fairbanks, Alaska. Dr Langsner was known for his theory on "brain waves" and for his ability, often demonstrated, in reading the thoughts of other people. He was engaged in research on this subject at the time of his death.

Dr Langsner was widely known, and his undoubted gifts had been made use of by Royalty. He had solved mysteries for the Shah of Persia, the King of Egypt and had helped the British Government in Asia. He will remembered, too, for the assistance he gave to many police departments faced with difficult cases.

When I looked up from reading the news clipping Detective Leslie had left the room.

UNGUARDED MOMENT

(Colin Pitchfork, UK 1986)

Joseph Wambaugh

DNA is the master molecule of life, carrying coded messages of heredity, governing everything from eye colour to allergies. It is present in trillions of cells in the human body. The structure of the DNA molecule was solved in the early 1950s by James Watson and Francis Crick, but the technique of so-called DNA fingerprinting is comparatively new. At first it was used to establish genetic relationships in paternity and immigration cases. It was based on a method developed in 1984 by a British geneticist, Dr Alec Jeffreys, in an attempt to identify genetic markers for disease. Jeffreys and his colleagues at Leicester University found a way of extracting DNA from a specimen of blood or other bodily fluid or tissue, slicing it into fragments and tagging them with a radioactive probe so that they would expose a piece of X-ray film. The resulting pattern of stripes on the film, resembling a supermarket barcode, is a DNA "fingerprint". In Britain in 1986, the technique resulted in a forensic triumph. Police had been searching for a man who'd been preying on girls in the East Midlands, raping and killing two fifteen-year-olds, Lynda Mann in 1983 and Dawn Ashworth in July 1986. At first, a seventeen-year-old kitchen porter was suspected of both murders, but he was released after DNA tests showed he could not have been the killer of Lynda Mann. Detectives knew that Lynda's killer was a Group A secretor, PGM 1+. Moreover, Dr Jeffreys' tests on the murdered girls had shown that the same man had killed both of them. There were few leads, only reports of a motorcyle seen near one of the murder sites, and an unknown man running along a footpath. The inquiry seemed stalled. So in early 1987, detectives announced "a revolutionary step", the mass screening of all young males living in the Leicestershire villages of Narborough, Littlethorpe and Enderby. Nevertheless the real killer, Colin Pitchfork, nearly managed to fool the police. He bribed a workmate to take his place at the screening. The friend, Ian Kelly, posed as Pitchfork with a passport altered to carry his photograph. The best-selling American crime writer Joseph Wambaugh (b. 1937), in his book The Blooding, *described how Pitchfork might have foiled the scientists, but for an unguarded remark in a Leicester pub.*

As the summer of 1987 began to burn itself out, the murder squad had some of their most difficult times. They drove blood buses to housing estates and factories in order to call people out. In larger work places they even took a doctor with them: a daunting display of mobile blooding. But they were exhausting their bloodlust.

They tried other tacks. They raided a travelling fair in Blaby with two dozen officers, searching the caravans of carnival workers. And they caught a flasher on a village footpath, a professional tennis player who was a psychiatric patient at Carlton Hayes. But he was good only for a few lame jokes about flashing and tennis balls. Always they returned to blooding for the answer.

The DI's, Pearce and Thomas, often went to the blooding. Those were long nights when they bloodied, and sometimes the doctors treated them to dinner. The DI's had to keep it lighthearted for nervous donors as well as weary cops. One night they conducted a lottery where everyone tossed in fifty pence and guessed how many they'd bloody by evening's end. Some of the frightened donors, many of whom had never been in contact with police before, wanted in.

Then one of them said, "Wait a minute! If I win, how will I know?"

"We'll drop the money in your letter box," Pearce told him. "If you can't trust us, who *can* you trust?"

"Okay, I'll have a go!" he said.

Then they planned a prank in which one of the local bobbies, himself scheduled for a blooding, was to pose as a civilian and come in protesting furiously, whereupon four of them were to pounce on him, snap on the handcuffs and carry him to whichever doctor looked most horrified. Superintendent Tony Painter got wind of it and stopped that one.

There was a travelling construction worker from Nottinghamshire whom they particularly wanted to bloody, but he was a fugitive on an assault charge and kept avoiding them. The best they could do after much effort was to leave a message for him to ring the incident room.

He complied, demanding to speak to a superior officer. Pearce handled the telephone call, and after a long conversation they struck a bargain. The fugitive agreed to be bloodied if Pearce would give his word of honour not to arrest him on the warrant.

Not only did the fugitive show up on schedule, he brought with him another travelling worker they'd been seeking. Both men were bloodied, and when they were finished and walking out the door, Pearce suddenly appeared and yelled, "Hold on! You can't just walk out!"

The fugitive crouched, ready to run or fight, or both, but he didn't know about the inspector's offbeat sense of humour.

Pearce grinned and said, "Fancy a pint or two?"

He took both men to a pub and stood them some drinks, after which it was discovered they didn't have bus fare. Pearce had to give them five pounds to get back home.

It was like that: trying to keep everybody interested, entertained and, above all, dedicated. Pearce's own dedication had gotten a boost just before the Ashworths left on their Australian holiday. When he'd taken a can of soda to gardener/cop Phil Beeken at the cemetery, he'd found Barbara Ashworth tending Dawn's grave. Pearce had met her on only one other occasion, but Barbara talked to him in the graveyard for thirty minutes.

When Pearce returned to the incident room he commented that whenever someone's killed you *always* hear that the victim was a nice person, but in this case it was true. "Lynda and Dawn were lovely, bubbly girls," he said to his detectives. "Pleasant, helpful, and *ever* so well liked, weren't they?"

He really didn't have to arouse any member of the small group that was left. The hunt for the footpath killer had consumed them all. They were becoming more fearful of the rumours that they were going to be closed down.

The squad held a meeting where everyone put forth arguments to be taken to Chief Superintendent David Baker and beyond. They wanted it noted that Dawn Ashworth II had been opened on a restricted budget because the first Dawn Ashworth inquiry had eaten up so much of the budgetary allowance. They pointed out that the reopening should have been treated as a *new* murder inquiry and budgeted accordingly. They promised not to drag in donors so indiscriminately, but said that in the long run it was still cheaper than a time-consuming verification of alibis. It wasn't their fault, they argued, that the laboratory was months behind in analyzing the blood, perhaps even the blood of the murderer, for all they knew.

They'd begun getting time-and-a-third pay for working more than eight hours in a day, as well as £5.54 for a meal allowance. They offered to give it up, as long as the inquiry was kept open.

They began a renewed search into computer print-outs of everyone in Britain who'd been imprisoned in the interim between the murders of Lynda Mann and Dawn Ashworth. It seemed a long time between murders for a serial sex killer, at least according to the psychiatric profile.

There had always been speculation that the kitchen porter, who seemed to know too much, could have had something to do with Dawn Ashworth's murder after all. There were bizarre theories about why samples taken from the vaginal and anal cavities had not shown a transfer of fluid back and forth, the implication being that perhaps two men had raped Dawn Ashworth, front and back, with only one leaving a sample. Perhaps one of them was a voyeur who had assaulted the dead body *after* the murderer was gone! There were macabre theories like that, because that's the way a murder cop's mind works after he's been in the business awhile.

Each of the sixteen officers still on the inquiry reiterated that morale was high, and that there was no doubt they'd flush him out sooner or later, one way or the other. They debated as to how the footpath phantom might try, or perhaps had *already* tried, to beat their system. The consensus was that he would induce a brother or close relative to take the test for him. A few thought he might be gambler enough to take it himself and hope that Jeffreys' system was not foolproof, and who among them could say it was?

Sergeant Mick Mason, like Inspector Mick Thomas, had been on the Lynda Mann inquiry as well as Dawn Ashworth I and II. Only the "two Micks," DC John Reid and Detective Policewoman Tracy Hitchcox had been on all three. Tracy Hitchcox worked with DC Roger Lattimore, who lived in the village and harboured personal fears for his own teenage daughter. Lattimore never forgot to ring the Ashworths or to stop by with hopeful reports as the hopeless months dragged on.

Mick Mason was the CID opposite of Derek Pearce. Where Pearce was fiery, the kind to shoot from the hip (sometimes hitting his own foot), Mason was deliberate, methodical, with a completeness compulsion. He didn't just dot his *i*'s and cross his *t*'s. They said he duplicated every bleedin *i* and every ruddy *t*. He was the kind to stress over the menu at a sandwich shop: Swiss or cheddar? Swiss or cheddar? Swiss or bloody cheddar! But when he finally made up his mind he was implacable.

Mick Mason would come to work fifteen minutes before he had to and might stay hours after he could have gone home. He was one of the first that Pearce and Mick Thomas had chosen when Superintendent Tony Painter wanted a squad on Dawn Ashworth II "to sort out the business once and for all."

Until you got to know the big middle-aged cop, he was the last you would imagine in a pub after an evening of blooding – after they got the music going and had a few pints – doing his version of Tom Jones doing "Delilah," complete with bumps and grinds! Mick Mason, "the pub singer," had that other side. But he'd been devoted to Kath Eastwood, Lynda Mann's mother, from the day her daughter had been murdered, and always promised her that he'd never forget Lynda, that they'd *get* the killer. The pub singer was, by his own admission, obsessed with this murder hunt. Possibly, he wanted the killer more than any of the rest of them.

When frustrated voices were raised in the incident room, when
the possibility of closure loomed, nobody even looked up if it was
Derek Pearce's voice; they were used to that. But when Mick
Thomas started raising his voice, as one later put it, "We'd think,
'Blimey! Maybe something *is* wrong!'"

The three-month duty charts had been changed to one-month
duty charts. As far as the top brass was concerned, the end was
near, and *that* was obvious to the two inspectors. The remaining
sixteen held a very tense meeting with Superintendent Tony
Painter. He informed them that Chief Superintendent David
Baker was getting great pressure from the chief constable who in
turn was being pressured by the Home Office. The inquiry could
not stay open indefinitely.

There was an extraordinary clamour at that meeting. People
wondered aloud what the Press would make of a surrender after
four years of hunting the footpath killer. Sergeant Mick Mason
openly suggested they should have the courage to begin blooding
other places. Like Whetstone, for instance.

Tony Painter became annoyed. He said, "You will not mention
Whetstone. We will not bloody Whetstone!" Of course, he didn't
know that Mick Mason was *already* blooding Whetstone.

Derek Pearce jumped in to say, "All right, let's pack it up and
go home!"

Painter rebuked Pearce about the need for a DI to control
himself, but the clamour persisted. Somebody actually said that if
the inquiry was closed, the Police Complaints Board should bring
a complaint against the chief constable himself!

Baker and Painter and their superiors were facing kamikaze
dedication here. Maybe they realized that these last sixteen were
foundering in a bloodlust frenzy. They might bloody every
goddamn mammal in Leicestershire!

A new television story was aired that didn't exude confidence.
Chief Superintendent David Baker, Superintendent Tony Painter, DI's Derek Pearce and Mick Thomas were all videotaped by
a news team during a blooding session. Baker made another
appeal. He said, "We have not got that vital piece of information
which allows us to put the jigsaw together completely."

When he was finished, newsmen made *sotto voce* comments about whether or not the squad had *any* puzzle pieces. The announcer called Baker's statement "a painful admission."

More painful to the murder squad was a visit by an inspection team from the deputy chief constable and the high sheriff of Leicester, who, after being given a brief summary of the mountain of work accomplished by the inquiry, had only one comment: the sign they'd posted for civilians that said, COFFEE 10P, TEA 5P, was "unprofessional."

Such is the policeman's lot, as Gilbert and Sullivan had long ago observed.

On a more upbeat note, a Midlands newscaster said, "As more men come forward the net slowly closes on the killer. If the police hunch is right, and he *is* a local man, he dare not run the risk of giving blood."

On the day of that newscast, David Baker offered a statement to the print media – a prayer almost – that proved to be prophetic. He said, "Somebody's *bound* to say something in an unguarded moment. Now *that's* the kind of information we need!"

The beginning of an answer to Baker's prayer had already taken place on the 1st of August, one year after Dawn Ashworth's murder. It happened in a pub.

The Clarendon Pub in Leicester was a pub for locals: students, university people, journalists. It was a bit Bohemian in an area that had become trendy. A nice pub, the Clarendon had salmon-coloured drapes and valances, co-ordinated wallpaper, and plush banquettes. It was near one of the Hampshires Bakery outlet shops, off Queens Road.

During the lunch break on that Saturday afternoon Ian Kelly went to the Clarendon, along with a twenty-six-year-old woman who managed one of the bakery outlets. Another woman and a young man, both Hampshires employees, tagged along.

They sat in the busy pub having a "cob," a Leicester snack consisting of a roll filled with meat, cheese or anything you fancy. The talk turned to bakery tittle-tattle, centering on Colin Pitchfork, whom the manager of the outlet shop knew by sight and reputation.

They gossiped about Pitchfork's girlfriends, Brown Eyes and her stillborn, and the fact that Colin couldn't stay away from women. As Ian Kelly sipped his drink, a bemused smile crossed his face and he blurted, "Colin had me take that blood test for him."

The bakery manager said, "*What* test?"

"For the murder inquiry?" the male companion asked. "That one, Ian?"

Ian Kelly got up and went to the bar for another pint. When he was gone the bakery manager turned to the other young man and said, "What's that all about?"

"It's odd," the young baker said. "Colin asked *me* to do it too. Offered me two hundred quid to take the blood test. He's just scared of coppers. A weird bloke, that Colin."

The shop manager was deeply disturbed. She tried to broach another question, but it was lightly dismissed as though the implication was preposterous.

Still she couldn't get it off her mind. A week passed, and she took aside the young baker who'd been offered the money and said, "What are we going to *do* about Colin Pitchfork?"

He said, "Leave it. He's a friend. You don't even know him."

She *couldn't* leave it, but she was fearful of involving someone in a double murder – someone who might be innocent – not to mention getting Ian Kelly into police trouble.

Three days later while the bakery manager stewed, history was made in London at the Old Bailey. Genetic fingerprinting was used in a criminal court for the first time in the case of a man accused of unlawful intercourse with a fourteen-year-old mentally handicapped girl who'd given birth to his baby.

Dr Alec Jeffreys was quoted as saying, "The use of the test in a court case is exciting for us. It is an historic occasion."

The bakery manager knew that the owner of the Clarendon Pub had a son who was a police constable. She inquired but found that the bobby was on holiday. It was six weeks before she rang him up.

It had been a good summer for Carole Pitchfork. She'd been

noticing a marked improvement in her husband's attitude since she had allowed him to return home in March. She felt that he was trying very hard to make a go of their marriage. He seemed to be maturing and accepting responsibility for his past actions. She didn't even have to nag him to change clothes anymore. He was dressing better, as beffitted a budding entrepreneur.

His scheme for opening the cake-decorating studio was beginning to jell at last. Colin had been to a banker, and was discussing things like cash flow with an accountant. He'd even accepted a small commission to make a birthday cake for a policeman's twenty-first birthday. It was cleverly conceived and skilfully executed. The policeman loved it. Colin had done an icing sculpture of a bobby's helmet, alongside a set of steel handcuffs.

Friday, the 18th of September, started off in a river of blood like all the others. Derek Pearce and Gwynne Chambers were on a London run to pick up four blood samples and to interview one man. Whenever they took trips like that they'd call in several times a day. But they got caught in motorway traffic coming back and it was some time before they could get to a phone box. They found one occupied by a girl who had about three pounds, all in tenpence coins, spread out in front of her.

She gave the impatient detectives a glance or two but wasn't about to give up the phone. They jumped back in the CID car and kept going.

When they got to the office at 9.00 p.m. there were messages all over the door. One said, "Don't go home!" Another said, "Got a job on!" A third said, "Don't go home. Got a job on!"

When Pearce got to his desk he found a huge one saying, "DON'T GO HOME!"

Phil Beeken had taken a telephone message that afternoon from a bobby whose father owned a pub near the Queens Road outlet shop of Hampshires Bakery. Beeky relayed the information from that telephone call directly to Inspector Mick Thomas and they pulled an old house-to-house *pro forma* from the Lynda Mann inquiry. They compared the signature of the resident of a semi-detached house in Littlethorpe with the *pro forma* from his blooding in January. The two signatures of Colin Pitchfork didn't match.

Mick Thomas and Phil Beeken tried to keep each other from getting too excited. After all, signatures can change over a period of three years, particularly with young people. But Pitchfork wasn't a kid. Then they looked at each other and decided, The hell with it! They were over the moon and rising!

Mick Mason was telephoned at home and given the job of immediately contacting the others from the bakery, who'd been present in the Clarendon Pub when Ian Kelly blurted an admission during an unguarded moment. Thomas and Beeken went to the manager's house and took her written statement.

She began by saying, "This is probably a waste of your time, but my conscience *forced* me to ring the police." She kept apologizing until they reassured her.

By the time Mick Thomas and Phil Beeken hooked up with Derek Pearce and Gwynne Chambers later that evening they were practically hyperventilating.

Mick Thomas said to Pearce, "Roger and Tracy are still in Yorkshire trying to bloody some bloke! You and Gwynne were in London! Everybody else had gone home! I was going crazy with no one to tell!"

One of them noticed something very peculiar. The conversation in the Clarendon Pub, that unguarded moment, had occurred exactly one year after the day that Dawn Ashworth's body lay undetected in a field by Ten Pound Lane. It seemed to be an omen.

They unanimously elected to go immediately to a pub, and they did. While drinking his second pint Pearce said that going to bed was out of the question. He wanted morning to come without having to sleep through the interim. Mick Thomas suggested that they'd better not get drunk because of the importance of the following day. But they didn't have to worry – the booze couldn't compete with the adrenaline rush.

Each man later reported that he spent a near-sleepless night. Each later reported that he felt he was facing the most important day in his police career.

As far as Pearce was concerned: "It was the most important day of our *lives*."

Ian Kelly had not been having an easy time at the bakery since he'd given blood for Colin Pitchfork. It seemed as though too many things were going wrong, and Colin Pitchfork was always around to "help" him. Once when they were making buns, Ian burned them. Colin observed the error and told Ian not to worry, he'd take care of it. Ian later heard that Colin "took care of it" by informing the foreman.

There was a more serious incident when Ian was making buns with another baker. A huge steel machine cover was propped against a wall. Ian pushed a baking trolley past it and was absolutely sure he had sufficient clearance, but somehow the heavy metal cover fell over and crashed into his partner's legs.

The man bellowed and swore and accused Ian of crippling him. It turned into such a row that the gaffer came out and shouted, "Stop behaving like kids, the two of you!"

The injured baker was so outraged he told the boss to stuff it. The baker quit his job that day, saying that Ian Kelly was the one who should've been sacked.

Ian went back to work, absolutely baffled as to how the machine cover could've fallen. Until he later learned that Colin Pitchfork had been standing nearby when it happened. It was *beginning* to look like somebody wanted him out of Hampshires Bakery.

On the morning of Saturday, September 19th, it was decided that Pearce and Chambers would arrest Ian Kelly. And they might arrest the young baker who'd been offered £200 by Colin Pitchfork, depending on his answers. Mick Thomas and Mick Mason were to call on that young man. Even though they were off duty, DC Brian Fentum and Phil Beeken insisted on being there. Nothing could've kept them away.

Ian Kelly opened his door that morning to a pair of visitors he knew weren't selling magazines. Derek Pearce showed his warrant card and said, "We're from the murder enquiry incident room at Narborough, investigating the murders of Lynda Mann and Dawn Ashworth. Have you given a blood sample regarding those enquiries?"

"No, not me!" Ian said.

"I don't believe you," Pearce said. "I have reason to believe you've given a blood sample."

"No, I haven't!" Ian said.

"We've talked to other people at the bakery," Pearce said. "I believe you *have*."

"Yes, you're right," Ian said. "I did it for another lad at work."

"Who's that?" Gwynne Chambers asked.

"Colin Pitchfork," Ian Kelly answered.

Pearce said, "I'm arresting you for conspiracy to pervert the course of justice and we're taking you to Wigston Police Station."

"Yes," said Ian Kelly. "I'll just put me shoes on."

They took Ian Kelly to the station, which was already humming, and put him into an interview room where his statement was recorded.

Pearce said, "I must tell you, you do not have to say anything unless you wish to do so, but anything you say may be given in evidence. Do you understand that?"

Ian began by saying, "Yes, well, the gentleman in question, Colin Pitchfork, he come up to me and asked if I'd do him a favour. I didn't know it were for them murders. I didn't know what it were really for cause he didn't explain what it were for. He just had to give a thingybob cause he got a letter from the police station."

Then Ian related the story that Colin Pitchfork had told him about giving a sample for the other bloke, and Ian told about the photo strip and altering the passport. But he stuck to his claim that he didn't know that the blooding was for anything as serious as murder.

Derek Pearce didn't look *quite* as dangerous as a Shi'ite with an AK-47 when he said, "Yeah, you're Mister Muggins. And you've just gone along and given the sample. And he got what he wanted: full protection. *You've delayed us eight months!*"

Ian started to understand what was facing him. He said, "Well, when I went to his house, more or less . . . well, the day before, he *told* me it were a murder enquiry. But I didn't know *which* murder it was at the time!"

And he admitted to having been given a little schooling on the dates of birth of the children and other personal information. He said, "I knew it were for a murder but I didn't know whose it were for, cause at the time when I walked in I were *that* sick. I'd got a temperature. I was feeling really low. I mean, when I began writing his signature I got shaking like a leaf!"

Supt. Tony Painter was called in that afternoon and found Derek Pearce bobbing and bouncing like a dinghy in a storm.

"Let's go nick him!" Pearce said to their commander.

"No, take it all down on paper," Painter said. "And *then* go get him."

Pearce said, "We want him *now!*"

"I'm the boss and I say paper first," Painter said.

"Quite right," Pearce said. "Paper first."

So they had to wait another two hours until all statements were transcribed and put in some semblance of order. By the time six of them got to the house in Haybarn Close, the blue Fiat was gone. There was nobody at the Pitchfork home. One stayed; the rest returned to the station, *trying* to be philosophical. After all, they'd waited four years.

THE FIRM OF PATRICK & JONES

(Albert T. Patrick, USA 1900)

Edmund Pearson

"What did he die of?"
  "Bananas."
  "What!"
  "Yes, baked bananas."
  In fact, William Marsh Rice was murdered in his sleep with chloroform, in the austere apartment in New York City he shared with his killer and valet Charles F. Jones. Young Jones had been recruited in a murder plot by a crooked lawyer called Albert T. Patrick. The scam to lay hands on old Rice's Texan millions might have worked, but for a couple of fatal slip-ups. One was down to simple nervousness. Patrick had forged a cheque on Rice's account, payable to himself, but had mis-spelt his own name as Abert. *There were more questioned documents in the case, principally Rice's so-called will which ran to four closely-typed pages, each of which was signed "W. M. Rice". The similarity of all four signatures contrasted sharply with other signatures made by Rice at the same time, which contained the kind of irregularities to be expected in the handwriting of an octogenarian. At Patrick's trial, the jury was satisfied that the attorney had copied Rice's signature by tracing it. An expert in questioned documents demonstrated how Patrick had done it. The jury declared the will a forgery and convicted Patrick of murder. The lawyer was sentenced to death, while young Jones (who'd confessed) was allowed to go free. In 1912, after years of*

*legal wranglings, and to general astonishment, Patrick was granted
an unconditional pardon. Between the wars, Edmund Lester Pearson (1880–1937) was America's pre-eminent dissector of murder
and its motives. He subscribed to George Lyman Kittredge's dictum
that, "Murder is the material of great literature." Pearson's telling
of the Patrick–Rice case dates from 1928, the year after he quit as
editor of publications at the New York Library to become a full-
time writer.*

A young man – not an especially attractive young man – came into
a banking house in Wall Street and pushed through the wicket a
cheque for $25,000. This was on a pleasant Monday morning
nearly thirty years ago. I do not really know anything about the
weather, but assume that the sun cannot be heavily overcast when
one goes to a bank with a cheque for $25,000.

The young man and the teller – naming the characters in the
order of their appearance – were David L. Short and J. H.
Wallace. The time – for those who care to be exact – was about
eleven o'clock on September 24, 1900.

It would have annoyed one, and perhaps both of them, had
they known that they were the performers in Act I, Scene 1 of a
legal tragedy of great length and appalling complexity. The
cheque was simple enough, and the sum could not stagger the
banking house of S. M. Swenson & Sons. The body of the cheque
was in a hand familiar to Mr Wallace, while the signature
appeared to be that of a depositor whose balance at the moment
was about $90,000. Had this depositor – Mr W. M. Rice – chosen
to send in a cheque for considerably more than his entire balance,
it is probable that the Messrs Swenson – knowing his resources
and his character and recalling his long association with them –
would have been glad to honour it.

The teller, however, did not count out the twenty-five crisp
one-thousand-dollar bills of romance. The request, I believe, was
not for cash, but for certification. Two things struck Mr Wallace:
the first name of the payee, and the writing in the signature. The
cheque was to the order of *Abert* T. Patrick, while the endorse-

ment had the name as Albert. And Mr Rice's signature looked a bit odd.

Which of these he noticed first is hard to discover: for the purpose of a good story, I prefer to believe that the omission of the letter "L" in the name of the payee was the tiny slip that set in motion an extraordinary series of events.

At any rate, Mr Wallace took the cheque to a rear office and showed it to another clerk, Mr Wetherbee. They compared the signature with some others on paid cheques of Mr Rice, and after a few moments returned it to Mr Short, asking for another endorsement, in accordance with the misspelled name on the face. Bankers love to perpetuate mistakes – just as the orchestra leader made one of his musicians play what appeared to be a note at a certain place on the score, although it was only a dead fly.

Mr Short departed, but returned within twenty minutes, with the new – and correctly incorrect – endorsement of *Abert* T. Patrick. Evidently Mr Patrick was far too busy to come to the bank, and evidently also he was somewhere just round the corner – like Mr Montague Tigg's friend, Chevy Slyme.

In the meanwhile, Mr Eric Swenson, a member of the firm, had arrived. He looked at the cheque and directed that Mr Rice's home should be called by telephone. The call was answered by Mr Jones, who was employed by Mr Rice. Mr Jones was secretary, or valet, or both, and, as the bankers knew, the body of the cheque was in his hand, according to custom. Mr Jones said:

"That cheque is all right."

Mr Swenson asked to speak with Mr Rice, but Mr Jones replied that Mr Rice could not come to the telephone – the only absolutely accurate and truthful statement that Mr Jones was to make for weeks and weeks.

Mr Wallace then stamped the cheque as certified, although shortly afterward Mr Swenson changed his mind and drew his pen through the stamp. The dim mark of the rubber stamp has vanished from the facsimile of the cheque, but the five vertical pen marks made by Mr Swenson are visible.

Possibly Mr Swenson knew as much about Mr Rice as anyone in New York. Nobody knew a very great deal about him. He was a valued depositor, although his account at another bank was – at this time – larger than at Swensons'. He had lived now in New York and now in Texas, off and on, for many years. His chief business interests were in Texas. He was an elderly gentleman, but he maintained an active control of his business affairs.

Mr Jones, the secretary-valet, typed Mr Rice's letters and made out cheques for his signature. The two lived by themselves in an apartment house at 500 Madison Avenue. The house was called The Berkshire – a red-brick building on the northwest corner of Madison Avenue and Fifty-second Street. As with almost everything in New York, one has to add: it was torn down a year or two ago. A new building, with the same name, is on its site.

There were more telephone conversations between the banker on Wall Street and the Madison Avenue apartment, and presently Mr Jones explained why his employer could not come to the telephone. Mr Rice was dead. He had died last night.

Mr Swenson was surprised but not astonished: Mr Rice was more than eighty-four years old. It was possibly at this point that Mr Swenson made the five strokes across the cheque: with the conservatism of a banker he declined to honour a cheque signed by a dead man – although, of course, the date of the cheque was the preceding Saturday.

After luncheon Mr Patrick at last came around the corner and appeared at the bank. He came to express regrets that they had not chosen to certify his cheque. He had an interview with Mr Swenson. To the banker it was surprising that Mr Patrick – who, it appeared, was a lawyer – should expect to have the cheque certified after the death of the man who drew it. There were more surprises for Mr Swenson. Mr Patrick said that he had another cheque on them from Mr Rice – and this for $65,000. This, with the first, equalled the total sum of Mr Rice's deposit.

Mr Swenson said that he now held the property of his late depositor at the disposal of the administrator of the estate. But Mr Patrick, who had an answer for everything, or almost everything, said that there would be no administration of the Rice property in New York State, as he held none there – having assigned it all to him, to Mr Patrick. The effect of all this was that one wealthy client was dead but another had appeared, well and

hearty, and disposed to be friendly with the Swensons and to do
business with them – if they chose.

Mr Patrick invited Mr Swenson to the funeral. Mr Rice's body
was to be cremated immediately.

"Cremated?" inquired the banker.

"Yes," said Mr Patrick, "you know the old man was a crank on
the subject of cremation."

"No," said the other, "I did not know anything of the kind."

"Well, he was."

"What did he die of?" asked Mr Swenson.

The reply was:

"Bananas."

"What!"

"Yes," said Mr Patrick, "baked bananas. You know Mrs Van
Alstyne, don't you?"

"Yes, I do."

"Well, old Mr Rice had indigestion, and Mrs Van Alstyne
advised him to eat baked bananas. Said they had agreed with her,
perfectly. He got nine of them and ate them, and I believe that is
what killed him."

There was other conversation; the bank adhered to its refusal to
honour the cheque, and Mr Patrick departed, concerned with
many affairs.

The people at Swensons' rubbed their heads and tried to think
what they had heard, if anything, of Mr Patrick. There was some
distant connection of his name with Mr Rice, but it did not spring
into mind. At last someone recalled that Mr Patrick, although a
member of the bar of New York, was a Texan by birth, and that
he had been engaged in some capacity in litigation over the will of
the late Mrs Rice. This was a suit involving a very large sum, and
Mr Patrick had been retained by the side opposing Mr Rice.

Well, old men sometimes do strange things in their last days.
Mr Rice was an elderly millionaire who lived, since the death of
his second wife, almost alone. All elderly millionaires, for the
purposes of novelists and writers of headlines, are "eccentric."
But his banker did not regard Mr Rice as eccentric – certainly not
in business. He was a shrewd but not necessarily tight-fisted old
gentleman who kept a firm control of affairs.

And yet, here was an obscure lawyer, whose only relations with Mr Rice had been antagonistic, now turning up as an heir, business manager, master of funeral ceremonies, confidant upon the subject of diet and disposal of remains, and generally as the late Mr Rice's bright-haired boy!

The interesting and valuable papers, of which Mr Patrick seemed to have a number, were uttered one by one. There was always something in his conjurer's hat when he put in his hand. He had two other cheques – on the Fifth Avenue Trust Company – one for $25,000 and one for $135,000. A kind friend had already been to the trust company that morning; presented the larger cheque, and the company had certified it without hesitation.

Thus it appeared that the dying hand of Mr Rice had dealt in no stingy spirit with his trusted counsellor, since the sum of these four cheques, $250,000, represented his entire deposits in New York banks.

At the New York Safe Deposit Company and at the vaults of the Fifth Avenue Trust Company, where Mr Patrick, in person or by deputy, presented assignments of all of Mr Rice's securities, the officials were not complaisant. The property held by these two companies was valued at about two and a half millions.

Mr Swenson was moved to action chiefly by the fact that he and all his clerks agreed that the shaky signature of "W. M. Rice" on the $25,000 cheque was a little too shaky. It was fair, but it was not the old master's. He talked with his lawyers, Messrs Bowers and Sands, and they talked with the District Attorney.

Late that evening, Mr J. W. Gerard, attorney from the office of Bowers and Sands, called on Mr Patrick at his boarding place, 316 West Fifty-eighth Street. Mr Gerard – who was afterward American Ambassador at Berlin, before the war – had with him another man who was actually a detective from the Central Office.

Mr Gerard told Mr Patrick that the Swensons had wished some investigation, as the circumstances seemed extraordinary to them. Mr Patrick said:

"I may as well tell you, in the first place, that I have a will in my possession in which I am executor; and I also have an assignment of all of Mr Rice's property of every kind. I expect to have the settlement of the estate in my hands. I intend to leave that with Swenson & Sons, and I hope we will have very pleasant relations. I hope there will not be any friction whatever between us. As far as these cheques go, why, I have arranged to get the money from another source, and I shall leave everything at present at Swensons'. Nothing will be disturbed there."

The detective, who had been introduced as another lawyer, asked:

"What is the use of having an assignment and a will, too?"

Said Mr Patrick:

"That is a secret."

The detective asked the cause of Mr Rice's death, and it appeared that his heir still laid the blame on the bananas. He further said that the body was to be kept until Thursday and then taken to Wisconsin to be buried beside that of the late Mrs Rice. Despite the old gentleman's fondness for cremation, described that morning on Wall Street, nothing was now said on the subject.

The two then departed; one of them to meditate at the Union Club, and the officer to make his report. Mr Patrick soon left his dwelling place, as he had business that kept him down town all night.

It appears that, on the previous night, Sunday night, after Mr Rice had died, his confidential servant Mr Jones had notified but three persons: first, Mr Patrick; second, his master's physician, Dr Curry; and third and later, a neighbouring undertaker, Mr Plowright. There were many other persons, in three or four different states, who had cause to be interested in the death of the old gentleman, but the first public announcement of it had almost been forced, by Mr Swenson's inquiries over the telephone.

Directly after that telephone conversation, on Monday afternoon, Mr Jones began sending telegrams to relatives. The funeral, said these telegrams, was to take place at ten o'clock next morning – on Tuesday. These messages elicited other messages, much stirring, and buying of railroad tickets.

A gentleman with no wife or children, but with property valued at millions, cannot die without causing other folk to break the regular current of their lives.

In the large and dismally furnished apartment at The Berkshire lay Mr Rice's body, skilfully embalmed by Mr Plowright's assistant, and very much at peace. His neatly trimmed white hair and beard, his good clothes, and his general tidiness made him look much as in life. He had never grown careless about his appearance as he grew older. About the apartment tiptoed Mr Jones: writing letters, answering the telephone, and looking as usual – neutral, uninteresting, and so much like thousands of other clean-shaven young men of twenty-five, that a portrait of him looks extraordinarily like nobody in particular.

But in Texas and elsewhere, boards of directors and trustees, operators of mines, managers of oil fields, ranchers, bankers, occupants of city offices, cattlemen and lawyers were busily thinking about the old man. In Massachusetts and New Jersey, sisters and nephews and nieces were also thinking of him; preparing, some of them, to come to New York; and thinking kindly of him, for he had not been a crusty old man. Probably some of them were wondering about the will.

It was nearly sixty years earlier, and long before the Civil War – that Mr Rice had left his birthplace in Springfield, Massachusetts, and gone to Texas. There he had prospered, until he owned whole townships, city blocks, and "so many stocks and bonds that he had to get someone to help him cut the coupons." In other states, as well, he was the owner of many broad acres – and these are much pleasanter to own than narrow, stingy acres.

He had lived at The Berkshire for four or five years, most of the time with Mr Jones as his only companion. Before that, he had lived at the Hotel Grenoble, which, about that time, had been widely known, because Rudyard Kipling lay there, seriously ill and near death. A woman came to Mr Rice's apartment twice a week to clean the rooms; there were no other servants. The barren walls – there was a map in one room, and no pictures at all – gave opportunity for many stories about his eccentricity. He was described as cooking his own food, while Mr Jones ate at restaurants.

Mr Rice was one of those wealthy men who have no taste for luxury and no intention of living up to the popular notion of a millionaire as a man who must drink champagne whether he

wishes it or not. He went out seldom, as he was slightly lame. His
health was generally good; he could have been called vigorous,
both physically and mentally. Because of his age and some attacks
of dyspepsia, he put himself on a diet: fresh eggs, which were
brought in by a man from Dunellen, New Jersey (where he had
once lived), and bouillon and bread, sent in from the Woman's
Exchange, on the same street. It is no hard fate to get one's food
from that source, and the notion of Mr Rice as a miser, starving
himself in a garret, is distant from the truth.

He was a childless widower, and chose to live a rather secluded
existence, with one man standing between him and the rest of the
world. For this, he paid dearly. He was not without friends, but
his callers were infrequent – a few New Yorkers, or now and then
a Texan who was visiting the city.

Many curious stories were set in circulation about him by his
worst enemy. Some of them bore on his parsimony. According to
one of these tales, Mr Rice, in going about the city, would pick up
an apple from a dealer's stand, bite it, and if it did not please him,
put it back and refuse to pay. As a result he was often in trouble
with Italian fruit vendors, who followed him about in their
righteous indignation. The same enemy, however, added that
"Rice was a master mind, and a great genius for making money."

Jones had been in his employ for three years. He was the son of
respectable parents; he originated in those surroundings which
(according to countless moral tales) insure integrity, loyalty, and
all the virtues: he was born on a farm. Texas was his native state:
the wide-open spaces; out where the West begins; out where
friendship's a little truer. He had been working in the Capitol
Hotel in Houston, when Mr Rice saw him, liked him, trusted
him, and brought him to New York.

Together they had experienced some of the vexations and legal
troubles of Mr Rice's old age. These were chiefly about wills.
The late Mrs Rice, his second wife, had availed herself of the so-
called community law. Texas, more progressive and modern in
her legislation than Mr Rice's native commonwealth, or than his
adopted State of New York, had recognized a woman's part in
building her husband's fortune and given her the right – or
privilege – of willing away half of her husband's property. It

was, therefore, not surprising, as a lawyer drily remarked, to learn that many Texans live in New York.

Mrs Rice, dying at some time between 1893 and 1896, prepared a surprise for her husband by willing away two or three millions of his dollars to her own relatives. This was valid if Mr Rice lived in Texas. But he, like so many wealthy persons, harried by tax commissioners and others, had a legal domicile that was a little mysterious. He firmly asserted that it was New York State, and that it had been New York ever since shortly after the Civil War. He was extremely indignant about this will of Mrs Rice's and was inclined to be bitter against all who were concerned in trying to put it in effect.

The head and front of this offending, in his eyes, was a Texan attorney, Mr Holt; the executor named in Mrs Rice's will. Mr Holt was opposed by Mr Rice's lawyers – a Texan firm of attorneys with the explosive name of Baker, Botts, Baker and Lovett.

Mr Rice had brought action to get a decision in a court of equity as to his legal residence. Many depositions were taken in New York; many affidavits were sworn to. For this, Mr Holt had employed an attorney, now of New York, formerly of Texas – no less than Albert T. Patrick, now the holder of the disputed cheques. So far as known, Mr Rice had never seen Mr Patrick but once in his life – and not then to know him. He merely knew his name – and hated it – as that of a lawyer engaged, as he believed, in procuring false depositions against his interest – or, as he put it, "hired by Holt to do the dirty work."

It becomes apparent why Mr Rice's business associates were astonished when the suave Mr Patrick turned up with so many documents to prove his claims on the Rice estate.

Mr Rice's own wills were interesting. His fancy was not to enrich his relatives – who seem to have been comfortably situated by their own efforts, but to found a college in the state where he had made his money. By a will in 1893 he left his relatives one fifteenth of his estate and endowed a scientific school to be called the William M. Rice Institute. This school was his residuary legatee; it had a legal existence only. No buildings had been erected. By a new will, in 1896, after the death of his wife, he specifically gave a fifteenth of his estate to various relatives, and fourteen fifteenths to the Institute.

His lawyers supposed that this was the final expression of his wishes – his true will. It does not appear that his brother, his sisters, or his one or two nephews had any ideas of tremendous inheritances. They knew him, and knew his ideas about the Rice Institute. As for the school, there were trustees, and there was a site, and that was all.

The telegrams sent out by Mr Jones on Monday afternoon had their effect. Relatives and lawyers began to arrive. To one of these Mr Patrick said, apropos of the cheques:

"I don't know how the old gentleman happened to send them to me."

To another, he explained:

"We had an understanding, Mr Rice and I did, that whenever he felt his end approaching he should send me cheques for $250,000."

It was an odd coincidence that Mr Rice should have felt that way on Saturday, September 22nd – the date of the cheques – and an unfortunate one for a business organization in Texas. This was the Merchants and Planters Oil Company, in which Mr Rice owned 75 per cent of the stock. Their plant had been burned, earlier that week, and the directors had applied by telegraph, asking Mr Rice to lend them $250,000 in order to rebuild. Mr Rice had agreed to do this, and the first draft – for $25,000 – arrived on Saturday. The whole loan would cover the amount of cash available in Mr Rice's bank deposits in New York. Yet, "feeling his end approaching," he had sent cheques – for $250,000 – to Mr Patrick. Or so it appeared.

When Dr Curry – and Mr Patrick – arrived at The Berkshire on Sunday night, within half an hour of the death, the lawyer took charge of the situation. He ordered the undertaker to have the body cremated immediately. The undertaker told him that at least twenty-four hours' notice was needed: the crematory was on Long Island. Mr Patrick then ordered embalming. He also, with the consent of Jones, filled a bag with papers, taking away a copy of the 1896 will, letters, documents, and about $400 in cash.

There is no doubt that Mr Rice had been ailing. The celebrated bananas had not agreed with him; and the burning of the property in Texas had caused him anxiety and annoyance. Dr Curry had seen him a number of times in the past week. Both Mr Jones and Mr Patrick had inquired, most solicitously, about the old man's health, and especially on Saturday. Mr Patrick was insistent on the point whether the patient would be able to go down town on Monday. He questioned Dr Curry, calling at his house for the purpose. The doctor tried to avoid any definite promise, but finally said that he did believe Mr Rice would be able to get up, go down town, and attend to business next week. He had seen no cause for alarm in his patient's condition when he called Sunday morning. Mr Rice spent part of the day in bed, but at times sitting up, looking out the window.

So Dr Curry, on Sunday evening, after a brief examination of the body, and after hearing what Mr Jones had to say, made out the certificate of death in entire good faith. He gave the causes as "old age, weak heart" and "collocratal diarrhœa with mental worry."

The telegrams, sent by Jones on Monday, to Mr Baker, the dead man's lawyer in Texas, and to one of the relatives, were as follows:

"Mr Rice died eight o'clock last night under care of physicians. Death certificate: old age, weak heart, delirium. Left instructions to be interred in Milwaukee with his wife. Funeral 10 am to-morrow at 500 Madison Avenue."

The reply came:

"Please make no disposition of Rice's remains until we arrive. We leave to-night, arrive New York Thursday morning."

Although Mr Patrick was ostensibly in charge, not all his directions and wishes were being obeyed. The cremation had had to be postponed, contrary to his expressed desire; the banks and trust companies had, for the most part, rejected his cheques and orders; and the telegram from Texas seemed charged with suspicion. Moreover, persons who looked unpleasantly like "plain-clothes" men had visited The Berkshire apartment, and there was the disturbing midnight call of Mr Gerard and the other inquisitive man.

His errand down town at one o'clock on Tuesday morning, after Mr Gerard had gone, took him to his own office. Here he brought little joy with him, for he tore up a great many letters and papers and tried to send the fragments down the toilet pipes. This blocked the pipes and caused an overflow of water, for which the janitor and a tenant had to be appeased. He spent the rest of the night at this work – incidentally countermanding to the undertaker, by telephone, his order for the cremation.

An autopsy had been ordered by the authorities. This took place on Tuesday. Two coroner's physicians, Drs Donlin and Williams, were assisted by Dr Rudolph Witthaus – the chemist who testified as an expert in such famous trials as those of Carlyle Harris, Dr Buchanan, and Roland Molineux.

All agreed that the body was in a healthy condition, and all the organs sound, with the exception of the lungs. These were congested as if by some irritant gas or vapour. There was no other discoverable cause of death. Dr Witthaus detected the presence of mercury in the body, and this was explained by calomel taken by Mr Rice. The embalming fluid would account neither for the congestion of the lungs nor for the mercury.

With the arrival in New York of Mr Baker, there was a man present who knew almost everyone concerned in the affair. He had long been Mr Rice's attorney, and had known Mr Patrick when that gentleman was practising law in Houston about 1890–91. He had had interviews with Mr Patrick in New York in 1899, when the latter came to him as representative of the executor of Mrs Rice's will and offered a settlement, if Mr Rice would pay the heirs of his wife $500,000. Mr Patrick made subsequent offers of $350,000 and $250,000 – all of which were declined.

The two now met and conversed, in the apartment at The Berkshire, with Mr Jones assisting, and the body of Mr Rice in another room. Said Mr Patrick:

"Well, Captain Baker, I suppose you are surprised to find me in charge."

The other replied:

"I certainly am!"

Mr Patrick then described the ruse by which he said he had become acquainted with Mr Rice. He had put an advertisement in a New Jersey paper for the heirs of Elizabeth Rice – the lady whose will had been disputed. He thus became acquainted with Mr Rice and became his confidential and trusted counsellor. The old gentleman, it seemed, had "lost confidence" in Baker.

This struck the Texan lawyer as especially strange, because, by the new will, the 1900 will, of which Mr Patrick was the guardian and exhibitor, he – Mr Baker – was one of the executors, together with the new favourite, Mr Patrick.

No explanation was forthcoming, but the rise of Patrick to favour was described as due to nothing short of downright admiration and affection.

"To be frank with you," said Mr Patrick, "the old man became, as it were, stuck on me. He thought I was the most wonderful man in the world."

Mr Baker and another Texan then went with Mr Patrick to the latter's home, to see this new will of the 1900 vintage. It was kept there, said its custodian, because the police had been "nosing around."

They were told, further, that Mr Rice had "tired of life and business," and had turned all his property over to Mr Patrick, only stipulating that the lawyer should pay him $10,000 a year during life and put up a monument costing at least $5,000 over his grave.

Mr Baker inspected the new will but did not become enthusiastic. He made a very pertinent remark to Mr Patrick. He said:

"In view of your antagonistic and hostile relation to Mr Rice, if you expect this will and this assignment to hold in any court in Christendom, why did you not have some friend of Mr Rice – the Swensons, for instance, who had known him for thirty years – or some other good people in New York who knew you and Mr Rice, go with you to Mr Rice's apartments and in their presence offer this will and this assignment, and tell those witnesses in the presence of Mr Rice that this was his act? Why didn't you do that?"

I take it that Mr Baker was a big, strong, broad-chested man, or he could never have repeated that sentence, except in relays.

However he did it, Mr Patrick acknowledged that it conveyed a good idea – alas, too late.

"I expect I ought to have done that," he admitted. "But Mr Rice, as you know, was peculiar, and he insisted always that our relations should be secret. As far as I know, not any one, no living man ever saw me in the presence of Mr Rice – unless it was C.F. Jones. And I don't know that he ever saw me with him."

At the funeral Mr Patrick was more than agreeable to everybody: shaking hands and whispering delightful bits of news about bequests. This charming lawyer had a greeting and something to say about five or ten or twenty thousand dollars to everyone.

"This is Mr Blinn, I think? Mr Joseph Blinn of Massachusetts? Yes. Mr Rice's nephew – oh, yes. Well, Mr Blinn, Mr Rice has left you $30,000. And $5,000 to your son."

He was easily the life of the party, and inevitably recalls the heir who arrived in time to inherit the fortune of Peter Wilks – that is, that inimitable inheritor, the king, in *Huckleberry Finn*:

Then the king begins to work his jaw again, and says how him and his nieces would be glad if a few of the main principal friends of the family would take supper here with them this evening, and help set up with the ashes of the diseased; and says if his poor brother laying yonder could speak he knows who he would name, for they was names that was very dear to him, and mentioned often in his letters; and so he will name the same, to wit, as follows, vizz: – Rev. Mr Hobson, and Deacon Lot Hovey and Mr Ben Rucker, and Abner Shackleford, and Levi Bell, and Dr Robinson, and their wives, and the widow Bartley.

Some time afterward, Mr Patrick unfolded and read to Mr Baker and to Captain F. A. Rice, brother of the dead man, another document, which explained his attempts to have the body cremated. This was a letter:

New York, Aug. 3, 1900.

ALBERT T. PATRICK, ESQ.
No. 277 Broadway, City.
DEAR SIR:—

Concerning the matter of cremation. I sent down to the United States Crematory office for information and got two circulars which are very interesting. I will show them to you when you come up. Ever since Col. Robert Ingasoll and Col. Waring were cremated, I have thought that I should like to be cremated also.

Col. Ingasoll was a very smart man, and a man of great judgment about all things which is possible for a man to know, but about religion a man cannot know. Ingersoll may be right or he may be wrong that is all guess work.

Col. Waring was a great sanitary man, and it seems to me that the law should not allow dead bodies to be buried all over the Country, after dying of all kinds of deseases. I would much rather have my body burned than eat by worms or stolen by some medical student and carved to pieces. If I should die I want you to see that I am not embalmed as they fill you with chemicals when they embalm you, but I want you to have my body cremated at once and my ashes put in an urn and interred with my late wife Elizabeth B. Rice. As to funerals I do not think my relatives would care to come to mine and I see no use having one until my ashes are interred with my wife.

I write these things because I happen to think of them although told me to give you written directions some time ago. But I expect to live twenty years, as I came of a long lived family and am in pretty good health for a man of my age.

Yours truly,

W. M. RICE.

It may be noticed that although in this letter Mr Rice desired that his body should not be embalmed, that it should be cremated at once, and that no funeral be held until after the burial of his ashes, his counsellor had not carried out one of these requests. Captain

Rice and Mr Baker neither opposed the cremation nor favoured it. They seem to have accepted this letter as expressing Mr Rice's wish, and so, as the body had been released by the police authorities, after the autopsy, it was accordingly cremated.

In the meantime, Mr Patrick surrendered to Mr Baker the cheques, assignments, and other documents. The Police Department had consulted experts as to the validity of the signatures of W. M. Rice on these papers, and on October 4th Messrs Patrick and Jones were arrested on the charge of forgery. Lacking bail, they were lodged in the Tombs.

Patrick said:

"If these cheques are forgeries, I cannot conceive that they are so" – whatever that meant.

The newspapers began to take a keener interest in this group of Texans whose activities were doing so much to confirm the impression that New York is a cesspool of iniquity.

The *World* published the results of its investigations about the central figure. Mr Patrick, said this paper, is only thirty-five, but he looks much older. He has "a fad for millions"; perhaps accounted for by the fact that his two sisters both married men of wealth, one in St Louis and one in Denver. He left Dr Robert Collyer's church and now goes to the Fifth Avenue Baptist Church. He tells his friends that he "goes to John D. Rockefeller's church."

He is an active member of the YMCA and spends three or four evenings a week at the West Side Branch, where he is a clever player of hand ball and basket ball.

The hair that remains to him is of a reddish brown; his beard is red, close-cropped, stubby, and aggressive looking. His eyes are steady and penetrating. His head, from forehead to back, is of unusual depth. He is as suave and gentle as a woman in manner; he talks easily and well and dresses in good taste.

He is a widower; his wife died three or four years ago, leaving him two little girls, who live in Austin, Texas. At his boarding house he is looked upon as wealthy; as the "star boarder." He had the telephone installed, and his many open conversations with Jones over the wire were cited as proof that their relations were frank and honest. Mr Patrick, said this writer, is always cool headed; he does not drink, and has none of the petty vices. At the Manhattan Club, where he was a member, he had many friends.

The *World* declared that its reports from Texas were not flattering to Mr Patrick. He was born in that state, graduated from its University, and admitted to practise law at twenty-five. But he "had the money fever badly." He was counsel for a man named Volk, who sued a railroad official for alienation of his wife's affections. Mr Patrick recovered for his client $5,000 – and took half of it as his fee. Then, rather unprofessionally, he became counsel for Mrs Volk, and on her behalf won a suit for divorce.

Next, he was heard from when he preferred charges of barratry against a member of Congress named Hutcheson. He sought to have him disbarred. The judge of the United States District Court, however, stopped the suit and later ordered the District Attorney to begin disbarment proceedings against Mr Patrick. The case was pending when the lawyer transferred himself to New York.

There was a curious difficulty with one Wronkow over a suite of offices on Irving Place. It was alleged that Mr Patrick sublet to a Negro club, and, while he was within his rights, succeeded in collecting a large sum from the landlord before he would induce the club to give up its sublease.

An aged millionaire named William H. Moore had, three or four years earlier, commenced litigation against Mr Patrick. Mr Moore had lived at the Hotel Occidental, and his confidential relations with Mr Patrick seemed to resemble those alleged to exist between Patrick and Mr Rice. Mr Moore was president of the Knickerbocker Phosphate Company: he held its notes for $5,500. He assigned these notes to Mr Patrick, and the latter collected the amounts. Mr Moore brought suit to recover, declaring that the assignment was only done on a technicality. Very shortly after suit was entered, Mr Moore died in his rooms at the Occidental. The doctor was questioned, and said that the old man suffered from debility, and that there was nothing suspicious about his death.

Mr Moore's relatives were inclined to mutter; they said that his fortune of $700,000 or more had dwindled to $30,000. But fortunes do dwindle, and expectant relatives do overestimate inheritances. The hotel employees said that Mr Moore had only one visitor, and this was a man.

These were the results of the newspaper investigations about the bald-headed lawyer, whose sudden emergence into notoriety and quick imprisonment covered the front pages of the journals. These facts were not proper matters for the jury who more than a year afterward, were to consider Mr Patrick's conduct, and did not reach them. Indeed, in all the years that the Patrick affair was before the public, it is doubtful if they were ever published again.

Events that took place in the Tombs within the next month are important. They rest on the statement of Jones; they came to be accepted by the State's attorneys and by the people generally, although denied by Mr Patrick and his defenders.

According to the story, at an interview between Patrick and his lawyer Mr House, the latter demanded to know if Mr Rice's death had been natural or the result of a crime. Patrick called Jones aside and ordered him to confess murder and to assume the entire guilt. Jones did not care to fall in with this plan, but insisted that his partner in the crime should be named. Together they spoke with Mr House, and Jones said that he had chloroformed his master by Patrick's instructions and at his advice.

After this, in the privacy of the Tombs, Patrick and Jones discussed suicide. Poison and a knife were both considered: Patrick had a bottle of oxalic acid and a penknife.

A few days later, Jones, talking to the Assistant District Attorney, began a series of conflicting statements: admissions, confessions, and accusations. Early one morning, alone in his cell, he made an attempt to cut his throat. He hurt himself badly enough to be taken to Bellevue Hospital, where for two weeks he was under treatment.

Finally, he made a long and detailed statement. It was, in the opinion of the prosecuting attorney, sufficiently corroborated by other known facts to form the basis for an indictment for murder. Both men were at last arrested for the crime, but Jones was admitted as State's evidence (on terms never satisfactorily made clear), and Patrick alone was put on trial for the murder of Mr Rice. This was sixteen months after the crime.

There had already appeared in New York a man who was to be

an important figure in the long struggle that began on that January morning. This was Patrick's brother-in-law, Mr John T. Milliken, described as "chemist, mine owner, and capitalist" of St Louis. Mr Milliken was to be Patrick's good angel – in the cant sense of the phrase rather more than in its original meaning. Mr Milliken is supposed to have provided a great share of the large sums of money spent in the amazing defence, and subsequent contention for the prisoner.

It is doubtful if this has ever been duplicated in the history of American criminal law. It resulted, according to one opinion, in the final salvation of the innocent; according to another opinion, very widely held, in bringing our criminal procedure, as an instrument of justice, into shame and disrepute.

The jury, drawn from a panel which in New York is especially chosen for homicide trials, was of unusual character and ability. There were in the jury two or three men of distinction, and, by chance, one lawyer, who, not being a member of the New York bar, was not exempt from jury service.

For ten weeks the trial continued: the record of it fills nearly three thousand pages. The backbone of the case for the State was the confession of Jones. He went on the witness stand on February 18th, and testified for five days. He described his early life, his meeting with Mr Rice in the Capitol Hotel, and his coming to New York on May 10, 1897.

Both in the direct and in the cross-examination, he was made to go into the minutest details, and he was questioned at length by the Court. Selecting from the many pages of testimony the principal facts, the statement was as follows:

My work for Mr Rice was clerical work; corresponding; writing letters for him on the typewriter. I drew cheques, and did collecting and depositing; did everything there was to be done. Mr Rice had no other companion beside myself.

I met Albert T. Patrick about the middle of November, 1899. He called at the house one evening, under the name of Smith. He wished to see Mr Rice; he said he was in some business – cotton, I think. We talked about Texas and I gave him some Texas newspapers.

He called again in about a week. Mr Rice was in his bedroom, preparing to go to bed. It took Mr Rice about two and a half hours to prepare for bed. At this visit or at the first visit, Mr Patrick spoke about the Holt case, and we talked about that, for we both knew all about it. At this visit he disclosed his identity; he then said his name was Albert T. Patrick. He said that his side needed a letter purporting to have been written by Mr Rice to Captain Baker stating that he, Mr Rice, was a citizen of Texas. He said that if I would write such a letter on the typewriter that he would arrange for the signing of it. He gave me the copy.

After that he called about every week. Thursday night was his night, and he would stay for two hours. He said that if I would write this letter he would give me two hundred and fifty dollars out of the five hundred he had received from Mr Holt. He was also to get $10,000, when the case was completed, and he promised also to pay me out of his $10,000.

I made the letter, but when I got ready to deliver it and asked for the $250 he refused to pay it, and I refused to give him the letter.

Mr Patrick asked what my salary was. I told him I was getting $55 a month and all expenses. He said that I was worth much more than that to Mr Rice; that I ought to have double that amount, and that if I were to go into a business deal with him, something of that kind, that he would see that I was well taken care of, or got much more than that.

He showed me a will he had made. It purported to be a draft of a will of W. M. Rice, giving half of his property to Albert T. Patrick, making numerous bequests to his relations and friends, and the rest was to go to the William M. Rice Institute. He said that if I would write this on the typewriter that he would arrange for the signing and witnessing of it. He wanted me to be a witness. I said that I would assist as far as the typewriting, and going on the witness stand and proving it to be genuine.

I wrote it on the typewriter, but there was a great many mistakes in it. Mr Patrick said it would not do, and he would

have it written by a young man in his office named Morris
Meyers.

According to Jones, Mr Rice never met Patrick. The secretary
had assured the lawyer that his master would refuse to see him;
that he knew of his part in the Holt case, and that all attempts to
bring about an interview would be useless.

Mr Rice looked into the living room, one evening, as the two
sat there – conspiring at every pore – and withdrew, with a
murmured apology. He afterward asked Jones who "that handsome bald-headed man" was, and Jones told him that it was a
friend of his own.

The picture is as curious as any that I can recall. The old man
undergoing his long preparations for bed while the two spiders
fashioned their web under his own roof. Mr Rice's method of
getting exercise was to wrap himself in a blanket, and then roll on
the floor for an hour at a time. Dr Curry forbade this as too
fatiguing.

Now comes one of the most delicious bits: Mr Patrick's holy
indignation at the injustice of Mr Rice's 1896 will. That not very
intelligent body of opinion sometimes called "the great heart of
the public" always throbs with resentment when a wealthy man
leaves more of his money to charity than to his relatives. Mr
Patrick and his aid reflected this noble sentiment.

Jones said:

I showed Mr Patrick the 1896 will. Mr Patrick thought it
was a very unjust will. He said that he did not think it right
that Mr Rice should leave so little of his property to his
relatives and give it all to charity, and I said that I thought
the same thing. I said I supposed we would have to destroy
this will of 1896, but he said he did not propose to destroy it
at all, but that he would use the 1896 will to force the heirs
to accept the will of 1900 that we proposed to make. Mr
Patrick told me it would be a good idea to have the same
witnesses that witnessed the will of 1896, and he told me to
speak to Mr Wetherbee about it.

This new will was shown to me, I suppose, in a dozen

different forms, changed and rechanged and redrafted in a
dozen different forms at least.

Mr Patrick's plan was based on his belief that every man has his
price, and that it is often a very cheap bargain. It is painful to have
to say anything contrary to this cynical theory, for it is always a
fashionable one. Many persons suffer complete loss of faith in the
intelligence of an author unless he maintains that human nature is
altogether base and degraded. But in the midst of this chronicle of
rascality it is necessary to record that the Patrick notion failed
completely. Not one of the bribes that he offered, in his will of
1900, did him any good. Relatives, lawyers, bank clerks, servants
– all came and testified, to their own hurt, that, in their belief, the
1896 will was genuine and the 1900 will was fraudulent.
Jones now described his visit to Mr Wetherbee:

Mr Wetherbee had asked me to call at his house and take
dinner with him. I did call toward the end of December and
talked with Mr Wetherbee two or three hours. I told him if
he would enter into a business arrangement with me I could
get him into something that would be very beneficial. I told
him that Mr Rice was in the habit of waking up suddenly
and was not exactly conscious of what he was doing, and
that he would sign any paper I would put before him, and if
he, Mr Wetherbee, would draw up a will and make himself
an executor, I would get Mr Rice to sign it.

Mr Wetherbee said that he would not have anything to do
with a matter of that kind. He said he would very much like
to be an executor of Mr Rice's will, but he would not go into
it under that arrangement. He asked me: "How came you to
make such a suggestion?" and I told him that I had been
approached by three lawyers in the matter.

I went to Mr Patrick's office the first time on the 15th of
March, 1900, and he introduced me to Morris Meyers. His
office was at 302 Broadway. He locked the door and got out
the will. He read it over to us and asked what we thought.
We both said it sounded all right. He then asked Meyers if
he should be willing to act as witness. Meyers said yes – as

soon as he became acquainted with Mr Rice and saw Mr Rice's handwriting. I said I would take Mr Meyers and introduce him to Mr Rice as a friend of mine, and when we needed a notary I would telephone for Mr Meyers to come up. In that way he could become acquainted with Mr Rice and connect his name on the papers with Mr Rice.

The witnesses to the 1896 will being unavailable, Mr Meyers and Mr Short were selected as substitutes. We have seen Mr Short, presenting the cheque at Swensons'.

Mr Jones continued, showing how Dr Curry was introduced as physician, first to Jones, and later, through him, to Mr Rice.

Soon afterwards I was taken ill and Mr Patrick telephoned me about it. He wanted to know if I had a good doctor, and said that he would recommend me a good doctor, and gave me the name of Dr Walter Curry. Mr Patrick also told me that he had been looking into the matter of having Mr Short appointed a notary public for the State of New York but decided instead to have him appointed a commissioner of deeds of the State of Texas. Mr Patrick and I had not agreed exactly on the will. I was still insistent that I wanted to be a beneficiary, but he said that in that case he could not have it probated.

Mr Patrick said it would be a good plan to have some letters from Mr Rice; that it would be advantageous to us to have letters on all matters of importance, practically a copy of letters that Rice wrote to his agents in Texas, in Louisiana, and in New Jersey. I wrote him some letters, and he added a great deal in a flattering way toward himself, saying that Mr Rice had the greatest confidence in Mr Patrick.

Short and Meyers both came to the apartment on May 26, 1900. They were introduced to Mr Rice and took some acknowledgements from him . . .

In the will Mr Patrick said he had left $5,000 to each and every one of the trustees of the William M. Rice Institute of Houston, Texas. I asked him what this was for, and he said that it was for the same purpose as the others – that they would allow this paper to be probated.

He said that he could buy any man in Houston, Texas, for $5,000.

He had agreed to give the two elevator men in the house $5,000 each, but afterwards he cut them down to $500 each, and said that if they needed anything more he would give it to them. He also cut down William Rice Carpenter's bequest.

About two months before Mr Rice's death Mr Patrick told me that he was going to draw up some transfers of property, transferring some of Mr Rice's property to himself. I typewrote these transfers or assignments according to his form. There was a transfer of all Mr Rice's property in the safe deposit vaults at the Fifth Avenue Trust Company, and an assignment of the contents of Mr Rice's safe at the New York Safe Deposit Company. There was a transfer of all the real estate that Mr Rice owned in the State of Texas, and another for all the real estate that Mr Rice owned in Louisiana, and there was one of all the property and real estate Mr Rice owned in New Jersey.

Having arranged the disposal of all Mr Rice's estate; having raised this person to prosperity, and cut down another to what he thought a more suitable figure, Mr Patrick now began to consider the time and manner of Mr Rice's departure from the world, and the disposal of his mortal remains.

Mr Patrick thought of everything.

The "cremation letter" was concocted, and it was dated August 3, 1900.

Jones testified:

In the early part of August, 1900, I was at Mr Patrick's office and he was inquiring about Mr Rice's health, and I told him Mr Rice had been getting along better than he had for a year or so.

He said to me: "Well, don't you think Rice is living too long for our interests?"

I told him that it did seem that way, and he asked me if I couldn't suggest some way to get him out of the way.

I told him that I couldn't unless we used a Gatling gun –
or some foolish remark like that.

He told me that if I would let him in some night when Mr
Rice was sleeping soundly he would come and put him out
of the way. I told him it would not do, for the reason that
Mr Rice did not sleep soundly enough.

Before this there had been some conversation between
Patrick and me about chloroform. He asked me if I could
get him some. He said he wanted to make toothache medicine. I told him I would get it for him from a nurse in the
Presbyterian Hospital. As a matter of fact, I got it from my
brother in Texas. I sent him $5 and he sent it to me by the
American Express.

Later I asked Dr Curry if anyone could tell whether a
person had or had not died by chloroform poisoning if his
heart was affected. He said that the amount required to kill a
person with an affected heart would be so slight that he
doubted very much whether it would show.

On the Saturday before Mr Rice's death on Sunday this
matter of the draft came up. This was the draft on Mr Rice
for the Merchants and Planters Oil Mill for $25,000.

I telephoned Mr Patrick and he asked me where I was
going to take lunch. I told him most likely at Third Avenue
and Fifty-third Street. He asked if I could not arrange to go
somewhere on the West Side, as he generally came up on
the elevated train. I told him that I would go to the Roma
Restaurant at Sixth Avenue and Fiftieth Street, and he
agreed to meet me there. He finally reached there after I
started to eat. He said he did not want any lunch. I told him
of Mr Rice's condition, and of the draft, and he said:

"Jones, whatever we do, Mr Rice cannot be here on
Monday, because there is more of these drafts to follow
and they will consume more money than Mr Rice has in the
bank."

There followed many conferences between the two; meetings on
the street and telephone conversations, both on Saturday and on
Sunday. It was on Saturday that Mr Patrick inquired so an-

xiously of Dr Curry about Mr Rice's health and his ability to go
down town on Monday.

Jones described, with great circumstantiality, the place of all
these meetings and the substance of the conversations. Patrick
had a bottle of oxalic acid, and this he gave to Jones, with the
suggestion that he mix it with water, and offer some of it to Mr
Rice as medicine. This was on Sunday.

Jones said:

> Mr Patrick and I had looked up in the encyclopædia to see
> what it said about oxalic acid. I mixed up some of it with
> water and offered it to Mr Rice, and he took a mouthful, but
> he spit it out and said he didn't want to drink it. Later I
> found him sitting up at the window and looking out on Fifth
> Avenue. I persuaded him to go to bed, but he seemed to be
> very weak, and every time he tried to get up he would drop
> down in his chair. I took him up in my arms and put him in
> bed and covered him up. He seemed to be dazed but he soon
> fell asleep.

At six o'clock, Sunday evening, Jones and Patrick again met, by
appointment, on the street.

> Mr Patrick gave me the bottle of chloroform and told me to
> take it to the house and administer it to Mr Rice, and
> according to the way he had told me. I refused, saying I
> had not promised to do anything of that kind, and did not
> expect to and would not do it. Patrick said:
> "I am a man of family and I can't afford to do this."
> He said that if I did not do it the draft would become due
> next day and would draw out all the money, and Captain
> Baker would be on very shortly, and probably all the
> scheme would be revealed and we would lose everything.
> After considerable persuasion I said that I would take the
> chloroform and do as he had instructed me, and I took the
> chloroform and went home.
> After looking some time for a sponge, I found one that Mr
> Rice had used for cleaning his clothes, and I made a cone of

a towel, placed the sponge in the small end, and took it and saturated it with chloroform and placed it over my own face. I got a very strong effect from it. I then added a little more and went into Mr Rice's room. I found he was still sleeping, and placed it over his face and ran out of the room.

Mr Patrick had given me these instructions, and I followed them out as near as I could. He told me also to leave the chloroform on his face about thirty minutes. I stayed out of the room thirty minutes, stayed in my room part of the time, part of the time in the hall, and part of the time in the dining room. At the expiration of the thirty minutes someone kept ringing the bell very frequently. Of course, I was very much excited that they should be ringing the bell at this moment, so that I went to the door and looked through, and I could see someone, but I did not know who they were. My impression was, it was two ladies at the door.

After the thirty minutes expired I went back to Mr Rice's room and found him in the same position that I had left him, with that cone shape over his face. I removed that and put it in the range in the kitchen and lit a match to it and burned it and returned to Mr Rice's rooms and opened all the windows, straightened everything around to its usual appearance, and telephoned Mr Patrick that Mr Rice was very ill.

That Mr Rice was "very ill" had been the phrase agreed upon between them as meaning that he was dead.

On Monday morning, and at Patrick's direction, as with every other step in the process, Jones had made out the four cheques that were designed to provide the money to carry on the business and litigation in proving the bogus will. Patrick provided the signatures. It was then that Jones misspelled Patrick's first name on one cheque.

During the recital of Jones' testimony, and during all the unfavourable evidence, Mr Patrick sat in court wearing an expression – as it has been described to me by a man who witnessed the entire trial – of sneering and contemptuous superiority.

Jones's story was told in a straightforward manner. Severe

cross-examination did not shake it in any important detail. As the confession of an accomplice, the actual perpetrator of the murder, it was necessary for the State to furnish corroboration. This was done in the minutest particulars, by a long array of witnesses.

The doctors testified that the congestion of the lungs was such as chloroform would produce. The purchase and delivery of the chloroform was proved by Jones's brother and by the express messengers. The forged will and other documents furnished a motive for desiring Mr Rice's death; the letter on cremation was evidence of a plan to commit murder; and the coincidence of the death, exactly in time to prevent the bank deposits from being diverted to Texas, was difficult to explain on any presumption of innocence.

Twelve expert witnesses testified for the State that the signatures on the 1900 will, the cheques, the cremation letter, and the assignments to Patrick were not in Rice's hand. Bankers and business associates gave what may have been still more impressive evidence to the same effect. One of the most convincing things done by handwriting experts was to bisect some of the forged signatures of Mr Rice and show that the sections would always fit, when rearranged, with the opposite half of one of the other forgeries. This showed that they had all been made from the same model.

Arthur Train, whose account of the case is practically the only one of literary value, written by a man with first-hand legal knowledge, says that "Technically the case against Patrick was not a strong one. Dramatically it was overwhelming."

One of the jurors has told me that the Government proved its case up to the hilt and beyond any shadow of doubt. He and the other jurors found that belief in Patrick's guilt was inescapable.

The defence denied that Mr Rice had died by violent means, or that his death had been procured by the prisoner. They asserted – without much assurance – that the forgeries had not been brought home to Patrick, or if they had, that this fact did not prove him guilty of the murder. As he was not charged with forgery, it was unnecessary to argue that point at great length, and this was fortunate, for by the time the trial was over it would have been next to impossible to convince any candid person that the 1900 will and the other documents produced by Patrick were genuine.

The main reliance of the defence was the fact that the chief witness for the prosecution was the self-confessed murderer of Mr Rice, and that the old gentleman was ill at the time, and might have died from natural causes, even if Jones did attempt the murder by chloroform, as he said.

The defence contended that Mr Rice died from œdema (dropsy) of the lungs. They further tried to show that a sleeping person so subjected to chloroform would wake up and struggle.

They produced expert witnesses on the medical points, and upon handwriting. Dr Curry, whose professional reputation was more or less at stake, appeared for the defence and testified that he did not smell chloroform about Mr Rice when he made the examination thirty or forty minutes after his death.

The defence also denied the motive; they asserted that Patrick took the residuary estate "for benevolent purposes" (it is not recorded that anybody laughed), and that he could not spend any of it for himself. Jones was denounced, and many of the people from Texas were called "vultures."

One or two witnesses said that they had seen Mr Rice and Mr Patrick together. Their testimony, even as it is read, does not sound convincing, and as it was heard by the jury it was probably even less impressive. David L. Short, one of the witnesses of the 1900 will, gave a full account of the scene when Mr Rice signed that document in his presence. Mr Short and Mr Meyers spent many months in the Tombs, on the charge of forgery, but Mr Short was able to appear because of the kindness of Mr John T. Milliken, who had furnished $7,500 cash bail.

The State had called one of two old ladies who had been at The Berkshire at the moment when Jones said he was engaged in chloroforming his master. They had brought some cakes and wine for their old friend, Mr Rice. It was their ringing at the bell that agitated Jones while he was waiting for death to occur.

According to the testimony of the lady, she did not go upstairs, but sent the elevator man and waited in the hall below. After an interval she sent up again, but still the man could get no answer from the Rice apartment. This tends to confirm Jones's story, although not that part of it in which he said that, on looking out, he thought he saw two ladies.

They were Texans, staying briefly at a New York hotel, and had eagerly planned this Sunday evening errand of friendliness. They appeal strongly to the imagination: tremulously standing below, with their little basket, while the murder was going forward inside. One pictures them as wearing much black jet and many bangles, and this fancy is strengthened on learning that one of them was named Martha Thompson.

Mr Patrick failed to go on the witness stand in his own defence, and his counsel fought vigorously to prevent the jury from hearing what he was reported to have told his lawyer, Mr House, in the Tombs. Jones had said that this was a confession of murder; but it was a "privileged" communication to counsel, and not legally proper for the jury.

On March 26, 1902, the jury found Patrick guilty as charged. They were out all the afternoon, but spent an hour or more of the time at luncheon. There seems to have been little debate, no doubt, and no dissension among them, but they went over the case, point by point, before reaching the verdict.

As in so many murder cases, the fight was but beginning. One of the early efforts of the friends and defenders of Patrick was to move on the jurors, individually, by means of affidavits and so-called "newly discovered evidence," to try to prevail on them to recant, and to join in the efforts for a new trial or for executive clemency.

At one time or another, some of the jurymen were prevailed upon to sign an appeal. Others, who refused, and who remained unmoved by the assertion that they would "have the blood of an innocent man on their heads," were treated to indignant and insulting letters.

It was the beginning of a long campaign, carried on, partly, by legal methods. Patrick had a succession of lawyers, including the late David B. Hill, who represented him before the Court of Appeals. His counsellors frequently ended their connection with him – for reasons which seemed sufficient to themselves – and others were engaged. All their efforts were aided or directed by his own knowledge of the law, and his ingenuity in finding schemes to escape the death sentence.

This legal fight was supplemented by other methods which left a trail of slime across the history of the state. A stench of corruption and fraud attended the whole affair, to the end that there might be saved from his legal sentence one of the most pernicious scoundrels known to our law.

In the two years following the conviction, a new trial was refused, and there were arguments before the Court of Appeals. That Court did not reach its final decision until June, 1905, more than three years after the sentence. The Court refused a new trial, dividing four to three against the appeal. This was a blow to the defence, but the fact of the division saved the prisoner's life.

Mr Justice Grey, in delivering the opinion of the Court, said that he was convinced that the jury "reached a just conclusion and that there is no warrant for . . . our interference with the judgment."

Further, "in my opinion no other verdict could have been reached upon a dispassionate and intelligent consideration of the evidence."

The complaints of the defence, upon which they based their appeal, were that they had been compelled by the trial Court to alter the phraseology of a hypothetical question to a witness; that Jones had been allowed to tell of his suicide attempt; and that parts of the conversation in the Tombs between Jones, Patrick, and Mr House had been admitted. It seemed to be the argument of the defence that, as Patrick's conversation with his counsel was excluded, so the conversation of Jones, Patrick's partner in the enterprise, should also have been kept out.

All the contentions of the defence seem highly technical, and although interesting to legalists, to have contained nothing whatever to show that any injustice had been worked at the trial.

But while these technicalities would probably not carry much weight in the same Court today, they were sufficient at that time to cause three justices to dissent for varying reasons.

Mr Justice O'Brien read a dissenting opinion. He began by saying:

"Let us look at the evidence, not in search of a victim, but to find the truth" – a familiar phrase from those who represent our courts as savage and vengeful. The learned Justice then said that

Jones could not swear that Rice was not already dead when he put
the sponge over his face; that the fact that Dr Curry did not smell
chloroform was important; and that, in spite of the physicians at
the autopsy, congestion of the lungs might have been caused by
the embalming fluid.

He criticized the treatment of Jones: "set at large, and maintained at public expense in a comfortable if not fashionable
boarding house" and "having earned his reward, he was allowed
to depart to his native State of Texas, where he now resides in
safety."

Apparently the Justice leaned to the belief that, if Jones had
actually been kept in a "fashionable" boarding house, Patrick
should have been set free instantly. Justice O'Brien said that "the
accused has not had a fair and impartial trial"; "the atmosphere
which surrounded" him made that impossible.

Translated out of the legal jargon, it seemed to come down to
this: nobody doubts Patrick's guilt, but his counsel have beauti-
fully split some hairs for our amusement, and three of us vote to
begin the farce all over again.

After his final sentence, Patrick was within four weeks of
execution. After his second sentence, the electric chair was but
two weeks away when the Court of Appeals granted a stay. In
January, 1906, the execution was within seven days when the
Governor granted an extension of time. There were two or three
other reprieves in this year. A bill once passed the Legislature to
grant Patrick another trial. The Governor vetoed it.

Finally, on December 20, 1906, Governor Higgins commuted
the sentence to life imprisonment. He issued a statement in which
he said that nothing would seem to warrant his interference with
the death sentence except that three of the seven justices of the
Court of Appeals were of the opinion that errors were committed
at the trial "which were substantially prejudicial to the rights of
Patrick . . . I feel that the death penalty ought not, under all the
circumstances, to be inflicted."

That is, nothing had shown that he was not guilty, but on
account of the opinion of the minority of the Court that technical
errors had been committed, he was given the lesser sentence.

At Sing Sing, next day, Patrick said:

"I am either innocent or I am guilty: I refuse to accept Governor Higgins' commutation of my sentence. I believe that to a certain extent its acceptance by me would be an admission of my guilt. I purpose to continue my fight for freedom."

His brother-in-law, John T. Milliken, also issued a bulletin saying that he would now spend twice as many thousands as he had already spent.

The New York *Tribune* said that Governor Higgins was within his rights. The whole thing, however, was a scandal. Now that Patrick's life had been saved, there would be demands for his release. If he got out, he would be invaluable as a counsellor to tell murderers how to escape.

He had been in the "death house" for four years and seven months. An anecdote of him in these surrounding shows him in genial mood. It appears in a book called *Life in Sing Sing*, written by "Number 1500." The author speaks of the games allowed to men in the condemned cells.

For pastime they play checkers and chess, each player being supplied with a board, and although they cannot see each other, they make up very entertaining tourneys by calling their moves. At one time when I was in the chamber in performance of some duty, and when seven men were confined there awaiting death, Patrick was playing the final group of three games with Flanagan, a Negro whose date of death was but a few days distant. Every inmate had his board, followed the play, and made the moves as they were called between the two contestants. At last Flanagan cried:

"I have you; if I win I'll get a reprieve."

He did win, and then the vastness of the stake and the uncertainty of its realization impressed him with the fear that Patrick had not exerted himself.

"You played off, you red-headed poisoner! You knew better than move that king on thirteen."

Patrick laughed heartily and all the rest joined in with as free and genuine an enjoyment of the rise that had been taken out of Flanagan as it is possible to imagine. Even in the shadow of the electric chair, care was driven away.

In spite of this, Patrick pretended to protest at the commutation of his sentence. Two days after he was removed from the "death house" to a life prisoner's cell, he handed the warden a statement:

> Please take notice I reject the warrant of the Governor of the State of New York commuting my death sentence to imprisonment for life, and that I refuse to accept or take any benefit under the same, and that I protest against the execution thereof on the ground that said warrant of the Governor, as well as the judgment of conviction upon which it is founded, is contrary to law and void.

He then settled down as a prisoner, to the work of making sashes. In his more than four years in the condemned cells, he had seen seventeen men taken to the electric chair, and said that all of them told him they preferred execution to life imprisonment.

A great many persons swallow this ancient buncombe about prisoners who would choose the death sentence rather than imprisonment for life. Its falsity is easily established by an inquiry for one instance of a prisoner, actually given the chance, and preferring death. By those who demand the abolition of capital punishment, on grounds of humanity, the curiously illogical argument is sometimes made that imprisonment should be inflicted, as the more *terrible* of the two penalties.

From time to time, during the next six years, Patrick was heard from in his constant and ingenious appeals. Those who can easily convert a murderer into a hero, if he keeps his name in the papers long enough, and is sufficiently persistent, began to sympathize with his, "brave fight for freedom." It was possible for some folk to see him as a "poor man" suffering for the alleged murder of a rich one; and therefore, by some specious reasoning, entitled to their best wishes. Of course, this was grotesque: the crime was committed in an attempt to divert money from public and educational uses into the pockets of a few. Moreover, the fight was now sustained by the backing of enormous wealth. The result of it all was actually to substantiate the belief that money will save a rich murderer from his just fate.

Patrick, for some reason, was allowed to go outside the prison to argue his case. In December, 1909, he insisted that he was "legally dead," and was taken to Brooklyn to argue this point before the Appellate Division of the Supreme Court.

His contention was that the Court of Appeals had acted without jurisdiction in signing a stay of execution after affirming his conviction. As a result of this stay, the warden stopped the execution, the week passed, and he became legally dead. It was therefore highly illegal that he should still be in Sing Sing.

It seems to me that this was the moment for the judges of the Appellate Division to show that they possessed logic, a feeling for justice, and a sense of humour. In all these respects they proved themselves painfully lacking. It was their chance to say:

"Mr Sheriff, we are convinced by the eloquent arguments of the prisoner that he is dead. That being the case, you are ordered to convey him back to Sing Sing and instantly bury him, within the prison walls. And, Mr Sheriff – it is too late to let the punishment fit the crime; the time of punishment is past. But, if the prisoner should care for the idea, just before the boards are nailed down – a cone made out of a towel – a sponge soaked in chloroform – we think you understand, Mr Sheriff."

The plea at Brooklyn having fallen on dull ears, no great stir in the matter was heard for a long time. Much, however, was going on behind the scenes.

On November 28, 1912, a few weeks before the expiration of his term of office, Governor John A. Dix surprised everyone by granting to Patrick a free and unconditional pardon. In an accompanying statement, the Governor said that "there had always been an air of mystery about the case." He quoted the minority opinion of the Court of Appeals, about the "atmosphere" which surrounded the defendant, and "precluded a fair trial."

He, the Governor, became acquainted with the case as far back as the time of Governor Higgins. Dean Huffcut of Columbia had told him that Governor Higgins believed Patrick innocent of murder, but that "he ought not to have a pardon at once." Governor Higgins had done enough when he saved Patrick from

the chair. He was leaving Patrick to "convince" some future
governor of his innocence.

Governor Dix made the further astonishing statement that:

> This pardon of Patrick really came to me as unfinished
> business from the Hughes administration. I have taken it up
> and devoted personal study to it periodically during two
> years, and I was only ready to act to-day . . . The pardon
> was strongly urged upon me by State Superintendent of
> Prisons, Joseph F. Scott.

That the Patrick pardon was "unfinished business" of the
Hughes administration would, I strongly believe, be altered by
any member of that administration to read, "untouched business." Patrick himself did not favour any appeal when Mr
Hughes was Governor; he knew the uselessness of an appeal
to a man of the clear mind and high character then at the head of
the State.

A newspaper account said that Governor Dix had been
strongly influenced by a report made by the "Medico-Legal
Society," which ridiculed the medical testimony at Patrick's
trial. Anyone who looks at this report of the "Medico-Legal
Society," and compares it with the testimony of the State's
medical witnesses will probably conclude that to be "strongly
influenced" by it, one must be strongly prejudiced in the beginning.

The *Sun* referred to various "societies and scientists" who had
kept up a never-ceasing and very mysterious agitation for Mr
Patrick.

"Back of all these societies and scientists has been the never-
ceasing efforts of John T. Milliken of St Louis, who married
Patrick's sister."

This man had met the Governor at a bankers' convention two
years earlier, and made this offer:

"I will deposit $100,000 in any financial institution in New
York City, which may be chosen, and I will forfeit that sum to
charity, if within a year after his release Albert T. Patrick does
not absolutely prove his innocence."

Mr Milliken's stake has long been forfeited, but news of its payment has not been heard. Herman H. Kohlsaat of Chicago, for some reason or other, gave out an interview on the glad news of the pardon, and said that all "credit" for the release should be given to Mr Milliken. But whatever joy Governor Dix and Mr Kohlsaat and Mr Milliken and the "Medico-Legal Society" may have felt – and it is believed that their first fine rapture was somewhat mitigated in later years – there was no mistaking the comment in responsible journals.

In the *Journal of Criminal Law*, Frederick B. Crossley wrote that Governor Dix had pardoned Patrick "after a secret hearing at which there were present pleaders whose identity the Governor declines to disclose." The Governor expressed the hope that *after his release* Patrick would demonstrate his innocence! The act of Governor Dix was "one of the most striking abuses of executive clemency in recent times, and an example to the entire country of the failure of the law to work justice."

One or two papers seemed to applaud the act. Thus, the Washington *Times* compared, for no obvious reasons, the case against Patrick with "the charges brought against people in witchcraft times" when "they burned folks to death." The Waterbury *American* also seemed to believe that it was a cause for joy that the bright spirit of Mr Patrick was again enlarged and at liberty.

But the Philadelphia *Times* said that Patrick had never fooled his judges, with all his shrewdness, his legal resources, and his "hair-splitting points." The Columbia (S. C.) *State* and the Springfield (Mass.) *Union* both denounced the pardon as unjustifiable. The *Union*, referring to Governor Dix's hope that Patrick would now prove his innocence, asked what proof he could bring that he could not have produced long ago.

The *Sun* of New York said that the incident was by no means closed. It said, and the Buffalo *Express* agreed, that the pardoning power should be taken from the Governor, and given to a board of pardons which would act openly, and not in secret.

Criminal lawyers denounced the Governor's act as outrageous, and pointed out that Patrick had committed forgeries which alone might have kept him in prison longer than he had served for

murder and forgery combined. The Governor had not claimed
that anything had shown him to be innocent, but merely cited the
minority opinions of the Court of Appeals that *technical errors* had
been made at the trial.

The New York *Evening Post* said that forgery of the will by
Patrick had been proved in a way that precluded reasonable
doubt. The Appellate Division had set aside the forged will;
and had affirmed the old one in language of exceptional emphasis.
The Court of Appeals had affirmed this judgment. Patrick had
not been tried for forgery, yet he must be considered as a forger of
the worst type. The reasons for which the Court of Appeals
divided on the murder were ones to which the practices of the
same Court would today give far less weight. There were no
indications that Governor Dix had given due consideration to the
case.

However editors and lawyers might denounce, the power of the
Governor was supreme, and his act final. The hundreds of
thousands spent in the efforts to free Patrick had not been
without result. The firm of Patrick & Jones was long ago dissolved; Jones is said to have died in Texas, and, of course, there
were the usual yarns about a recantation of his testimony,
probably on his "death-bed."

Mr Patrick was free to go westward, to the arms of his loving
friends. As with the maid of Fall River, who was restored, by a
jury, to her admirers in her native town, the arms grew chill as the
years went by. Yet for a time, at least, the lawyer dwelt in St
Louis – a mysterious and romantic figure to those of the younger
generation who grew up since his celebrity. The atmosphere
which surrounded him was one of injured innocence; it was
subtly conveyed that he had been a notable martyr; he was
now in dignified retirement, after he had suffered greatly – for
the sins of another!

But the rôle of martyr did not altogether suit. The call was too
strong, and it is even said that in a southwestern state he is once
more "Attorney and Counsellor-at-Law." There was always,
always, the callure of bonds, deeds, and assignments. And of
wills; especially of wills. He has been known to visit New York, to

look upon those centres of financial power in which his gentle voice so nearly became a tone of authority.

Says a pamphlet, printed by De Vinne in 1915:

> The Rice Institute, a university of liberal and technical learning, founded in the city of Houston, Texas, by William Marsh Rice, and dedicated by him to the advancement of letters, science and art, opened for the reception of students in the autumn of nineteen hundred and twelve. Edgar Odell Lovett, president.

I hear, that after years of litigation, about ten millions became available and that Rice is the richest educational institution in the South. The grounds are beautiful; and the men and maidens of Texas flocked to them, in 1915, to the number of 384. Forty instructors awaited them. Doubtless, these numbers are trebled to-day.

Somewhere on the campus – an American college feels miserable without a campus – there must be a statue, or in the Hall of Administration there may be a portrait, of the Founder – the white-bearded, trim, little old gentleman who perished (A voice: "From bananas!") that these youths might, in such pleasant groves, study arts and letters.

Wherever Mr Patrick goes in his travels, I fancy it is not toward Texas. He is not – it is fair to suppose – summoned to Rice Institute at Commencement to receive its degree in science, or in laws. And however he might be greeted at the Institute, his appearance on the streets of Houston would seem extra-hazardous – considering the opinion he once expressed of the price, *per capita*, of the men of that city.

THE BIRMINGHAM SIX

(Paddy Hill and others, UK 1974)

Ludovic Kennedy

Most of the cases in this book show how forensic science was harnessed by the prosecution to prove guilt, but there are occasions where it has been used to establish innocence. In the 1990s, some twenty years after the original trial, the case against the Birmingham Six finally crumbled when the defence exposed weaknesses in the original forensic evidence. The story opens in November 1974. The bombing of two crowded pubs in Birmingham, in which 21 people were murdered and 162 wounded, was the worst IRA atrocity on the British mainland since the "Troubles" began in 1969. Most of the victims were young people thronging the city centre on what should have been a carefree night out. Public anger and outrage at the carnage put pressure on the police to track down the culprits. Later the same evening, six Irishmen booked on the boat to Belfast were arrested at the ferry port of Heysham in Lancashire. Traces of nitroglycerine were found on their hands. They were beaten, tortured and threatened by detectives. At the end of this violent intimidation, four of the suspects signed written "confessions" while the other two made oral ones. All six were convicted of murder at their Old Bailey trial the following year and sentenced to life imprisonment. But there were doubts in the case. Twelve years later, in 1987, following an inquiry by the Devon and Cornwall police, the case of the Birmingham Six was referred back to the Court of Appeal. The appeal judges heard fresh evidence. Part of this new evidence concerned the "confessions" and part concerned the tell-tale chemical traces on the Irishmen's hands found when they were picked up at Heysham. The men's lawyers claimed that it could no longer be concluded that any of the six had been in contact with explosives. All six appeals were dismissed, however, and it seemed that the convictions would stand. But the campaigning author and journalist Ludovic Kennedy (b. 1919) took up the case, convinced that a gross miscarriage of justice had occurred. Over the winter of 1989–90 he examined the documents in the case and set out his findings and conclusions in an article for The Sunday Times. *This expanded version appeared the following year.*

Just over two years ago the Court of Appeal in the shape of Lord Lane the Lord Chief Justice, Lord Justice O'Connor and Lord Justice Stephen Brown heard fresh evidence in the case of the six Irish drinking companions, convicted in 1975 for the murder of those killed in the IRA bombing of two Birmingham pubs. Evidence was led on the two heads that had resulted in the men's convictions: firstly that it could no longer be concluded that any of them had been in contact with explosives, and secondly that their alleged "confessions" had been obtained by threats and violence (as in the case of the Guildford Four). The court rejected both submissions. "The longer this case has gone on", they said, "the more convinced this court has become that the verdict of the jury was correct." The appeals would be dismissed.

Yet the case refuses to die . . . which in itself and like so many other cases, indicates that whatever the opinions of judges may be, there are others no less worthy of belief who continue to assert that justice has miscarried. So were the judges in the recent appeal of the Birmingham Six right in their judgement or wrong?

Whenever in the past I have looked into a case of an alleged miscarriage of justice, I have always gone first to the convicted men's solicitors because they are least likely to be conned by the guilty proclaiming innocence. Ivan Geffen has been solicitor of two of the six for twelve years and Gareth Peirce of the other four for nine years. Neither has the slightest doubt about their innocence. Peirce has called the findings of the Court "disgraceful", Geffen says, "It's only what one has come to expect from this Court of Appeal."

The three counsel for the men take a broadly similar view. Lord Gifford, QC, told me, "The judges had no business dismissing the evidence of police malpractice and violence. To come to the conclusions they did on evidence which was 90 per cent written and only 5 per cent oral is to assume powers of divination which no-one should arrogate to themselves," Richard Ferguson, QC, said the findings had sickened him. "The whole demeanour of the judges was not to find the truth but how to counter the good arguments of our side. They were also gratuitously offensive. Coming as I do from Northern Ireland, I find it particularly distressing when justice fails to live up to the high standards we were brought up to believe in." And Michael Mansfield, QC, who thinks there should have been a retrial, most of the participants being still alive, said that the judgement had left him angry and upset. "I think it did incomparable damage to people's concept of justice."

It was the same with the three distinguished scientists whose evidence clashed with that of Dr Frank Skuse, the forensic scientist who had appeared for the prosecution and was later dismissed on the grounds of limited efficiency. David Baldock, a former senior scientific officer at the Home Office Laboratories, told me, "When I turned up at the Old Bailey to give evidence, Michael Mansfield said; 'We're wasting our time. They're not listening. I think the judges quite failed to grasp the nettle of the scientific evidence.' Dr Brian Caddy, head of the University of Strathclyde's Forensic Science Unit agreed, and Dr Hugh Black, former Chief Inspector of Explosives at the Home Office, went further. "Their decision", he wrote to me, "was an outrage."

Having myself read the Court's judgement and the evidence presented to it; having spoken personally to some of the new witnesses; having visited Birmingham's Queens Road Police Station where the alleged beatings of the prisoners and the "confessions" that followed took place; and having also read Chris Mullin MP's well-documented book on the case, I am led inexorably to the same conclusions. So if we are all right in our views, how was it that the Court's findings came to be so at variance with the evidence presented?

In many murder cases where justice is later found to have

miscarried, it often happens that quite early in their investigations the police light on some small but seemingly convincing piece of evidence that leads them to draw the wrong conclusions; and which, if pursued tenaciously, leads in turn to wrongful prosecution, conviction and sentence. In the 10 Rillington Place case they assumed that Timothy Evans would not have sold his furniture and fled to Wales had he not murdered his wife and child whose bodies they had discovered in the ground-floor wash-house; and from there it was a short step to their manufacturing a false confession which led to his conviction and hanging. In the Ayr murder case Patrick Meehan's life sentence originated from his admission to the police that he and his friend Jim Griffiths had been engaged on a criminal enterprise near the scene of the crime when the only firm evidence the police then had was that the two intruders had called each other "Pat" and "Jim"; and to make certain of a conviction the police planted false evidence in Jim Griffiths's coat pocket. Similarly in the Lindbergh baby kidnapping case the discovery of $14,000 of marked ransom money under the floorboards of Hauptmann's garage in the Bronx was enough to convince New York and New Jersey police of his guilt, and with a wealth of fabricated evidence to railroad him to the electric chair.

In the case of the Birmingham Six their undoing was their association with an IRA bomber named James McDade who on 14 November 1974 blew himself up while planting a bomb in the Coventry Telephone Exchange. Five of the six (Gerry Hunter, Paddy Hill, Richard McIlkenny, Billy Power and Hughie Callaghan) had grown up with McDade in the small Roman Catholic enclave of the Ardoyne in West Belfast, where as children they had suffered abuse and discrimination from the surrounding Protestant majority. All had come to Birmingham to seek work, mostly in the 1960s, and it was there that the sixth member of the group, Johnny Walker from Londonderry, came to know McDade and the others. Until McDade blew himself up, only one of the six, Walker, suspected that McDade was an IRA activist. They themselves were not members of the IRA, or even of Sinn Fein. But they were staunch supporters of the Republican cause and its belief in a United Ireland, and they all helped to raise money to send to dependants of Ulster fellow Catholics who had been imprisoned or interned.

On 21 November 1974 the body of James McDade was to be flown from Birmingham to Belfast, and to show Ardoyne solidarity five of the six agreed to combine attendance at his funeral with a visit to their families. Their friend Hughie Callaghan saw them off at Birmingham's New Street Station on the 7.55 p.m. train which would connect with the night boat from Heysham. At 8.17 p.m. the first bomb went off in the Mulberry Bush pub and a few minutes later the second in the Tavern in the Town, both near to the station, and resulting in the horrific casualties of 21 dead and 162 injured. Ports and airports were immediately alerted, and when the booking clerk at New Street reported that he had sold consecutive numbered tickets to a group of Irishmen travelling to Belfast, the Lancashire Police were asked to interview them at Heysham.

The five reached Heysham at 10.45, having spent most of the journey smoking and playing cards and having been observed by a British Rail guard as being in good humour. Paddy Hill was out first, and after showing the contents of his luggage to the waiting police and told them he was going to see his grandmother and aunt in Belfast, he was allowed through to the boat where he settled himself in the bar to wait for the others. They also were interrogated and had their luggage examined. If they were innocent, they knew nothing of the explosions in the two Birmingham pubs; but because of the IRA bombs that had gone off in the Birmingham area in recent months, they said nothing about going to McDade's funeral. Then their clothing was searched, and in Walker's coat were found Roman Catholic mass cards for the funeral of McDade. The local police called up the head of Lancashire CID who ordered the men to be taken to Morecambe police station for further interrogation, and for Dr Frank Skuse to be there with his equipment for detecting traces of explosive. As the four men were being taken away, they asked what had happened to their mate. They were asked what mate, and when they said Paddy Hill, he was taken off the ferry to join them.

If the six were guilty, there are already two things wrong with this scenario. Firstly, as Lord Scarman has pointed out to me, as trained IRA men they would hardly have been so foolish as to set the bombs to explode at a time which they knew would give the police two and a half hours to alert the Lancashire Police to their arrival at Heysham. And secondly, they would not have called the police's attention to the missing Paddy Hill; they would have been glad that at least one of their number looked like getting away.

There is evidence that on the journey to Morecambe all five of the group appeared relaxed which, if innocent, they had every reason to be. On arrival they were put in different cells. In the small hours of the morning Dr Skuse arrived, also Superintendent George Reade from Birmingham and detectives from the West Midland Serious Crime Squad, now disbanded because of misconduct of many of its officers. One by one the five men were escorted in to Dr Skuse to have their hands swabbed in what was called the Griess test, then regarded as a reliable method of detecting nitroglycerine but now, like Dr Skuse himself, considered unreliable. McIlkenny's, Hunter's and Walker's hands proved negative, as did the left hands of Power and Hill. But the right hands of Power and Hill proved positive. This, said Frank Skuse, made him 99 per cent certain that both Power and Hill had recently been in contact with explosives.

Before considering the "confessions" that followed, let us follow the forensic evidence which began with Dr Skuse's findings at Morecambe right through to the final verdict on them at the 1987–8 Court of Appeal. At the trial of the six in Lancaster, Mr Justice Bridge said that the forensic test was one of two "absolutely critical" chapters in the prosecution's case. Yet Skuse in evidence had to admit that when he subjected the traces of Power's and Hill's right hands to two further tests, one of which, the GCMS at Aldermaston, was said to be a hundred times more sensitive than Griess, both registered negative. But he stuck to his 99 per cent certainty of the tests at Morecambe, and added that in the GCMS test a trace from Hill's *left* hand (which was found negative at Morecambe) had also proved positive. However, Dr Hugh Black for the defence said he had seen a print-out of this GCMS test and that it had *not* proved positive.

Nor was that all. In May 1985 the Granada television programme, *World In Action*, invited Mr David Baldock and Dr
Brian Caddy, the two forensic scientists referred to earlier, to
carry out the Griess test on a variety of common substances.
Between them they found that items containing nitro-cellulose,
such as lacquer, aerosol spray, cigarette packets and old playing
cards, all gave Griess positive. It will be remembered that the
men were smoking and playing cards on their journey to Heysham. Asked later if he was surprised that Dr Skuse had been so
certain of his findings at Morecambe, Mr Baldock said he was
amazed. Also asked to comment on Skuse's findings of nitro-
glycerine on the GCMS on Hill's left hand, both he and Dr Black
said that the test had not been properly carried out. "What Skuse
should have told the Court," said Baldock, "was that it did *not*
confirm the presence of nitro-glycerine." This was also the view
of Mr R.A. Hall, Director of the Northern Ireland Forensic
Laboratory and vastly experienced in the science of detecting
explosives.

In the appeal of the Birmingham Six, the evidence of Mr
Baldock and Drs Black and Caddy again clashed head on with
that of Dr Skuse; with the result that the judges found themselves
obliged to admit that "in our judgement the Griess test at
Morecambe *should not be regarded as specific for nitro-glycerine.*"
One would have thought that that left all of Dr Skuse's evidence
in ruins. But like shipwrecked sailors on a spar, the judges clung
to Dr Skuse's positive finding on Hill's left hand in the GCMS
test, and indeed found another spar in the evidence of a Dr Janet
Drayton who had conducted the GCMS test with Skuse. But she
would go no further than to say of Hill's left hand, "*possible* ng
present, very small increase".

So on this flimsy edifice and disregarding the evidence of Mr
Baldock and Dr Black that the test had not been properly carried
out, and of Dr Black that when he had seen the GCMS print-out
thirteen years before it had not registered positive, the Court
came up with this:

So far from creating any doubt the fresh evidence on this
topic [Dr Drayton's] makes us sure that Hill's left hand is

proven to have nitro-glycerine upon it, for which there is, and can be no innocent explanation. That conclusion is fatal to the appellants.

Some conclusion!

I should say here that some months after this article was published, I succeeded in tracking down Dr Janet Drayton at her home in Woking with the help of Heather Mills, home affairs correspondent of the *Independent*. I showed her the above extract from the Court's judgment which she had not seen before. She told us that the Court had no business in saying that Hill's left hand was *proved* to have nitro-glycerine on it when she had gone no further than to say it was *possible* (She even thought her findings could have been "a rogue result".) She also said that she could not see how any findings about Hill could have any bearing on the guilt or innocence of the other five. Nor could we. But that is the sort of perverse reasoning we have come to expect from senior judges in recent times.

Let us now turn to the "confessions", the first of which (that of Billy Power) was obtained at Morecambe at about lunchtime on the Friday, and a further three (those of McIlkenny, Walker and Callaghan) on the Saturday after the return of the prisoners to Birmingham. But first it is necessary to look at the background circumstances in which the "confessions" were obtained.

When the news of the pub bombings with their appalling casualties became known, there was hardly a man in Birmingham who would not have been ready and willing, such was their anger, personally to lynch any of those responsible. When the six arrived at Winson Green Prison on remand only three days later, they were beaten up mercilessly both by prison staff and inmates. Even the wives suffered. Sandra Hunter experienced paint and beer glasses being thrown at her house, bangings on the door in the middle of the night, nooses left hanging on the front gate and daubed on the walls the words HANG IRA BASTARDS. And after Theresa Walker had taken her children to Londonderry, their house was broken into and vandalized, the television set and coins from the gas meter stolen.

It would have been extraordinary if the Birmingham police at Morecambe, once the Griess test had shown positive on Power and Hill, had not also felt, and to some degree shown, their sense of outrage and anger. It is well known that when routinely interrogating suspects police invariably simulate belief in their guilt so that, if guilty, the suspects will be encouraged to admit to it. "They have to be certain," Lord Devlin once wrote of police attitudes, "they are no use if they aren't." On this occasion they did not have to simulate certainty: they *were* certain. The scum of the earth, those who had killed and mutilated nearly two hundred people, many of them young girls and boys, had been delivered into their hands; and they had the power to do to them what they wanted.

Yet if we are to believe those who interrogated the Birmingham Six, they did not so much as lay a finger on them. Reading their evidence, one would be entitled to assume that they never even raised their voices, and that all the "confessions" were given freely and voluntarily.

But those arrested told a different story. This is part of Power's, taken from evidence at his trial and after his right hand was proved Griess positive. Two officers called Watson and French led him to an upstairs room.

> As I walked through the door French punched me on the back of the head. I stumbled forward and they both set about me. I was pushed into a chair. They were shouting, "You dirty, murdering IRA bastard. You got gelly on your hands."

They and another officer, said Power, beat him up again, and then French said they would throw him out of the car on the way back to Birmingham, and explain it by saying he was trying to escape.

> Then they started telling me there was a mob outside my home ready to lynch my wife and children. All that was

saving them was the police who were searching it. The only way to save my wife and children was to tell them what they wanted to know.

He was taken to another room where, he said, several more officers set on him:

> From all sides I was punched, hit and kicked. When I slid down the wall, I was dragged up by the hair. This was repeated three or four times.

It was at this stage, said Power, that he fouled his trousers. Then one officer said, "Stretch his balls", and another bellowed into his ear, "You'll never have sex with your wife again." "I screamed 'OK OK.' I had to say something to stop them. I couldn't take any more."

Yet even then they hadn't done with him. When he stalled over answering a question, someone shouted, "Throw him out of the fucking window." Power was not to know that the window was sealed. They dragged him over to it, and another officer said, "If the fall doesn't kill him, the crowd will."

Power screamed, "I'll tell you anything you want me to say," and they prepared to write his confession.

The others told broadly similar stories: of being slapped and punched and kicked, and hearing the screams of their friends as they were punched and kicked in other rooms. Hill said he was dragged round the room by his hair, told he would be shot and his body dumped on the motorway, but that if he signed a statement saying he'd planted the bombs, they would stop beating him. Walker said he was punched repeatedly on an operation scar on his stomach, was also told he would be shot and had a gun pressed against his head and the trigger pulled, had a cigarette stubbed out on a blister on his toe. "In the end I became completely deranged."

In the late afternoon the five men, without shoes and socks, were bundled into police cars. Hunter said that as soon as he got in Superintendent Reade, who was smelling of drink, started slapping and punching him. In another car, Walker said that an officer called Kelly who also smelt of drink, head-butted him. In a third car, Hill complained that a Sergeant Bennett whipped his testicles with the leather thong of his truncheon. Later, he said, an Inspector Moore put a revolver into his mouth, "said he was going to blow my fucking head off", pulled the trigger so that it clicked, then laughed.

Although the prisoners were all kept segregated from each other the police maintained that all these stories, so similar in what they claimed, were total inventions; that they did not assault any of them.

Yet worse was to come. Late that Friday night the five were taken to Birmingham's Queens Road police station where they were joined by Hugh Callaghan, and kept there until the Sunday afternoon. During this time they claimed that they were further savagely assaulted, that they were kept awake all Friday night by the bangings of the cell-door hatches and by an Alsatian dog that was made repeatedly to bark at them, that they were continually made to stand up or sit down and that they were continually abused; and that it was this sustained intimidation and violence that led all but Hill and Hunter to sign written "confessions". (These two allegedly gave oral ones.)

The "confessions" themselves were a mass of contradictions and untruths. Three of the four referred to the bombs being carried in plastic bags (in which, only the police knew, previous unexploded bombs had been found). In fact they had no plastic bags with them, and forensic examination of the remains showed that the bombs had been carried in holdalls or briefcases. Callaghan said he put his bomb *outside* the Mulberry Bush on one side and that Hunter had put his *outside* on the other. Forensic evidence showed that the bomb or bombs had been placed *inside* the pub. Despite Callaghan's claim that he and Hunter had bombed the Mulberry Bush, Walker claimed that Hunter had been with him bombing the Tavern. Callaghan said there were six bombs, Walker and McIlkenny said three.

Subsequently all six denied the voluntariness of the confessions. Callaghan said, "I was in a state of shock. I do not know what I said. They said things to me. I agreed. At the end one of the officers put a pen in my right hand, placed it over the paper

and guided my hand as I signed." Similar assertions were made
by the Guildford Four.

At their trial neither judge nor jury believed the allegations of
beatings or disbelieved the "confessions". With amazing naivety
Mr Justice Bridge spoke of the allegations against the police as
being "of the most bizarre and grotesque character". If the
defendants were telling the truth, he said, "I would have to
suppose that a team of fifteen officers had conspired among
themselves to use violence on the prisoners and to fabricate
evidence." Poor innocent, he did not seem the least aware that
when the police feel sure they have the right man or men, this sort
of conduct is not unusual: there was no need for a conspiracy
because everyone reacted spontaneously. He concluded, "All the
police officers who gave their evidence of the circumstances in
which the statements were taken, impressed me as being straightforward and honest witnesses." But this is how they are trained to
appear; that is how they were with the Guildford Four; that is
why they lie and lie and know they will be believed.

In November 1977 the six men brought a civil action against
the police and the Home Office for injuries they had received
while in police custody; for fresh evidence they were relying on
the findings of a Dr David Paul, a former police surgeon and City
of London coroner, and a specialist in the interpretation of
injuries from photographs. Shown enlarged photographs of the
six taken while they were in custody at Queens Road, he found
signs of injuries on all.

The action was allowed and application made for legal aid. But
the police appealed and in an uncharacteristically depraved
judgement Lord Denning upheld them. If the action were to
succeed, he said, it would show evidence of police perjury and
violence, and the six might have to be pardoned; this was such an
appalling vista that the action could not be allowed to proceed; ie
better that the six rot in jail than to find there had been police
wrongdoing.

But the supporters of the six, including some of the media,
continued to press their case; and in December 1986 a retired
police officer by the name of Tom Clarke, who had been at
Queens Road at the material time, appeared on Granada Tele-

vision to say what he had seen and heard there. Seven weeks later the Home Secretary announced that he was sending the case back to the Court of Appeal and was ordering an inquiry into it by the Devon and Cornwall Police.

At the Appeal hearing Clarke confirmed the prisoners' claims of police intimidation and ill-treatment, even admitting that he himself had joined in verbal abuse of the prisoners ('I was thrilled to know we had got the right people"). He supported what they had said about being kept awake all night, the dog barking at them, the cell-door hatches being banged up and down, their being made to stand up or sit down. He described one prisoner, whose blanket had slipped from him, as having on his stomach a red weal turning bluish and measuring about six inches by four. "He had been hit so badly that, although I wanted to see him dead, I was worried about him. He had had the hell of a hefty thump." When he went off duty at 5.30 a.m. on the Saturday morning he said, the prisoners were "scared out of their wits"; and when he came back on duty that night, he observed puffiness over and under their eyes and red faces. "They had", he told the Court, "been hammered." By the time he left on the Sunday morning, the prisoners were "all in a petrified state, all physical wrecks" . . . an observation which the photographs of them taken at Queens Road tend to confirm.

Tom Clarke knew when he came to give evidence that he would be discredited as a witness for having been dismissed from the police force for having stolen £5 from a prisoner. He contests that verdict, and having read his papers on the case and spoken to him, I would say there could be a doubt in the matter (it was his word against another's). But he was supported in his Appeal Court evidence by a former member of his first-aid team, a Sergeant Brierley, who said that Clarke had told him within weeks or months of the bombings that cell doors had been banged, the prisoners had been kept standing up and that police dogs had been let into the cell block to bark at them. Another former policeman, Paul Berry, also told the Court of having called in at Queens Road at this time on a routine matter and seeing in the cell block a prisoner "whose left eye and lip were puffed and swollen".

Yet the most impressive witness for the appellants was Joyce Lynas, who was on duty at Queens Road as a police cadet. She gave evidence to the Court on two occasions. On the first she said that on arrival the prisoners were pushed through her office to the cells fairly roughly and had been called "fucking bastards" and "murdering bastards". She also remembered the dog inside the cell block and the cell-door hatches being banged up and down. But she denied having witnessed any prisoners being assaulted.

But a few days later she was back in court to say that she *had* witnessed a prisoner being assaulted. Asked why she had not said so at her first appearance, she said that she had been frightened off by two telephone conversations: the first in the summer when she rang Queens Road to enquire about the *bona fides* of the Devon and Cornwall inquiry and was told by an officer to whom she was put through, "You know what you saw and heard, but remember we have families", and the second, an anonymous call to her home before the hearing began, "Don't forget that you have children." However on the Saturday after her first appearance, she had seen a television programme about bullying in the army and people not reporting it, and after talking to her husband and her minister, she volunteered to return to court, even though it meant having to admit to perjury. This required the same sort of courage as I had witnessed at the trial of Stephen Ward when Ronna Ricardo, having been blackmailed by the police into saying at the Magistrates' Court that Ward had procured clients for her, refused to substantiate it at his trial.

And what new evidence did Joyce Lynas have to offer? Quite simply that when she took tea to officers who were interviewing the prisoners in a room upstairs, she saw two officers holding one by the arms while a third kneed him in the groin. As she entered she heard the third man say, "This is what we do to fucking, murdering bastards," and what she called "other vile words". In court she declined to say what these were, but when I asked her, she told me: "You won't be having sex with your wife again because I'm going to put your balls where your brains are." I asked if she was certain about this, and she said that it was not the kind of thing you could forget.

There was other confirmatory evidence of the prisoners having

been beaten up. Prison officer Brian Sharp of Winson Green was
on duty when they arrived at the prison on the Monday morning.
He said that when Walker undressed, "his torso from the neck to
the middle had numerous amounts of bruising, purple, blackish,
some had tinges of yellow", which he thought were a day or two
old. At the trial of the six, another officer called Murtagh
confirmed this, speaking of "a long yellowing bruise" running
from Walker's waist up across the front of his ribs, and which he
thought was two or three days old. Sharp thought the injuries so
bad that he telephoned for a hospital officer to come down and
examine them.

And then the former Superintendent Reade appeared, the man
who had arrested the six at Morecambe and claimed never to have
touched them, and had to admit that later in his career he had led
a party of officers on a raid in a house at Walsall at which a Mr
Buckley had, in Reade's presence, been punched, kicked and
thrown down the stairs; and Mr Reade had to admit that later Mr
Buckley had sued the police and been awarded £800. Mr Reade
was also found to have altered a document relating to interviews
with the six; and Dr Skuse, too, admitted to altering certain
timings at the police's request.

And how did the three Appeal Court judges respond to the
overwhelming evidence that over a period of three days the
appellants had been assaulted and intimidated by the police
and that their "confessions" were therefore no longer tenable?
Until 1966 it was obligatory on the Court of Appeal when
reaching a decision about new evidence, to put themselves in the
minds of the original trial jury and say what verdict they might
have given in the light of the totality of all the evidence, old and
new. This is the course which Lord Devlin thinks should have
been taken; and had the three judges done so, they must surely
have said that doubts in the minds of the jury would have led to
acquittals for all six. But the judges, as they are now entitled to,
took it on themselves to decide the truth of the facts – an
unfortunate decision for, as lawyers and others have pointed
out, judges are notoriously shaky when it comes to assessing
the facts.

Those who attended the court, and in particular the appellants' counsel, said it was clear from the start that the judges had made up their minds that the appeals were not going to succeed, although even they had not bargained for the manner in which their witnesses would be rubbished. This is what the judges said of them:

Tom Clarke: "a most unconvincing witness and an embittered man. His motive was . . . at first at least to make money and secondly to blacken the reputation of the West Midlands Police Force." (A year later the reputation of the West Midlands Serious Crime Squad had become so blackened that it had to be disbanded.) Whatever Mr Clarke's motives, the judges did not seem to have asked themselves the only question that mattered: were his observations, corroborated by the appellants, true?

Paul Berry: who had glimpsed a prisoner with a puffed and swollen face, was "mistaken". But how could he have been mistaken? All the cells in the cell blocks were occupied by the appellants: there were no other prisoners there.

Brian Sharp: who had said that Walker's body was covered with bruises on his arrival at Winson Green, was, the judges said, trying to conceal or minimize the violence that prison staff and inmates had inflicted on the prisoners and so "forfeited any credibility that he might otherwise have had". But Sharp had no motive to conceal anything: he had been tried for assaulting the appellants and been acquitted. And again, was his evidence true? If the bruises he and Murtagh saw were coloured yellow, purple and black, they must have been a day or two old and therefore incurred at Queens Road rather than Winson Green.

Joyce Lynas: the writer Robert Kee was in court on the day of her second appearance. He wrote in *The Times* that the way in which she gave her evidence "was so totally convincing that had I been a member of a jury asked to judge her credibility there would have been no question in my mind that she was speaking anything but the truth, or that in consequence very considerable doubt attached to the validity of the men's confessions." Richard Ferguson, QC, agreed: "Anyone who heard her give evidence must have known she was speaking the truth." But the judges described her as "a witness not worthy of belief" and her reasons for changing her story "not acceptable". Mrs Lynas is a committed Christian whose character while in the police force was assessed as "Exemplary" and she was upset and angered by these attacks on her integrity. "I did not have to go back," she told me. "I went because I felt I ought to, and I told the absolute truth."

For the judges to declare, in the light of all they had heard, that the original verdicts were *safe* and *satisfactory* seems to me both an abuse of the English language and an insult to anyone's intelligence. So why did they do it? The harsh truth is that just as the CID have corrupted themselves by their readiness to fabricate evidence against those who they have wrongly convinced themselves are guilty, so the judges, otherwise honourable men, have also corrupted themselves by refusing to recognize police fabrication, even when it is staring them in the face.

All that is new about this is that cases like the Guildford Four and the Maguire Seven and the disbandment of the West Midlands Serious Crimes Squad have brought the corruption to the surface. But it is an old story. "British justice is in ruins," said Lord Denning after the release of the Guildford Four. But it had been in ruins for a long time. Judges at trials of first instance, as well as judges in the Appeal Court, have consistently refused to entertain the ideas of police fabrication unless it is so clear cut that they have no alternative. And every judicial inquiry into miscarriages of justice in recent years – Scott Henderson and Brabin in the two Evans inquiries, Fisher in the Confait inquiry, Hawser in the Hanratty inquiry, Hunter in the Meehan inquiry, as well as Lawton and Roskill in the fourth Luton appeal, Roskill at the appeal of the Guildford Four and again of the Maguire Seven – all have preferred to accept dubious police evidence rather than give the people concerned a clean bill of health; and in so doing they have done both themselves and British justice a grave disservice. Lord Hunter spoke for them all when he wrote, "Reliance is rightly placed on the integrity and competence of police officers." He could not bring himself to believe that the police in question had planted incriminating evidence in a dead man's pocket.

It can, I think, only be a matter of time before the Home Secretary decides that it is time for the ordeal of the Birmingham Six to end and for them to receive proper compensation for all their years inside. And when that has happened, the three judges who had the evidence and power to open the prison gates for them and yet failed to do so, and in whose judgment not only the public but some members of their own profession have lost faith, might care, as honourable men, to consider their position. For collectively they have gravely undermined confidence in British justice.

Towards the end of 1990 and as a result of fresh evidence obtained by the Devon and Cornwall Police, the case was once again referred back to the Court of Appeal. As with the appeal of the Guildford Four, the Director of Public Prosecutions [DPP] announced that he would not contest the case, but unlike that of the Guildford Four, the three judges appointed to hear the case decided that they wished to hear the new evidence which, according to the DPP, made the convictions unsafe.

The appeal was heard at the Old Bailey between 4 and 14 March 1991, and was based on two grounds, both forensic. The first was the final discrediting of Dr Skuse's Griess test which expert evidence said was not and never had been specific for nitro-glycerine. When writing my *Sunday Times* piece I had omitted to say that Dr Hugh Black, the former Chief Explosives officer for the Home Office had in fact said this for the defence at the trial. But Mr Justice Bridge had clung to Dr Skuse's findings as though they were holy writ and told Dr Black in no uncertain terms that his opinions were worthless and he was wasting the court's time. Further expert evidence at the appeal supported Dr Black's trial evidence that Dr Drayton's findings on the GCMS test had not proved positive, and in the witness-box she herself confirmed what she had said to me about her findings possibly being "a rogue result".

The second piece of new forensic evidence concerned what has been called the Electrostatic Document Analysis test, or ESDA, which showed that some police officers' statements of interviews with the accused were not contemporaneous as they had claimed at the trial but had been written at different times on different pads with different pens, and that some parts had been added to or altered afterwards; and an interview which the police claimed to have had with McIlkenny was denied by McIlkenny as ever having taken place. Faced with both these heads of new evidence, the judges concluded that had they been available to the trial jury, they must have made a considerable impact. The convictions therefore were unsafe and unsatisfactory, and the appeals would be allowed.

For me one of the most refreshing aspects of the appeal was that, with the Crown having conceded defeat, this was the nearest I had seen in a British court to the inquisitorial system as practised on the continent. In contrast to the impatience and hostility displayed by Lord Lane at the previous appeal, the three judges here (Lloyd, Mustill, Farquharson) really did want to understand what was being put to them, and for the appellants Mr Michael Mansfield, QC, guided them most skilfully through the maze of highly technical forensic evidence. The only sour note came at the end of the submissions when Mr Graham Boal, QC for the Crown, powerless to challenge the new forensic evidence, solemnly told the judges that *circumstantial evidence alone* would have been sufficient to secure convictions against all six. This was not only dotty and untrue but, said in the presence of six men who he knew had just endured sixteen years of wrongful imprisonment, extremely distasteful. But that is the adversarial system for you: in an inquisitorial system such a submission would not be made.

I was sorry that Mr Mansfield did not raise the matter of the Six's allegations that their "confessions" had been beaten out of them by the police, as this partly enabled the judges to belittle the claim by saying there was no evidence that they had suffered any injuries before their first appearance in court, and then to join with Lord Lane's rubbishing of the witnesses at the 1987 appeal who said they *had* seen evidence of injuries inflicted on the Six when they were at Birmingham's Queens Road police station. The new evidence had shown that the Six were not guilty as charged, and if they were not guilty as charged, what other explanation could there be of their "confessions" – which were detailed, varied and contradictory – than that they were beaten out of them by the police?

Afterwards the judgement of Lord Lane and his colleagues in the 1987 appeal was seen to have been so crass and to have so undermined public confidence in the administration of criminal justice that there were many calls for his resignation. *The Times* urged him to take early retirement and more than 140 MPs signed a motion calling on the Queen to remove him from office; but he gave not the slightest indication that he intended to do other than remain where he was; and he would presumably have considered any sort of apology for his ineptitude, *infra dig.* Yet one cannot think of any other profession or business where had the managing director been guilty of similar incompetence (in this instance a further three years incarceration for six innocent men) he would not have been faced with a call for his immediate resignation or dismissal.

Predictably the legal establishment closed ranks. The Lord Chancellor, who had earlier described my *Sunday Times* article as "clamour", made soothing noises about judicial integrity. The Attorney-General said that all judges do is to see that the rules are kept, while former judges such as Sir Frederick Lawton were quick to point out that it is not they but juries who reach verdicts and judges can only be as good as the evidence put before them – conveniently forgetting that judges do not hesitate to discount good evidence they don't agree with, as Bridge did at the trial of the Birmingham Six, as Lane did at their appeal, and as Lawton himself did at one of the Luton appeals. The *Independent* summed it up:

> Instead of taking a hard look at its own failings, the Court of Appeal has sought to exculpate itself. There could be no clearer evidence that judges are temperamentally inclined to protect the legal system rather than the lives of those with

whom it deals. To them the dignity of the law too often seems to be more important than justice itself.

Thankfully the Home Secretary realized that after the cases of the Guildford Four, the Maguire Seven and the Birmingham Six, things could not be allowed to continue as before and announced the appointment of a Royal Commission under Lord Runciman to inquire into the whole criminal justice system; and to make every effort to report within two years.

I cannot think of any public pronouncement in recent times which has given me so much satisfaction. Indeed, with the real possibility it brings of change, I see it as a justification of part of my life's work.

The Birmingham Six were released in March 1991 by the Court of Appeal, which concluded that the prosecution's scientific evidence and confessions taken under duress failed to meet British legal standards. Two years later, the Royal Commission on Criminal Justice under Lord Runciman produced a long string of recommended reforms. But critics complained that subsequent legislation put into effect proposals favourable to the prosecution, and largely ignored those that favoured the defence. Furthermore, it was argued, the new measures seriously encroached on the defendant's right to silence.

THE MYSTERY OF THE FLYING BLOOD

(Dr Sam Sheppard, USA 1954)

Leo Grex

The questions and curiosities in the Sheppard affair have established it as one of the most celebrated murder cases in American history. Dr Sam Sheppard was accused of killing his wife Marilyn, apparently striking her twenty-seven times on the head with a blunt surgical instrument while she was asleep. Sheppard himself blamed the murder on a "bushy-haired intruder" who knocked him unconscious at their home in suburban Cleveland. The bedroom was ransacked and steeped in blood. Sheppard was an immediate suspect and soon arrested. At his trial, an affair with another woman (which he had denied at first) was suggested as the motive for murdering his wife. He was convicted of second-degree murder and sentenced to life imprisonment. But in 1966, aided by his lawyer F. Lee Bailey, Dr Sheppard secured a retrial. Bailey dismissed the prosecution case as "ten pounds of hogwash in a five pound bag". This time, the jury was persuaded of Sheppard's innocence and acquitted him, after an expert reassessed the blood evidence. The case of Dr Sheppard inspired the 1960s TV series The Fugitive. *The author here is Leo Grex, one of several aliases used by Leonard Gribble (1908–86), one of the most prolific British crime writers of all time. As well as producing a torrent of detective fiction, Leonard Gribble wrote nearly seventy factual books on crime and detection, invariably collections of cases with such gung-ho titles as* Famous Stories of Scientific Detection *and* They Had A Way With Women. *"The*

*most appropriate description of Gribble's non-fiction," declared one
critic, "would be that it is enthralling and entertaining; concentrat-
ing as he often does upon the stranger aspects of crime and the more
bizarre cases of murder, they certainly hold the imagination."*

One of the strangest mysteries of America in the fifties was
undoubtedly that of the man most Americans thought of as Dr
Sam after his incredible story had received coast-to-coast publicity. It had resulted in two widely reported trials of sensational
interest for the murder of his wife Marilyn. At least one major
film had been made of the story and several books written about
the mystery, and today, years after Sam Sheppard's death, there
are many who feel that the last word has not been said on the
subject of what happened on a very windy day in July 1954.

It was July 3rd when Dr Sheppard, a popular man of considerable personal charm as well as professional standing as an
osteopath among the people of Bay Village, a small community on
the shores of Lake Erie, decided to mark the forthcoming 4th of
July celebrations with a party for his friends the Aherns. The
visitors consisted of Don Ahern and his wife Nancy and their
children. Like the Sheppards they lived only a short distance
away in West Lake Road, where their garden plot ran down to a
private beach.

It was decided that the Aherns should come to the Sheppards
as Dr Sam, as everyone called him familiarly, had to attend a call
at the local hospital and couldn't get away again for about an
hour. The womenfolk elected to get dinner and wait for him.

The Aherns arrived at about six o'clock, when Marilyn told
Chip, the Sheppards' young son of six, to go out and play with the
Ahern children, leaving the adults to their drinks and gossip.

They all seemed relaxed. Later the two women finished preparing a summer meal while their husbands sauntered down to
the nearby beach after Sam had returned from his hospital visit.

"These white-caps won't make it very smooth for skiing across
the lake," Sam Sheppard mused, watching curling breakers
washing the sand bordering a steep embankment. "There's

another hospital picnic fixed for tomorrow, and if this wind keeps up I don't fancy their chances for a ski run."

Ahern agreed.

"That's the best of sticking to golf," he grinned. "At least you can't drown."

When dinner was announced Don Ahern collected his children and took them home to put them to bed. Then he returned to the women and Dr Sam and the two couples settled down in the comfortable lounge. Chip had already been put to bed. Sheppard switched on the television and tuned to a film, but his eyes drooped. He had performed a tricky operation earlier and felt sleepy. His head slipped back on the couch. The film ended at twelve-thirty and Marilyn, who was four months pregnant, felt as tired as Sam looked.

"I can hardly keep my eyes open," she apologized to the Aherns.

"Well, it's high time we were making tracks," said Nancy. "I'll just look in on the children – oh, and that reminds me, Marilyn," – she went on. "Make sure you latch and chain the front door. One can't be too careful about taking precautions, as I keep telling Don."

Marilyn nodded and said goodnight to her guests, patted her mouth to smother a yawn, and then stood waving to them as she closed the front door. The latch clicked and she switched off the light.

Five hours later a 'phone rang in the home of Bay Village's mayor, Spencer Houk, which was only three houses away from the Sheppard residence.

He woke and scowled at the insistent instrument and threw back the bedclothes.

"Who the devil is it at this hour?" he demanded irritably.

A voice he could only with difficulty recognize as Sam Sheppard's called urgently, "Get over here quick, Spence. My God, they've killed Marilyn!"

"Who – what –" the roused mayor stammered and broke off, for Sheppard had already slammed down the receiver and the only sound was the broken bleeping of the familiar dialling tone.

His wife had already been roused, and the pair, now wide

awake, hurriedly scrambled into their clothes and in little more than ten minutes arrived at the Sheppards' front door, which they found unlocked and wide. It was first light, and on the floor of the hall the mayor saw a doctor's bag which had been up-ended with its contents spilled across the carpet. Sam Sheppard was slumped down in an easy chair by a desk in his den.

"What's this all about, Sam?" inquired the mayor, looking at his wife in puzzlement.

Sheppard groaned, shaking his head.

"I don't know," he said, the words clearing. "But someone ought to look at Marilyn."

Esther Houk climbed the stairs to the first floor, while her husband was taking stock of observable details. Three drawers from the desk had been stacked on the floor and Sam Sheppard was clad only in socks, shoes, and slacks. His torso was bare. As he stepped into the living-room Houk glimpsed a tan corduroy jacket on a settee or couch and saw that the drawers of another desk had been pulled out and a pile of papers was strewn across the floor.

He was interrupted by his wife's hurrying feet on the stairs.

"Get the police!" she called. "And get an ambulance – only hurry!"

The mayor snatched up the 'phone and alerted the police. He then rang Dr Richard Sheppard, Sam's eldest brother, who lived only a short distance away. Uniformed officers were quickly at the scene, and the mayor accompanied them to the bedroom at the top of the stairs, where they found Marilyn lying battered in a blood-soaked bed. More than a dozen heavy blows had smashed her skull, destroying her head. Her face, arms, and upper body had also been bludgeoned. She was sprawled on her back, with her legs dangling over the bed's foot. A stained sheet partly covered the remains. The body was clad in pyjamas, one leg free of the trousers and the top tugged down. There was a copious amount of blood. The brother of Dr Sam took only a few moments to inform the police that his sister-in-law was dead. He was clearly shocked by the brutality of the crime, which was destined to become one of the most notorious mysteries of the age.

Meantime, Dr Sam had collapsed and was removed to hospital, while young Chip, who had slept through his mother's murder, was dressed and hurriedly taken to the home of another of the Sheppard brothers, Dr Stephen Sheppard.

Then the police began their questioning. They heard from the Aherns of the informal party which continued until after midnight, when Nancy Ahern herself secured the door into the yard on the Lake Erie side of the house.

"Marilyn was asleep on her feet. In fact, they both were," she admitted. "I believe Sam went to sleep on the couch, which was why Marilyn didn't waken him. He was bushed after a long day at the hospital."

Dr Sam, the Aherns said, had gone home wearing a white T-shirt, slacks, and the corduroy jacket. They said he was frequently sleepy and given to dozing because of his long hours in the hospital. To the police, after listening to the Aherns' story, it seemed a case of a burglar being disturbed by Marilyn Sheppard and being viciously struck down to prevent an alarm being raised. But a rational enlargement suggested that Dr Sam had been awakened by his wife. He then ran to her aid and was struck down by the intruder, who was by then anxious only to escape.

The coroner agreed with the enlargement when the husband explained that he had been awakened by his wife's cries of "Sam! Sam!" He had rushed upstairs and was met by a blow on the back of the head.

"I was rendered unconscious," he told Dr Samuel Gerber.

He had no idea how long he remained unconscious, but it could not have been long for he came to when he heard a noise in the living-room and ran back downstairs in time to see what he said was "a form" running towards the disturbed waters of the lake. He gave chase to a beach hut where he confronted the mystery man. They struggled and he was knocked down, losing consciousness again and coming to with his face in the lake and his legs in deeper water. When he collected his scattered wits he groped his way back to the house, climbed the stairs, and discovered the horror of the battered Marilyn.

He could hardly credit what had happened and he was incoherent when he rang Houk, but he could not say how long had passed in that wild interval. Later he varied his dramatic story. He told a couple of Cleveland detectives from his hospital bed on the Sunday morning that he now thought there had been two intruders, one who attacked Marilyn Sheppard and a second man who had hammered himself. While recovering consciousness at the head of the stairs he saw his wallet on the floor. In it were three dollar bills and three twenty-dollar notes. When the detectives withdrew he lay listening to the noises of a typical Fourth of July Sunday when everyone seemed to be *en fête*, except the doctor who had lost a wife. His head ached and he fell asleep.

It was Larry Houk, the mayor's son, who made an early find. In some scrub not far from the lake he came upon a green bag containing Dr Sam's automatic winding watch. There were several water drops under the wrist-watch's glass and several dried spots of blood on the band. The green bag, which usually held tools for the doctor's outboard motor, also contained his key-chain and signet ring. The contents of this bag had been spilled on to the floor of the den in the Sheppards' home, and among them lay Marilyn's watch, stained with blood. There was more money in the den and other sums in an upstairs room.

But one seeming discrepancy puzzled the police. The Aherns had reported that Sam Sheppard had gone to sleep wearing a T-shirt under his tan jacket. But when he summoned the Houks he had been stripped naked from the waist up. The corduroy jacket had been neatly folded on the couch.

The detectives broadened their inquiries, but did so discreetly. They had learned that Sam and Marilyn Sheppard had been childhood sweethearts, but that a red-headed hospital technician called Susan Hayes had attracted the doctor's roving eye until she had left Bay Village in February to secure a post in Los Angeles. A month later the Sheppards journeyed to California to attend an osteopathic convention Dr Sam felt was important to his career. But when Sheppard said he had not indulged in an affair with the redhead, it was Susan Hayes who revealed that she had spent a week with him in Los Angeles while Marilyn was staying with another doctor's family near Oakland, some four hundred miles away. Sheppard had bought a watch for the redhead to replace one she had lost at a wedding party attended by both of them. He had also bought her a ring, and she said she had been Dr Sam's lover for more than a year.

While the threads of the Sheppard episode in California were being woven and taking shape Detectives Schottke and Careau in Cleveland were getting down to further details. They asked Sheppard how badly he had been hurt.

"My brother can tell you," said the man whose wife had been murdered brutally. "I'm told that my neck is broken."

Stephen Sheppard said that an X-ray plate revealed that a vertebrae joint in his brother's neck was chipped and that he was suffering from shock and bruises.

"It is possible," he told the police, "that he has suffered brain injury."

At the best it wasn't conclusive.

The post-mortem had given the time of death as somewhere between three and four in the morning, and Sheppard's self-winding watch had stopped at four-fifteen. On the Monday the Cleveland pair returned to ask the man in the hospital bed if he could recall any further details of the man he had chased towards the lake.

Sheppard shook his head and said, "Only that he was a biggish man with bushy hair."

Stephen Sheppard came into the room at this point. He looked serious as he informed his listeners that he had retained counsel for his brother.

"So I can't allow you to ask any further questions," he told the detectives, who shared a glance and withdrew in silence.

A few days later Sheppard, wearing a surgical collar, left the hospital to attend his wife's funeral; he avoided both Press and police. In fact his avoidance of anything in the nature of news or publicity so annoyed the coroner that Gerber threatened him with a subpoena. Possibly due to this on July 10th Sam Sheppard signed a nine-page formal statement in which he stated that his wife "may have tried to awaken him and get him to go to bed." But he was not sure, he said, for he remained on the couch, until he was roused by her cries and heard her moaning. He ran upstairs, sure that she was suffering from a convulsion of the sort she had had in the early days of her pregnancy. But then he was given a blow on the head, which rendered him unconscious until he came to beside Marilyn's bed.

"I looked at my wife," he related. "I believe I felt her pulse and felt that she was gone."

He looked into Chip's room and found him still sleeping, but when he heard a noise downstairs he turned and gave chase. However, the man landed a blow that knocked the doctor out.

Probed about the Sheppards' home life, he claimed it was ideal and firmly denied ever becoming enraged and angry with Marilyn when discussing what he called marital problems. All the same, it was obvious that the questions were becoming more pointed and penetrating the longer the process of asking and answering continued.

"Do you know of any reason why someone else would take her life?" was one rapier-like thrust from which Sheppard flinched visibly.

He wiped his mouth.

"Possibly," he said uncertainly. "I have heard of individuals who are maniacal enough that when they start something, an act like that, it becomes a compulsion." Then more certainly he added, "She has spurned lovers, potential lovers."

There was sudden silence while the coroner considered what had been said.

"How many of these potential lovers did she have?"

"Three I know of, and I am pretty sure more. I am certain that there were more."

While notes were being transcribed he suddenly seemed to take a mental plunge. He named three men. One was Spencer Houk, a second was Dr Hoversten, and the third a distant relative of Marilyn Sheppard. The unravelling threads explained, at least partially, several new facts. For instance, on the 3rd of July it was established that Sam Sheppard had been both preoccupied and morose, but on the 4th, the day of the murder, Dr Hoversten had hastened to Bay Village to express his commiseration with the appalling news of the tragedy. The police had quietly checked his alibi. It could not be faulted. Nor could the alibis of both Houk and Marilyn's relative.

By this time the police were indulging in fresh thoughts about the crime, and a growing query was expressed by them about the possible motive of a husband who could have slaughtered his wife so brutally. For one thing was not explained away. Why had someone apparently taken the trouble to remove so many smudged fingerprints in the Sheppards' home? Who was incriminated and why was a trail of blood cleaned up, howbeit not very thoroughly?

After a further discussion with the police and Dr Gerber the latter announced that a formal inquest would be heard on the 22nd of July. By this time the case was accumulating vast public interest throughout the Middle West, and Sam Sheppard swore on oath that he had not been guilty of murdering his wife nor had he indulged in a love affair with Susan Hayes.

But there was, the police learned, evidence to refute this latter claim and the story of Sheppard's week spent in Susan Hayes's company and the watch lost at a wedding party became current news. The case widened into the dimensions of a *cause célèbre* when Sam Sheppard was arrested for murder and charged. Then began a three-month period before the hearing of the trial in October 1954. The police were busy checking on likely clues, "To sew up the case," as the District Attorney explained to impatient newsmen.

However, there was a good deal of speculation about the merits of the case, and a good many people believed that the popular Dr Sam would be able to clear his name of all imputation in the sordid crime, and as month followed month into the autumn the arguments as to the complicity or otherwise of the doctor grew more voluble and heated.

At last, with the concentrated and riveted gaze of America on the figure of Dr Sam seated at his counsel's table, the trial opened on the 18th of October. The court was crowded to hear the opening words by Judge Edward Blythin, but it did not take long for the first dramatic development. It was provided by the prosecution's first witness, who was Dr Lester Adelson, the deputy coroner. He began by showing a series of colour slides on a screen, including photographs of the terrible wounds inflicted on the victim's smashed head.

They brought an audible gasp from the persons in court, who after showing their revulsion turned to stare at the defendant. Sam Sheppard's shoulders were seen to quiver and tremble beneath the fabric of his neat blue serge. He resolutely turned his gaze away from the slides. Seconds later he broke into convulsive sobbing. But Dr Adelson continued and paid no attention to the side-drama. Using a ruler, he pointed out the thirty-five wounds for the jurors' benefit as he admitted there had been no sex attack on the victim, but turned to declare that "the cause of death is plain enough".

There was utter silence in the court.

Sheppard's counsel, Attorney William J. Corrigan, rose to cross-examine the witness and a wrangle ensued. Adelson admitted that there had been no microscopic study of the various wounds, neither had there been a toxicologist's examination of the victim's internal organs. He made the point that seven gashes in her forehead were just one inch apart and parallel, and he developed the argument that death had been caused by a seven-pronged instrument, and then he insinuated that Marilyn could have been poisoned, and even that she might have drowned in her own blood.

By this time the court was sitting erect.

"It's all circumstantial," he declared waspishly, and said he intended to question every statement made by the prosecution.

The spectators settled down for an intensive session.

Attorney Corrigan claimed he knew what the murder weapon was, but was careful not to define it; he said that a four-month-old male foetus taken from Marilyn's body was not buried with her, but possibly it was for further use in the examination. The cross-examination ground on.

So did the arguments.

For instance, the prosecution insisted that if Sheppard had indeed been knocked out and left unconscious on the beach on a night of growing storm conditions, he would have drowned. But it was Spencer Houk's telling of the 'phone call that produced a real surprise. He claimed that when Richard Sheppard first told Sam that Marilyn was dead the elder brother asked a curious question.

"He said either, 'Did you do this?' or 'Did you have anything to do with this?' and Sam replied, 'Hell, no!'" Houk told the court.

He also claimed that on the day before the inquest he said to Sheppard, "If you did this crime come out and say you did. If it was done by you, it was done in a fit of rage. If you did it, all your family and friends will be behind you."

Sheppard's reply was a dogged, "I couldn't have done it."

However, the defence attorney mounted a special attack on the coroner, whom he claimed had disregarded many clues pointing to Sheppard's innocence. But Dr Gerber came up with a surprise of his own and produced a ghoulish exhibit, a bloodstained pillow removed from the slain woman's bed. He said he had found an impression of a two-bladed instrument, which he said must have been the murder weapon. But the surgical instrument, or whatever it was, had been removed and the pillow turned over. But in contrast, Marilyn's wrist-watch had not been taken off until the blood had dried. In view of Sheppard's claim to have followed the intruder to the beach it seemed extremely unlikely that he would in the circumstances have removed his wife's watch and left it in the den. The case was assuming improbables. Also some snide remarks.

For instance, when Corrigan had asked of the coroner whether there had at any time been a projected divorce and he had replied, "Yes, sir," he had rejoined, "Well, you're divorced, aren't you?"

There had been instant objection by the prosecutor.

"He was asking about divorce," said Corrigan with mock-mildness.

"But his wife wasn't killed," snapped the prosecutor.

"And Dr Sam didn't kill his wife," shouted the defence attorney.

It was a ding-dong legal battle until Susan Hayes appeared, dressed demurely, and related events that occurred in California. She stated in a low voice that she had never seen Sheppard lose his temper, that she had always been aware that he was a married man, and that he only used the word "love" in signing her letters, when he inscribed them, "Love, Sam". Corrigan took the legal bull by the horns and moved for a direct acquittal. But the motion was denied by the judge, and so Dr Stephen Sheppard took the stand as the first of the defence's witnesses, and said, "Sam is the most level-headed one in our family. I have never seen him rise in anger. I have never seen him speak in any way to indicate that he had lost his head. As a child, when he got into arguments, he always refrained from fighting."

He contested the prosecution's evidence at almost every turn, flatly denying that his brother's jacket had been carefully folded and placed on the couch. It had been flung down on the floor. He contended also that his brother had suffered a spinal contusion in his grappling with the intruder, and insisted that police photographs of his sister-in-law's body while on the bed showed both her clothing and an arm in postures and positions different from those he noted upon first seeing her and when he saw her a short time later.

However, on the following day he wavered in cross-examination. Thomas Parrino, the assistant prosecutor, forced him to admit that he had "erred somewhat" in his testimony about the position of the body, but he hedged about the photographs and their actual position. His defensive stand was a prelude to the defendant taking the stand to give his own testimony, which the assembled court awaited with bated breath.

For here was the crux of mystery.

Would the defendant's testimony prove him to be innocent or otherwise?

Garbed in a dark grey suit with a white shirt, and wearing a sober-hued knitted tie, Dr Sam Sheppard turned and addressed his words to the jury. He spoke in a sequence of what many felt were stilted sentences and phrases interspersed with hesitant pauses, so that he cannot be said to have made the best impression on his listeners.

An example was when he referred to his hurry to bring help to his calling wife. The words he chose in such a threatening and dramatic moment fraught with danger sounded contrived and not spontaneous.

"I initiated an attempt," he said, wiping dry lips, "to gather enough senses to navigate the stairs."

Small wonder the jury and other members of the court stared at him with a frown. It was as though he was speaking of a stranger. He told the court that his marriage had always been an ideal one and that he was a man who had welcomed his wife's second pregnancy, refuting all suggestion that he had not wanted the baby.

He was given some help at times by Attorney Corrigan in painting a glowing and warm picture of his marital life with a loving son and contented wife, whom he had no reason to harm. But Parrino, the assistant prosecutor, spoiled the effect of this picture. He asked a number of questions all directed to get Sheppard to admit that it was Marilyn's attacker whom he chased down the stairs and out of the house.

"I had that sensation," was the way Sam Sheppard put it.

But Parrino wanted more than a sensation.

"Did you make any effort to get a weapon?" he demanded.

"No, sir."

"Did you make an outcry?"

"I may have," said Sheppard, hedging again. "I don't know. I have never gone after anyone with a weapon."

Suddenly Parrino changed direction.

"Isn't it a fact that you slapped your wife that morning?"

Again came the flat negative. "No, sir."

The assistant prosecutor slyly posed the next question to inquire expansively, "After you killed her, Doctor, you rushed down those stairs, jumped from the platform on to the beach and fell and injured yourself?"

Sheppard reacted sharply.

"That is absolutely untrue and unfair!"

The needling went on, with the court seemingly mesmerized as were the jury, with the assistant prosecutor listing various items underlining the weaknesses in Sheppard's testimony, including the woman witness who had seen two lights on in the Sheppard home at a quarter past two in the morning of the crime. In rebuttal the defence stressed the defendant's injuries received during the struggle with the intruder, and eventually Judge Blythin summed up a difficult case and the jury filed out to consider their verdict.

They remained debating all aspects of it for a week before the foreman handed a folded paper to a court bailiff who duly offered it to the judge. All eyes were fixed on Edward Blythin as he read the slip of paper and started to read aloud: "We, the jury, find the defendant not guilty of murder—"

There was a stir in court and Dr Sam was suddenly smiling. But the stirring was quelled and the smiling withered as the judge continued – "in the first degree, but guilty of murder in the second degree."

There was a sound like an exhaled overcharged sigh.

Sam Sheppard's eyes went curiously blank, as though actual sight had left them as well as awareness. He made a choking sound, but no words came to his lips. A fearful anti-climax had already begun to set in. It was as though he was seeing a re-run of a secret truth that was not to be shared and must remain a mystery for all time.

Then the judge was speaking again, sentencing Sam Sheppard to imprisonment for life in the Ohio Penitentiary. There was a scramble and the reporters were suddenly busy at a line of telephones, for the trial had been snowballing in mounting interest.

But at last the longest-run trial in US legal history was over. The decision was to be argued to and fro, pro and con, for years, for whatever else the trial had proved it was to be considered inconclusive. But tragedy came to persons concerned with it. A month after Dr Sam was sentenced came the news that his mother had committed suicide. Shortly afterwards his father died. Death followed several other people connected with the case, and a member of the trial jury committed suicide, while until his death in 1961 William J. Corrigan maintained a legal fight to obtain his client's release.

The famous trial lawyer F. Lee Bailey stepped into the dead Corrigan's shoes, and in typical fighting form and fettle vowed he would earn for Sheppard a retrial, and his efforts were successful when the Supreme Court decided that such a hearing should take place as the previous trial had been prejudiced by an hysterical Press campaign.

It was on 24th October, 1966, almost a dozen years later, that Dr Sam arrived in court for yet another hearing to clear his name, and straight away the militant Lee Bailey went into the attack,

claiming that there had never been an opportunity for fingerprints to be taken from the various items listed in the defendant's
possession. But it was a medical technologist whose evidence gave
Bailey pause for special consideration. She was Mary Cowan,
who had examined the contents of the green bag at the time of the
murder. She showed colour photographs to the court of the
contents, and these photographs revealed Sheppard's watch as
it was originally found, spotted with blood. Such spots, she
informed the court, were made by "flying blood". Lee Bailey
had a real task explaining the spots, especially when the prosecutor claimed that they must have got on to the watch while
Sheppard was beating his wife to death.

Bailey spent days trying to overcome this evidence of "flying
blood". He finally claimed there was further evidence of similar
particles on the inside of the watch strap, which meant that they
had got on to it after it had been removed from Sheppard's wrist.
It was a clever legal interpretation and on November 16th, 1966,
the fresh jury accepted his words, and Dr Sam Sheppard was
duly found not guilty.

But by this time he was a broken man, both rejected and
dejected in his former profession, and his marriage to his second
wife, a divorcee, did not last long. He died in 1970.

For years after Dr Sheppard's death his son Sam Reese Sheppard
campaigned to have his father's name cleared. In 1997 he exhumed
his father's body to get genetic material to support his $2 million
lawsuit against the State of Ohio for wrongful imprisonment. DNA
tests on four bloodstains from the 1954 crime scene showed they did
not belong to Dr Sheppard, but did match the genetic make-up of an
odd-job man, Richard Eberling, serving a life term for the murder of
a widow in 1984. As we have seen, Dr Sheppard consistently blamed
a "bushy-haired intruder" who knocked him unconscious during the
attack on his wife.

MURDER IN DEPTFORD

(The Stratton Brothers, UK 1905)

Jurgen Thorwald

Fingerprinting was used as a weapon of detection as early as 1890, but it was some years before the science of dactyloscopy became accepted in a court of law. In 1902, following the theft of billiard balls in Denmark Hill, south London, the culprit was identified from the print of his left thumb and was convicted largely on this evidence. The first murder trial to turn on fingerprints was in 1905, when a couple named Farrow were found brutally murdered at their shop in Deptford. The investigation was personally supervised by Scotland Yard's CID chief Melville Macnaghten. Beyond two black stocking masks, the only clue was a cash box made of black tin, which had been broken open. On it was a single mark which looked like that of a finger or thumb. Two brothers called Stratton were arrested and fingerprinted: the mark on the cash box exactly matched the print of the right thumb of the elder brother. But the judge at their trial urged caution. He pointed out that the fingerprint evidence was the strongest point in the prosecution's case. The resemblance between the two prints was certainly remarkable, but he warned the jury to take the whole of the evidence together in reaching a verdict. They did, and the Strattons were convicted. They were hanged together, blaming each other. Jurgen Thorwald (b. 1916) has written several award-winning books on the history of crime and science. Born Heinz Bongartz, he adopted the pseudonym Jurgen Thorwald to avoid harassment in Soviet-occupied Germany while researching a book after World War II; the book did so well that he took it as his legal name in 1949. Thorwald now lives in Switzerland.

The streets of Deptford, a drab borough of south-eastern London on the south bank of the Thames, were still almost empty at 7.15 a.m. on 27 March 1905. A milkman saw two young men rush out of a small paint shop at 34 High Street and vanish around a corner. They were in such a hurry that they did not close the shop door behind them.

The milkman paid little attention. Life in Deptford was rough and ready; people did not meddle with each other more than they could help.

About ten minutes later a little girl came walking along the High Street. She saw a man with blood all over his clothes who thrust his head out the door of the paint shop, but immediately withdrew and locked the door from inside. The child was not particularly surprised by this sight. Blood flowed in streams in the slaughter-houses of Deptford – bloody faces and smocks were a commonplace in these streets.

It was not until 7.30 a.m. that a boy sounded the alarm. He worked as an apprentice in the paint shop. When he went to work he found the door locked – an unusual circumstance. His employer, Mr Farrow, a kindly old man past seventy, always rose very early to serve the painters who stopped in on their way to their jobs to buy paint or tools. So the door was always open when the apprentice arrived. But this morning it was locked, and there was no response when the apprentice rang the bell. Finally he climbed over the wall of the adjacent property into the courtyard. He glanced through the rear window – and ran screaming for help into the nearest store.

Detective Inspector Fox, accompanied by several detectives, arrived at the High Street within twenty minutes. Shortly afterwards Melville Macnaghten in person appeared.

The small room behind the shop, which served as office and storage space, presented a picture of total devastation. All the furniture had been overturned. Drawers were pulled out, blood was everywhere. Old Farrow lay on the floor in a crumpled heap, barely recognizable as a human being. His bloody head rested on the hob of the fireplace. Under his trousers and jacket the old man was still wearing his nightshirt. From the numerous traces of blood in the shop and on the narrow staircase that led to the upper floor, Fox concluded that Farrow had come down from his bedroom to serve what he must have assumed to be an early customer. He must have been attacked and knocked down in the shop. Apparently the old man had succeeded in pulling himself to his feet and had attempted to keep the murderer (or murderers?) from going upstairs, where Mrs Farrow was asleep. A large pool of blood on the stairs plainly indicated where he had collapsed for the second time. Yet, incredibly, he seemed to have got up again, this time after the assailants had fled. He had crawled to the still open door and looked out. Perhaps he had wanted to call for help. But then, since there was no one in sight, he had bolted the door from inside – perhaps fearing another attack. Then he must have dragged himself into the back room, where death had overtaken him.

In the bedroom upstairs lay Mrs Farrow, a feeble old woman, her head crushed. She was still breathing and was taken to the Greenwich hospital, where she died four days later, without having been able to say a word.

Meanwhile, Fox had discovered two masks made out of women's black stockings. He concluded from this that there must have been two assailants. At first it seemed that they had left no other clues. But then a small money-box was found under Mrs Farrow's bed. It had been broken open and everything but a sixpenny piece taken. From an account slip in the box the detectives concluded that the loot had amounted to no more than £9. Macnaghten, who was closely connected with the development of dactyloscopy, at once examined the money-box for fingerprints. Sure enough, there was a significant smudge on its smoothly varnished inner surface. He promptly ordered Fox and his men, as well as Farrow's distraught apprentice, who were waiting in the shop, to come upstairs. He asked whether any of them had touched the money-box. A young sergeant spoke up with some embarrassment. He had pushed the box further under the bed, so that the stretcher-bearers who had carried Mrs Farrow out would not stumble over it.

Macnaghten had the box carefully wrapped and taken at once to Chief Inspector Collins. The young sergeant was also sent to the fingerprinting division. To make perfectly sure, Macnaghten also had the fingerprints of the apprentice and the two victims taken. (This was the first time that the fingerprints of a corpse had ever been taken in London.) Then Macnaghten informed his superior, Edward Henry, of his actions. Both men tensely awaited the results of the investigation.

Collins reported the following morning. The smudge on the money-box was a thumbprint. It did not correspond with the prints of the apprentice, the victims, or any of the police officers at the scene. Its mate had not been found among the 80,000 fingerprints so far on record. Collins' report concluded with the statement that the print on the money-box proved to be, when photographically enlarged, unusually clear. Should the person who had made this print be arrested, he could be identified without the slightest difficulty.

Meanwhile Fox had begun a house-by-house investigation of the neighbourhood. In the course of it he spoke with a young woman named Ethel Stanton. At approximately the same time as the milkman, she had seen two young men running up the High Street, one of them wearing a brown overcoat. And one of Fox's detectives, eavesdropping in a Deptford pub, overheard a discussion of the murder, in which the names of two brothers, Alfred and Albert Stratton, were mentioned as being "capable of it".

Alfred and Albert Stratton were not altogether unknown to Scotland Yard, although as yet they had never been arrested. Respectively twenty-two and twenty, they were considered good-for-nothings who had never found employment but lived off various girls and women. They had no regular address. Nevertheless, within a few days Fox learned that Albert Stratton had taken lodgings in a shabby house on Knott Street. His landlady, Mrs Kate Wade, was thoroughly afraid of her lodger: that came to light when the detectives questioned her. Once, in cleaning Stratton's room she had come upon several masks made of black stockings hidden under the mattress. Fox also learned that Albert Stratton's brother Alfred had a mistress named Hannah Cromarty. He found the girl living in a wretched room on the ground floor of a house in Brookmill Road. The room's single window gave on to the street. The girl showed traces of a recent beating. Sure enough, Alfred Stratton had beaten her, and she was furious enough to "squeal". He came whenever he felt like it, she said, and she had to do as he said. He had slept with her on Sunday night. Late in the evening a man had come to the window, and Alfred had talked with him. Later, towards morning, there had been a knock at the window, and Alfred had dressed. Then she had fallen asleep. When she awoke, it was broad daylight, and Alfred was standing in the room, fully dressed. He had done this often before, she said, departing through the window at night and coming back the same way. This time he had warned her that if anyone asked she must say that he had spent the entire night with her and had not left until Monday morning, after nine o'clock.

Hannah Cromarty added one significant detail. Since that night, Alfred no longer had his brown coat. When she asked where it was, he had told her harshly that he had given it to a friend. Also, he had dyed his brown shoes black.

Macnaghten issued orders for the arrest of the Stratton brothers, wherever they were found. A first attempt to surprise them at a soccer match in the Crystal Palace failed. Meanwhile Hannah Cromarty vanished from her room. But on the following Sunday Alfred was captured in a pub, and his brother was caught the next day. Both of them were strapping young men with brutal faces. They made a great ruckus when they were brought into the Tower Bridge police station. Macnaghten was well aware that the evidence Fox had gathered would never suffice to secure an indictment. But he wanted to have their fingerprints.

The old police magistrate who had to decide whether the Strattons were to be held proved, in fact, to be scarcely impressed by Fox's arguments. How much evidence did he have? The gossip-mongering of a landlady and a loose woman! But after a good deal of argument back and forth, he agreed to let the suspects be held for a week, and fingerprinted. He had heard only the vaguest rumours about dactyloscopy, and was curious to see it in action. Collins came forward with his apparatus. The Stratton brothers were highly amused when their fingers were blackened and pressed against the filing cards. It "tickled", they innocently blustered.

Macnaghten recorded in his memoirs: "I had returned to the office in the forenoon, and shall never forget the dramatic entry made into my room by the expert an hour or two later. 'Good God, sir,' he exclaimed, with pardonable excitement, 'I have found that the mark on the cash-box tray is in exact correspondence with the print of the right thumb of the elder prisoner.' "

Alfred was the elder of the brothers. Henry, who had since become Police Commissioner of London, was informed immediately. He at once got in touch with the prosecutor, Richard Muir. For he saw that this case was as if made to order to dramatize the usefulness of fingerprinting. The eyes of all England would be upon the trial of the Stratton brothers – for the whole country had been shocked by the brutal murder.

Richard Muir went to Scotland Yard for a lesson in fingerprinting by Macnaghten and Collins. He arrived just in time to learn that the Stratton brothers had been shown to the milkman who had seen two men running out of Farrow's shop on the day of the murder. The milkman had failed to recognize them. Ethel Stanton, however, was prepared to swear that Alfred Stratton had been one of the two running men. Thus the one witness weakened the case, the other reinforced it. The only tangible evidence was the thumbprint on the money-box.

Muir realized fully how frail his case was. Everything would stand or fall on the fingerprint question. Would the jury accept a fingerprint as conclusive evidence, or as any kind of evidence at all? Muir mulled over the problem for two days before he made his decision. Then he announced his willingness to prosecute Alfred and Albert Stratton.

The arraignment took place in the Tower Bridge police court on 18 April. Two policemen stood guard over Muir's table, on which stood the money-box. Muir himself watched that money-box like a hawk. He knew that the judge and jurymen knew too little about the whole procedure of fingerprinting to accept a mere photograph of the thumbprint. He needed the original. "Careful, don't touch," he warned everyone who came near. "There are fingerprints on it."

Collins waited beside Muir, prepared to expound on the science of fingerprinting. The Strattons' lawyer let it be known that if the case were brought to trial, he would call two experts to the witness stand to prove that Henry's fingerprint system was

undependable. He did not give the names of his experts. Muir
and Collins racked their brains wondering who these mysterious
experts could be. How many persons in England had the faintest
knowledge of the subject?

They obtained their indictment, and on 5 May Alfred and
Albert Stratton appeared in the dock at the Old Bailey, with
Judge Channell on the bench. This was the judge's first experience with dactyloscopy; the jurymen had also never heard of the
technique. Booth, the defendants' lawyer, had selected two
barristers to plead the case, Curtis Bennett and Harold Morris,
the former of whom was to reach the front ranks of British
jurisprudence during the next few decades. It was not they,
however, who presented any particular threat. Muir kept glancing at two other persons who had taken seats beside them. The
secret of the counter-experts was out. The first of the men was Dr
Garson, who had so long argued the cause of *bertillonage* and had
then developed his own, quite inadequate fingerprinting system.
He had been worsted in the rivalry with Henry. Did he mean to
discredit the system which had proved better than his own?

Beside Garson, however, sat Dr Henry Faulds! Through a
chain of unlucky accidents, the name of this man, who had first
solved a crime by means of fingerprints found at the scene, had
been overshadowed by the names of Herschel, Galton, and
Henry. Ever since Galton had hailed Herschel as the discoverer
of fingerprinting, Faulds had been bitterly fighting to wrest from
the other man the fame he felt was rightly his. He had grown
more and more paranoiac about the whole situation and by now
believed there had been a conspiracy to deprive him of his
priority. Over the years he had abandoned all moderation; in
articles, open letters, and pamphlets he not only tried to prove his
priority in on-the-scene fingerprints – for which he undoubtedly
deserved the credit – but also for the discovery of finger-printing
in general. Was he going to testify against fingerprinting out of
blind spite – and thus, at bottom, repudiate his own discovery?

Muir glared at his antagonists. When he stood up to speak, a
hush fell over the courtroom. As Muir's biographer, Felstead,
later wrote:

In the hundreds of murder cases in which he prosecuted for the Crown, Muir never revealed such animosity towards prisoners in the dock as he did towards the two Strattons. He looked upon it as the most brutal crime he had ever come across, saying that the manner in which the faces of the poor old couple had been battered about made it quite impossible to extend the slightest human consideration towards the murderers. He spoke perhaps even more slowly and deliberately than usual, but with a deadly effect which made the men in the dock look at him as though he, and not the judge, might at any moment order their execution.

And a Sunday newspaper wrote: "His words rang out as though it was the execution bell at Newgate prison tolling."

Muir called up his parade of witnesses, such as Kate Wade and Ethel Stanton. From their testimony, he constructed a complete picture of the murder, even to the preparations for the alibi. Only after he had presented the whole picture did he bring up the fingerprint. He pointed to the money-box and declared: "There is not the shadow of a doubt that the thumbprint on this money-box, which once belonged to the murdered Mr Farrow, comes from the right thumb of the defendant Alfred Stratton."

Then he called Collins to the witness stand. Behind Collins was a large blackboard, so that Collins could clarify some of his points by means of sketches. Collins gave an even more convincing exposition than he had done three years earlier in the case of the burglar Jackson. He displayed the greatly enlarged photographs of the thumbprint on the box, and set beside it the print which had been taken of Alfred Stratton's thumb. He pointed out that the two prints were identical on at least eleven counts. There was a deep hush over the court while Collins spoke.

The cross-examination by Booth and Bennett quickly exposed the weakness of their position. They themselves were totally without experience in the field of dactyloscopy, and had leaned upon Faulds and Garson without realizing the irrational hatreds that motivated these men. Innocently and in good faith they argued a theory Faulds had suggested to them. Collins' photographs showed discrepancies, they said, which were obvious to any careful eye and demonstrated irresponsible negligence on the part of Scotland Yard.

The discrepancies they made so much of were those small differences which must occur when fingerprints are taken because it is impossible always to roll the fingers over the paper with the same pressure. Muir and Collins met this with a dramatic demonstration. Collins took the thumbprints of the jurymen several times in succession. He then showed the jury that the prints contained the same "discrepancies" which the defence insisted invalidated the prosecution's case. Each juryman was able to convince himself with his own eyes that these differences had nothing to do with the characteristic patterns which alone mattered. The cavillings of the defence were shattered. Moreover, a violent altercation broke out between Booth and Dr Faulds, with the latter relapsing into grim silence.

Troubled and uncertain, their faith in their experts severely reduced, Booth and Bennett hesitated to call Dr Garson to the witness stand. Perhaps, too, they saw a spark in Muir's eyes that suggested he might have a surprise in store and was prepared to annihilate Garson in cross-examination. But at last, for lack of any other ammunition, the defence decided to call Garson after all.

That decision proved even more fatal than their reliance on Dr Faulds. Muir produced a letter. Had Dr Garson written this letter to him? he asked rhetorically. In this letter had not Dr Garson proposed to aid the prosecution as an expert in fingerprints, before he offered his services to the defence? How did Dr Garson wish to explain this duplicity?

Everyone understood Muir's unspoken charge: that Dr Garson had been prepared to testify the exact contrary of his testimony for the defence, if the prosecution had been willing to have him and feed his self-importance. Garson threw one nervous look around the courtroom. Then he replied defiantly: "I am an independent witness." He was not allowed to go on. "I would say," Judge Channell interposed, "a completely untrustworthy witness . . ." He ordered Garson to leave the stand.

That was Muir's victory. In his instructions to the jury, Judge Channell cautiously observed that the fingerprint should certainly be regarded as valid evidence to a certain measure. The jury retired for only two hours. When they filed back, another suspense-filled hush descended upon the courtroom. Then the spokesman pronounced the verdict: Guilty. Judge Channell condemned Alfred and Albert Stratton to death by hanging. And the torrent of mutual abuse that burst from the two of them proved that they richly deserved their punishment.

The Stratton trial was a first milestone on the road to full legal recognition of dactyloscopy. Henry's system spread through Great Britain, Scotland, Ireland, and the British dominions and colonies. Concurrently, it began to be adopted all over Europe and throughout the inhabited globe.

THE COPPOLINO CASE

(Dr Carl Coppolino, USA 1965)

James A. Brussel

Carmela Coppolino died suddenly, allegedly after receiving a fatal dose of the "undetectable" drug succinylcholine chloride at the hands of her husband, an anaesthetist. Dr Carl Coppolino had become infatuated with Marjorie Farber, the attractive middle-aged wife of a retired army colonel who also died suddenly after being attended by Dr Coppolino. The bodies of both the wife and the colonel were exhumed. A needle puncture was found on Carmela's body, and the colonel showed signs of having been strangled. Coppolino was tried for the murder of both, and after much confusing and conflicting forensic evidence was found guilty of second-degree murder and sentenced to life imprisonment. For Dr Milton Helpern, the chief medical examiner of the City of New York, it was "the most extraordinary case ever to come my way." Coppolino gambled on his chosen weapon of murder, succinylcholine chloride, being impossible to detect. But he overlooked the fact that science is constantly pushing back the frontiers of ignorance in the fight against crime. Coppolino's story is told by James A. Brussel, a psychiatrist and criminologist, described as "the Sherlock Holmes of the couch". He came to public attention in 1957 in the case of New York's notorious Mad Bomber. Author Gerold Frank believed that Dr Brussel's ability to study a crime and from it reconstruct the criminal gave him a charmed name in police circles.

It started, as most of my adventures seem to do, with a phone call. It came on a dismal gray morning in December, 1966. The caller was Teri Plaut, Lee Bailey's charming girl Friday. She said: "Doctor, get down here as soon as possible."

By "down here" she meant Freehold, New Jersey, where her boss was at that moment appearing as defence counsel in one of the most bizarre criminal trials of the 1960s. I knew from reading the papers that this new trial was now in its second day. Something unexpected must have happened to make Lee Bailey call on me so suddenly. Normally he is a man who plans ahead, outlines his trial strategy, and lines up his witnesses well in advance of any court appearance. I had learned this while working with him on the Boston Strangler case. What was going on? What did he need me for?

Intrigued, I hastily reviewed my day's schedule in my mind. There was nothing on my calendar that couldn't be postponed. "All right," I told Teri, "I'll be there by noon."

"Wonderful" she said. She sounded relieved. "Mr Bailey will be grateful."

"Maybe he won't be when he gets my bill," I said.

"Pardon?"

"Nothing. I'll see you later."

And thus I entered the strange, baffling, multifaceted case of Dr Carl Coppolino. By the time my part in it had ended, I wished my phone had been out of order on that December morning. The Coppolino case was one of very few I've come up against in which I never formed a clear idea of who the criminal was – or, indeed, precisely what crime or crimes, if any, had been committed. It was perhaps the most mystifying case of my career. It was a case made of shadowy half-truths and vague suppositions, a case involving many people behaved in devious, sometimes inexplicable ways. Many lies were told, but it was hard to expose them as such. Undoubtedly, some truths were also told, but they were impossible to prove. In the end, as still today, there were as many theories about the case as there were people trying to get to the bottom of it.

Some of the cases I've worked on have been relatively simple and straightforward. I tell the Coppolino story to show that it isn't always so, to demonstrate just how complicated human circumstances can become.

In the early 1960s a housing developer bought a large expanse of gently rolling woodland and meadowland in suburban Middletown, New Jersey. Planning with care in order to save as many of the larger trees as possible, he carved out roadways and mapped plots for houses in the $35,000 price range. He called the section Fox Run. It was to be a development for people in the upper-middle-income bracket.

Buyers came quickly, for Fox Run showed promise of maturing into an attractive neighbourhood. They were people from varying social and economic backgrounds. Many of the men were commuters to Manhattan. Perhaps the developer wondered, as he met them, how they would get along as neighbours.

One plot of land, at 35 Wallace Road, was bought by a family named Coppolino. The Coppolinos were both physicians. Dr Carl Coppolino was a lean, dark, intensely nervous man of thirty with heavy black eyebrows and a prominent beak of a nose; he was a full-time anaesthesiologist at a nearby hospital. Carmela Anne Coppolino, twenty-nine, was a slim, attractive, dark-haired woman with an outwardly calm, sunny disposition. She worked at a pharmaceutical laboratory in Nutley, New Jersey. The Coppolinos had two children.

While the Coppolinos' new colonial-style house was rising, another house was taking shape diagonally across the street. This house, at 50 Wallace Road, was being built for a somewhat older couple named Farber. Lieutenant Colonel William Farber, fifty, was a medalled war veteran who had recently retired from the Army. He was drawing disability pay because of a heart ailment. He now held an executive job in a New York insurance office. He was a stocky man with a square, good-humoured face. His wife, Marjorie, looked far younger than he, though she was in fact forty-seven. She was a former divorcée. She had a round, pretty face and a figure that any college girl would have been proud of. The Farbers had two daughters.

Fox Run gradually changed from a sea of mud to a well-tended neighbourhood. The houses were finished. Families moved in and began to turn the houses into homes. Terraced lawns and shrubs covered the bulldozed earth. Slowly, families got to know each other.

The Coppolinos and Farbers met at a neighbourhood party and took an immediate liking to one another. Through late 1962 and the winter and spring of 1963, the foursome got together almost every weekend. Sometimes with other couples and sometimes not, the four played cards, dined, and went to parties and the theater. They became the nucleus of a social clique typical of upper-middle-class suburban neighbourhoods. At least, for a while, it seemed typical.

But changes were taking place – some of them overt, some beneath the surface. Signs of dissatisfaction were beginning to show in the Farber household. Colonel Farber, who had seen enough action in World War II and Korea to last a lifetime, had hoped that his new life in Fox Run would give him peace and quiet. Though he was an affable man, he didn't want to spend every evening and weekend on a merry-go-round of social activity. For much of the time, he preferred to be left alone, puttering in the tranquil solitude of his garden. His wife, Marge, wanted to be out where the action was. She grew increasingly restless, took lessons in golf and interior decorating; joined a riding club, more and more often went to parties without her husband.

In the Coppolino household, there were more abrupt changes. Carl came home one day and announced to the neighbourhood that he had resigned his hospital post because of a heart ailment. The heart ailment may have been a partial cause of his resignation, but there was in fact another that he didn't tell the neighbours about (and that came out later in court); he had become involved in a bitter quarrel with a nurse anaesthetist, and had sent her a threatening letter. The contents of this letter and circumstances of the quarrel have never been revealed, but somehow the FBI became involved. Fearing unfavourable publicity, the hospital authorities decided to end their relationship with Coppolino.

He did not seek another post. Instead, he and his wife (Carm, he called her) went to work on a book about alcoholism, *The*

Billion Dollar Hangover. She kept her daytime laboratory job and helped Carl with the book each night.

During the days, with Carmela and Colonel Farber away at work, Carl Coppolino and Marge Farber saw each other frequently. They made an odd pair. Marge was vivacious, outgoing, a woman who loved to be where there were lots of people and lots of noise. Carl had always been a singularly quiet man. In fact, as *Newsweek* later reported, he had been so shy and retiring at Fordham University that the editors of his class yearbook could think of only one thing to say about him beyond the bare outline of his biography: "He specialized in chemistry." Yet the lively Marge Farber was strongly attracted to this darkly taciturn man.

One thing led to another. At first he used to go to her house, or she to his, to discuss his book. She was a former alcoholic and had belonged to Alcoholics Anonymous. She occasionally chauffeured him around town when he complained that his heart ailment made him feel too weak to drive. Marge was a heavy smoker; and one day – following a laughing suggestion from Carmela – Carl offered to help her break the habit through a series of treatments with hypnosis. He hypnotized her several times, and she did in fact stop smoking for a while. In repayment, Marge – an accomplished amateur artist – painted his portrait.

Carl and Marge became lovers. This much is known. Very little else about the subsequent events is known for sure.

Did Colonel Farber and Carmela Coppolino know what went on at Fox Run while they were away at work? Perhaps not. Perhaps, on the other hand, they did know – and didn't care. They certainly behaved with supreme nonchalance. One winter night, while the four were sitting around drinking coffee and chatting, Carl remarked that he'd like to go to Florida for a few weeks to hasten his convalescence and perhaps speed up work on his book. Since his wife couldn't leave her job, he said, wouldn't it be a good idea if Marge were to go with him and take care of him? Strangely, the suggestion carried both houses unanimously. And so, early in 1963, Carl and Marge went off to Florida while their spouses cheerfully stayed home in Fox Run. To some of the neighbours, this seemed to be carrying broad-mindedness to an extreme.

Suntanned and happy, the two lovers came home to Fox Run a few weeks later, and life went on more or less as before. Carl spoke in ecstatic tones of Florida. While there, he told neighbours, he had looked around at some properties with an idea of buying or building a home there one day. He particularly liked the idea of living on one of Florida's coastal islands or keys. The seclusion of island life appealed to him.

On July 30, 1963, Lieutenant Colonel William Farber suddenly died in his home.

Understandably, people panic at times like that; they become disoriented and confused, later cannot recall precisely what happened. Such was the case when Farber died. Nobody seemed quite sure, later, who had done what during the hour or so after the tragedy. All that is known for certain is that Carmela went to the Farbers' house and, in her capacity as a physician, made out the death certificate. She listed the cause of death as coronary thrombosis.

Now there were three. The trio stayed together, attended cocktail parties and even church as a group. The neighbours thought it was good of the Coppolinos thus to take Marge under their wing in her bereavement.

In the spring of 1965, Carl Coppolino finally realized his dream of living in Florida. He and Carmela sold their house in Fox Run and moved into a modest but pretty white stucco house on fashionable Longboat Key, near Sarasota. Marge Farber seemed unable to get along without them. Two months later, she, too, sold her house in Fox Run and with her two daughters moved into a house next door to the Coppolinos on Longboat Key.

On August 28, 1965, Carmela Coppolino abruptly died in her home at the age of thirty-two. Dr Juliette Karow, a Sarasota physician, was called in to complete the death certificate. She talked to Carl, who (she said later) told her Carmela had been suffering chest pains the day before. He said he had found her dead in bed that morning. Dr Karow examined the body and listed the cause of death as coronary occlusion.

Now there were two.

Or so Marge may have thought. Unhappily for her, however, Carl was no longer the ardent lover he had been in Fox Run. He

and Carmela had been going out socially without Marge, and he
had been looking appreciatively at other women. One, whom he
had met at a bridge game, was a pretty, dark-haired, thirty-eight-
year-old divorcée named Mary Gibson. Mary later testified in
court that her income was a mere, $8,000 to $10,000 a year, but
she was rumoured to have won an enormous lump-sum divorce
settlement and she owned an elegant villa in the wealthy Forest
Lakes Country Club area of Sarasota. Six weeks after Carmela's
death, Carl married Mary Gibson and moved into her villa.

Now there was only one: Marge Farber, lonely and stranded on
Longboat Key. How did she feel? Angry, certainly. Full of hate
for Carl, who had jilted her? Perhaps. The question of what went
on in Marge Farber's mind later became an important one, but it
was never answered completely.

What is known is that, late in 1965, she talked to Carmela's
father and to Sarasota County Sheriff Ross Boyer. She said there
was "something odd" about Carmela's death – and also about
Colonel Farber's death two years before.

Boyer listened to her story. It seemed to him (as to others later)
that she was highly confused; the story she told was internally
inconsistent, full of holes and implausibilities. Moreover, when
asked to repeat parts of the story, she told it a different way each
time. All the same, Sheriff Boyer felt that some checking into the
story was warranted. He couldn't just file the story and forget it.
It was too shocking. Marge Farber was accusing Carl Coppolino
of murder.

Sheriff Boyer began a discrete investigation that slowly widened and deepened until it included police authorities in both
Florida and New Jersey. The bodies of Colonel Farber and
Carmela Coppolino were disinterred. Physicians, chemists, and
other experts examined the corpses and gave their opinions. The
case exploded into the public news media. It was a sensational
story that could be played large on page one – a story of sex and
murder in a high-income suburb.

Murder? Well, possibly. It was hard to say for sure.

The main theme of Marge Farber's story was that her husband
– and, she suspected, also Carmela – had been murdered with a
drug called succinylcholine chloride. As an anaesthesiologist,

Carl Coppolino would have been well acquainted with this drug. According to Marge, he had talked several times about it as an ideal weapon for murder – one which, he said, would be impossible to trace in a dead body and would leave no outward evidence of its having been the cause of death. In one version of her story, Marge said that Carl had handed her a lethal dose of the drug and that she, acting on his instructions, had injected it into her husband. In another version, she said that she had stood by while Carl injected it. In still another version, she said the drug didn't kill her husband fast enough, and she and Carl had suffocated him with a pillow.

Which version, if any, was true? Nobody could find out. There is no doubt that succinylcholine chloride could be used for murder. It is a common drug, available to physicians under various trade names such as Sucostrin (Squibb) and Anectine (Burrough Wellcome). It is packaged as a white powder which when it is to be used, is introduced into a glass container of sterile fluid. It can be given either by hypodermic injection or intravenous drip. Its main effect is muscle relaxation. In psychiatry, we use light dosages of it during electric shock therapy. Heavier dosages are used in surgery, dosages that would be lethal if there were no anaesthesiologist present to counter their effects. In these dosages, the drug renders all the patient's muscles completely flaccid – including the muscles that are used for breathing. The patient can no longer breathe for himself; the anaesthesiologist keeps him alive by pumping gases in and out of his lungs. Without this artificial breathing aid the patient would die very quickly, looking relaxed and peaceful.

Did Colonel Farber and Carmela Coppolino die this way? Examining the body tissues, some experts thought they detected chemical residues of succinylcholine chloride. But other experts, equally eminent, thought they found evidence that both the colonel and Carmela had died of heart attacks, as the death certificates said.

There was circumstantial evidence against Carl Coppolino, however. He had had access to supplies of succinylcholine chloride before both deaths. He had been in the neighbourhood at the time of both deaths. Moreover, it turned out, Carmela had increased her life insurance coverage shortly before her death. It wasn't a big boost, from $50,000 to $65,000. But it was enough to add to the mounting suspicion.

In July 1966, a New Jersey grand jury returned an indictment against Carl Coppolino, charging that he had murdered Colonel Farber. A few days later, a Florida grand jury charged him with murdering his wife.

In December, 1966, his first trial opened at Freehold, New Jersey.

I'd been following this sensational and confusing case as it developed in the newspapers. As a psychiatrist, I'd been particularly interested in the question of motive.

Why would Carl Coppolino have wanted to kill Colonel Farber? Because Carl wanted to have Farber's wife for himself? This was the suggestion being offered in the newspapers; yet, to me, it didn't quite add up. Carl was having his way with Marge Farber even though Colonel Farber was alive. Why take the risk of committing murder? Even if Carl were passionately in love with Marge, would the risk have been necessary I wondered. And, as Carl later demonstrated by marrying Mary Gibson, he was not passionately in love with Marge. In what way, then, did he profit by the colonel's death?

And what of his wife? The alleged motive in this case seemed a little more clear-cut. It was suggested that he had killed her so that he could marry Mary Gibson, share Mary's wealth, and simultaneously collect Carmela's $65,000 life insurance benefit. But the evidence was circumstantial and leaky.

Marge Farber's motives were still harder to fathom. It was generally supposed that she felt bitterly vengeful toward Carl and that this was why she had blown the whistle on him. In fact, Lee Bailey's main strategy in defending Carl Coppolino was to portray Marge Farber as a woman scorned – a woman who would make up fantastic fictions in order to get revenge. Yet, in some versions of her ever-changing story, she implicated herself in the murder of her husband: told of injecting the lethal drug into him or of helping suffocate him with a pillow. If the story were fiction, why did she thus jeopardize herself?

Perhaps to make the story more believable? To give it an "I was-there" quality?

It seemed possible. Assume for a moment, as Lee Bailey hoped to show, that Marge had made up the whole story. Picture her being questioned over and over again by police officers. She is in a highly emotional state, bitterly angry at Carl, eager to punish him at almost any cost to herself. To make her accusation of murder seem like more than conjecture, she says, "All right, I'll admit it. I was in the room when he killed my husband. In fact, I *helped*."

Later, perhaps, she would regret having implicated herself thus. But, at the time, in her passionate eagerness to hurt the man who had jilted her, it may have seemed like the only thing to do.

This was merely conjecture on my part. Marge's story may have been wholly or partly true. And yet . . .

And yet, if it were true in part, why did she keep changing it? Her explanation was that she had been frightened and confused at the time of her husband's death – so much so that she couldn't remember sequences of events clearly nor separate fact from her own bewildered imaginings. Such a mental state is conceivable. People's recollections are seldom clear after some terrifying event – a fact that irritates the police when questioning witnesses to a crime. There are often as many diverse versions of the story as there are witnesses. Thus Marge could have been simply confused. On the other hand, as Lee Bailey hoped to show, she could have been lying deliberately in some versions of the story or in all versions.

Either way, it was impossible to know the truth. Had Carl alone murdered the colonel? Had Marge helped? Had Marge done the deed by herself? Or had Colonel Farber actually died of an ordinary heart attack?

These questions were in my mind as I drove to Freehold that December morning. I arrived at the courthouse shortly before the noon recess.

Freehold is an attractive suburban community. Once principally a farm town, it has been engulfed by the inexorable spreading-out of the New York metropolitan area and now it exists largely as a bedroom town for commuters and their families. Its courthouse is an old brick structure that, under the bleak winter skies, looked impenetrably mysterious. I felt pessimistic. Would the mystery now housed in this building ever be unravelled?

After a hurried lunch, Lee Bailey took me into the court library and handed me a transcript of Marge Farber's testimony of the day before. "When you read this," he said, "you'll see why I need you on the stand. Marge Farber has changed her story one more time."

I looked at him, puzzled. "A new version?"

"Right," said Bailey, "and it took everybody by surprise, including the prosecution. Do you know what she's saying now? She says she helped kill her husband because Coppolino hypnotized her and made her do it."

"*Hypnotized* her?"

"That's what she says. She claims she was under his spell for a year or more after he hypnotized her out of a smoking habit. She says she had no free will, had to do whatever Coppolino told her to do. Is it possible?"

"Not likely," I said.

"I didn't think so. And that's what I want you to testify on."

I settled down to skim through the transcript. I didn't have much time, but I managed to digest the meat of Marge's testimony. She explained her entire part in the affair by reference to an alleged hypnotic influence. Carl Coppolino had hypnotized her to help her stop smoking, she said, and had then carried the hypnosis into other areas of her life. She hadn't known what was happening to her. She became a puppet, with Carl pulling the strings. When he ordered her to help him murder her husband, she claimed, she felt irresistibly compelled to obey without knowing why.

The story seemed wild to me. And, I wondered, what was the point of it? Why had Marge suddenly brought it up, after having said nothing about the hypnosis through all the months before the trial?

One possibility suggested itself. Perhaps, as I'd suspected could happen, Marge was now sorry she had implicated herself in the alleged murder of her husband. Perhaps this new hypnosis story was designed to get her out of trouble – to lighten or remove the criminal responsibility of which she had accused herself.

Perhaps. On the other hand, perhaps she really believed she had been hypnotized into helping a murderer. The case seemed to be growing more complex by the hour. My pessimism increased. I had the baffled feeling that the truth was slipping out of sight, irretrievably lost like a jewel sinking in swirling, muddy waters.

I went into the courtroom and took my place as the afternoon session began. Lee Bailey was relying mainly only on medical men to clear Coppolino of the murder charge. First there were Drs Richard Ford and Joseph W. Spelman, medical examiners, respectively of Boston and Philadelphia. These two men produced evidence showing that William Farber had had a diseased heart and could have died of a heart attack. They doubted that he had died either of a fatal drug injection or of suffocation or strangulation with a pillow; at least, they showed that there was no reliable evidence to support either conclusion. The jury listened to these two men attentively. Prosecutor Vincent Keuper could not find any chinks in their professional armor.

Next on the witness stand were two men who knew about hypnosis. One was Dr Leo Wollman, an obstetrician and president of the New York Society of Clinical and Experimental Hypnosis. I was the other.

After having me qualify myself as a psychiatrist who knew how to use hypnosis, Lee Bailey asked me: "Is it possible for someone to be forced into a criminal act under hypnosis? I mean an act that he wouldn't otherwise be willing to perform?"

I answered flatly: "No. No amount of hypnosis could make him do it if he weren't at least unconsciously willing to begin with." I pointed out that, if hypnosis could compel people to do what they didn't want to do, despots like Hitler could have had whole populations hypnotized into slavish obedience. Troops could be hypnotized into a total disregard of their own safety. No such magic spell has ever been invented, except in science-fiction novels. "If Mrs Farber wanted to do something under hypnosis," I said, "she would do it. If she didn't want to, no amount of hypnosis could make her do it."

Prosecutor Keuper now tried to tear my testimony apart. He wanted me to concede that "anyone can be hypnotized into doing something." He began by getting me to concede one point, then went on to try to make me concede others.

Keuper: Mrs Farber said that she was, at times, under a compulsion to perform certain acts. At other times, though, shortly before or shortly after, she would have complete freedom from any compulsions. Doctor, is this consistent with what we know about the hypnotic state?

Brussel: Yes, it is.

Keuper: If I were a smoker and came to you because I wanted to stop smoking, could you implant a posthypnotic suggestion in my mind so that I wouldn't smoke for the rest the week?

Brussel: Yes – because you didn't want to continue smoking.

Keuper: If at the end of the week I wanted to continue not smoking, could you do something, like snapping your fingers, to prolong your posthypnotic suggestion?

Brussel: I can't answer that question. No two minds are the same.

Keuper: Could you plant a posthypnotic suggestion that would last a lifetime?

Brussel: Possibly, but all I can tell you honestly is that no one would know whether you were reacting to my hypnosis, or reacting to your own desire to stop smoking. I'm being as honest as I can.

Keuper: But the suggestion that I stop smoking came to me from a hypnotist?

Brussel: No, the suggestion really started with you. You wouldn't have consulted a hypnotist unless you wanted to stop smoking.

Keuper: Are you able to tell this jury what hypnosis actually is?

Brussel: No one can.

Keuper: If a posthypnotic suggestion lasts a lifetime,

couldn't you give some credit to the hypnosis – and not to the subject's willingness?

Brussel: There's no honest answer . . .

Prosecutor Keuper kept returning to the subject of smoking, no doubt because this is how Marge Farber's alleged compulsion to obey Carl Coppolino got started.

Keuper: Now, then, if I wanted to stop smoking and I came to you, could you hypnotize me out of the habit?

Brussel: If your conscious desire was backed up by an unconscious desire – that is, if your unconscious mind was fearful of smoking as a threat to life. In that case, I could. If this unconscious desire was absent, I could not.

Keuper: Oh, come, doctor! Could you or couldn't you hypnotize me out of smoking?

Brussel: If your unconscious wanted it, yes. If not, no.

Keuper: All right, we'll say you *did* succeed in hypnotizing me. How long would the spell last? Forever? A year? A month?

Brussel: As long as your unconscious feared smoking.

Prosecutor Keuper was getting nowhere. He grew increasingly irritable. Lee Bailey, who senses people's moods very quickly and seizes every opportunity to take advantage of them, deliberately added to Keuper's discomfort. Bailey kept turning around in his chair and looking at the prosecutor with a faint smile. As the tide of the trial swung ever more heavily against him, Keuper found this harder and harder to ignore. Finally he could stand it no longer.

"Judge," he shouted, "make him stop looking at me!"

The judge sighed. "Mr Bailey," he said, "please stop looking at Mr Keuper."

"Yes, Your Honour," said Bailey contritely, "I'm sorry."

This was one of the few points Prosecutor Keuper won. The jury deliberated for four and a half hours and returned with the fully expected verdict: Carl Coppolino was innocent of any complicity in Colonel William Farber's death.

Marge Farber looked angry. Carl Coppolino, neatly dressed in a dark suit, smiled as he was escorted from the courtroom under guard. He was taken immediately to Florida, where he next had to stand trial for the murder of his wife.

In May, 1967, a Florida jury found Carl Coppolino guilty of murdering his wife with succinylcholine chloride.

Oddly, the verdict was for second-degree murder – which under Florida law, means murder without premeditation. To many observers, the verdict seemed to contain a built in paradox. How can you obtain supplies of a drug and prepare an injection without premeditation?

That was the verdict, however. Carl Coppolino was sentenced to life imprisonment. Lee Bailey immediately appealed the verdict, and a new trial awaits Carl sometime in the future.

Did he really commit a murder? Were any murders, in fact committed? If so, who really killed Colonel Farber and Carmela Coppolino – or did they die a natural death?

Shortly after the close of Coppolino's New Jersey trial, Prosecutor Vincent Keuper tried to approach the mystery from a new angle. He asked a grand jury to indict Marge Faber for the murder of her husband. The jury refused on the ground of insufficient evidence.

Since then, I've often been asked for my opinion of the case. But I have no answers. I don't even have anything strong enough to be called a hunch.

The Coppolino–Farber episode remains my most baffling case. I puzzle over it sometimes, but I get nowhere. I assemble one group of facts into what seems like a workable hypothesis, but then another group of facts knocks it down. In the end I can only agree with Hamlet: there are more things in Heaven and earth, Jim Brussel, than are dreamt of in your philosophy. Or your psychiatry.

It may seem strange, in a way, for me to end this book with a failure. Or, if not a failure, certainly not a total success. I've ended the book thus for what I think is a good reason. I want to remain humble. Only a humble man can go on learning.

Perhaps, in some of these stories of my encounters with crime, I have made myself seem less than humble. I may have seemed too much impressed with my own deductive and intuitive victories. This last story is here to make amends. And to keep me lean and hungry ready for the next time my phone rings and a police officer says, "Dr Brussel, we've got a case here that's giving us some trouble—"

MURDER BY ACCIDENT

(Richard Brinkley, USA 1907)

C. Ainsworth Mitchell

This was the first case of its kind to involve the forensic analysis of ink. For a simple, unvarnished carpenter, Richard Brinkley had something of an inky history. He claimed to have a wife and four children, but his family (if it existed) kept out of the limelight. Before his arrest, Brinkley had cut a dashing Edwardian figure, sporting a fine head of black hair and a black moustache which curled up at the ends. But when he shuffled into the dock at his trial for murder, stripped of his wig, black dye, wax and curling tongs, he was almost bald with a drooping, grey walrus moustache. Brinkley was trapped by scientific evidence concerning the ink used to forge a signature. The carpenter's fraudulent collection of witnesses' signatures on the will of his elderly neighbour was exposed by an expert chemist, Dr Charles Ainsworth Mitchell (1867–1948). He was a past president of the Medico-Legal Society, the author of several books on criminal investigation, and the editor of a scientific journal called The Analyst. *Many years after the Brinkley affair, Dr Mitchell published this recollection of the case and his role in it.*

The criminal laws of England provide for murder by mistake, for if a man means to kill one person and unintentionally kills another, he is none the less guilty of murder. It would be difficult to find a better illustration of this law than the case of the poisoner, Brinkley, who had not the slightest wish to do away with his two victims, who died as the result of a criminal accident. The story is a remarkable one.

In 1906, Mrs Blume, or Blombery as she preferred to be called to conceal her German origin, was living in a house that she owned in Maxwell Road, Fulham. She was a retired maternity nurse, seventy-seven years of age, and was looked after by her unmarried daughter, Caroline. There was also a granddaughter, Augusta Glanville, a young actress, who lived with them when she was not on tour. Towards the end of the year the old lady was taken suddenly ill and on December 19th, Augusta, hurrying back from a rehearsal at the Fulham Theatre, was shocked to find that her grandmother had died while she was out. After the funeral a thorough search was made for a will, for Mrs Blume had a small income from the securities in which she had invested her savings, but nowhere could it be found. While Miss Blume and Augusta were still looking in every conceivable place, they had a visit from a neighbour, Richard Brinkley, who gave them the unwelcome information that they need not search any further because he had the will and it left everything to him. The two women were astounded and incredulous, but Brinkley then produced the will, written on a half sheet of foolscap paper and signed "Johanna Maria Blume," in presence of two witnesses, Parker and Herd. Although Brinkley had gradually gained a strong influence over her mother, Miss Blume was convinced that there was something wrong about this will. Some seven or eight years previously Brinkley, who was a carpenter, had been called in to do sundry odd jobs in the house, and this had led to a friendship which gradually became more intimate, until at last Mrs Blume came to rely upon him for advice in all her business affairs. He called her "Grannie," and would help her with her rates and income tax returns. But, although he was thus accepted as a family friend, Miss Blume knew that her mother had not had the slightest intention of leaving her house away from her daughter and grandaughter. Brinkley, however, told a circumstantial story about the signing of the will, and, acting as executor, entered the will for probate, turned Miss Blume and Miss Glanville out of the house and went to live there himself. Miss Blume consulted a solicitor, who issued a *caveat* (ie a notice a giving a general warning against anyone doing anything in the matter of an estate without notice to the issuing solicitor), and thus, although Brinkley was in possession of the house, he was prevented from touching the money. It came as a shock to him to find that the will was to be contested, and his next move was to try and get the matter settled by agreement. Dressed in a new suit of mourning, and with his grizzled moustache dyed black, he paid a call upon Miss Caroline Blume. He began by saying that he was sorry that she should have taken steps to contest the will, for he detested lawyers. It would be much better to have a friendly settlement. Only a few days before her death "Grannie" had told him how happy she would feel if only Caroline were the wife of such a man as Richard Brinkley. "I have been thinking it over," he sighed. "Of course, her wishes are very sacred to me – as no doubt they are to you. Let us be married and settle the matter." Much to his chagrin Miss Blume declined this prosaic offer of marriage. "The matter," she replied, "would never be settled that way."

This move having failed, Brinkley was faced with the certainty that the will would have to be subjected to close scrutiny in the Probate Court, and he had, therefore, now to rely upon the evidence of the "witnesses" to the will, and he began with the more important of them, Reginald Parker, whom he had known for some years as a dealer in household pets. Early in 1907, Brinkley asked Parker to procure for him a savage dog to protect his new home at Maxwell Road from burglars while he was away, and arranged that he would call at Parker's lodgings in South Croydon to see it. On Saturday afternoon, April 20th, Parker brought home a large white bulldog and told his landlady, Mrs Beck, that a prospective purchaser was coming to see it that evening. While the Beck family were out Brinkley arrived, and Parker, placing a bottle of ale and two glasses on the table, invited him to have a drink with him. But his visitor refused, saying that he had become a teetotaller and that his doctor had ordered him to take oatmeal stout, a bottle of which he produced from his pocket. As Parker refused to join him in drinking the stout, Brinkley drank some himself. Shortly afterwards he asked for a glass of water and Parker was out of the room for about a minute getting it. On his return he was again pressed to have some of the oatmeal stout, but still declined. Then, having concluded their business, the two men left the house together, leaving on the table the empty glasses, the empty bottle of ale and the bottle of oatmeal stout brought by Brinkley.

At about a quarter to eleven Daisy Beck came home and found the house empty. Peeping into Parker's sitting room she noticed that the fire was burning brightly and that there were bottles and glasses on the table. Soon after Mr and Mrs Beck returned and, attracted by the fire, went into Parker's sitting room. Then, noticing the oatmeal stout, they called for Daisy and asked her if she would like some. She came in and tasted it, but, finding it bitter, refused to drink any and returned to the kitchen. A few minutes later she heard a groan and then a cry of alarm and rushed back to find her mother lying on the floor and her father writhing in a chair. A doctor who lived near was called in, but within a few minutes both his patients were dead. The doctor noticed the distinctive almond-like odour of prussic acid in the few drops of stout left in the glasses and in the bottle, and immediately informed the police.

Their first task was to interrogate Reginald Parker, who came in soon after and was horrified at the tragedy in his sitting room. He made a statement about the affairs of the evening and what had led up to them; if what he said was true, it was evident that Brinkley had put poison into the stout in the short interval while he was alone, and had left the bottle on the table in the hope that Parker, when he returned, would notice it and drink it. Unfortunately for them he was forestalled by Mr and Mrs Beck.

Next arose the question of motive. Why should Brinkley wish to poison Parker, who was only a casual acquaintance with whom he had never had any dispute? But the police, who meanwhile had been looking into Brinkley's antecedents, soon found that the challenged will supplied the answer.

"You are one of the witnesses to the will of the late Mrs Blume," said the inspector.

"Mrs Blume," exclaimed Parker, "who is she? I never heard of the lady. What are you talking about? I never witnessed any will."

In reply the will was produced, subscribed with the name

"Reginald Clifford Parker," as having been signed by the testatrix in his presence. Parker, staring at the signature, admitted that it was in his handwriting, but reiterated positively that he had never heard of Mrs Blume, had never been in her house, and had not witnessed the will.

A scrutiny of the disputed will showed creases indicating that it had been folded over in such a way that only the space in which the signature would be written could have been visible. Parker then recalled that some months previously he had been sitting with Brinkley in a Brixton public house and had signed his name in a blank space on such a piece of paper, having been told by Brinkley that the paper contained merely a list of persons who wished to join in a pleasure excursion.

It thus became obvious that Brinkley's motive for wishing to murder Parker was to get an alleged witness to the will out of the way, since otherwise his story must break down. It was, however, essential to have corroboration of Parker's story. Accordingly the police secured the bottle of ink from the public house in Effra Road, Brixton, and submitted it to me for examination, to see whether it was the same ink as that in Parker's signature on the will. Before chemical tests may be applied to any part of a will, it is necessary to obtain the permission of the President of the Probate Court. On this, the first occasion on which the point had arisen, permission was refused, and it was therefore necessary to rely upon optical methods of examination. Fortunately the ink (Mordan's Azuryte) happened to be the bluest of the blue-black inks then sold, and it was possible to demonstrate beyond doubt that it agreed exactly with the ink in Parker's signature on the will.

Brinkley was arrested late on the Sunday night, the day after the murder, and was kept in custody pending further enquiries. Parker was released, but was subpoenaed to appear as witness for the Crown.

New evidence was forthcoming to link Brinkley with the crime. A boy in the grocer's shop where Brinkley had bought the bottle of oatmeal stout had seen him take it away and was able to identify him. The source of the prussic acid was also discovered. Brinkley had procured it from a man who described himself as "the friend of our dumb fellow creatures," stating that he required the poison to put a sick dog out of its misery.

After the preliminary hearing of the case before the magistrate, Brinkley was committed for trial at the summer assizes at Guildford. As there was no suitable accommodation in the town, the prisoner had to be brought each day from Brixton prison by the same train in which the counsel, solicitors and many of the witnesses travelled. The case was tried before Mr Justice Bigham (afterwards Lord Mersey), who had the reputation of being a very humane judge with a kindly sense of humour. Mr (afterwards Sir) Richard Muir, then Senior Counsel to the Treasury, led for the prosecution and the prisoner was defended by the late Mr Walter Frampton. Owing to its unusual nature the case had attracted much attention and the London Press was well represented. In those days no objection was taken to photographing in court, and a number of court scenes, some showing the prisoner in the witness box, were reproduced in the newspapers. Taking photographs in or near a court is now prohibited.

Mr Muir, after first explaining the law relating to a murder such as this, outlined the case against Brinkley in quiet measured tones, allowing the facts to speak for themselves and making no attempt at rhetorical appeal. He laid stress upon the scientific evidence – the presence of prussic acid in the bodies of the victims and in the remains of the stout (both prussic acid and stout having been bought by Brinkley), and the corroboration of Parker's story that the ink in his signature on the will was of the same kind as that in the bottle obtained from the public house.

The chief toxicological evidence on the poison in the bodies of Mr and Mrs Beck was given by Sir Thomas Stevenson (then Senior Official Analyst to the Home Office), whose name is associated with many celebrated trials, notably that of Dr Lamson, who poisoned his young brother-in-law with aconite under the impression that it could not be detected. Stevenson was an excellent witness, sure of his facts and of himself, and he gave his evidence simply and clearly, and refused to be drawn into making the admissions that the prisoner's counsel tried to obtain. The proof that the remains of the stout contained prussic acid was given by Richard Bodmer, a public analyst. Evidence was also given that the writing of the signature of Mrs Blume on the will did not agree with her ordinary writing. The body of the will itself was admittedly in the handwriting of Brinkley.

The lines upon which Mr Walter Frampton conducted the defence were that no one had seen Brinkley taking the oatmeal stout to Parker's lodgings, and that no one except Parker, who was himself implicated in the matter, had seen him going away. Brinkley had bought more than one bottle of stout, and his explanation that he had procured prussic acid to destroy a dog which annoyed him might well be true. The evidence against the prisoner was purely circumstantial, and therefore carried much less weight than direct testimony. In any event, the evidence was speculative, and it was conceivable that some other person with a grudge against Parker might have stolen the stout from Brinkley, put poison into it and left it in Parker's sitting room, with the object of making Brinkley appear the criminal.

The only witness called for the defence was the prisoner himself. He denied all knowledge of the poisoned stout and stuck to his story about the signing and witnessing of the will in Mrs Blume's room.

In the witness box Brinkley, who was fifty-three years of age, appeared as a tall, thin figure with grey hair and a clipped grey moustache (it was dyed black when he was arrested). He was fluent in his replies in cross-examination, but in no vital matter could he produce any corroboration. For instance, when he was asked how he accounted for the fact (upon which I had given evidence) that there were three different inks upon the will, he replied that Mrs Blume had three different kinds in the house. As only one make (Stephens), in which the body of the will had been written, had been found there, he was asked what had become of the other two bottles, and replied that he had given them to a little girl; naturally she was not forthcoming.

While Brinkley was giving his evidence a sudden thunderstorm burst over Guildford. The court room was almost blacked out, while frequent flashes lit up the figures of the prisoner standing motionless in the witness box and of counsel imperturbably continuing his cross-examination. It was more like a scene in a stage melodrama than a trial for murder. The macabre possibi-

lities of the scene appealed strongly to a London journalist, and
he observed to me: "If only this could have happened when the
death sentence was being passed."

Mr Justice Bigham opened his summing up by corroborating
what counsel for the prosecution had said about the law relating
to murder, and then proceeded to correct the assertion put
forward by counsel for the defence, that circumstantial evidence
is less conclusive than direct evidence. In few poison cases, he
pointed out, can anyone be found who can say, "I saw the deed
done," and it is only by the circumstantial evidence of facts, each
linked together and pointing unmistakably to the criminal, that
such murders can be proved. At the same time the facts must be
such as to leave no reasonable doubt of the guilt of the prisoner in
the minds of the jury; if there should be any doubt, they must give
him the benefit of it. The judge then summarized the whole of the
evidence, bringing out clearly the points that had been put in
favour of the accused, and the jury retired to consider their
verdict.

It has often been observed that cold-blooded murderers never
seem to realize the gravity of their position. For example, to
mention only one notorious instance, all the contemporary accounts of the poisoner, Dr Palmer, referred to his nonchalance
and jocular bearing at his trial in 1856. Brinkley's behaviour was
fully in keeping with this tradition. In the intervals while he was
in the dock waiting for his trial to be resumed, he laughed and
chatted unconcernedly with the warders, apparently not even
admitting the possibility that he could be convicted. Those who
had followed the evidence, however, had little doubt what the
result would be, and the short time that the jury took to arrive at
their verdict of guilty showed that there was no material difference of opinion among them. Sentence of death was passed, and a
few weeks later Brinkley was executed at Wandsworth.

Had Brinkley achieved his aim of poisoning Parker, he would
have had only a local and short notoriety, but when instead he
unintentionally killed two other persons, the crime became what
Dr Ingleby Oddie (at that time Junior Counsel to the Treasury)
has described as a classical example of this type of murder.

THE VAMPIRE RAPIST

(Wayne Boden, Canada 1971)

Clifford L. Linedecker

The Canadian press dubbed Wayne Boden "The Vampire Rapist" because he sank his teeth into his victims' breasts with such force that his teeth-marks were plainly visible at the autopsies. Boden had a sadistic obsession with women's breasts, and killed and raped several times before being caught and convicted on the clinching evidence of an orthodontist. This expert identified the teeth-marks on one of the women's breasts as having twenty-nine points of similarity as Boden's. The assaults began in the summer of 1968 in Montreal and by early 1970 the killer was wanted for four rape-murders in and around that city. But despite massive publicity and a huge manhunt, Canada's most notorious killer remained at large. The next killing occurred 2,500 miles away in Calgary in May 1971. This time the killer was glimpsed at the wheel of his car and Boden was picked up the following day. He was sentenced to life imprisonment for the murder of the Calgary victim, and received three more life terms for three of the Montreal murders, always denying responsibility for the first killing. Clifford L. Linedecker (b. 1931) worked as a reporter and rewrite man for various American newspapers before switching to magazines in the 1970s. For much of the 1980s he was executive editor of the weekly tabloid National Examiner *and is now a full-time author and freelance writer. He has written nearly thirty books, most of them on true-life crime, and lives in Florida.*

Despite the serene expression on the face of the petite young schoolteacher who looked almost as if she had merely dropped off to sleep after a few pleasant moments of romance, homicide investigators realized as soon as they saw her that they were dealing with the grisly handiwork of a murderous sexual psychopath.

Attractive twenty-one-year-old Norma Vaillancourt was dead. And the peaceful expression on her face was spoiled by an ugly purple-and-red bruise that circled her throat – and by ragged, bloody marks left by human teeth that had savaged her bare breasts. She was nude.

The teacher's macabre death marked the beginning of a ghastly sex, mutilation, and murder spree that would make headlines throughout Canada and baffle the Montreal police department's top homicide investigators for nearly four years.

And ironically, the horror that began in Canada's largest city on a hot midsummer day in 1968 would not end until the psychopath that both journalists and police called the Vampire Rapist moved more than twenty-three hundred miles away to the western province of Alberta.

Homicide detectives summoned to Miss Vaillancourt's Montreal apartment a few minutes after 1 p.m. on July 23, however, could hardly have known that they would soon be looking for a perverted serial killer with an amazing ability to exert a hypnotic-like charm over trusting young women. Like Miss Vaillancourt, most of the victims would be lured into romantic trysts that ended not in the promised glamour and excitement of a love affair but in savage mutilation and violent death.

Except for clues collected from the body itself – semen, foreign pubic hairs, and the telltale bite marks – investigators were unable to collect much helpful evidence in the victim's apartment. There were no signs of a struggle, such as overturned furniture or torn flesh under her fingernails or bruises, to indicate she may have tried to scratch and fight off an assailant. Nor was there any indication that any of her personal property had been stolen.

Detectives quickly turned to the circle of acquaintances she had formed since moving from the small town of Ste Anne-des-

Monts, along the southeast shore of the St Lawrence Seaway, to taste the big-city life of Montreal. She had loved the excitement of the city and was as vivacious and popular as she was pretty. Investigators quickly put together a long list of boyfriends. They learned, in fact, that she was seen with three different men on the day before her death.

After an autopsy was performed, pathologists estimated the time of death at about 10 p.m. the night before the body was discovered.

But although investigators patiently tracked down her friends and acquaintances, paying special attention to the men she had known, their efforts didn't produce a single solid suspect. Contacts with other law-enforcement agencies in Canada and in the United States in efforts to turn up reports of similar crimes were also fruitless.

The popular young schoolteacher had been dead more than a year when twenty-year-old Shirley Audette died. Like Norma Vaillancourt, she had brown hair and was petite, weighing in at around one hundred pounds. She had also had sex with a man shortly before her death, her breasts were shredded and bloodied by a series of savage bite marks, and she had been strangled.

Unlike the other woman, she was almost fully clothed, except for her brassiere, which had been forcefully ripped off before her body was found in a courtyard at the rear of an apartment complex about a block from her own. But like Norma Vaillancourt, she was a small-town girl; she had moved to the city from suburban Longueuil.

Investigators theorized that the victim was strangled and raped in one of the hundreds of apartments in the neighbourhood, then dressed by her killer, carried to the courtyard, and dumped.

Questioning of acquaintances quickly turned up indications that the young woman not only had known her killer but had also suspected that he was dangerous. Detectives learned that she had confided her apprehension to a friend at the shop where she worked as a clerk. "I'm embarked on something which I'm not sure I'll be able to get out of," she had said.

The dead woman's boyfriend provided even stronger indications of her distress when he told police that he telephoned her at about 3 a.m., during his 7 p.m. to 7 a.m. shift at an area factory.

"I'm scared," she said.

When he asked her what she was frightened of, she replied that she was "just scared." She refused to elaborate.

The boyfriend was the last person known to have talked to her, except for her killer.

More than a year later, twenty-year-old Marielle Archambault was murdered. The body of the pretty jewellery-store clerk was found in her apartment at about 1 p.m. on November 24, 1969. She was sprawled on the living-room floor, partly covered with a blanket. Her panty hose were pulled down under her knees, and her brassiere had been ripped and torn down the middle.

The Vampire Rapist had left his macabre calling card on her breasts and neck. They were torn and bloodied with the marks of human teeth.

This time, however, there were signs that a minor struggle had occurred, and the killer had left behind what appeared to be a promising clue: a crumpled photograph of a handsome young man.

The photograph itself was too badly damaged to permit making reproductions with a camera, but a police artist provided a sketch that was quickly flashed to law-enforcement agencies and the news media throughout Canada. Other officers began contacting acquaintances and friends of the slain young woman for questioning and viewing of the sketch.

Her employer and other co-workers quickly agreed that the drawing resembled a young man who had twice stopped at the store to chat with Marielle on the last afternoon they had seen her alive. They said he first stopped in at about 4:30 p.m., then an hour later. She seemed to be pleased, and the second time she told him to wait, because she would be getting off work in a few minutes. He nodded in agreement, and the couple left the shop together at about 6 p.m.

The shopkeeper and his employees said that the first time Marielle talked with the young man she spoke French, then switched to English. She called him Bill.

Because her first language was French, the fact that she had called to him in English when she suggested he wait for her led investigators to believe that English was his primary language.

The mystery man was described as about twenty-five years old, five feet, nine inches tall, 160 to 165 pounds, and well dressed, with moderately long, carefully styled hair.

Delving further into Marielle's background, detectives learned that she had come to the big city from nearby Jolliette, and liked to party and have a good time with other fun-loving singles at popular local night spots.

Bill was also apparently a regular at many of the discotheques, and several young people pointed out that they frequently saw him around on the club, scene. But no one was able to provide a last name, address, place of employment, or any other information helpful in leading police to the slippery man-about-town. And despite his obvious fondness for nightclubs and pretty girls, he dropped abruptly from sight. He wasn't seen around at the discos anymore.

But he was a hot suspect in at least three grisly sex-and-mutilation murders, and investigators felt almost certain that it was only a matter of time and opportunity before the Vampire Rapist would strike again. They renewed the public warnings to young women to beware of strangers, no matter how charming they might appear to be.

A new year and new decade were ushered in without incident. Then, barely three weeks later, Jean Way died. The lovely twenty-four-year-old brokerage-firm secretary was apparently raped and strangled in her apartment while a boyfriend stood impatiently outside, ringing the doorbell to pick her up for a date.

The date had been set for 8:30 p.m., but the boy-friend arrived about fifteen minutes early and was surprised and disappointed when she didn't answer the bell. He later told investigators that he just couldn't believe she had broken their date without notifying him.

Disappointed but not yet ready to give up seeing the lovely secretary, he walked to a nearby tavern, where he had a couple of beers, then he tried to telephone her at about 9:15 p.m. When she failed to answer the phone, he returned to the apartment. This time when she didn't respond to the bell, he tried the door. It was unlocked, and he swung it open and walked in.

His girlfriend was stretched out naked on the front-room sofa with a leather belt knotted around her neck. Her clothes were lying all over the floor, where they had been thrown as they were ripped from her body. Her breasts were covered with bloody bite marks.

A window was open, leading police to speculate later that the killer had planned to leap from the second-floor apartment after the boyfriend's unexpected arrival interrupted the murder and rape.

Jean roomed with a nurse who worked a 4 p.m. to midnight shift at a local hospital. The room-mate told detectives that she telephoned her friend at about 7 p.m., and Jean said that she was with a male friend. Jean named him, but the nurse could remember only the first name, Bill.

Detectives also learned that on the afternoon of the day before she died, Jean had stopped in a photo studio to have some film developed. When she left she pleaded to use the back door. The proprietor said she told him that she was frightened of a man outside who had been annoying her.

"I'm scared," she said.

Of four victims, she was the third who had confided to friends or acquaintances shortly before their deaths that they were afraid of someone.

An autopsy confirmed evidence of sexual intercourse between the victim and a man shortly before or at about the same time of her death. And although she had died of strangulation, the weapon was the killer's hands. The belt had apparently been looped around her neck and tightened after she was killed, to make sure that she was dead.

But the age and appearance of the victim, including her petite build, as well as the location of the murder and the mutilated breasts, clearly marked the slaying as the handiwork of the same killer who had been terrorizing young Montreal women for nearly three years. And like the other women, Jean Way was not a native of the city. The second of three children of a surveyor and his wife, she was a native of Hare Bay, Newfoundland.

Some of the most experienced homicide detectives on the Montreal Police Department had devoted two years to the investigation of the sex stranglings, and yet it seemed there was nothing they could do to put a stop to the horror. They had few leads to work on, and one of the most promising – the crumpled photograph – had distintegrated when they learned that the man in the picture had died before the first murder in the series occurred. Police had spent hundreds of man-hours trying to match a suspect to the photograph.

And despite repeated warnings, naive and trusting young women continued to fall under the evil Svengali-like spell of the bloodthirsty killer. "If the fiend isn't a hypnotist, he has a hypnotic way about him," a frustrated police spokesman declared at a press conference. "He seduces and strangles with such a delicate touch that the victims show no agonized expression."

Among themselves, some investigators speculated that the killer might have selected young women he instinctively felt were a bit masochistic and would permit some delicate biting and strangling during sex. But sometimes their lover would get carried away, lose his gentle touch, and become homicidal.

Detective Lieutenant Marcel Allard, who was in charge of the special ten-man squad working almost full-time on the case, warned that investigators were certain the strangler would strike again. "We're dealing with a psychopath," he continued. "We've had dozens of psychiatrists tell us that he must hate women, or that he hated his mother, or sister, or wife, etc, etc. But that still doesn't help find him."

Although police weren't yet aware of it, the nightmare had in fact ended at last for the shaken citizens of Montreal. It hadn't yet started more than two thousand miles away, in Calgary.

Known worldwide for its famous rodeo, the annual Calgary Stampede, the city of nearly a half million people is broad-shouldered and brash, and peopled by citizens who pride themselves on self-reliance and minding their own business.

But the entire community was stunned when it was learned that one of the most sadistic and ghoulish killers in Canada's history had apparently shifted his nightmare activities from Montreal to their city.

The first hint of trouble surfaced when Elizabeth Anne Porteous, a skilled and well-liked business education teacher at Bowness High School, failed to show up for morning classes or to notify her principal that she was ill. She didn't answer telephone calls from other school employees, and she failed to respond after the manager of the high-rise apartment hotel she lived in was notified and knocked at her door.

Another teacher who lived in the same building had knocked at the door earlier on her way to work and had gotten the same results. There was no response.

By early afternoon, the concern of the thirty-three-year-old teacher's colleagues was turning to dread. She had a reputation for dependability and efficiency and wasn't the kind of person who would suddenly decide she needed an unscheduled day off or would leave town because of family problems without notifying her employers. The building manager was contacted again and was asked to enter her apartment to check on her.

The manager let himself in with a pass-key. The apartment was a shambles. Furniture was overturned, and papers were scattered over the floor. The manager quickly retreated and called for police.

The schoolteacher was lying on her back on the bedroom floor. Her dress was ripped open and her brassiere had been violently torn from her body. Her breasts and neck were smeared with blood and punctured with the imprints of human teeth.

It was May 18, 1971, nearly a year and a half since Jean Way died in Montreal. An alert news reporter quickly recognized the ghastly trademark of the Vampire Rapist, and after confirming his suspicions with a phone call to Montreal, he passed on his information to Calgary police.

Had Canada's most-sought-after serial slayer moved to Calgary from Montreal? The media wanted to know. Or were police looking at the work of a copycat killer?

Like three, possibly four of the Montreal victims, the schoolteacher had been slain in her own apartment, and like all four, her breasts had been mutilated with bites from human teeth. And like the others, she had grown up as a small-town girl. The only child of a banker and his wife, she was a native of Dundas, in Ontario.

But despite the similarities to the Vampire Rapist's dark deeds, there were also several glaring differences in the teacher's slaying. The condition of the apartment and of the body left no doubt that she had put up a fierce fight for her life. Not only was the front room a shambles, but the fight had apparently extended into the bathroom as well. A corner of the water closet on the toilet had been shattered, and the medicine cabinet was pulled from the wall. Bright red buttons from the victim's dress were scattered over the floors of both rooms, like malignant drops of blood. A woman's shoes, with the heel ripped off, lay on its side in the hallway.

And there was no sign of the serene expression on the teacher's face that had added such a bizarre dimension to the Montreal murders. Her agonized grimace showed clearly that she had died in terrible fear and pain.

After police technicians had photographed the body at the crime scene, and its location on the floor had been pinpointed as precisely as possible, the corpse was removed for autopsy to the morgue at Calgary General Hospital. As the body was being raised at the hospital to remove the shredded remains of the dress, a man's cufflink clattered onto the metal examining table. It would become a valuable piece of evidence.

As expected, the autopsy disclosed that the victim had been raped. And, true to the murder style of the Vampire Rapist, she had been strangled: either with the killer's hands, or from pressure applied to her throat with his forearm.

Pathologists also discovered five fresh burn marks on her back, which they believed were inflicted with the tip of a lighted cigarette.

As news of the tragedy flashed throughout Calgary, friends and acquaintances of the dead woman began to contact police with information. A man-and-wife pair of educators told police that the night before Elizabeth's body was discovered, they had seen her with a man who appeared to be in his mid-twenties. They said they were stopped at a traffic light when she and her well-dressed companion pulled up beside them. They recalled that the car was an older-model light blue Mercedes, and it had the small figure of a steer visible in the rear window.

A description of the vehicle was disseminated to all uniform and plain-clothes officers in Calgary, and they were told to be on the lookout for it. The owner, or driver, was wanted for questioning.

One of Elizabeth's friends told police that the teacher had talked to her about a date she had set up for the night of May 17. But, unfortunately, she hadn't named her escort or provided any other helpful background about him.

But another friend, a former teacher at the high school, informed detectives that they were in the nearby mountain resort town of Banff about a month earlier when Elizabeth met a handsome young man in a cocktail lounge. The good-looking stranger appeared to be in his mid-twenties, had stylishly long brown hair, and was well dressed.

While exchanging the usual cocktail banter, he had identified himself as a car salesman and said he drove a Mercedes. He said his name was Bill. Surprisingly, the couple learned, they had grown up in the same town, Dundas, Ontario.

Elizabeth was impressed with the smooth-talking stranger, and before leaving the lounge she scribbled her name, address, and telephone number on a piece of paper and suggested that he give her a call sometime.

The day after the grisly discovery of the teacher's body, a policeman spotted an older-model light blue Mercedes parked a few blocks from her high-rise apartment. A stakeout was set up, and after a brief wait a young man was apprehended as he approached the vehicle.

He readily admitted the car was his, but said he didn't know anything about the man called Bill, whom police were looking for. He said his name was Wayne Clifford Boden, he was twenty-three, and he had been in Calgary about eighteen months since leaving his native Ontario. He was a traveling salesman, and was originally from Dundas – Elizabeth Porteous's hometown.

Transported to police headquarters for interrogation, Boden conceded that he had dated the unfortunate schoolteacher, but insisted that he knew nothing about her murder. He said they had gone to a nightclub for a few drinks and dancing, and that he had her back at her apartment before midnight. She invited him in for coffee, he said, but explained that he declined because it was late and both of them had to work the next morning. He added that he heard her latch the door as he left.

"Elizabeth was alive when I saw her last," he declared.

When police interrogators showed him the cufflink that dropped from her dress, he admitted it was his but said he lost it at the apartment before they went out nightclubbing. They had looked all over the apartment for it, he claimed.

Despite Boden's smooth replies and repeated protestations of innocence, he was charged with first-degree murder in the teacher's slaying and lodged in jail.

But the investigation was still a long way from over. Police in Montreal were notified of the arrest and sent Criminal Investigation Bureau detectives to question Boden about the serial killings there.

Their difficulties with the bizarre case hadn't yet ended, however, and by a curious twist of fate, as the three detectives were returning to Montreal, their Air Canada jet was hijacked. They were eventually rescued, along with 115 other passengers and crewmen.

In Calgary, homicide officers spread out on a variety of assignments aimed at putting together an undeniable chain of evidence against the suspected sex strangler. Some detectives continued questioning acquaintances of the victim, and others began assembling information about Boden's background.

Checks with authorities in Dundas, and in the larger nearby city of Hamilton where Boden had also lived for a time, revealed that he had no record of trouble with police in either community. Police in Dundas, in fact, recalled him as a mild-mannered youth. He appeared to be well behaved and well liked.

A search warrant was also obtained from the Alberta courts, and police began a painstaking search of Boden's apartment. The search turned up a red button similar to those ripped from Elizabeth's dress. It had been discarded in a paper wastebasket. Detectives also confiscated a cartoon book filled with drawings of women, which someone had crudely sketched over with gross exaggerations of the breasts and nipples.

A young woman who had been living with Boden as his

common-law wife told investigators that they had come to Calgary from Montreal about eighteen months earlier. On the night the schoolteacher was murdered, he had told his sweetheart that he was going to a sales meeting. He returned about midnight, looking very tired.

The slender, soft-spoken salesman went on trial for the Porteous murder on Feburary 15, 1972, in the Alberta Supreme Court before Chief Justice J. V. H. Milvain. As anticipated, both the cufflink and the button recovered from the wastebasket figured as important pieces of physical evidence.

But some of the most sensational testimony was provided by a Calgary orthodontist who confirmed that the bite marks on the breasts and neck of the victim were inflicted by the teeth of the defendant. The unique character of Boden's teeth and bite matched the wounds on the victim.

Appearing as an expert witness, the orthodontist testified that an analysis of the wounds showed twenty-nine points of similarity to the formation of Boden's teeth. Thirteen points were matched on the right breast and sixteen on the left. The minimum total number of corcordant points required by law for identification was thirteen, he told the court.

He added that his findings were confirmed by a skilled British orthodontist who was also an experienced consultant on similar wounds and a respected expert witness.

The dental expert's testimony made judicial history in Canada, where it marked the first time such evidence was admitted in court for the purpose of identifying a defendant.

A crime technician with the Royal Canadian Mounted Police crime-detection laboratory in Edmonton identified a pair of men's shorts, removed from Boden and found to be stained with seminal fluid. The technician testified that strands of hair found in the shorts were identical in color and texture to hairs taken from the body of the victim. He also identified hair taken from the rug in her apartment as matching hair taken from Boden.

But the most startling testimony of all dealt with a conversation Boden had at police headquarters with his live-in lover three days after the victim's body was discovered.

The chief of the Calgary Police Department's homicide squad

said he was present when Boden, in effect, confessed the murder to his girlfriend. Detective Sergeant Ernest Reimer testified that Boden told the woman he was going to plead not guilty by reason of insanity, then asked if she knew what he meant. He said Boden repeated the question, then declared:

"You understand? I am the one. That is why I am charged. I did it but I don't know why. It's not in my character to do something like that."

Boden's girlfriend also testified, confirming the homicide sergeant's statements about the conversation. She said that her boyfriend appeared to be "pretty shook up" when he told her about his plans for the insanity plea.

Boden did not testify, and his defence counsel did not call any witnesses.

At the conclusion of the trial, conducted without a jury, Boden was pronounced guilty by Chief Justice Milvain of non-capital murder. He was given the mandatory sentence: life in prison.

But the young sex strangler's troubles weren't yet over. He was still wanted in Montreal, where he was suspected as the Vampire Rapist who had terrorized the city for more than two years.

Although he had previously denied being the killer, he waived extradition to Ontario, then gave statements to police admitting three of the Montreal slayings. Police learned that he had known and dated Jean Way for about a year before she was killed. He had also lived in an apartment near Shirley Audette's home, and he hung around the same discotheques as Marielle Archambault.

When he appeared before Justice Jacques Ducros, in the Court of Queen's Bench in Montreal, Boden disregarded the advice of his court-appointed attorney and pleaded guilty to the three murders. He admitted that he had strangled Shirley Audette, Marielle Archambault, and Jean Way.

But he denied that he was responsible for murdering Norma Vaillancourt, the first victim in the shocking string of sex-and-mutilation slayings on Montreal's West End that had been blamed on the Vampire Rapist.

Despite the best efforts of the Montreal Police Department's homicide investigators, Crown prosecutors determined that there was insufficient evidence to convict Boden of the Archambault killing, so he was not charged and brought to trial in that case. Officially, the murder was left unsolved.

Boden, however, was sentenced to separate life prison terms for the other three slayings that he had confessed to.

The Canadian justice system hadn't yet heard the last of him, however.

Barely more than twelve years after he was sentenced to four life terms behind bars, he walked away from an unarmed guard in downtown Montreal while he was on an authorized strangler's day off from a federal maximum-security prison. The prison arts-and-crafts teacher assigned to accompany him on his daylong holiday gave him permission to go to the washroom in a hotel restaurant by himself – and he never returned.

Instead, the onetime Vampire Rapist who had held the city hostage to a nightmare more than a decade earlier not only left his escort without a prisoner to return with but also stuck him with the dinner bill as well. Then he looked up an old friend he had met in prison, and they went out on the town together.

Police caught up with Boden the next evening when patrons at a bar where he was drinking recognized him from the old days and turned him in. He was sitting quietly in the artificial twilight of the bar, wearing dark glasses, and casually sipping a beer.

According to his ex-convict pal, Boden had spent a good part of the previous evening drinking with a woman he met at another hotel bar in the same neighbourhood he roamed when he had held the city hostage to a nightmare of sexual assault, mutilation, and murder. He financed his spree with three hundred dollars in prison earnings and with a credit card he had been issued while behind bars in 1977.

Police and citizens were apprehensive and outraged when they learned that the Vampire Rapist had been allowed to so casually resume his old bar-hopping habits. When Louis Way, the father of one of the Montreal victims, was contacted by a newspaper reporter, he was shocked: "What's the world coming to when you have people like that prowling the streets?" he asked. "As far as I'm concerned, they should bring back the death penalty."

But the thirty-six-year-old killer was convinced that it was he who had been wronged, and when he appeared before Sessions

Court Judge André Chalous he complained that he pulled off the high-profile escape merely to get media attention. He was angry that he had been kept in prison so long without parole.

"I want someone to go to Ottawa and find out why I have been put off for thirteen years," he complained.

"You killed three people in Montreal," the judge sternly reminded him.

Boden was returned to the federal government's Laval Correctional Development Centre, with a new one-year prison sentence to serve for escape. He had fled the same prison during the second of two outings allowed outside the walls.

Asked about future security measures for the notorious Vampire Rapist, a corrections official told newsmen that it would be "a good while" before he was awarded another day on the town.

CONFLICT OF EVIDENCE

(Sidney Fox, UK 1930)

Sydney Smith

For Bernard Spilsbury, the Crippen case was a personal triumph, a turning-point. He was retained as a pathologist by the Home Office for the next thirty-seven years, and his appearance as an expert Crown witness in a series of important murder trials between the wars brought him celebrity status. "To the man in the street," explained Edgar Lustgarten, "he stood for pathology as Hobbs stood for cricket or Dempsey for boxing or Capablanca for chess." Spilsbury's good looks, easy courtroom manner and his knack of explaining complex forensic points in clear, simple language mesmerized juries. But in 1930 he found himself pitted against a younger, ambitious pathologist called Sydney Smith, who'd been retained by the defence in the sad and sordid case of Sidney Fox, a homosexual drifter accused of murdering his own white-haired mother. Fox was believed to have strangled her and set fire to her room in order to collect on her life insurance, which he had recently increased. Spilsbury, Smith and two other medical experts disagreed in court over the evidence of strangulation. Spilsbury (by now Sir Bernard), who conducted the post-mortem examination of Mrs Rosaline Fox, believed she had been strangled before the fire started, and that she had died from asphyxia due to manual strangulation. Sydney Smith, making his debut as an expert witness for the defence, gave it as his definite opinion that Mrs Fox had died of heart failure, brought on by exertion and fright, having woken to find her room full of smoke. Born in New Zealand, Sir Sydney Smith (1883–1969) was Regius professor of forensic medicine at Edinburgh University for twenty-

five years. The Fox case (Smith hyped it as "one of the causes célébres of the century") was the first of his frequent court clashes with Spilsbury. Although Fox's trial is said to have involved a direct conflict of medical evidence, the truth is less clear-cut. The evidence on which the two sets of expert witnesses (prosecution and defence) base their opinions is seldom the same: in this case, as in others, the pathologist summoned by the Crown was first in the field. Spilsbury saw the bruise on Mrs Fox's larynx, but Smith did not, because by the time he examined the larynx several months later, the bruise had disappeared.

Sidney Harry Fox was not a good citizen. He was in the hands of the police before he was twelve, and in prison at nineteen; and he was in and out of gaol throughout the remaining eleven years of his life.

He was a forger, a blackmailer, a swindler, and a thief. He was also a homosexual, although when he appeared at his last trial he had just been cited as a co-respondent in an action for divorce. He admitted the adultery but denied any pleasure in it. He was proud of his inversion, and claimed that he had never been with a woman except as a means to get her money.

Clever and plausible, and something of a charmer, he had lived by his wits all his life. Yet as a criminal he had not been a success. At the time of his final arrest, when he was thirty, he possessed nothing in the world but a long record of convictions and a number of debts. He had even been hard put to it to find two shillings for the premium on an accident insurance he took out on his mother's life.

They made a pretty picture, the dear old lady with the shuffling gait – she suffered from paralysis agitans – and the devoted son. She was undoubtedly fond of him, although hardly a model parent. Her husband was probably not Sidney's father, and she was a confederate in most of her son's crimes. When he was not in prison they lived mainly in hotels, moving round the country and leaving a trail of unpaid bills and dud cheques. It was a hand-to-mouth existence, and they had no luggage at all when they arrived at the Hotel Metropole, Margate, on October 16, 1929. Six days later Fox went to London and arranged for two accident insurances that he had taken out on his mother's life to be extended until midnight the following day. At 11.40 p.m. that day Mrs Fox was dead.

Fox himself had raised the alarm about ten minutes earlier. He ran down the hotel stairs, wearing only a shirt and shouting that there was a fire. It was in his mother's bedroom. A commercial traveller ran up with him, and succeeded in dragging her out of the smoke-filled room. Artificial respiration was applied, and two doctors were called. By the time the first of them – Dr Austin – arrived Mrs Fox was already dead. Dr Austin examined her, and certified her death as due to shock and suffocation. His colleague, Dr Nichol, arrived soon after, and did not question Dr Austin's opinion.

An inquest was held the next day. The proceedings were brief, and the expected verdict of accidental death was returned. Five days later Mrs Fox was buried in her native village of Great Fransham, in Norfolk. So far as the police were concerned the case was closed.

Fox put in for the insurance. His claims were investigated. An official of one of the insurance companies wired his head office, "Extremely muddy water in this business." Scotland Yard was informed. The case was re-opened, and eleven days after the funeral the body of Mrs Fox was exhumed. A post-mortem examination was performed by Sir Bernard Spilsbury, who said she had been strangled. Fox was charged with murder, and eventually committed for trial. I was asked by his solicitor to give evidence in his defence. After examining the medical part of the case for the Crown, I agreed to appear in the role of expert witness.

I had, of course, given evidence in this role hundreds of times before, but always for the prosecution. I was always available to the Crown in cases occurring in and around Edinburgh, and was commonly asked by them to investigate cases in other parts of the country; but I could also give expert evidence for the defence in cases outside Edinburgh.

It is, I think, to the credit of the British legal system that expert witnesses are made available to the defence by the Crown, and paid by them in cases in which the defendant is without means. Apart from this, I believe that any expert witness should be prepared at any time to place his special knowledge at the disposal of the defence, whether it is in a position to pay him a fee or not. The Crown has all possible resources at its disposal; it can afford to call in as many experts as it wishes, it has access to all records, and has control of the whole machinery of the police, including the Criminal Investigation Department and the police laboratories. The defence usually has only limited resources, is often short or entirely devoid of funds, and must depend to a great extent on a critical appraisement of the evidence produced by the Crown.

The attitude of a scientific witness should be the same whether he is called in by the Crown or by the defence. It is not for him to concern himself with the previous character of the accused or with other evidence in the case. As a scientist he should be completely detached: he must not let himself be influenced in any way by emotional considerations such as sympathy or antipathy. His sole function is to examine the facts which come to his knowledge in his special capacity, to decide what is the true or the most probable interpretation of them, and to indicate to the court that interpretation, along with the grounds on which it is based.

I have often been asked why I have given evidence for the defence in cases in which the accused seemed to be guilty or in which he seemed to be a scoundrel who was not worth saving. In a particular instance the life of the accused may not be worth saving, but the principles of justice always are. Once concede the possibility of conviction on insufficient evidence because the accused is a worthless scamp, and you open the way to flouting the fundamental proposition of our law that every man is innocent until he is proved guilty.

Fox was a bad hat, and he would be in every way, as an eminent Scottish judge said of another rogue, "nane the waur o' a hangin'." It was clear from the start of the case that the circumstantial evidence, especially that relating to the fire and to the insurance policies, might be strong enough to earn him one. That was no concern of mine. My interest was limited to the medical evidence, which I found remarkable.

It depended almost entirely on Spilsbury's post-mortem report. The surprising thing about this came at the end – "Cause of death: asphyxia due to manual strangulation."

A person being strangled fights like mad. Even if the victim is a feeble old woman, Nature will supply her with unsuspected additional strength to help her in her fight for life. She will struggle furiously to wrench the strangler's hands away from her throat. She may fail, but some marks of the struggle will remain. Nearly always there will be scratches about the neck.

There were none here. According to Spilsbury's report, there was no trace of external injury at all – no sign of injury about the mouth or nose or in the skin of the neck, no marks left by the indentation of finger-nails or pressure of finger-tips.

Nor were there any of the usual signs of manual strangulation under the skin or in the tissues, such as bruises in the muscles surrounding the neck and in the larynx where the fingers would grip. Most remarkable of all, there was no fracture of either the thyroid cartilage or the hyoid bone. In elderly persons the hyoid becomes brittle and is easily broken, and this is one of the most characteristic marks of strangling. Yet Mrs Fox's hyoid was unbroken – until Spilsbury broke it himself unintentionally while taking it out. For all his care he could not avoid breaking it in two places. It was as brittle as that.

A strangler's victim is usually not a pretty sight. Bluish or purple lips and ears, change of colour of the nails, froth and possibly blood-staining about the nose or mouth, the tongue forced outward, the hands clenched – these are the typical signs of death from asphyxia.

There were none on Mrs Fox.

There were none of the usual internal signs of asphyxia, either. Instead Spilsbury found, on opening the body, natural disorders that pointed to a different conclusion. Her kidneys were cirrhosed, her arteries diseased, and her heart was in an advanced state of degeneration. The state of the heart alone, as described in Spilsbury's report, seemed to me to have been bad enough to cause death at any time.

Spilsbury himself emphatically rejected this possibility. "Cause of death: asphyxia due to manual strangulation." The oracle had spoken. There was nothing more to be said.

At the trial, under cross-examination, Spilsbury agreed that he had never known of a case of strangulation with fewer signs. He agreed cheerfully, for by then the point was immaterial to him. Spilsbury, like the rest of us, could make mistakes. He was unique, I think, in that he never admitted a mistake. Once he had committed himself to an opinion he would never change it.

"The injuries could, in my opinion, only have been produced by strangulation by the hand." That was Spilsbury's opinion at the beginning and the end, in spite of all that went between.

This opinion was based on four signs. These were hæmorrhage in the epiglottis and three bruises – one on the tongue, one at the back of the larynx, and the third on the thyroid gland. On these he based his theory of strangulation, which he subsequently outlined to the court. Firm pressure, he said, between the thumb and fingers applied to the larynx could have produced the bruise on the thyroid and the hæmorrhage in the epiglottis; the bruise on the larynx might have been caused by forcibly pressing that organ upward; and this pressure could also have closed the victim's jaws and forced her to bite and thus bruise her tongue. With his use of tentative verbs like "could" and "might" the theory sounded so plausible that the unwary could forget it was only a theory, not hard fact.

Spilsbury gave evidence at the proceedings before the Margate magistrates, which began on January 9, 1930. As is usual in such cases, the defence was reserved and no witnesses were called, but Fox's solicitor, George Hindle, cross-examined the Crown witnesses very thoroughly. His purpose was to get them to commit themselves as far as possible – to make definite statements of which they might be reminded, if necessary, at the trial; and also to try to find out as much as possible about the prosecution's line without giving away any clue to the line of the defence.

Thus Hindle sent me an account of Dr Nichol's evidence with a request for any observations that might help him in cross-examination. In fact there was not much that could be asked, as Dr Nichol had neither examined Mrs Fox nor noticed anything special about her appearance. I advised Hindle to ask Nichol to confirm that he saw no signs of death from asphyxia, no marks of violence of any kind, no signs of froth or blood-staining at the mouth or nose; and that the appearances were quite consistent with death from heart-failure. Hindle followed my advice, and in cross-examining Dr Austin also he asked the same questions and received similar answers; but while Dr Nichol thought the appearances were not consistent with heart failure, Dr Austin thought they were.

Spilsbury gave his evidence in his usual clear and definite way, and he was too experienced in being cross-examined for Hindle to get much out of him.

"Is it not extraordinary that there were no marks of violence on the neck?" Hindle asked.

"It is not," Spilsbury replied. "It is unusual in a case of manual strangulation, but that is another matter."

The case was transferred from Kent to the Sussex Assizes, and the trial was fixed to begin at Lewes on Wednesday, March 12. On the preceding Saturday I went to Spilsbury's laboratory at the University College Hospital in London to look at the various specimens he had removed at the exhumation.

It was my first professional encounter with the Honorary Pathologist to the Home Office, a prelude to our first conflict in court. He could not have been more courteous or helpful. He showed me the whole of the exhibits.

Among the parts he had preserved was the larynx, which I was particularly interested to see. Spilsbury regarded the bruise on this as the main prop of his strangulation theory. I was inclined to think it was the only prop, and not a very good one at that, for I regarded the whole theory as flimsy. At the same time I was intrigued by this bruise. Spilsbury had said in his report that it was behind the larynx and about the size of a half-crown. I could not imagine how such a large bruise could have been inflicted there without damage to the tissues on the side of the larynx or the neck.

Spilsbury said nothing while I examined the larynx. He just stood beside me silently, while I looked – not at, but for, the bruise.

There was none to be seen.

Putrefactive discoloration, yes. No doubt about that. But not even a sixpenny bruise, let alone one the size of half-a-crown.

With me in the laboratory was Dr R. M. Brontë, formerly Crown Pathologist for All Ireland, who had also been asked to appear for the defence. He had crossed swords with Spilsbury in court before. He also examined the larynx, and finally shook his head.

"I can't see any sign of a bruise, Spilsbury," I said at length.

"Nor can I," said Brontë.

"No," agreed Spilsbury. "You can't see it now. But it was there when I exhumed the body."

That fairly staggered me. The larynx had been preserved in formalin ever since the exhumation.

"Where's the bruise gone, then?" I asked.

"It became obscure," said Spilsbury, "before I put the larynx in formalin. That is why I did not take a section."

A microscopical section would have been of inestimable value in showing whether the patch of discoloration Spilsbury had seen was a bruise or not. Personally I was pretty sure it was not. A bruise is caused by the breaking of small vessels which allows blood to be forced out of the vessels into the tissues, where it clots. To get a bruise the size of a half-crown quite a lot of blood would have to be extruded. The blood remains in the tissues, and cannot be removed by post-mortem changes.

"I don't see how a bruise of that size could have just disappeared," I said.

"It became obscure," he repeated. "It was there. I saw it myself."

"Spilsbury, I don't doubt that you saw something," I said. "But I put it to you that it might not have been a bruise. It could have been a patch of discoloration from post-mortem staining or putrefaction." Brontë nodded agreement. "We all know how difficult it is to diagnose a bruise with the naked eye after partial putrefaction has occurred."

Spilsbury listened attentively and was very polite, but he would not argue the point. I had the feeling that nothing I said would make any difference, that his mind was closed. Had I known him then as well as I came to later I would have realized why I was wasting my time. He could not change his opinion now because he had already given it. He had described the alleged bruise in his report and given evidence about it before the magistrates. His belief in himself was so strong that he could not conceive the possibility of error either in his observation or interpretation.

We looked at the other signs of alleged injury. The haemorrhage in the epiglottis was there – a spot the size of the head of a pin, such as might be found on five out of six cases of death from natural causes. There was the bruise on the side of the tongue, which might well have been caused during strangulation – and, just as easily, by the old lady biting her tongue, as she could so easily have done with the badly fitting dentures she wore. Finally there was the alleged bruise on the thyroid gland, and this led to another difference of opinion. It consisted of a few stray red blood corpuscles such as might be found in a section of any ordinary thyroid.

"I cannot accept that as a bruise," I said emphatically.

"Nor can I," said Brontë.

Spilsbury said nothing, but we found an ally in Dr Henry Weir, a pathologist of standing whom the Crown had engaged to support Spilsbury's evidence for the prosecution. He also said it was not a bruise.

The four of us discussed it in the laboratory, and I thought Spilsbury yielded to our view. He said little himself, but I went away with the definite impression that he accepted that on this relatively small point we were right and he was wrong.

Brontë knew him better than I did.

"Not Spilsbury," he said as we left. "You wait till we're in court."

The case for the Crown was that Fox had strangled his mother and then set fire to the room to cover up his crime. Spilsbury had looked for soot on the linings of the air passages, and had tested the blood for carbon monoxide, with negative results in each case. He was therefore satisfied that Mrs Fox had not died through suffocation by smoke. So was I. In my opinion she had not died of asphyxia at all. I thought she might very well have died of heart failure brought on by sudden exertion or fright. The shock of waking up and finding the room full of smoke, and the effort to get out of bed and escape, might well have put a fatal additional strain on her already weakened heart.

One would have thought that any pathologist would have agreed that this was a possibility, but though Weir agreed Spilsbury would not.

The prosecution of Fox was led by the Attorney-General, Sir William (later Lord) Jowitt, and he seemed determined to hang Fox. It is, of course, not the proper function of the Crown counsel to press the case against the accused. An eminent authority, Mr Justice Crompton, once said that the duty of prosecuting counsel was to acquit themselves as ministers of justice, aiding in the administration of the criminal law, and not as advocates attempting to secure a conviction.

Jowitt's attitude was anything but judicial. His treatment of the medical evidence in his opening speech was open to criticism, especially the part dealing with the half-crown bruise. "It will be said, how could the inside bruise be done without an outside bruise? This much is plain: the inside bruise is there. It is there—"

It was not there. Spilsbury himself was to testify that it had vanished from sight four months before.

The first five days of the trial were taken up mainly with nonmedical evidence, which was heavy against Fox. Of course, nothing was said about his criminal record, and when Chief-Inspector Hambrook of Scotland Yard gave evidence on his conduct of the case the jury had no inkling that he had arrested Fox for forgery thirteen years before. The evidence that could properly be brought, however, made it pretty clear how he normally obtained his living. There was adequate evidence of motive in the insurances he had taken out on his mother's life. His conduct on the night of her death was at least suspicious.

Dr Austin was the first medical witness. He repeated the evidence he had given at the proceedings before magistrates. Cross-examining for the defence, Mr J. D. Cassels asked him if he saw any signs of death by asphyxia.

"No, except that the face was very flushed, which you find in a case of asphyxia."

"Did you see any marks of violence?"

"No."

"Or appearances consistent with death by heart-failure?"

"Well, I should hardly think so."

Cassels' next question brought out the value of Hindle's careful cross-examination at the preliminary hearing.

"Did you say, in examination at the police court, 'I saw no signs of death from asphyxiation and no marks of violence. As far as I was able to see, the appearances were consistent with heart-failure'?"

"If I am reported to have done so I must have done," Dr Austin replied. "It is five months ago."

Dr Nichol also was cross-examined to good effect. He said that after death Mrs Fox's face was composed, pale, and presented no special significance, that he saw no marks of violence, and that "the woman did not give me the impression of having died from asphyxia."

But all this was of little consequence compared with Spilsbury's evidence, which was given clearly and with great sincerity – and complete conviction.

To explain his theory of how Mrs Fox died, Spilsbury produced a porcelain model of the human mouth and neck.

"At the back of the larynx," he said, pointing to the spot, "I found a large, recent bruise about the size of half-a-crown. It was then that I had the first indication of the conclusions to which I finally came, that death was due to strangulation."

Spilsbury repeated his previous evidence about the bruise on the tongue and the very small haemorrhages on the epiglottis. Then he came to the alleged bruise on the thyroid gland.

"I found a small dark area just on the surface which I thought might be a bruise," he said. "I made microscopical preparations of it which in my view confirmed the presence of a little bruising. I showed the preparations to Dr Weir, Professor Smith, and Dr Brontë, who, however, did not take the same view, and for that reason I prefer that the bruise shall not be considered as a possible injury caused at that time."

"Apart from the thyroid gland," he was then asked, "are we, in your view, outside the region of doubt?"

"Yes."

This answer implied that Spilsbury accepted that there was doubt about the bruise he claimed to have seen on the thyroid gland. With Weir against him as well as us he could hardly do otherwise. But when he was cross-examined he made it clear that he still thought that he was right and the rest of us wrong.

"Is your opinion upon this part of the case as definite as it is on the other parts of the case?" Cassels asked.

"Yes."

The judge asked, "Your opinion is still that the thyroid gland was bruised?"

"That is so."

Since he was still so sure of this, it was not surprising that he refused to admit even the possibility of doubt in the matter of the alleged bruise on the larynx, which only he had seen or would ever see.

Cassels suggested it might have been a mark of putrefaction.

"It was a bruise and nothing else," Spilsbury answered shortly. "There are no two opinions about it."

Certainly only he had seen it. This sort of thing is a common handicap to medical expert witnesses appearing for the defence. The Crown's experts are there from the start, and often there is nothing left to see when the experts for the defence come in. Spilsbury was scrupulously careful and painstaking in his work, but once he had given an opinion nothing would make him change it. The supposed bruise on the thyroid gland was a case in point. No doubt if he alone had seen it he would have put that also outside the region of doubt.

He was an excellent witness, especially for the Crown. I listened attentively while he gave evidence, making notes and passing them to Cassels whenever a fresh line of questioning occurred to me. But there was very little to be got out of Spilsbury, and as usual he made a good impression on the jury. Even the admission that this was the first exhumation he had done in a case of what he thought was manual strangulation did not detract from the effect of his undoubted reputation and complete assurance.

Spilsbury was followed by Dr Weir, who was pathologist to the National Hospital for Diseases of the Heart. He had not seen any more of the remains than I had, but he accepted Spilsbury's statement about the half-crown bruise. However, he did not share Spilsbury's view that death was caused by asphyxia, but agreed with us that it was due to heart-failure, and he was an expert on diseases of the heart. He attributed it to commencing strangulation – but "in my opinion, except for the bruises, there was sufficient disease in the heart to account for death from natural causes."

So the conflict of medical evidence was not only between the prosecution and the defence.

Weir was the last witness called by the Crown. Fox himself was the first witness for the defence, and probably he did himself much more harm than good. He made what was considered his worst mistake when Jowitt questioned him about his actions after discovering the fire in his mother's room.

"Can you explain to me why it was that you closed the door instead of flinging it wide open?" Jowitt asked.

"My explanation for that now is that the smoke should not spread into the hotel."

"Rather that your mother should suffocate in that room than that smoke should get about in the hotel?"

"Most certainly not, sir" – and then, realizing the implication of his answer, Fox half-denied that he had closed the door. But by then the damage was done.

I was called later the same day.

In the course of the years I had learnt a number of lessons about giving evidence in court. One was to confine one's answers to the questions asked; another was not to try to score off counsel. I had also found that it pays to be reticent, and to keep back a few odds and ends to release under cross-examination; this makes the opposing advocate more careful in his approach.

Until this case I had always been treated with consideration and courtesy, and my evidence had not been seriously challenged.

Over many years and in many different courts I had always tried to give my evidence on the facts as I saw them without any regard as to whether my opinions were helpful to the prosecution or the defence. This was my first experience of the clashes between counsel and expert witness that are a feature of British criminal courts.

In my examination-in-chief I gave my opinion that there was not sufficient medical evidence to support a charge of strangulation.

Jowitt began his cross-examination the next morning.

"You stated in your evidence-in-chief that you had a very long experience in cases involving manual strangulation?"

"Yes."

"Were they cases of strangulation by a young man of an old woman as the old woman lay in bed?"

"I have had many cases of strangulation of elderly men and elderly women."

"Will you try to answer my question?"

"I will think of the special conditions for one moment. Yes, I have had."

"Do you mean to tell us you had not considered that question before you came to give evidence in this case?"

"I have considered the question."

"Then I take it you have brought your notes of a person being strangled in bed."

"No, I have not."

"Was there one case, or more than one case?"

"I have had many cases of a somewhat similar nature. May I explain?"

"Please answer my question. It may be difficult for a gentleman who gives lectures to answer questions, but I want you to answer mine."

So it began, and so it went on: sharp, harsh, and somewhat blustering. Jowitt had been well briefed. After a series of questions about the signs of asphyxia he read out a passage from Taylor's *Medical Jurisprudence* and asked me if I agreed. As my name was on the title-page of the book as the current editor I could not have easily disowned it. In fact, however, it was not in conflict with the opinions I had expressed in evidence, as I was able to explain.

Jowitt continued to press his questions in a rather hectoring way.

"Do you think that is being quite candid with me?" he asked once. Then, "If the answer is 'No' say 'No.' You are not trying to make it difficult for me, are you? I want you to try to help."

"I am, to the best of my ability," I replied, "but you won't give me an opportunity of putting you right. If I begin to explain you say, 'Please answer my question.' It makes it very difficult."

Jowitt went on to the matter of the half-crown bruise.

"You said yesterday that in training assistants you had to be careful in distinguishing in post-mortem examination between bruises and discoloration marks. Do you put Sir Bernard Spilsbury on a par with one of your assistants?"

This was a catch-question. Jowitt was trying to make me belittle Spilsbury.

"Do you suggest Sir Bernard would not know the difference between the two?" he persisted.

"Nobody can tell merely by looking," I replied. "I do not think anyone should say a bruise is a bruise until it has been proved that it is."

"Do you say that you would not say a bruise was a bruise until you put it under a microscope?"

"No, I should cut into it."

"If you saw a fellow with a black eye would you say, 'Let me put it under a microscope before I say it is a black eye'?"

This question surprised me. It was not the sort of thing I would have expected from the Attorney-General.

"Sir Bernard says there can be no two opinions about it," he went on.

"It is very obvious there can be," I pointed out.

"You are bound to accept the evidence of the man who saw the bruise?"

"I do not think so."

"How can you say there was not a bruise there?"

"Because if there was a bruise there it should be there now. It should be there for ever. The larynx is there to be examined by anybody."

With that Jowitt left the half-crown bruise, and the rest of his cross-examination was in a slightly milder tone.

He began pressing again when he cross-examined Brontë, who confirmed my evidence and went on to give the opinion that putrefactive changes "would magnify the bruise and make it easier to detect." He quoted a case in which Spilsbury himself had said the same thing.

Jowitt asked more pointed questions about Spilsbury and the half-crown bruise.

"Are you suggesting Sir Bernard did not see what he said he saw?"

"Far be it from me to make such a suggestion."

"Did you suggest that Sir Bernard Spilsbury was wrong, and that it was a post-mortem change? If Sir Bernard made this mistake it would be a very elementary mistake to make? It is a sort of mistake that every laboratory assistant is warned against?"

Cassels put the matter back into perspective in his closing speech. He recalled the two bruises on which Spilsbury based his theory of strangulation.

"There was, of course, another at one time," he reminded the jury. "Another pinpoint mark, which under a microscope was said to be a sign of bruising upon the thyroid gland – that mark which Sir Bernard Spilsbury still retains his opinion about, but does not desire to have as much importance attached to it as to the other two, because Dr Weir, Professor Smith, and Dr Brontë did not agree with him. If Sir Bernard Spilsbury is wrong about one thing might he not be wrong about something else? No one can say that an individual, whatever his position and skill, is never likely to be mistaken. No one can claim for anybody infallibility."

Mr Justice Rowlatt summed up with perfect fairness.

"There were no external indications of asphyxia. There were no external marks on the throat. Sir Bernard Spilsbury has said it was quite possible there would be none, but you and I might think it difficult to believe it. As regards the brittle bone in the throat known as the hyoid, it is a very curious coincidence that that bone was not broken in this case. That is a very strong point in favour of the accused. As to the mark at the back of the larynx, alleged by the prosecution to be a bruise, there is no doubt that

Sir Bernard Spilsbury saw some object there. It is unfortunate that those tissues could not have been preserved for others to see. The defence have said – and are justified in saying it – that that point rests on the testimony of what one skilled man observed, and observed at one moment only . . ."

Perhaps the judge did not quite appreciate the dangerously high esteem in which that one skilled man was held. Perhaps Spilsbury did not fully realize that fame brings responsibility as well as honour. I do not think the jury would have returned the verdict they did if his evidence had been given by anyone else but Spilsbury.

One hour and ten minutes was all they needed to find Fox guilty.

"My lord," he whispered, "I did not murder my mother. I am innocent."

I believe he was.

I certainly would not have put it past him to murder his mother. He was bad enough for any crime, and the evidence about the renewal of the insurances was heavy against him.

There were many suspicious circumstances in the case, but Fox was specifically charged with and was hanged for strangling his mother. I thought then – and I still think now – that he was innocent of that.

"ACT OF MERCY"

(Dr Hermann Sander, USA 1949)

David Rowan

The case of Dr Sander, the first to involve an act of so-called mercy killing, caused a sensation in the early months of 1950. It arose from Dr Sander's open admission that while treating a dying patient, Mrs Abbie Borroto, he had injected 40cc of air into her arm, causing an embolism. The injection had been witnessed by a nurse at Dr Sander's side, and although bowel cancer was given as the cause of death, the doctor declined to alter his written record of how he had treated Mrs Borroto, and he was widely applauded for his act of euthanasia. Dr Sander stood trial for murdering Mrs Borroto, and there was much evidential confusion over whether the patient was actually already dead when Dr Sander administered the injection of air. The doctor was acquitted and eventually resumed his career.

No place on earth can be so silent as a room of imminent death. Outside Hillsborough County Hospital, New Hampshire, a bitter wind moans relentlessly through the snow-laden trees. Inside, the noise is blanketed by the comfortable central heating and double windows; even the nurses chattering about Christmas to come are only a distant murmur. But in all the hospital on this December morning in 1949, no room is more still than that of one middle-aged patient, Mrs Abbie Borroto.

For over a year, Mrs Borroto has been ill with cancer. She has wasted away to little more than half her usual weight. Now the dread disease has reached its climax. Death is only a matter of hours, perhaps of minutes. Already it is almost impossible to detect signs of life. A pretty, grave-faced nurse tries in vain to find the pulse. White-clad shapes move soundlessly out of the room. Finally one doctor and a lone nurse are left. The doctor bends over the bed, syringe in hand. Then he straightens himself and, with shock effect, speaks in his normal voice. It is all over . . .

To the medical profession, that scene may be a commonplace. In large hospitals, it happens several times a day. This time, however, the scene was to become the subject of tall headlines in newspapers throughout the world – and was to rekindle a controversy that is likely to remain unsettled for many generations.

The first clue that the commonplace had a distinctly uncommon feature was detected by a young nurse-secretary, Miss Josephine Connor, to whom the doctor in charge of Mrs Borroto had dictated his notes on the case. The clue appeared amid the welter of medical detail certifying the cause of death as cancer. Meticulously, the doctor had recorded the fact that, on the morning the patient died, he had injected a small amount of air into her veins. It might have seemed insignificant, but it led the young nurse to inform the hospital authorities immediately. For injecting air into a victim's veins is one of the classic murder methods beloved of the thriller writers. On reaching the heart, the air bubble supposedly has the same effect as a blood clot, causing an embolism, or blockage, which brings death within minutes of the injection.

For the hospital authorities who opened an enquiry into the strange entry, the inference was plain – Mrs Borroto had been eased through death's door before her time. It might have been a mere hour or so before, but there was still only one word for it. Murder.

On December 29th, as the suspect walked into Goffstown Hospital to attend another patient, two detectives stepped forward.

"Dr Hermann Sander?"

"Ah, yes, gentlemen. I've been expecting you."

The charge: first-degree murder. The maximum penalty: death.

And the motive? Nothing like so clear cut. Material gain, revenge, or any other of the usual motives for murder were all out of the question. The prosecution's answer, provided at a preliminary court hearing the following day, had far wider implications. It emerged from an alleged statement by Dr Sander, denying that he had committed murder and saying: "I did it as an act of mercy. There was no malice on my part." It was further alleged that he told the county prosecutor, Mr William Craig: "Her family had asked me if anything could be done to end her agony."

From that moment on, it was certain that the trial of Dr Hermann Sander would arouse the strongest feelings throughout the US. In a country which calmly accepts such a phenomenon as the Forest Lawn cemetery (as dissected by Evelyn Waugh in *The Loved One*), and where the fear of pain often transcends even that of death itself, there are probably more protagonists of euthanasia than in any other nation in the world. These are the people who favour the "putting to sleep" of the incurably sick, to save them from terrible pain before their inevitable deaths. Resolutely entrenched against them, however, are millions of Church-goers, particularly the Roman Catholics, whose religious teaching is utterly opposed to such an idea. It is fair to say, therefore, that this case split the American nation violently in two – emotion versus Church discipline, "modern" thinking against twenty centuries of spiritual belief.

Nowhere was that general picture more acute than in the accused's own little New England community. At least two-thirds of the local population were Roman Catholics – many of them simple immigrant French-Canadians from over the border. On the other hand, within hours of Dr Sander's arrest, more than six hundred people in his home-village of Candia had signed a petition on his behalf, expressing their "unshakable faith" in his integrity. The petition added: "We respect him as a man of Christian virtue, devoted to the higher interests of human welfare at all times." To add bitter piquancy to the situation, the lawyer who was to lead for the prosecution, Attorney-General William Phinney, had been at school with the accused and was a lifelong friend and neighbour. Finally, although Phinney promised that he would show no leniency in pressing for a conviction, bail was set at $25,000 (nearly £9,000) – which, although a stiff sum, was just within Sander's reach and enabled him to remain at liberty until the Grand Jury hearing.

At first glance, the forty-one-year-old man who had inspired such a wealth of sentiment and bitter arguments seemed an unlikely figure for the role. A long, rather sallow face; dark hair, parted in the middle; a pencil moustache; spectacles; mild brown eyes; a slight, not very strong physique. Study of his career, however, showed that he had some of the stuff of which martyrs are made. Friends told of his long hours of selfless work, of how he usually "forgot" to send the bill to his poorer patients. He was evidently a man who knew his own mind, even if one might not always agree with his views. Earlier in the year, he had toured Great Britain to inspect the National Health Service. On his return, he expressed frank admiration for it (contrary to general American opinion at that time), but still said he opposed the idea for the US – on the somewhat dogmatic ground that "the Government should keep out of medicine".

It was characteristic of him that, when the question of a police charge arose, he told his secretary not to cancel any of his appointments. A few hours after his release on bail, he was helping to bring a baby into the world. He had been "booked" by a Mrs Louise Crocker and, though he had only just returned home, he did not fail her – duly delivering her of a 5 lb 12 oz daughter.

Great play was made with such details in the Press. There were long stories of how, on Sunday, New Year's Day, he had left his white-timbered home on the outskirts of Candia and gone to church with his wife, Alice, an ex-nurse, and their three young daughters. The following day, the newspapers reported faithfully, he had gone on his country rounds as usual, calling, first on Mrs Crocker and her baby, then on a young boy on whom he had performed a minor operation on New Year's Eve, and then on twelve more patients. The doctor was quoted as saying: "It is tremendous what people have said and done. I am rather overwhelmed. From every walk of life they have called to sympathise with me. I have never seen so much sentiment." When asked about the circumstances of Mrs Borroto's death, according to another report, he replied: "Doctors tell me these things have happened many times but have never been put in the records. They say I'm a couple of decades ahead of my time."

If the last report were accurate, it seemed pretty damning. For, despite the whipping up of mass emotion, nothing could get over the cold fact that, in law, there is no such thing as "mercy killing". It remains murder, pure and simple.

Pure it may have been, but simple, no. The complexities were typified by statements made by the victim's family. Her husband, sixty-five-year-old Mr Reginald Borroto, a retired oil salesman, might have been expected to appear as an injured party, yet he said openly that he was "terribly saddened" at the charge against Dr Sander, whom he described as the "biggest man I ever knew". One of Mrs Borroto's brothers, Louis Constantino, agreed: "I bear him absolutely no ill-will." But two other brothers strongly disagreed. The first, Bernard Constantino, declared: "My sister was at death's door, but she had great courage and refused to give up hope. I still insist that he had no right at all to take her life." The second, Thomas Constantino, denied that he had made any suggestion for ending Mrs Borroto's pain. "It should have been left to the will of God."

On Thursday, January 5th, 1950, Sander drove with his wife to the nearby town of Manchester to face the Grand Jury. Long before the couple climbed the stairs together to the second floor of the red brick courthouse, the building was crammed to over-flowing. Outside was another big crowd, with newsreel cameras and a large jostle of Press photographers. The accused's cheeks were hollowed and his eyes black-ringed, but his voice was unexpectedly strong as he answered "not guilty" to the charge.

"Hark to the indictment," intoned the clerk, and Sander's hands clenched tight as the clerk went on: ". . . feloniously, wilfully and of his malice aforethought did inject ten cubic centimetres of air four times in close succession into the veins of Mrs Abbie Borroto, fifty-nine, his patient."

Four times. Most people in the room sat up with a jolt. That was a total of forty cc – far more than they had been led to believe by the early newspaper reports.

Nevertheless, at the end of the short hearing, Dr Sander was again granted bail in the sum of $25,000, although this time on condition that he treated no more patients before his trial.

Just over two weeks later, Mrs Borroto's body was exhumed and three pathologists made a post-mortem examination lasting ten hours. A month afterwards – on Monday, February 20th – the trial opened in Manchester.

By now, outside interest knew no bounds. Dr Sander had received some 3,000 letters from sympathizers all over the world, including Britain. Many Euthanasia Societies had offered to help pay for the defence – offers which were declined. Every hotel room in the town had been taken. Special writers sent to cover the trial included such personalities as John O'Hara and Fanny Hurst. Among the boilers in the courthouse cellar, space had been cleared for telegraphic equipment, tables for typewriters and even a broadcasting studio. It was uncomfortably hot in this makeshift news-centre, and the stifling atmosphere was aggravated by the fact that the temperature in the street outside was several degrees below zero.

The effect of all this on the people of Manchester was somewhat revealing. Feelings had run so high that for weeks past the local newspapers had refused to comment editorially on the case or to print readers' letters about it – a most unusual step in the US, where the strictures of *sub judice* do not apply as under British law. At the same time, the town could not quite get over its astonishment at finding itself the centre of world attention, whatever the cause. The presence of four correspondents from London newspapers was an item on the local radio, and the last-minute arrival of Nicholas Chatelaine, of the Paris *Le Figaro*, earned him a front-page picture in the *Manchester Evening Leader*.

That was superficial parochialism, however. Only two factors really counted: (1) In this tightly knit community, Dr Sander had been a familiar and respected figure all his adult life; and (2) Roughly 50,000 of Manchester's 80,000 population were Roman Catholics.

Clearly, the task of selecting an unbiased jury would be extremely difficult. Under American law, counsel are allowed to cross-examine prospective jurors and, if desired, to reject them. It is nearly always a tedious business, but this time it promised to take longer than ever.

When the accused arrived – wearing a heavy overcoat and a bright red scarf against the icy cold – he found a panel of no fewer than 145 candidates for the jury in the courtroom. Hour by hour, the slow process dragged on. A surprising number of the candidates immediately disqualified themselves by stating that they had already formed definite views which would not be changed by any evidence they might hear. By the end of the day, only nine of the thirteen necessary jurors (including a substitute) had been chosen. The following day was even worse. Still more jurors were dismissed from service after saying that they must put a "higher law" before the laws or evidence of the court. Another setback came when one of the jurors selected the previous day (a naturalized American of British birth, who had come to this little Manchester from the great Lancashire city of the same name) was successfully challenged by the prosecution – following a one-and-a-quarter-hour conference between the judge and prosecuting and defence counsel.

It was not until the third morning that an all-male jury satisfactory to both sides was at last completed. The jurors' average age was fifty-four, and they comprised nine Catholics, one Episcopalian, a Baptist and a Methodist.

Throughout the frustrating delay, Dr Sander and his wife, who had left a sick bed to attend court, had sat listening patiently. Sometimes they held hands. Between sessions they went for a stroll round the block. Every day a police car brought them to and from their home eleven miles away. Otherwise the doctor was a free man – an ironic situation for the unfortunate jurors, who had to remain locked up in their hotel.

Throughout this period, too, despite the somewhat premature objections of the dismissed jury candidates, there had been no official mention of the phrase "mercy killing". But now Attorney-General William Phinney, in his opening speech for the prosecution, underlined the unusual nature of the case by announcing that agreement had been reached under which the State would *not* ask for the death penalty. Although he did not elaborate, one possible explanation of this clemency lay in his use of a

single word. Medical evidence would show, he said, that forty cc
of air injected into a woman in Mrs Borroto's condition would
probably cause death and that the air which Sander administered
was in fact the cause of her death. "Probably" was a most
unexpected qualification. Until this moment, it had been assumed that the State's assertion would be categorical. Now the
lists were wide open for a conflict of expert opinion.

A minor clash occurred during cross-examination of the very
first witness, Dr Harold Loverud, director of the Hillsborough
Hospital, who had told of the discovery of the fateful entry in the
victim's medical records. Rising to his feet, the chief defence
counsel, Mr Louis Wyman, put a long but deceptively simple
question. Had another member of the hospital staff, Dr Albert
Snay, seen Mrs Borroto at 11.10 or 11.15 on the morning of her
death, just before Dr Sander entered the room and just before any
injection of air; and could Dr Loverud say, he concluded, "if Dr
Snay at that time examined Mrs Borroto and pronounced her
dead, would he be able to give pretty reliable information?"

Mr Phinney jumped up immediately and objected to the
question. It should not be admitted, he insisted, unless evidence
were to be produced to support the suggestion. A pronounced stir
rippled along the two hundred and fifty public seats in the court
as grey-haired Mr Wyman assured him: "In due course we
expect evidence to that effect."

Behind the involved language, this was the first open sign by
the defence that they intended to fight the case by arguing that
Mrs Borroto was already dead when the air was injected – and
that they believed they could prove the claim.

The hitherto rather bored reporters seized the news gleefully,
correctly envisaging the largest possible headlines. From across
the Atlantic, five hours ahead in time, the results of the British
general election on the same day were flowing in. It was the
election in which the Labour Party only just held on to power,
with the barest majority. Most Americans, accustomed to "root-
ing" unabashedly for the team of their choice, no matter where its
home ground, had been hoping for a Conservative victory. Yet
even this close struggle had to take second place to reports of the
Sander trial in the US popular Press.

The following day, Friday, February 24th, produced significant details of the notes with which Dr Sander had trapped
himself. Nurse Josephine Connor, to whom he had dictated
them, confirmed in evidence that he had said the patient was
"practically moribund" on the day before her death and that she
"expired within ten minutes" after he started injecting air on the
following day. She then described a conversation between the
accused and Dr Robert Biron, the county medical referee, after
she had drawn the hospital authorities' attention to the notes.
"Dr Biron asked if Dr Sander realised he had broken the law. Dr
Sander said, 'Yes, he had broken laws before – he had been
through stop signs.' Dr Biron said this was more serious; this was
murder. Dr Sander said he did realise he had broken the law but
the law should be changed. Dr Biron said, 'Why didn't you
change it first – before you did this?'"

When asked if he realized the seriousness of the situation, Miss
Connor said, Dr Sander replied that he assumed the Medical
Association would probably reprimand him for it, "tell him not to
do it again."

This had been damning evidence, and not least for the phrase
"the law should be changed", with its apparent acquiescence in
the principle of euthanasia. Moreover, the light-heartedness of
some of the alleged replies struck an unhappy note. Another blow
followed almost immediately, although this time the defence
parried it more successfully. It came when the prosecution tried
to squash once and for all the rumours, repeated in evidence, that
Mrs Borroto's husband had pleaded with Dr Sander to end her
suffering. A police witness, Sheriff O'Brien, took the stand to
testify that the prosecutor had obtained from Mr Borroto "a
signed, sworn statement . . . that he had nothing to do with Dr
Sander in this". This brought an immediate defence protest.
Justifiably, for Mr Borroto himself was on the list of witnesses.
The court, concurring, sustained the objection and ordered the
sheriff's remark to be struck out. To demonstrate that he had
nothing to hide, however, Mr Wyman told reporters later that the
defence would probably call Mr Borroto if the prosecution
decided not to do so.

Before that happened, there was vital evidence to hear from a twenty-four-year old, slim and attractive nurse who set necks craning as she walked forward. Her name, Elizabeth Rose, suited her blue eyes and blonde hair to perfection. But there was a macabre incongruity about the minor diversion caused by her appearance. For Miss Rose was the nurse who had been alone with Dr Sander at the time he made the injection.

It was not long before she caused a stir of another kind. Reading from the notes she had made at the bedside, she told the court that, shortly before Dr Sander entered the room, three people had been unable to detect Mrs Borroto's pulse.

Sensation! If this meant what it seemed to mean – that the patient was already dead – the case was virtually over. The Attorney-General, however, evidently had reason to think otherwise. Step by step, he took the witness through the events of the victim's last morning. When she went on duty at 7.00 a.m., Miss Rose said, the patient was asleep and her respiration was very shallow. A little later she sipped coffee and said she was uncomfortable. "At 11.00 a.m.," the young nurse went on calmly, "I was unable to get her pulse."

Another nurse, Miss Garrard, was also unable to find a pulse and Miss Rose then went into the corridor and met Dr Albert Snay. He, too, said he could not get any pulse. He asked for a stethoscope but could hear nothing.

Mr Phinney: "Did Dr Snay say the patient was dead?"
Miss Rose "No."
"There is no question of that in your mind?" – "No."

At this point, the witness continued, Dr Sander arrived and talked briefly to Dr Snay. She did not overhear the conversation.

Mr Phinney: "Did you notice Mrs Borroto after Dr Snay left?"
Miss Rose: "Yes. *There was some gasping.*"

So here was the goal for which the Attorney-General had been aiming. Firstly, he had established that, despite the failure to detect Mrs Borroto's pulse, no authoritative confirmation of the fact of death had been given at the time. Secondly, although Dr Snay might counter this when he gave evidence later, he would have to do so in the face of the nurse's testimony about the subsequent gasping. The prosecution had certainly turned the tables . . .

Miss Rose's description of the final scene enabled Mr Phinney to drive home his advantage still further. After Dr Snay left the room, she said, Dr Sander also tried to find Mrs Borroto's pulse. He made no comment about this, but asked her for a syringe. She saw him apply the syringe, which was empty, to the patient. Then, she asserted, "I heard a gasp from Mrs Borroto," and Dr Sander, turning to her, had said: "Air in the veins would act like an embolus."

The accused's face flushed as he listened from the defence table, only a few feet from the witness stand. It was a bad moment – the prosecution had now shown twice what appeared to be proof that the victim was alive when the injection was made. Moreover, what would the jury read into his alleged comment about an embolus?

Mr Phinney paused to give the witness' last words their full dramatic effect, before asking: "What happened next?"

Miss Rose: "I looked at the syringe. The plunger was down on the barrel. After two or three minutes, Dr Sander turned and handed me the syringe and needle. He said he would notify Mrs Borroto's people and call the undertaker."

Mr Phinney: "What did that indicate to you?" – "That the patient was dead."

For the defence, at this juncture, the sole hope seemed to lie in re-emphasising the first half of the young nurse's evidence. Cross-examining, Mr Wyman went straight to the point. "On January 2nd," he asked, "did you say Dr Sander did not kill her because she was dead before the injection was made?"

Miss Rose: "I couldn't get her pulse."

This failure to answer the question directly incurred its own penalty. Fishing a typewritten sheet of paper from the mass of documents on his table, the chief defence counsel read out, in a flat, dry voice, a statement made by Miss Rose during enquiries before the Grand Jury hearing. The key words of this statement were: "Dr Sander did not kill her because she was already dead."

One point retrieved for the defence . . . By itself it could hardly overcome the image in everyone's mind of a dying woman gasping, but – particularly since the judge admitted the statement as a defence exhibit – it had at least reopened the door to doubt.

Hitherto the conflict had been mainly on a medical plane, if at a minor level. Now, with the long-awaited appearance of Mr Reginald Borroto, the dead woman's husband, it swung back towards the latent euthanasia controversy and the by-play of mass sentiment. The Attorney-General, sticking to the guns which had been temporarily spiked when Sheriff O'Brien took the stand, asked at once: "Did you at anytime, directly or indirectly, ask Dr Sander to shorten your wife's life?"

"No."

Despite this denial – which anyway came as no surprise – Mr Borroto obviously disliked his position. The State had decided to call him as a prosecution witness after all, doubtless to Mr Wyman's disappointment. Yet, for the job of re-establishing public sympathy, the defence could hardly have asked for a better ally. Had the accused been his own brother, Mr Borroto said, he could not feel more kindly towards him. "If my wife had been Dr Sander's mother or sister, he could not have done more to minister to her." The doctor had made many gifts to her, he went on. "Once he brought her a canary in a cage, complete with all the fittings. She became very fond of the bird." And it had done much to distract her attention from her suffering . . .

All this gave abundant heart-rending material to the weepier writers at the trial. But a court of law is supposedly concerned only with the facts at issue before it – and the most important tests had yet to come.

As a first step, one vital point had to be cleared up. Of the three people who had failed to find Mrs Borroto's pulse, only one could say with authority whether she was dead – Dr Albert Snay, the staff doctor who had examined her only a few minutes before Dr Sander entered the room.

To the audible relief of the accused's sympathizers, Dr Snay seemed to have little doubt. On examining the patient, he said, he found no pulse, no reflex of the eyeball and no sound through the stethoscope. "I concluded then that she was dead. I remarked to Miss Rose that the patient appeared to be gone. Dr Sander walked in and I said something to the effect that there was nothing to be done." He did not make a report because he knew it was Dr Sander's case. Later he met the accused, who said: "She was dead." Dr Snay added: "From her appearance it was amazing to me that she had lived as long as she did. Nothing Dr Sander or anyone else could have done could have affected her condition."

On the surface, this was definite enough. It looked once more as though the defence had triumphed. Yet close observers noted that, despite his strong emphasis, Dr Snay had still not committed himself fully. He had *concluded* that the patient was dead . . . He had remarked that she *appeared* to be gone. Moreover, the stumbling-block remained: How was his evidence to be reconciled with that of Miss Rose – the nurse who said she heard Mrs Borroto gasp when the needle was applied?

Quick to widen any available loophole, the Attorney-General called Dr Robert Biron, the county medical referee who had first questioned Dr Sander. Wheezing stoutly from the heavy witness chair, Dr Biron quoted hospital records as stating: "Patient given ten cc of air, repeated four times, and expired ten minutes after this was started." He had asked Dr Sander if he realized that Mrs Borroto died of an air injection. Dr Sander had said he did. "I asked him if he knew he had broken the law. He stated that he had the permission of Mr Borroto and that he thought the law was not correct in this case, that he might have broken the law but that the law ought to be changed." Much of this was repetition, merely amplifying earlier evidence, but it was a reminder that came at a telling moment.

As a climax, the Attorney-General now produced his most powerful ammunition – impressive medical evidence from two experts who had attended the exhumation and post-mortem and who both asserted flatly that the air injection had led to death . . . And no quibbles about the possibility of Mrs Borroto being dead beforehand.

The first of the two, Dr Miller, said that, in his opinion, death was caused by a pulmonary embolism (a blood clot in the lungs) after air had been injected. The second expert, Dr Milton Helpern, Deputy Medical examiner for New York City, went into greater detail. Using a large black-board to explain to the jury how the air would travel through the veins to the heart, he said: "A big bubble of air would be just as effective in blocking circulation as a big clot of blood." The autopsy, of course, could not disclose the presence of air. But, he added, "it was significant that it did not reveal any other cause of death which would have caused as rapid a death." He concluded: "In my opinion, death was caused by an air embolism resulting from the injection of forty cc of air."

Dr Helpern's evidence ended the case for the prosecution. It seemed an effective case, with weighty answers to any doubts which the defence had succeeded in arousing. Inevitably, though, the defence immediately called for the charge to be dismissed, basing the plea on two grounds:

(a) Failure to establish that death was of a felonious nature; and

(b) Failure to show that air injections and not cancer killed Mrs Borroto.

Just as inevitably, the plea was rejected. Still, there was no harm in trying . . .

It was now Thursday, March 2nd, so it had taken more than a week, excluding the time for selecting the jury, to reach the half-way point of the trial. In most criminal cases, except those in which defending counsel has a major surprise up his sleeve, it is often possible at this stage to gauge the probable verdict. This time, however, it still looked anybody's guess. The fact that Dr Sander had made the injections was not in dispute. In effect, therefore, the issue boiled down to three questions: (1) Was Mrs Borroto already dead when the air was injected? (2) If so, why did the accused inject the air? (3) If not, was the air responsible for death?

The prosecution had claimed that the answer was "No" to the first question and "Yes" to the third. The defence had said that the answer to the first question was "Yes". Failing that, they could seek for a "No" to question No. 3, by trying to prove that, in any case, the amount of air was insufficient to cause death. But a really convincing answer to the second question would still be all-important. What possible reason could there be for an act which, by their own submissions, was completely pointless? Without a good explanation, it would be impossible to satisfy the jury over the other two questions.

The defence jumped straight into the deep end. Dr Sander,

counsel said, would admit making the air injections "on the impulse of the moment" and in spite of the fact that "he was satisfied she was already dead". To understand why, it was necessary to understand his background, his character, the tensions of everyday life. This information would be given.

In other words, as one cynical American reporter put it, the court was in for a psychological blood-bath . . . That may have been as inaccurate as it was cruel. But at least it was clear that, although the "mercy killing" theme was taboo, the defence would have to invoke much that would appeal to popular emotion – as demonstrated by their first witness, Mrs Borroto's pretty nineteen-year-old daughter, Elise. Wearing a grey suit with a black sweater and an incongruous little sailor hat, she told the court that Dr Sander "seemed to feel almost as badly" as she did about her mother's death. After it occurred, he had invited her and her father to stay at his home, "not overnight or for a day, but for a week or as long as we wanted".

Further tributes to the accused's humanitarian qualities were paid by his blonde medical secretary, Helen Maciolek, who testified: "He was not an ordinary doctor – he was a saint. He was a twenty-four-hour doctor and did not take a proper day off, so that he would be available when other doctors were not." Other witnesses told how he started a clinic for under-privileged children and had collected $6,000 for a new hospital wing. His poorer patients, it was stated, were often asked to stay at his home for their convalescence – and were never charged.

This picture of Dr Sander, as a dedicated, honourable physician, explained why nearly all his patients had already contributed a total of more than $11,000 (some £4,000) towards a fund for his defence. Yet, to acquit him of murder, character references were not enough. Quickly, therefore, the defence switched back to its first claim; that no crime could have been committed because the patient had already gone. Among witnesses who supported this view was Mrs Cecilia Smith, duty sister in the part of the hospital where Mrs Borroto died. A few minutes before the air was injected, she said, Mrs Borroto had a death pallor and was not breathing. "I thought she was dead."

Defending counsel had shown skilful timing throughout the

case and it was at this point, with the words of the last witness still
in the jury's ears, that they launched a frontal attack on their most
difficult obstacle . . . Just *why* had Dr Sander asked for that
syringe? From in front of the jury box, counsel nodded across at
him and said with slow emphasis: "He saw that Mrs Borroto was
lifeless. Her heart was not beating. He thought she was dead. A
doubt, however, did cross his mind. He was thinking of giving
assurance that the pain which she had conquered would not
return. He injected the needle." And with that, almost before
the spectators had time to murmur, Dr Sander was before the
witness stand, his right hand raised to take the oath.

The trial had now been in progress for two weeks. In that
time, the accused's composure had been remarkable. There were
dark rings under his eyes, betokening some sleepless nights, and
it was noted that he avoided looking at the Attorney-General
face to face, even when his old friend was pacing up and down
only a few feet in front of him. Outwardly, though, he had
betrayed no sign of nervousness and it was as if chatting with old
friends that he gave the requisite detailed account of his career,
recalling how a famous book about a doctor, *The Magnificent
Obsession*, had made him decide to become one himself. In
recent years, he said, his wife had felt that he was working
too hard.

Imperceptibly, something of that strain began to make itself
felt in court – and at last, as he told of Mrs Borroto's closing days,
Dr Sander's own calm was broken and his voice sometimes
choked with emotion. Two weeks before her death, he said,
"she could hardly move. She could not eat. All she ate during
the last month would not make a single normal meal. We had to
go by the expression on her face to tell if she was having pain." In
the final week, she "looked like a dead person". When she did die,
he believed the cause was cancer and had signed the death
certificate accordingly.

At the behest of the second defence counsel, Mr Ralph Langdell, he described what happened when he called for the syringe.
"It was my opinion then that she was dead. I can't explain exactly
what action I took then. Something snapped. Why I did it, I can't
tell. It doesn't make sense."

Mr Langdell: "Did you have any intention of killing Mrs Borroto?"

Dr Sander: "I never had any intention of killing Mrs Borroto."

"Did you ever agree to kill Mrs Borroto?" – "I never agreed to kill her."

"Did you know what you intended to do with the syringe?" – "I don't know what I intended to do. I remember trying to get into her vein."

"Was there blood on her arm?" – "There was never any blood anywhere. I tried to get into the vein. I did not use a tourniquet to bring up the vein. Her veins were collapsed."

Dr Sander said he had a ten cubic centimetre syringe. "I withdrew the plunger to make suction, but nothing came out – there was no blood."

Mr Langdell: "What did you do next?" – "I injected a couple of cubic centimetres and I injected a couple more – and nothing happened. There was a slight swelling around the needle. I continued to inject small amounts of air until the entire ten cubic centimetres was gone."

"Was there any change in her expression at any time?"
– "During this entire procedure there was no indication of life, no reaction."

Dr Sander went on: "I detached the syringe by holding the needle with my left hand and unscrewing the syringe. I repeated the process with five or six cubic centimetres, two cubic centimetres at a time, till the syringe was empty."

"Was there any change in her expression, appearance or reaction?" – "No, sir."

"You repeated the same procedure a third time?" – "I did."

"Did you note any change in her expression, any motion or activity at any time?" – "No, sir."

Altogether, Dr Sander said, he had injected a total of "between twenty-five and twenty-eight cc" of air – as compared with the prosecution claim that it was a full forty cc Asked why he had dictated the entry in the medical records which had trapped him, he explained: "I think it is the duty of every doctor to put down on the charts what he has done for every patient, whether it has any effect or not."

Why, then, had he said that the patient "died within ten minutes" of the injections?

"I probably was not being fair to myself. It was casual dictation. The fact that I say she expired at that time does not mean she died at that time. It is merely a means of closing out the case on the chart."

The atmosphere in court became tenser than ever as Attorney-General William Phinney rose to cross-examine. pressing yet again for an explanation of the injections. Looking at him squarely for the first time since the trial started, Dr Sander replied: "I was influenced by the expression on her face – the long suffering – also the suffering of her husband. The expression on her face touched me off. What I did does not make sense."

Mr Phinney: "Why did you put the needle into the vein?" – "I don't know."

"Do you want to tell the jury that?" – "That's right."

"You said something snapped in your mind?" – "What I was thinking at that time is hard to explain. I realized I had not taken a life. I told Craig (the county prosecutor) I had not committed a crime. I meant by that I had not taken a life. The whole behaviour was an irrational behaviour."

Once more Mr Phinney demanded a practical explanation and once more the accused insisted firmly: "I was terribly upset inwardly and I tried to preserve an outward calm. I knew I had not committed any sin. My conscience has been clear throughout the whole affair. I do not know why I did all these things. I was upset to do this and I do not know why I kept on nor why I stopped."

Mr Phinney: "You knew Mrs Borroto was unconscious?"

Dr Sander, emphatically: "I knew she was dead."

"Yet you had this obsession to pump air into this poor dead soul?" – "That's right."

"Have you ever been of the opinion that a patient might be better served by being dead?" – "I have never thought that."

"You said you knew you had broken the law?" – "I do not recall any such answer."

And that was that. After nearly four hours on the witness stand, the only reason Dr Sander had given for his action was that it was an "irrational behaviour" – that there was no reason. Nothing could have seemed weaker, yet in that might lie its very strength. Just as honest witnesses of the same incident almost always differ about what they see, so a jury might be more impressed by a confused mind than by one which thinks with complete clarity – particularly when, as here, evidence is provided to show how the confused mental state arose.

The following day, the defence rounded off this character evidence by calling Mrs Alice Sander, the accused's wife. Since February 20th, she had been away from his side only while he was on the witness stand. Now, wearing a quiet grey suit and speaking in a soft, pleasant voice, she told the court that she had first met her husband when they worked together at a New Jersey hospital. She had admired him because "he respected the poorest patients". The former nurse smiled at the jury as she confessed: "I never wanted to marry a doctor. I knew most doctors spend long hours at work and put that ahead of their families. After we were married, I was never allowed to say he was not in to any patient."

Mrs Sander was followed briefly by Nurse Gertrude Morency, who said that the doctor had given his own blood to a patient. "He told me: 'They need it more than I'."

At this climax of *vox humana*, the defence abruptly switched their line of attack again. They had elaborated their assertion that Mrs Borroto was dead before the injection occurred; they had built up a picture of the psychology which, they claimed, lay behind their client's strange deed. It was time to tackle the third outstanding question: Was the amount of air injected actually sufficient to cause death? The prosecution had produced two experts to answer "Yes" to this question. The defence called only one, although the balance had been made up a few days beforehand, in effect, by a widely publicised challenge from Dr Harry Robinson of the University of Maryland Medical School. From Baltimore, nearly four hundred miles away, Dr Robinson had boldly offered to receive an injection of forty cc of air to prove it would not be fatal, asserting: "Injections of air into the veins cannot cause death." He was quoted as saying that he had given such injections to patients and: "There are no results – good or bad."

The printing of such stories as this, even before the defence had broached the subject, is among the more surprising features of the American scene – particularly to people accustomed to the *sub judice* principle of British Law, under which, once a charge is preferred, no outside comment about a case may be published until the trial is over. Fortunately, it is the rule that all references to their case are cut out of the newspapers before the jurors, locked up in their hotel, are allowed to read them. Moreover, the defence expert whom they were invited to hear in the proper place, before them in court, did not need anyone else to help him. The name alone of Dr Richard Ford, head of the Department of Legal Medicine at Harvard University, was enough to bring a buzz of anticipation from the spectators. For here was one of the country's most celebrated pathologists, an American Spilsbury.

Dr Ford, who had performed the autopsy on Mrs Borroto at the defence request, declared roundly that the patient could not have died from the air injected. The argument between prosecution and defence, as to whether it was forty cc or only twenty-eight cc at the most, was immaterial. Forty cc of air – and he demonstrated – was the equivalent of a small whisky and was not enough to kill. During the past year. Dr Ford said, he had been engaged in the study of air embolism. In his opinion, between two hundred and three hundred cc, delivered within twenty-five seconds, would be required to cause death. "Forty cubic centimetres is not enough to block any appreciable part of the arterial system leading to the human lung." And, he concluded, the fact that a human being's heart action was poor at the time of injection would not make any difference.

Pity the poor jury that had to make up its mind between this authoritative evidence and the equally definite statement to the contrary by the prosecution's chief expert, Dr Helpern!

At last, on Thursday, March 9th, seventeen days after the trial opened, the jurors retired to consider their verdict. They were out for sixty-nine minutes. As they shuffled back into their box, Dr Sander stared intently across the court.

"What say you?" asked the clerk of the court. "Guilty of first-degree murder, guilty of second-degree murder, or not guilty?"

"Not guilty."

Immediately a hubbub that nothing could suppress. A burst of
clapping, cheers – and above them, a man's voice crying: "Thank
God!" Throughout it all, Dr Sander still stared, though now tears
came to his eyes. Beside him, his wife bowed her head and wept
unashamedly.

It is strange, at this distance of time, to note the way in which
the character of the case had changed. At first, the tremendous
controversy over "mercy killing", the sweeping assumption that
this was the sole issue. Gradually, as the trial went on, the theme
was pushed more and more into the background until it appeared
to have been forgotten. In the final analysis, the defence fought
and won on grounds of medical fact. No other way could have
been successful. Yet the outburst of emotion after Dr Sander's
acquittal showed that, under the surface, many people still
regarded him in the light of what they had originally believed
to have been his role.

Indeed, the doctor's ordeal was not over. His medical peers, as
was their right, could still impose punishment for professional
misconduct. A few days later, he was barred by a Roman Catholic
hospital in Manchester. The following month, the State Board of
Registration in Medicine revoked his licence. Even if the air
injections were made after death, the Board said, they were
"morally reprehensible". However, it was indicated that he could
apply for reinstatement after June 19th.

Well-wishers had raised the amazing sum of $21,000 for Dr
Sander, but all had gone to pay his legal expenses. For two
months, he supported his family by working as a ploughman,
using his own electrically-driven plough, for $4 an hour. For-
tunately for him, the professional "sentence" imposed on him
proved to be indulgent. On June 28th, the Board announced that
his licence had been restored – and his first patient called just ten
minutes later.

Whatever view one takes of euthanasia, and of Dr Sander's
temporary, unwitting position as a hero of its supporters, three
additional points emerge from the trial. The first is that, despite
the partisan fervour which greeted his acquittal, no comparable
case has since come to public notice in the United States. The
second is best illustrated by a confession made to me some years

ago by the late Sir James Purves-Stewart, the great British neurologist, who died in 1949 at the age of eighty. (Since he also told this story to a medical meeting. I am not breaking his confidence now.) Sir James said that he was once called to the bedside of a friend, "a charming, cultured woman", who was dying of an incurable disease. She asked him to kill her. "I cannot promise you anything," he replied, "but goodbye and God bless you." Sir James concluded: "I will not say what action I took, but the next day the sufferer failed to awake. Had I been placed in the dock, I might, perhaps, have been convicted and condemned."

The third and last point arises from the sad circumstance that, six months after his acquittal, Dr Sander's pretty young secretary, Helen Maciolek, committed suicide. The doctor, who led search parties all night until her body was found, said that she had recently been "emotionally upset". There is not the slightest evidence that her act resulted in any way from her employer's trial. Yet it may well serve as an indication of the dangerous strains – on people indirectly as well as directly involved – which might arise even if "mercy killing" one day has the full sanction of the law.

THE ACID-BATH VIRTUOSO

(John George Haigh, UK 1949)

Edgar Lustgarten

Haigh's was one of the most sensational murder trials in England, in which dental evidence clinched the the identity of the victim. Haigh's mistake was to believe that without a body, there could be no conviction. As he cheerfully told the police: "Mrs Durand Deacon no longer exists. She has disappeared completely and no trace of her can ever be found again. I have destroyed her with acid. Every trace has gone. How can you prove murder if there is no body?" But in spite of Haigh's boasts, a team of forensic scientists was able to prove that even after a lengthy immersion in sulphuric acid, enough of a human body would survive to provide conclusive evidence. In this case, Mrs Durand Deacon's new acrylic resin dentures were found, buried but intact, in several hundred pounds of greasy, oily sludge recovered from Haigh's premises in Crawley, Sussex. The dentures were conclusively identified by her dentist, and even though the question of his sanity loomed large at the trial, Haigh was hanged. Edgar Lustgarten (1907–78) was a prolific journalist and broadcaster, perhaps remembered best for hosting a series of black-and-white television programmes telling the stories of famous trials with the demeanour of a weary lizard. Lustgarten, a former president of the Oxford Union, came from a generation that scorned sympathy for the likes of Haigh, believing that (like many other notorious killers) he actively enjoyed murdering, being insensitive and indifferent. "I rejoice that they were executed," Lustgarten declared, "every one of them."

For many years I acted as commentator and narrator of a film series with a self-explanatory title – *Scotland Yard*. During the early fifties, in one of these films it was my privilege to be associated with Sir Travers Humphreys, the famous High Court judge, who had recently retired.

On the evening before his scenes were scheduled I was asked whether I would call for him and escort him to the studio. On the way you can tell him the form, suggested the producer.

I said I should be delighted, and inquired where Sir Travers lived.

"He lives now," the producer said, "at the Onslow Court Hotel."

A shiver shook my spine, as if some unrevealed and unaccountable cosmic irony reposed in that impeccably respectable establishment. I could not immediately construe my own reactions. Then, after a moment's reflection, understanding dawned.

Travers Humphreys was the judge, who, only a few years earlier, almost at the close of his memorable career, had tried the acid-bath multi-murderer Haigh, and had dispatched that chemical virtuoso to the gallows. And Haigh, although he had committed his crimes elsewhere – a storeroom at Crawley, a cellar on Gloucester Road – had latterly quartered himself in, and involved himself with, and operated from, the Onslow Court Hotel.

There are hotels and hotels; the term is now so wide that it has ceased to be descriptive. Nor do I know whether the Onslow Court Hotel, in particular, corresponds exactly with its earlier image. It certainly could have served once as the prototype of those hotels which do not desire to attract a floating clientele – in contrast equally to international stop-offs and commercial taverns. With their discreet comfort, orderly routine, and close resemblance to a well-conducted home, they form a communal permanent retreat for unhoused members of the English upper-middle class.

The preponderant characteristic of such hotels is Quiet. Lowered voices in the lounge. Soft footfalls in the corridors. Modest entries and inconspicuous exits. Subdued greetings and sedate farewells. A quietness of bearing, too, as well as of speech and movement: the formidable reserve of the consciously well-bred.

This austere tradition of calm correctitude was firmly established by the earliest residents, and ever since has been maintained by recruiting others like them. Ex-Army officers, pensioned civil servants, former Church dignitaries – and, of course, their relicts. Indeed, the female almost always outnumbers the male, though not to the same extent that the old outnumber the young. But sex and age are negligible elements in a relatively ageless and entirely sexless world. You are of it, or not of it. You belong, or you do not belong. It is a world painstakingly secured against the vulgar and the sordid and – above all – the violent; those notorious, lamentable, excesses of inappropriate parentage and indifferent education. It is a world conceived and born in the nineteenth century, jealously preserving its corporate exclusiveness against the social explosions of the twentieth.

Only if your individual personality – from which is deduced your birth and upbringing – stands up to the critical scrutiny of your fellows can you hope for more than temporary survival in such a dedicated bastion of good form. Their freezing disapproval – silently conveyed – has, within its narrow scope, finality.

Pass that test, and you are politely welcomed. Fail, and it is made clear that you do not fit in.

Olive Durand-Deacon – to the porter, One-One-Five – fitted in as perfectly and as harmoniously as anyone who has ever stayed at the Onslow Court Hotel.

She was a widow, once endowed with more than average good looks, and still possessing a certain mellow comeliness which – quite justifiably – she made the very most of. Her hair was nicely done. Her face was skilfully made up. She liked gay handbags and an orthodox show of jewellery: earrings, a string of pearls, a diamond wristlet watch. She had a taste for hats and her wardrobe included that acknowledged status symbol, a coat of Persian lamb. Her status, though, had deeper and more assured roots – in the fine set of her head, in the rich tones of her voice, in her unassuming and effortless good manners. No-one could doubt for a moment she belonged.

Mrs Durand-Deacon, none the less, had avoided the most dangerous pitfall of belonging. She had not allowed her mind to atrophy or rust. She relished leisure, but did not equate it with passivity. She cherished friends, but did not engage in vacant chatter. Within the permissible frontiers of her environment, she thought and talked to practical effect. Particularly she was inclined to ventilate ideas for minor business ventures in which she could participate; ventures ingeniously designed both to increase her income and occupy her time.

In 1949 – the year that she was to be murdered – Mrs Durand-Deacon was sixty-nine years old, and she had lived at the Onslow Court Hotel for the past six.

John George Haigh – to the porter, Four-Oh-Four – also fitted in at the Onslow Court Hotel, at least up to the point of gaining qualified acceptance. But whereas Mrs Durand-Deacon fitted in by nature, Haigh only did so by studious contrivance.

He was a bachelor, smooth, persuasive, charming; the type that Kensington mamas of bygone days would have considered – on first impressions – an eligible match. He was well-dressed (even to those with an eye for dressing) and well-spoken (even to those with an ear for speech). His small moustache was neatly trimmed, his dark hair neatly cut, his behaviour courteous, his smile agreeable. And yet . . . you couldn't quite put your finger on it, could you? . . . and yet, with all these marketable, assets, he didn't quite – did he? – he didn't quite belong.

The residents still adhered to that opinion after they had warily allowed him in their circle. But they were relying solely upon instinct. The manageress and book-keepers knew what they did not – that Haigh was a bad payer, a poor financial prospect; existing, apparently, from hand to mouth, from day to day. But that, in turn, marked the limits of their knowledge. That he had served several sentences for theft and fraud – including one of penal servitude – was then only known to a remote and scattered few. That he had done deeds so black and terrible that they would spread his evil fame across the earth was then not known to anyone at all.

In 1949 – the year that he was to be hanged – John George

Haigh was thirty-nine years old, and he had lived at the Onslow
Court Hotel for the past four.

They sat at adjacent tables in the dining-room. Civilities were
exchanged, and sometimes conversation. Mrs Durand-Deacon's estimate of Haigh remains conjectural; probably it coin-
cided with that of her neighbours. He wasn't quite – not quite.
But for her, unlike them, one aspect of him aroused interest.
Haigh was an agent of sorts, active and in touch with contemporary business, who might on occasion prove a useful
intermediary. That had always been the trouble: she hadn't –
inevitably couldn't have – the contacts. Next time I devise a
saleable project, this man – so Mrs Durand-Deacon hoped –
can do the selling.

Once such a project had taken viable shape, like all enthusiastic
amateurs she couldn't wait.

On 14th February, Mrs Durand-Deacon entertained a woman
friend to lunch. Her name was Gwendoline Birin, and some may
detect a mystical significance in the fact that she was an official of
the Francis Bacon Society, and hence, through that great Stuart
Chancellor, tenuously linked with the sanctions of the law.
Although theirs was a regular lunch engagement between inti-
mates, normally absorbed by each other's company, this time the
hostess brought in a small box, which she placed beside herself in
obvious readiness. It had nothing to do with Mrs Birin. It had to
do with Haigh.

When presently the latter took his seat at the next table, Mrs
Durand-Deacon begged her guest's pardon, and turned round.

"Mr Haigh, would you glance at those?"

She passed over the box. Haigh opened it and took a look
inside.

"I see," he said. "Novel, aren't they?"

"They have a strong appeal to women," Mrs Durand-Deacon
said.

"Possibly."

"For sure. All I need is a manufacturer." She exerted her
considerable charm. "You know *so* many people. Now, think, Mr
Haigh. Think hard, Mr Haigh. Please."

Haigh thought hard – harder than Mrs Durand-Deacon guessed. "I know a chap in Crawley," he said. "I'm seeing him in the morning. If I could get him interested – just as a start – perhaps I could arrange for both of us to go and see him."

"That would be splendid. Thank you very much, Mr Haigh."

He passed back the box. Mrs Birin could not refrain from eyeing it. Mrs Durand-Deacon laughed at her friend's curiosity.

"Artificial fingernails," she said.

On 18th February – it won't surprise the superstitious that it was a Friday – Haigh drove Mrs Durand-Deacon down to Crawley. Ostensibly they were going there for discussions about the manufacture of artificial fingernails.

Haigh had spoken to the chap in Crawley – in view of what was brewing, it is not clear why. In any event, the chap wasn't enamoured of the notion. Fingernails – artificial fingernails? Technically it would be a most expensive process. No, not worth bringing along the other person.

Haigh did not argue, but continued with his plans.

The chap at Crawley was head of an engineering firm with premises in West Street and at Giles Yard, Leopold Road. Giles Yard was used almost solely as a storeroom, and Haigh – the firm's unpaid London representative – had made a practice of borrowing the keys from time to time. "For a conversion job," he said on one occasion, but generally he was not required to explain.

During the hours that mattered on 18th February, the keys of the storeroom were reposing in his pocket . . .

Between four and five o'clock that afternoon, Haigh called for a minute or two at the George Hotel in Crawley. He arrived with Mrs Durand-Deacon and he left with her.

At a quarter to seven that evening, Haigh called at the Ancient Prior's restaurant in Crawley and stayed for a quarter of an hour. He had an egg on toast, a cup of tea, and a chat with the proprietor.

He arrived and left alone.

"Do you know anything about Mrs Durand-Deacon? Is she ill? Do you know where she is?"

Mrs Lane – residing nine years at the Onslow Court Hotel – looked up from her breakfast almost angrily. She did not care for Haigh, and she was greatly worried at Mrs Durand-Deacon's unexpected absence.

"Do *I* know? Don't *you* know?" she retorted. "I understood from her that you wanted to take her to a factory."

"Yes, but I wasn't ready," Haigh parried Mrs Lane with his customary blandness. "I hadn't had lunch, and she wanted to go to the Army and Navy Stores, and asked me to pick her up. I waited there an hour, and she did not arrive."

Nobody would have felt, or need have felt, alarm, if Mrs Durand-Deacon had not been of such methodical habits. She hardly ever stayed a night away from the hotel, and certainly never without notifying the staff. And yet she had gone out early yesterday afternoon, and since then not a word, nor a message, nor a sign. Little wonder that as Saturday passed by, Mrs Lane's concern steadily increased.

At Sunday breakfast Haigh again came over.

"Have you had any news?"

"No," snapped Mrs Lane. It is in the highest degree improbable that, at this stage, she had even an inkling of the truth. A jumble of emotions fuelled her resentment: against Haigh as an Outsider with impermissible aspirations, against Mrs Durand-Deacon as a Lady with impermissible condescensions, against herself for connecting their innocuous relationship with the catastrophe she vaguely apprehended. "No, I have not had any news. This afternoon I shall go to the police-station and ask them to take the matter up at once."

Haigh nodded thoughtfully, and withdrew. After breakfast Mrs Lane went into the Tudor Room, and there Haigh approached her yet again.

"I think," he said, "that we had better go together to the police-station."

"I think so, too."

"I'll drive you there," said Haigh.

So it came about that her murderer went with her best friend to report Mrs Durand-Deacon's disappearance to the police.

★   ★   ★

In the days following – on the Monday and the Thursday – Haigh made two lengthy Statements. The gist of them, however, can be put into a sentence: when Mrs Durand-Deacon failed to keep her appointment on Friday afternoon at the Army and Navy Stores, he went by himself to Crawley, where he "attended to some business", returning to London in the evening on his own.

With the police, Haigh seemed neither reticent nor nervous. He exuded frankness as he exuded confidence: the frankness of a man who had nothing whatever to hide, the confidence of a man who had nothing whatever to fear. If the frankness was counterfeit, the confidence was authentic. Deceived by past experiences and lulled by present vanity, Haigh believed the precautions he had taken were cast-iron.

Police scepticism determined otherwise.

Both their professional *nous* and their professional records forbade them to accept a man like Haigh on trust. On Saturday – two days after Haigh's second Statement – with the owner's consent they forced the storeroom at Giles Yard. In this building – the keys of which Haigh still retained – a singular collection of objects greeted them.

Three acid carboys: full, half full and empty. A stirrup pump. A rubber apron. A pair of rubber gloves. A leather box, containing a revolver (lately fired), together with eight rounds of appropriate ammunition.

And – transforming baulked perplexity into sharp suspicion – a cleaning firm's receipt for a coat of Persian lamb.

The case that gradually built up from these beginnings was as formidable as any in the history of crime. Of course the Persian lamb coat was Mrs Durand-Deacon's. A watch that Haigh had sold on 19th February at a shop in Putney was Mrs Durand-Deacon's. Jewellery that Haigh had sold on 22nd February at a shop in Horsham was Mrs Durand-Deacon's. And a chain belonging to Mrs Durand-Deacon was found on 8th March beneath a hedge at Buxted, exactly where Haigh had said it would be.

More conclusive – and more grisly – evidence, however, came from an intensive search through Giles Yard itself. The least conclusive evidence lay in the bloodstains on the wall (as there were bloodstains on the rubber apron), and the hairpin embedded in a sea of grease coating the bottom of a forty-five-gallon tank. The most conclusive evidence lay in a quantity of sludge which had been deposited over the soil outside.

The sludge was removed to Scotland Yard, and for three days Dr Keith Simpson, the pathologist, accompanied by Dr Henry Holden, the Director of the Metropolitan Police Laboratory, sieved and sifted it in minutest detail. The principal fruits of this investigation were some fragmentary human remains (elderly female), the handle of a red plastic handbag (Mrs Durand-Deacon's), and – hardly less infallible than fingerprints – an upper and lower pair of dentures, both intact, which were identified by Mrs Durand-Deacon's dentist.

Many of these discoveries were still to be unearthed – in some instances quite literally unearthed – when the police reviewed their situation at the end of one full week's consistent work. But they were now seized of sufficient information to justify a further interview with Haigh; an interview at which they threw in what they had.

Haigh's statement of Monday, 28th February – his most veracious as well as his most macabre utterance – furnishes a lesson in criminal flexibility. Confident as he was, like any prudent general he had doubtless devised provisional measures to counter and cushion an unforeseen reverse.

Only under irresistible compulsion, though, would he drop the mask of innocence and bring them into play.

"I have continued my inquiries into the death of Mrs Durand-Deacon," said Detective Inspector Shelley Symes, as Haigh settled himself comfortably in a chair. "And I want you to answer some more questions."

"I'm quite willing," Haigh said amiably, "to answer anything I can and to help you all I can."

"Have you anything to say about a coat of Persian lamb?" The Inspector smoothed a crumpled ticket between his fingers. "Or about this jewellery?" He spread the items on the table. "I would like you to tell me about them, if you will."

Haigh preserved unaccustomed silence. They had got on the trail all right. His bluff was fairly called.

"How did you come by this property, and where is Mrs Durand-Deacon?"

The interposing of a formal caution granted Haigh a little time. He had hardly begun to speak when he was granted more; Inspector Symes was called out of the room.

Left waiting with another officer, Haigh had opportunity to deliberate. Plainly now they *knew* that he had done it. And, having got so far, they might conceivably *prove* that he had done it. But not necessarily – and even if they did there were ways and means of escaping from the worst.

Haigh's reactions at this crucial moment held important implications for the future. Certainly – to quote the Attorney-General at the trial – there was no sign of reason tottering on its throne.

"Tell me frankly," he said to Detective Inspector Webb, "what are the chances of anyone being released from Broadmoor?"

Haigh was not discouraged by Inspector Webb's refusal to enter into a discussion of that kind. He had now reorganized his dispositions, and was impelled to behave accordingly.

"If I told you the truth," he went on, "you would not believe me; it sounds too fantastic."

"You are not obliged to say anything," began Inspector Webb, but Haigh heard out this second caution with impatience.

"I understand all that. I will tell you all about it. Mrs Durand-Deacon no longer exists. She has disappeared completely, and no trace of her can ever be found again."

"What has happened to her?" asked Inspector Webb.

"I have destroyed her with acid. You will find the sludge that remains at Leopold Road."

But even as Haigh – for a rarity – told the truth, and thereby, in effect, committed himself to an insanity defence, he still cherished a modicum of hope that there might be no need for any defence at all. He did not know yet – not did the police themselves – that Mrs Durand-Deacon had not "disappeared completely";

that certain plastic substances – for example, dentures – resist erosion even by sulphuric acid; and that – perhaps because he had moved with too much haste – even certain perishable constituents had survived. And Haigh embraced a common delusion, still shared by many, despite an outstanding demonstration of its falsity in the Porthole murder trial of 1948.

His next question to Inspector Webb was thus half interrogatory and half rhetorical.

"How can you prove" – Haigh looked right and left and centre – "how can you prove murder if there is no body?"

> We went to Crawley together in my car. She was inveigled into going by me in view of her interest in artificial fingernails. Having taken her into the storeroom at Leopold Road, I shot her in the back of the head while she was examining some paper for use as fingernails. Then I went out to the car and fetched in a drinking glass and made an incision, I think with a penknife, in the side of the throat, and collected a glass of blood, which I then drank. Following that, I removed the coat she was wearing, a Persian lamb, and the jewellery, rings, necklace, earrings, and crucifix, and put her in a forty-five-gallon tank. I then filled the tank up with sulphuric acid, by means of the stirrup pump, from the carboy.

That is the core of Haigh's Statement to Inspector Symes about the murder of Mrs Durand-Deacon – a Statement which also confirmed what was already known (that he had previously "fenced" about the matter), admitted what could no longer be denied (his abstraction and sale of her personal possessions), and factually reported on his calls at Giles Yard to observe the advance of acid dissolution. *Saturday* . . . "Not satisfactorily completed." *Monday* . . . "A piece of fat and bone still floating in the sludge. I emptied off the sludge with a bucket and tipped it on the ground opposite the shed, and pumped a further quantity of acid into the tank to decompose the remaining fat and bone." *Tuesday* . . . "I found decomposition complete and emptied the tank off." (What had seemed complete to him was not complete to eyes more expert.)

"I emptied the tank off" – those words marked the gruesome end of the lady with an interest in artificial fingernails. But they did not mark the end of all that Haigh desired to say. There had been a hint of nameless revelations yet to come in that remarkable allusion to a glass of blood. It suggested – and I think it was intended to suggest – that the murder of Mrs Durand-Deacon had resulted from a lunatic compulsion on Haigh's part. Such a compulsion, by its character, must, almost always, be repetitive. And sure enough, when he had dealt with the subject then in hand, and when he had no doubt that he would be detained, and when he had briefly scanned the hazards of detention, he insisted on widening the compass of his Statement; he laid to his own account several other murders, of which, up till that moment, the police had never heard.

"In 1944," Haigh declared, dictating, "I disposed of William McSwan in a similar manner in the basement of 79 Gloucester Road, SW 7. And of Donald McSwan, and of Amy McSwan, in 1946* at the same address. And in 1948, Dr Archibald Henderson and his wife Rosalie, also in a similar manner, at Leopold Road, Crawley."

The McSwans were a family Haigh had known for many years. William was the son, and they met one evening – Haigh told Inspector Symes – at a public-house in Kensington High Street called The Goat.

"From there we went to 79 Gloucester Road, where in the basement, which I had rented, I hit him on the head with a cosh, withdrew a glass of blood from his throat, and drank it. He was dead within five minutes or so. I put him in a forty-gallon tank and disposed of him with acid."

The War and its by-products had been handy as a cover; Haigh put William's parents off the scent by intimating that their son had gone away to dodge the call-up. Subsequently, from Scotland, he posted bogus letters to them (Haigh was a fluent and proficient forger). But the parents' turn, too, eventually came. "I took separately to the basement the father, Donald, and the

* That date was given by Haigh in error. He should have said 1945.

mother, Amy, disposing of them in exactly the same way as the son."

Inspector Symes continued to write it down as though taking particulars of a stolen bicycle. Training and discipline count on such occasions.

"I met the Hendersons by answering an advertisement offering for sale their property at Ladbroke Square. I went with them to Brighton where they stayed at the Metropole."

As a surgeon might recall his operations, so Haigh recalled how, one February morning, he had taken Dr Henderson to Crawley, where he shot him through the head and put him in a tank of acid; and how, that afternoon, by saying her husband had been taken ill, he tricked Mrs Henderson into making the same journey. "I shot her and put her in another tank. In each of the last four cases, I had my glass of blood, as before."

In every case – or so he *said* – he had his glass of blood. In every case – or so he *thought* – he had got rid of the corpse.

These two facts may not be disassociated from his – imperfect – understanding of the law.

I am not affirming, or insinuating, that Haigh's Statement of 28th February, taken in its broader aspects, was untrue. One may make a reservation in respect of "my glass of blood" without attacking the entire fabric. That he did kill, not only Mrs Durand-Deacon, but the McSwans and Hendersons, by the means described, does appear in retrospect a virtual certainty.

Less credence can be accorded to his Statement of 4th March – what may be described as the Haigh apocrypha.

Held in jail on a capital charge, with every waking hour devoted to a single theme, Haigh could refine and elaborate his plans. During that long session with Inspectors Symes and Webb, he had vaguely staked a claim – the term is used advisedly – to several further killings, then unspecified, which he did not choose to incorporate in his Statement. Four days' solitary reflection apparently convinced him that this was a mistake. At his own request, Inspector Webb visited him in custody, to hear and record whatever else he should impart.

There were three victims – more precisely, alleged victims –

that Haigh now added to his ample catalogue. A woman about thirty-five ("slim, dark"), casually encountered in the streets of Hammersmith, and "duly" destroyed (1945) at Gloucester Road. A "youngish" man ("about my height and build") persuaded from the Goat public house to Gloucester Road, where (1945) "the same thing happened". A girl ("Mary"), picked up on the front at Eastbourne, and put in an acid tank at Crawley (1948).

In one respect, these three supplementary murders – according to Haigh's considered narrative – followed the common pattern of the six for which he had earlier held himself responsible. Each time he had "tapped" his victim's blood. But in another respect, the six and the three were differentiated. Each of the six had meant financial gain to Haigh (secured, as he admitted, by forgery and fraud); none of the three had done, or ever looked like doing so. The slim woman "had next to nothing in her handbag". The youngish man "had no more than a pound". Mary "had little or no property". Such a complete absence of material inducement – so laboriously and clearly pointed out – conveniently left "my glass of blood" as the sole motive.

The police – who checked Haigh's Statements by their own inquiries, and had confirmed much in that of 28th February – could not find any confirmatory evidence for the assertions in his Statement of 4th March. Lord Dunboyne, a recognized authority on the case, wrote thus in his preface to the transcript of the trial: "Though not impossible, it is, in all the circumstances, highly improbable" that Haigh ever murdered anyone other than those whom he expressly named in full. I do not doubt that Lord Dunboyne is right, and that the Statement of 4th March is a cunning fraud.

Some may suppose that Haigh was merely getting it off his chest, that the Statements of 28th February and 4th March constitute an undesigned catharsis of confession. Others – of whom I am one – prefer to take the view that he had skilfully prepared his counsel's brief and given a useful lead to his psychiatrist.

The trial of Haigh took place at Lewes in July. From every point of view it was a memorable occasion: the greatest criminal judge in England on the bench, the greatest criminal in England in the dock, and the two most eminent members of the English Bar (Sir Hartley Shawcross and Sir David Maxwell Fyfe) appearing respectively to prosecute and defend.

Haigh was tried for the murder of Mrs Durand-Deacon only. Sir Hartley Shawcross – then, as Attorney-General, the senior Law Officer – scrupulously refrained from introducing any other. Nothing about the McSwans and Hendersons; nothing about the slim woman, the youngish man, and Mary. Those references were deliberately excluded when the Crown put Haigh's State- ments in as evidence. It was Sir David Maxwell Fyfe who subsequently brought them to the notice of the jury. Actually they tended to support, not to prejudice, his case.

For there was no dispute at all upon the facts. Neither the murder nor the method was contested. Out of thirty-three prosecution witnesses, Sir David cross-examined only four, and never to mark a disagreement or a challenge. His questions, without exception, were designed to underline Haigh's mental abnormality. Sane or insane? That was the sole issue. Must Haigh bear responsibility for his deed according to the tests prescribed by the M'Naghten Rules?

Even those who most persistently attack the M'Naghten Rules would concede them one great merit: simplicity. They do not require the expert intervention of initiates; they can be grasped and applied by an ordinary group of citizens exercising their ordinary sense. Although formulated at a full conclave of judges – after a man named Daniel M'Naghten had shot the Premier's secretary in 1843 – the Rules are not an arbitrary innovation by that conclave, but a solemn and authoritative statement of the law as it was, and had been for centuries. This statement declared that an onus rested on every person raising an insanity defence – the onus of proving that *either* he did not know what he was doing, *or* that he did not know what he was doing was wrong.

Did Haigh know what he was doing when he killed Mrs Durand-Deacon at Giles Yard? And if he knew what he was doing, did he know that it was wrong?

It constitutes an essential feature of the M'Naghten Rules – without which they would lose much of their realism – that the prisoner's state of mind is only relevant as "at the time" when the act was committed. None-the-less, a moment cannot be judged in isolation; it demands recourse to what went before and to what came after.

Immediately prior to the murder of Mrs Durand-Deacon, Haigh was facing an acute financial crisis. He had no assured and regular source of income. He was overdrawn at the bank by £83 5s 10d. His hotel bills, accumulated over several weeks, totalled about £50 on 15th February, and he felt constrained to borrow that amount, out of which he pacified an insistent management. The loan, however, afforded him only the shortest breathing-space for it had been made conditional on repayment by the weekend, so that the lender could discharge a premium then due. (Part was, in fact, repaid on 22nd February.) Haigh, therefore, on the morning of the murder was more than ever impecunious and sorely pressed.

The murder, though, did not occur on sudden impulse. Very few in history have been so premeditated – or premeditated to such practical effect. During the two preceding days Haigh methodically assembled the necessary instruments to carry out his purpose. He ordered sulphuric acid from a firm in Clerkenwell. He arranged with a local mechanic to collect it. He bought the forty-five-gallon tank from a firm in Barking – a tank especially lined to resist corrosive chemicals. He took a stirrup pump to have the foot sawn off (which would make it possible to insert the body of the pump through the narrow neck of a sulphuric acid carboy). And lest anything should be overlooked or forgotten, Haigh, like a prudent housewife, made a shopping-list ("Stirrup Pump, Gloves, Apron, Rags", and so forth) which the police discovered later in his room. Nothing was left to improvisation or to chance.

Nor did his prudence vanish after the event. While he was making those solicitous inquiries, he was also paying those visits to Giles Yard; surveying his handiwork, pumping in fresh acid, and finally pouring away that residual sludge which yielded up its shocking mysteries at Scotland Yard. Simultaneously the spoils of his crime were turned into the cash he so desperately needed. He obtained £10 for Mrs Durand-Deacon's watch. He obtained

£100 for Mrs Durand-Deacon's jewellery. He took the loose coins from her bag and slipped them in his pocket. He had not realized the coat before arrest, but it needs no great flight of imagination to divine the reason for which it was being cleaned . . .

Didn't know what he was doing? Didn't know that it was wrong? It is against the background of these facts – all either stated by Haigh or else accepted by him – that his insanity defence should be examined.

An insanity defence is generally based on alleged abnormalities of behaviour observed by others (especially by experts). The best testimony, therefore, is that of such observers.

The case for Haigh's insanity, though, assumed a different character.

His alleged abnormalities had not been manifest; indeed, the persona he presented to the world might have passed for that lawyer's incarnation of plain sense, the reasonable man on the Clapham omnibus. The jury were asked to infer insanity, not from any overt and visible phenomena, but from what Haigh was supposed to have thought and felt and done in the recesses of his mind or in the secrecy of solitude. The best testimony, therefore, would be that of Haigh.

But Haigh did not go into the box. Had he done so he could have given, as no-one else could give, a first-hand, direct, immediate description of the thoughts and the feelings and the hidden acts on which his counsel was constrained to place reliance. Had he done so, he would have provided, as nothing else could provide, an opportunity for the court to study his mental composition. Had he done so, however, he would have also been liable, in both respects, to cross-examination.

That liability being declined, and Haigh holding fast to the sanctuary of the dock, the only witness called on his behalf was a Harley Street psychiatrist, Dr Henry Yellowlees. That witness's credentials and experience were – and are – impressive. He was a Fellow of the London Royal College of Physicians (where he held a Diploma in Psychological Medicine), a Fellow of the Edinburgh College of Physicians, and a Fellow of the Glasgow Royal

Faculty of Physicians and Surgeons. He had been honorary Consulting Physician, Physician for Mental Diseases, and Lecturer in Psychological Medicine at St Thomas's Hospital. He had been examiner in Mental Diseases and Psychology at the University of London. During the Second World War, as a colonel in the Army Medical Service, he occupied the post of Consulting Psychiatrist to the British Expeditionary Force in France. When the judge subsequently referred to him as "a highly qualified gentleman" and "a gentleman of position" he gave Dr Yellowlees no more than his due.

Doubtless it was his misfortune rather than his fault that he enacted two distinct roles at the trial of Haigh – roles which neither complemented nor sustained each other. On the one hand, the trained and impartial diagnostician; on the other, the accused's sole channel of communication with those to whom he must communicate. Dr Yellowlees had to tell Haigh's story before he could submit his own assessment of it. That put him at a grave disadvantage straightaway. The more effective he proved as Haigh's expositor and spokesman, the more suspect he became as Haigh's examiner and analyst.

The dilemma was inescapable – and so was the handicap of being, in his prior capacity, a mere agent for an available principal. "Members of the jury," said Sir David Maxwell Fyfe in opening the defence, "I am not going to detail it [Haigh's actions, reactions, and accounts of them] because *it is much better that you have it from Dr Yellowlees.*"

The jury cannot be blamed if they reflected, as Dr Yellowlees stepped up and took the oath, that it would have been better still if they had had it from Haigh.

Dr Yellowlees had seen Haigh on three occasions, in jail, within three weeks of his impending trial. The time they spent together totalled two hours and ten minutes, during which Haigh appears to have unfolded a psychopathological conspectus of his life. Dr Yellowlees now faithfully passed this on, interspersed, as opportune, with the conclusions that he drew.

The story reached right back into the roots of childhood. I was brought up in a fanatic religious atmosphere (Haigh had said); my parents were Plymouth Brethren, and the vengeance of God broke over my head for each trifling misdemeanour. My mother was given to telling the future from dreams (Haigh had said); books on the subject were always around for me to read. I was a solitary youngster (Haigh had said); no friends, no comrades, odd man out at school. In my teens, I became attached – first as chorister, then as organist – to Wakefield Cathedral, which was High Church (Haigh had said); the opposite extreme from the services I knew. "About that time I began to get recurring dreams in which I saw either the head or the whole body of Christ on the Cross with the blood pouring from His wounds."

From this data Dr Yellowlees deduced that the adolescent Haigh had "a paranoid constitution".

That is not a disease of the mind, Dr Yellowlees explained, but it can be a preliminary state in mental aberration. It makes the psychiatrist alert for further symptons – which, in this instance, the psychiatrist discovered. Or rather, Haigh reported, during those talks in jail, what had been to him (he said) mystical revelations, but were medical symptoms to Dr Yellowlees.

His first "revelation" occurred (Haigh had said) when he was only sixteen or seventeen years of age. "Divinely guided", he construed a phrase in the Old Testament as an instruction to drink his own urine. Haigh told Dr Yellowlees he had obeyed that instruction, and had continued to obey it ever since.

The second "revelation" came much later (Haigh had said), not until 1944 or 1945; another recurring dream in which a forest of what he thought were crucifixes, but found were trees, dripped with what he thought was rain or dew, but found was blood. One tree presently turned into a man, who invited Haigh to drink blood collected in a bowl; but before Haigh could reach it and satisfy himself, the man receded and the dream resolved. These dreams (Haigh had said) confirmed his belief that he was divinely guided; created a feeling of uneasiness and distress during their cycle; and often – or always – culminated in his killing.

The third "revelation" (Haigh had said) embraced the killings themselves. In these, he acted as the instrument of the outside power. They concerned – he could not be more definite – eternal life. He drank – Dr Yellowlees was "pretty sure" he at any rate tasted – the blood of his prey on every occasion. "I have a destiny," Haigh had asserted, "to fulfil."

From this data Dr Yellowlees deduced that the adult Haigh had developed paranoia.

What is paranoia?

Sir David Maxwell Fyfe had already apprised the jury. "Paranoia," he said, "brings a complete and permanent alteration of the entire personality which overwhelms the mental outlook and the character and the conduct. Broadly and fundamentally, it is the result of the patient's interest and energies being turned in upon himself and withdrawn from the real world around. It really amounts to, practically, self-worship, and that is commonly expressed by a conviction that he is in some mystic way under the control of a guiding spirit which means infinitely more to him and is of infinitely greater authority than any human laws or rules of society. The defect, and at the same time, the badge of this disorder is that the victim who suffers from it knows that his secret life of fantasy has got to be lived alongside the ordinary life of the world; and the paranoiac is, therefore, lucid, astute, and shrewd, when he is not actually acting under the influence of his fantasy. In such cases, he takes the steps which one would expect in order to avoid trouble."

That was an adroit and skilful definition which, while wholly unexceptionable from a general standpoint, corresponded closely with the particular facts. Dr Yellowlees qualified it only by limiting its application to "completely well-established paranoia". As he maintained that Haigh's paranoia had "gone over the line", this qualification had no practical significance.

But while "completely well-established paranoia" might count as insanity in a consulting-room, it did not necessarily do so in a court of law. Is a paranoiac spared by the M'Naghten Rules? Does a paranoiac not know what he is doing, or – in relevant circumstances – that what he is doing is wrong? Can this "self-worship", or this "guiding spirit", eliminate consciousness of ordinary values and ordinary sanctions?

"Taking the last question of the legal test," Maxwell Fyfe said finally to Dr Yellowlees, "would it be right to say at once that you are not prepared to express an opinion on whether he knew that what he was doing was wrong?"

It skipped the initial step, but with ample justification. Nobody himself in his right mind would be convinced that Haigh did not at least know what he was doing.

"You are not prepared to express an opinion on whether he knew what he was doing was wrong?"

"Yes," replied Dr Yellowlees. "That is so."

"In your view what amount of contact with the accused and what opportunities of observation would be necessary in order to answer that question?"

"I do not think," said Yellowlees, "that any psychiatrist could even attempt to answer that question unless he had lived with such a paranoid patient for years."

The Attorney-General began to cross-examine with a paramount target that all could plainly see.

Dr Yellowlees had given a physician's diagnosis; he had declined to comment on its implications. The question remained at present in the air: Did Haigh know what he was doing was wrong? The whole of the Attorney's admirably succinct interrogation, therefore, was designed to extract an affirmative reply.

After a short preliminary exchange which put the witness at initial disadvantage (he had confused the number of his interviews with Haigh), Sir Hartley Shawcross set about his task.

"You would agree, would you not, that the prisoner is a person on whose word it would be utterly unsafe to rely?"

"Yes," said Dr Yellowlees.

"But you have, as a matter of fact, relied on it entirely as the main basis of your opinion in this case?"

"No," said Dr Yellowlees.

"Have you not?"

"No."

"What *objective* signs of insanity are there in the prisoner?"

"I should have to repeat all my evidence to show you."

"Far be it from me to ask you to do that." The Attorney's gentle sarcasm followed on an examination-in-chief which had occupied the court for a full hour and a half. "What objective signs of insanity are there, apart from what the prisoner has said to you?"

Yellowlees replied.

"There are no such things as isolated objective signs of insanity. It is one of the oldest fallacies."

"Then you are relying in the main on what the prisoner said to you?"

Yellowlees was encountering a clear-headed and tenacious cross-examiner. But he continued to present his thesis with manifest sincerity.

"No, I am relying in the main upon my lifelong knowledge of such cases, and my observation of a *cumulative* series of symptoms, as I said."

"What symptoms are you referring to, apart from what the prisoner said to you? Mention one."

"I am relying on his verbosity, his egocentricity, the fact that he is unable to speak the truth, the fact that he has no shadow of shame or remorse for his deeds, the stories that he tells me about his dreams, and the fact that paranoia is, I think, the most difficult of all mental disorders to simulate, and I do not think – I may be wrong – but I do not think I would have been hoodwinked."

"That may be so," Shawcross said impassively, "but all the things you have mentioned are things the prisoner said to you?"

"He has not told me he is verbose," retorted Yellowlees.

"Of course not. But he has talked to you with verbosity?"

"Very well."

"All those symptoms" – there was an iron will behind that velvet voice – "arise, do they not, from what the prisoner has said – except the last one which is not a symptom at all?"

"I do not think," Yellowlees said, "that I can help you further."

Shawcross now proceeded to drive his point home with the minimum of words.

"Do you attach importance to the dreams?"

"Yes, great importance."

"Whether this man dreamed or not is a matter you can only judge by what he told you?"

"Yes."

"You said a moment ago that he is unable to speak the truth?"

"Yes."

Thus smartly was that outsize chicken sent back home to roost.

"You know, do you not, from the prisoner's statements in this case, that he is a man who, in connection with the various murders, has practised an elaborate system of forgery and false pretences in order to possess himself of his victims' property?"

"I don't know whether he did it in order to possess himself — that is not a question for me, but he has done so, I believe."

"With the *result* that he possessed himself of his victims' property?"

"Yes."

"Do you think it is an impossibility that he might have deceived you about his dreams and other symptoms?"

The doctor's answer was inconclusive.

"I will put it to you quite frankly," Shawcross said, "that this man has been inventing a defence and has been deceiving you in regard to these symptoms upon which you have relied for your opinion that he is a paranoiac."

Yellowlees, to his honour, refrained from dogmatism.

"I do not think I am likely to be deceived on this subject, but I may well be."

"You may well be deceived?"

"Undoubtedly."

Whatever possibilities of escape for Haigh had ever reposed in the evidence of Dr Yellowlees, these were receding as each moment passed. It says much for Maxwell Fyfe's professional aplomb that he gave no outward sign of pressure or anxiety as Shawcross pursued his devastating course.

"Did you ever ask the prisoner how much he realized in pounds, shillings and pence from the murders of the Hendersons and McSwans?"

"No, I do not regard that as my province."

This rejoinder may have fairly reflected psychiatric method. Those who were not psychiatrists, though, could perhaps be forgiven if they registered shock.

"Were you not considering it as part of your province to discover what the motives for these offences were – whether it was a motive which lay in the field of insanity or a motive which belonged to a more mercenary field?"

"It was quite obvious from the first interview with him that there was no question of motive in the popular sense at all."

Mr Justice Humphreys had been following closely. Now he intervened.

"Did you in fact inquire, or were you told, whether this man made large sums of money or not from the murder of the persons whom he said he murdered?"

Dr Yellowlees thought he had read as much in some of the statements, "but I do not remember inquiring specifically myself."

Mr Justice Humphreys rubbed his cheek with his bent knuckles.

"In your opinion, is it of any importance whatever in this case whether he made money or whether he did not?"

"In my opinion," Dr Yellowlees said, "no."

"That is what I thought you'd say," observed the judge.

The ground was crumbling under an honest – but, as I think, misled – witness when the Attorney-General moved in close for the finale.

"This man knew the nature and quality of what he was doing?"

"Perfectly."

"Did he know that what he was doing was wrong?"

Yellowlees maintained his previous position.

"I have no opinion to give on that," he said.

"You have given evidence in a great many cases where the defence has been insanity?"

"Yes."

"And you have not previously had difficulty, have you, in saying whether you thought the prisoner concerned knew or did not know that what he was doing was wrong?"

"It depends," said Yellowlees, "on what you mean by difficulty."

"You have given evidence upon the point, at all events?"

"Yes."

"This is the first case, is it not, in which you have been unable to say whether, in your view, the prisoner knew that what he was doing was wrong?"

"Yes," said Yellowlees, "I think that is true."

"Is your difficulty really this – that you realized from the preparations which the prisoner made that he *must* have known that it was wrong?"

"No." The rejection was categorical. "If that had been my difficulty I shouldn't have dreamed of coming to give evidence."

"Why do you think he procured sulphuric acid in advance in order to destroy the body?"

"You have answered the question, haven't you? In order to destroy the body."

"Why do you think he thought it necessary to destroy the body?"

"Because he wished to escape detection."

"Why do you think he wished to escape detection?"

"Because he did not wish to be punished."

Three short jabs. But deeply penetrating. And, moreover, opening wide the way – as Shawcross had intended – for the Crown case to be deployed at full strength.

"Does it not follow that he knew if he were detected he would be punished?"

"I think he certainly knew that murder is punishable by law, as a general proposition."

"Is it your opinion, then, that he was acting in obedience to a higher law?"

"Yes." Dr Yellowlees made his last stand. "He said so."

"Whether he believed he was acting under the guidance of a higher law or not, did he believe that, *according to the law of this country*, what he was doing was wrong?"

"He cannot have, if he believed he was acting under a power above the law."

Shawcross repeated and persisted.

"I asked you whether this man, thinking, as he may have done, according to you, that he was acting under the guidance of some higher power, still believed that what he was doing was wrong *according to our law*?"

"I don't know."

The Attorney only needed to ask a very few more questions.

"Can you draw any other possible conclusion from the elaborate preparations he made in advance and the attempts made subsequently to conceal what he had done?"

"No, it looks like it." Dr Yellowlees might have been communing with himself. "On the other hand, I know, or I would not be here, how little this question of knowledge of right and wrong has to do with patients in the condition I believe this man to be. It is a difficulty with all disorders to express it satisfactorily in a legal way, and I can only say I do not know."

"I am not asking you" – Shawcross pressed with remorseless relevance – "whether this man decided in obedience to a higher power to do what he realized was wrong. I am asking you to look at the facts and tell the jury whether there is any doubt that he must have known that *according to English law* he was preparing to do, and subsequently had done, something which was wrong?"

Dr Yellowlees examined the situation.

"I will say 'Yes' to that if you say 'punishable by law' instead of 'wrong'."

It delayed the final thrust by seconds only.

"Punishable by law," said Shawcross, "and therefore wrong by the law of this country?"

"Yes, I think he knew that," said Dr Yellowlees.

The trial was virtually over.

In vain did Maxwell Fyfe, with all the eloquence and force at his command, plead that Haigh's "divine control" had operated so as to annul his sense of right and wrong. The defender was not merely asking the jury to say something that Dr Yellowlees would not say himself. He was asking them to say something in contradiction of what Dr Yellowlees had already said.

It is not surprising that they preferred to accept the Attorney-General's pithy phrase for Haigh – "Not mad, but bad." It is not surprising that they needed only seventeen minutes to reach their verdict – guilty, without qualification or proviso. It is not surprising that no appeal was launched (rare though that is when the sentence has been death). It is not surprising that a special medical inquiry – appointed under statute – pronounced that Haigh was simulating insanity, and that he was neither irresponsible by legal standards *nor insane by medical standards either*.

It is certainly not surprising that the Home Secretary found no sufficient ground to justify him in advising His Majesty to interfere with the process of the law.

A whole host of legends has collected around Haigh. That he was either sub- or super-human; a werewolf, a demon, a ghoul, an incubus. That he installed a mincing-machine at Gloucester Road, and expelled the sliced remnants of his corpses down the drains. That his victims numbered, not the six we know nor the nine he claimed, but many hundreds who have wholly disappeared.

Those, though, were the fancies or the fantasies of others. The legend Haigh devised himself has lasted best of all.

There are still people who believe that there was "something in it" – something in that second-best and second-hand defence; something in that dream of weeping crucifixes; something in that thirst for drinking human blood. They believe it because it is the solitary alternative to facing a stark and disagreeable fact.

That fact is easier to state than to digest. Occasionally human beings are begotten who combine a complete sanity of mind with an infinite capacity for evil. Their mental equipment is unexceptionable, but they are morally uninhibited and emotionally void. Haigh furnishes an excellent example.

He was intelligent, rational, sensible, and acute; even – though it doesn't bear on sanity – quite cultured. On any IQ test, Haigh was somewhere above average. I do not think he had any defect of reason whatsoever, nor that he had – as one writer has proclaimed – a lust for killing. If Haigh had any lust at all, it was a lust for money; and for money he would kill as readily as others might back a horse or take a job.

It is illuminating in this regard to note the profits he extracted from his earlier – authenticated – murders, and also the means that he adopted to extract them.

From the three McSwans, through forgery and personation, he realized securities, freehold properties, furniture, and personal belongings amounting in value to about £4000. From the two Hendersons, through forgery and theft, he realized a house, a motor-car, jewellery, and other possessions amounting in value to an even larger sum (during the twelve months after they were murdered his famished bank account was fed with over £7000). Fortunate indeed – as Sir Hartley Shawcross commented on the loot that Haigh derived from Mrs Durand-Deacon – fortunate indeed the man whose irresistible impulses and monetary interests lead to exactly the same result.

By comparison, of course, Haigh's murder of that lady harvested only modest dividends. But two considerations must not be overlooked. Beggars can't be choosers, and in February, 1949, even a hundred pounds to Haigh spelt temporary salvation. Moreover, detection followed too closely upon crime for anyone to gauge how far his schemes lay uncompleted.

It must have been galling – especially for a man with Haigh's high pride in his professional achievements – to forfeit all in an attempt to win so little. He did not waste time, though, on fruitless lamentation. He applied those quick wits to a revised purpose; if they failed at one level, they might prosper at another. So he set out to feign insanity ("What are the chances of anyone being released from Broadmoor?"), and it must be admitted that he did it very well. But not quite well enough.

None need regret his failure. The verdict did him absolute as well as instant justice. It assigned him his rightful place in criminal history – that of a passionless and calculating murderer for gain, who planned his killings with a chess-player's precision, executed them with a slaughterer's indifference, and exploited them with a usurer's rapacity.

"IF—"

(Emile Gourbin, France 1912)

George Dilnot

Every contact leaves a trace. The French criminologist Edmond Locard (1877–1966) established one of the key precepts of forensic science while working at the University of Lyon in 1910. His theory was that a criminal will always take something away from the scene of his crime and leave something behind. Two years later, Locard was able to prove his theory while investigating the case of Emile Gourbin. Gourbin was suspected of having strangled his mistress, but detectives failed to shake his alibi. When Locard scraped beneath Gourbin's fingernails, he was able to analyze the resulting debris under a microscope. As expected, Locard found flakes of skin from the victim's neck. But crucially he saw that the flakes were coated with a fine powder, the same cosmetic she used as make-up. Gourbin confessed. George Dilnot (1883–1951) was general editor of the Famous Trials *series, and the author of a dozen factual books on crime. He was also a prolific writer of crime and detective fiction.*

The most significant word in the language is "if."

There are men and women who have died because of an "if" and this is the story of one of them. If Emile Gourbin had thought of visiting a manicurist – if he had been a better actor . . . Search, if you like, the archives of the principal detective bureaux in the world – in London, Paris, New York, Berlin, Vienna – and you

will understand how frequently fate plays a grim game with an
"if."

The fact of the matter is that, nowadays, the lady or gentleman
who takes a step outside the criminal code often does not get a
sporting chance. The law has no scruples in potting its game
sitting. It has made a profound study of "ifs." It is rarely possible
for any human being, however farseeing, to dodge them all. The
detective has called to his service so many allies in the realms of
science that "ifs" are multiplied beyond the conception of most
criminals.

There was a time when the law-breaker knew to some extent
the type of detective against whom he would be pitted, the
methods that would be adopted in the hue and cry. Now he
cannot be sure. He may have his guilt made manifest by some
man he never sees. Some enthusiastic specialist working in a
laboratory, not necessarily with test tubes, but even with so
prosaic an instrument as a vacuum cleaner, may glean a story
which nothing can controvert. The microscopist, the bacteriol-
ogist, the analyst, the photographer, and a score of other experts
in the domain of science are mobilized in that search for "if." It
will be found – almost to a certainty they will find it.

All this is preliminary to the case of Emile Gourbin. Now,
Emile Gourbin was a clerk with a post at a bank in Lyons. It has
been the fashion since the days of Lombroso to dwell on the
abnormality of murderers – observe that I make no secret of the
fact that Gourbin was a murderer. As a fact, murderers are much
like other people. You and I, gentle reader, are quite capable in
certain circumstances of killing someone. That is one of the
difficulties of investigating cases of homicide.

Therefore, I regret that I cannot paint Gourbin as otherwise
than a very ordinary young man to all external appearances. He
was of a type familiar everywhere in the world – an amiable fellow
of convivial disposition, perhaps a trifle neurotic, with plenty of
friends, and ambitious of ultimate promotion in the bank.

There was, of course, the girl. Marie Latelle was as fragrant
and piquant a piece of femininity as ever caused a bank clerk's
heart to miss a beat. It is not to be supposed that this gay and
debonair young lady was without her string of admirers. For

besides her personal attractions was a "dot," which would serve
to solve many of the difficulties of starting housekeeping for one
with the modest emoluments of a bank clerk. Her family if not
wealthy was at least well-to-do, and they had a neat little villa on
the outskirts of Lyons. Yet I would not do Gourbin an injustice.
He was very much in love, and if Marie Latelle had been without
a sou it would possibly have made little difference.

Here it will be noticed that I break all the rules of the detective
story-writer. I have given away my murderer instead of reserving
him for the last paragraph, and the astute reader will already have
gleaned some conception of motives. Things, outside fiction, do
not happen that way, and I am bound to my facts. Young
Gourbin and Marie fell in love. There came a day when they
were betrothed. Then it was that Gourbin touched the limits of
ecstasy. He swam in dizzy heights, no longer a bank clerk but a
silken prince of romance, the affianced of a princess of dreams.

Thus the days passed. Gourbin was an assiduous lover – too
assiduous it might have been for the little lady, who had hitherto
thrown her kerchief to any gallant as her butterfly whim dictated.
I would not be misunderstood. There was no harm in Marie. She
was young and volatile. Her dainty feet scarce touched the
ground. The inhibitions of her lover were a matter of jest –
but more than once of tears and passionate defiance.

The psychology of a man fiercely in love baffled even Solomon.
Why, therefore, should I attempt to define it? There were morose
brooding fits of sulky jealousy – futile outbursts of anger. He was
suspicious and contrite by turns, but always at the back of his
mind was the morbid fear that she was playing with him. Such a
frame of mind reacting on a temperament such as Gourbin's
might have been the subject of either comedy or tragedy. Destiny
decided that it should be tragedy.

The days grew into months. And one morning it befell that
they found little Marie dead in the parlour of her parents' home.
There were the marks of a man's fingers about her throat, but
beyond that there was no clue by which the crime might be
brought home to the assassin. The doctors said that she must
have been killed shortly before midnight. So far as any of the
family knew she had had no visitors that evening.

The house lay just outside the boundaries of the Lyons police district, but the local gendarmes felt that they were confronted with a mystery that was beyond their powers. They, therefore, turned the case over to the city authorities, and the complicated but highly efficient French system of criminal investigation began at once to work.

Unlike British procedure, a magistrate invariably takes a prominent part in the investigation of a crime in France. The detectives, the *police judiciare*, are apart from the police proper, are especially recruited, and have never worn a police uniform.

These, then, were the skilled and experienced officials who began to probe the mystery. The usual formulae were sedulously observed. Nothing that might be of moment in their search was overlooked. They probed relentlessly in every direction. Beyond the marks on the white neck of the girl, which on a superficial examination they took to be fingerprints too blurred to be of use, there was no tangible thing on which they could fasten. There was not a shadow or a shred of proof which might open some avenue of inquiry. They were baffled, against a blank wall.

That terrible snowball, the *process verbal*, which is unknown to British jurisprudence, but which is so formidable a weapon in the hands of Continental police, was commenced. Anyone and everyone who might have had any connection with the crime, or who conceivably might throw light upon it, was submitted to interrogation. All the tittle-tattle and gossip of fifty tongues was reduced to writing to be used – when there should be someone to use it against.

Even here there was nothing solid against which the detectives could lean. Suspicion there was, but an utterly unsubstantiated and flimsy suspicion.

In the wide cast that was taken, it was of course, inevitable that Emile Gourbin should be sought. Among the whispers that had been caught by the detectives was word of his jealousy. That might mean anything or nothing; but he, at least, had a possible motive. So they talked with him. They plied him with subtle questions. He was badgered and browbeaten and coaxed. They were seeking for an "if" – a little "if" – but the examining magistrate and his *confréres* were ready to snatch at the most tenuous trifle. In the beginning it had nothing to do with manicuring. Their methods were as old as crime itself. Gourbin was cunningly cross-examined; but he had expected that.

The young man was utterly grief-stricken, garrulously desolate. He was very ready to tell them anything he knew, anything that might aid them. Alas, it was very little. Through his streaming tears he answered brokenly. Yes, he had been foolishly, insanely in love with his beautiful Marie. There was now nothing in the world for him to look forward to but death. Ere that came, no doubt, messieurs would have found the dastard who had done this thing. With vengeance inflicted on the murderer of his heart's life he would die happy. Yes, it was true that he had been a little – the *Bon Dieu* forgive him – a little jealous. He had even – yes, messieurs – reproved his rosebud for little freedoms with other men. She was young. She did not understand that it was a censorious world. Messieurs would pardon his uncontrollable emotion. She was gone, the incomparable . . .

A wise man, it was once laid down by an eminent Persian philosopher, sometimes does not know when to begin; a fool never knows when to stop. So it was with Emile Gourbin. His grief was just a little too grievous; he was a shade too insistent on his emotions.

"That man," whispered one veteran police official to another, "is the murderer of Marie Latelle."

"True, friend," agreed his colleagues. "But how are we going to prove it?"

This may be an age of detective science, but science is not always necessary in certain aspects of human nature. These men knew a liar when they met one. But it is very difficult, even in France, to substantiate a charge of murder against a man because he has paraded a grief he has not felt.

Nothing that the young bank clerk had said in his examination was accepted. Every point was probed and tested. Again the officers ran against a blank wall. There is nothing more exasperating for a police officer than to feel a moral certainty of the guilt of a person, and yet to find that every fact he unearths bears apparent testimony to that person's innocence.

In practically every particular the story told by Gourbin was

borne out. He had given what appeared to be an unassailable
alibi. On the evening of the murder he had been entertained by
friends at a house some miles away from that in which Marie
Latelle had been found dead. These friends had been sought out.
Not only did they assert that Gourbin had dined with them, but
he had remained playing cards until about one o'clock in the
morning, and then gone to his room.

Now if that was true, and the conclusion of the doctors that the
girl had been killed before midnight was also true, the young
bank clerk could not have been the assassin. It seemed pure
madness to put Gourbin under arrest. That, however, was just
what the police did. They were convinced that there was a nigger
in the fence somewhere. There was nothing to go upon but an
impression, and that impression had been utterly shattered by the
alibi. British police officers would certainly and properly have
hesitated at such a drastic step. It looked like courting trouble.

But the Lyons men played their hunch and took a chance. If
the prisoner was innocent – why, so much the better for him. If he
was guilty – well, certain of them held their own views. It could
do no harm to put him under lock and key till they had decided
the next step.

Gourbin, also, was no doubt quite content. They were fools,
these detectives, if they thought to match their wits against his.
And it was perfectly true that they were in a quandary. Any legal
tribunal in the world would have laughed them out of court had
they dared to take their case for trial.

We have now reached a point at which the story of Emile
Gourbin becomes different from that of other murderers. Things
had gone in some degree as he had expected. He had reckoned
that his alibi was airtight – that it would place the police in just
such a cul-de-sac as they had in fact reached. He had not thought
of Dr Edmond Locard; it is doubtful if he even knew of his
existence. What interest has the ordinary, obscure bank clerk in
scientific matters?

Yet, all the same, Dr Locard was quite a well known person in
circles of the world alien to those in which Gourbin moved,
though perhaps not as well known as he has since become. His
reputation as a criminological scientist was worldwide. He was,

and is, among that select few which includes people like Hans Gross in Prague, Sir Bernard Spilsbury in London, and Dr Réné Faralicq in Paris. By a chance unfortunate for Gourbin, his efficiently equipped police laboratory was situated in Lyons itself.

It was not unnatural, therefore, that in their dilemma the Lyons officials should turn to this calm student, who, with his strong face, thick black hair, and dark moustache with a slightly aggressive little tilt at each corner, looked quite unlike a student or a professor, and least of all like Sherlock Holmes.

He listened thoughtfully to the story that was told to him. Quite frankly the police assured him that, unless he could find some way out, the man whom they were convinced was a brutal murderer would have to go free. He was their last hope.

"I had better look at this girl," he said.

So he was taken in a motor-car to where the still body of Marie Latelle lay. He studied it with close attention, and then proceeded to adjust a singular photographic microscope of his own invention.

This instrument, eight feet long, is capable of magnifying objects up to fifty thousand times their natural size. It was rather a pet of Locard's, for it had more than once been of service in simplifying many extraordinary cases when other methods had failed.

I step aside for the moment from the episode of Gourbin to recount that of Josef Holle, whom the police of Paris had good reason to suppose was doing a flourishing coining business by using nickel and an alloy to manufacture bogus franc pieces. Against him, however, they could get no positive evidence. They referred the matter to Locard, and on his advice Holle was arrested on a trumped up charge, which had nothing to do with coining. He was provided with a new suit of clothes and his own were taken away from him and sent to Locard, who had them beaten in a dust-proof bag – a vacuum cleaner is now used in similar cases – and then photographed the dust through his microscope. When the negatives were developed a large proportion of nickel and alloy particles were disclosed. The scientist followed this up with a chemical analysis. Those bits of metal were exactly similar to those which had been used in the false coins. That finished Holle.

Then there was the murder case which resulted from the quarrel of two men employed in a timber yard. One of them had been killed in a desperate struggle to and fro over the ground. There were no eyewitnesses, and the suspected man declared that he had not either quarrelled or fought. From his clothes, however, Locard extracted dust, among which, as well as sawdust and wood fibre, were infinitesmal fragments of soil which showed that he had at least been in contact with the soil of the timber yard. The dead man's clothes showed an exactly similar result. This evidence provided the missing link and convicted the prisoner.

As I have said, it was with this appliance that Dr Locard examined the body of Marie Latelle. He almost at once established beyond cavil or doubt that the marks on the neck were not blurred fingerprints, but superficial scratches that must have been inflicted by her assailant during the death struggle. The skin of the throat had in places been slightly scraped away.

The police glumly accepted his conclusion. Here, it seemed, was the last chance of a clue washed out. If the great criminologist, with his wealth of knowledge and resource, could not help them, where were they to turn? The case was at an end. Gourbin had beaten them after all.

Something of their feelings they conveyed to the black-haired scientist, who shrugged his shoulders and shook his head with a whimsical smile.

"Oh no," was the effect of his reply. "Give me an hour or two. Meanwhile I would like to see this young man."

They brought the prisoner to him. Gourbin was a little confused, a little doubtful of what it all meant. But he met the swift, first scrutiny of the scientist with confident self-possession. What harm could this keen-eyed, stern-faced man do to him? Had he not established an impregnable alibi?

"So you are Gourbin," said the scientist quietly. "Sit down, I want to see your hands."

The bank clerk silently obeyed. Locard drew his chair nearer to that of the prisoner and studied the hand that the other had thrust forward. Those who were present in the room beheld the strange sight of a great scientist acting with infinite care as manicurist to the nails of a suspected murderer.

"What are you doing?" demanded the mystified Gourbin.

"You will know in time," answered the absorbed scientist. "Keep your hand still."

Gourbin was not the only person who was mystified by the action of the scientist. The police officials themselves were puzzled to some extent. But they had enough confidence in Locard to be sure that there was profound significance in any action he took, however fantastic it might seem. He had some practical end in view, and it boded no good to the murderer of Marie Latelle.

"That will do," announced Locard. "I must get back to the laboratory. In a few hours I may be able to tell you something."

Back in the laboratory the scientist and his assistants set to work with businesslike zeal – for even a wizard of crime investigation has to be businesslike if he is to succeed. Also in matters of this kind speed is frequently of importance. Locard knew that he had obtained the clue which had hitherto been overlooked. A very short while would either demonstrate the guilt of Gourbin or his innocence.

There are many great scientists in the world; there are many great police detectives. In this case Locard displayed some of the qualities of both. Science had provided the instrument, but shrewd reasoning from effect to cause had really given the clue. Ninety-nine men out of a hundred had they made the discovery that the marks on the throat of the victim were scratches and not fingerprints would have left it at that. Not so Locard. He recognized that the scratches might be almost as infallible as fingerprints in bringing home the crime.

It is not fair to hold the reader longer in suspense. Locard had reasoned that the person who was responsible for the crime had carried away *beneath his fingernails* the chief evidence that was needed in the case. With that point fixed on his mind, he had seen his course clear. He had acted as a manicurist, and it was on the material he had found beneath Gourbin's nails that he set to work.

The first fact that the microscopic photographs revealed was that in the dirt taken from the nails there were unmistakable blood corpuscles. That, by itself, was enormously significant, but by no means conclusive. It was quite possible for an innocent man to have had his hands in contact with blood. A second discovery carried the case a step farther. Some very tiny fragments of flesh were found – just such fragments as the murderer must have carried away. Again there was the remote possibility of coincidence. These two things combined were of enormous value, and a strong case against Gourbin might have been built on them, notwithstanding the alibi to which he so resolutely held. All the same, there was not that precision of proof which Locard wanted. It was circumstantial evidence without absolute certainty. A jury might have preferred to believe the alibi of the accused man.

Once Locard had found the tiny pores of a murderer's hands clogged with blood, which he believed that he had washed away. With a remembrance of this case before him, he scanned the photographs again and again, seeking for he scarcely knew what. He asked the police to examine the personal belongings of the dead girl, and at long last he was able to put his finger on the point that was to send Gourbin to the guillotine.

The photographs disclosed traces of something that, on experiment, proved to be nothing else than the face powder which Marie Latelle had been in the habit of using. Coincidence could not stretch so far as that. The blood corpuscles, the fragments of flesh, and the face powder could not be explained away.

These facts were placed in the hands of the examining magistrate, and the confident Gourbin brought once more before him. Then one by one the proofs were stressed to him. For a time he held out, but when the damning fact of the face powder was made clear to him, in the dramatic style affected in French criminal procedure, he broke down and confessed.

It was all very simple. Those people who had substantiated the alibi had been perfectly sincere. Time flies fast during a convivial evening, and who would suspect a guest of altering a clock? Thus Gourbin had gone to his room much earlier than was supposed. He had slipped out while his companions imagined that he was in bed, had that fatal interview with Marie, returned, and put the clock right without rousing any suspicion.

He had luck – to a point. If he had thought of those fingernails the mystery of Marie Latelle would have remained a mystery and the guillotine would have been cheated after all. "If—"

A RIDDLE OF MAGGOTS

(William Brittle, UK 1965)

Keith Simpson

Fixing the time of death can be crucial in a murder investigation. In the case of William Brittle, accused of murdering Peter Thomas, the Home Office pathologist Professor Keith Simpson used some school- boy biology to establish this all-important fact. Having found blue- bottle maggots on Thomas's body, Simpson was able to show that the fact they had not pupated meant the victim had been dead for at least nine or ten days, a fact that destroyed Brittle's alibi. Simpson recalled the case in his memoirs Forty Years of Murder.

The police record for clearing up murders in England and Wales could hardly be better. Of the 150 or so real murders – not technical homicides – they hear about each year, only a handful have to be written off as unsolved. But how many more are unknown to the police? How many murdered persons are buried or, worse, cremated, as ordinary natural or accidental deaths? How many are hidden so successfully that their bodies are never found and recognized as human remains?

It's anybody's guess, of course. But it seems certain that some murders escape detection, for some come to light by pure chance. The body of Peter Thomas, for instance, could have remained for ever half buried in a Berkshire wood but for its unlikely discovery by two thirteen-year-old boys looking for bait for a Sunday fishing expedition.

The bait they were after was maggots, the larvae of flies that lay their eggs on the carcasses of dead animals. So off they went one Sunday, young Tony King and Paul Fay, to Bracknell Woods, in the hope of finding a dead pigeon or rabbit, as they had several times before. On this occasion, 28 June 1964, they found the maggots before the carcass – a seething mass of fat white maggots, on a mound of rough sods of turf loosely covered with beech cuttings lying a few feet off a forest path. The boys at once started to pull the turf away, and were so pleased that they hardly noticed the stench as they dragged the sods aside to get at the maggots – until they caught sight of a decomposing forearm with the remains of a hand at the end.

The fishing expedition ended before it had begun. Being sensible boys, they left everything, including the precious white maggots, and ran to the nearest police station.

"There's a dead body buried in the woods," they told the duty sergeant in their commendably matter-of-fact style.

Shortly after I was rung up out of my Sunday afternoon snooze in the garden at my cottage at Tring, and by 5 p.m. I had joined Detective Superintendent Arthur Lawson, chief of the Berkshire CID, at the scene, where I set about a more scientific disinterment of the lightly buried body. I stopped to allow photographs to be taken at every stage as I removed the turf cuttings and sprays of beech wood; looking around, I noticed there were no beeches in the vicinity. From Lawson I learnt there were none in Bracknell Woods. Had the body been brought there dead, then? The police searched very thoroughly but found no appropriate tyre tracks or footprints.

It was the body of a man, lying on his back, fully clothed, with his head wrapped in towelling. How long had he been there; or, rather, how long had he been dead? It was much too late to try to measure the loss of body temperature, and rigor mortis would certainly have come and passed off again long before. The body was disintegrating, and the police assumed it must have been dead for six or eight weeks.

"At least nine or ten days, but probably not more than twelve," I told Lawson, who stared at me in disbelief. "It's astonishing how quickly maggots will eat up the flesh," I reminded him. "I've seen a body reduced to this state in *as little as ten days*."

I thought it safe to assume the maggots were larvae of the bluebottle *Calliphora erythrocephalus*, but I preserved samples because the maggots of other flies of the calliphorine type, with slightly different hatching times, are not dissimilar to the naked eye. The ordinary life history of the bluebottle is quite simple. The eggs are laid in day-light, usually sunlight, and in warm weather they hatch on the first day. The tiny "first instar" maggot sheds its skin after eight to fourteen hours, and the second instar after a further two to three days. The third instar, the fisherman's maggot, feeds voraciously for five or six days before going into a pupa case. The larvae I was looking at were mature, indeed elderly, fat, indolent, third-stage maggots, but they were not in pupa cases. Therefore I estimated that the eggs had been laid nine or ten days earlier. Adding a little more time to allow for the bluebottles getting to the dead body, I reckoned death had occurred on 16 June or 17 June.

Lawson telephoned the Scotland Yard missing persons bureau and learnt that a Peter Thomas had disappeared from his home at Lydney, in Gloucestershire, on 16 June, and that Detective Superintendent Horace Faber of the Yard had been down there helping the local police in their investigation. Faber was so interested in the report of the body in Bracknell Woods, though it lay more than a hundred miles from Lydney, that he joined us at the scene the same afternoon.

Because of the extensive decomposition and maggot infestation I had decided to examine the exposed parts – head and neck and hands – as they lay. This was a fortunate decision, for as the neck came into view I saw a pool of liquid blood over the left side of the voice box – and not at any other site. (I found later it was the only pool anywhere in the body.) The small bones of the larynx were crushed on this side, and I picked them out loose.

"He received a blow across the throat," I said. "Not a violent constriction but a blow."

"What sort of a blow, doctor?" asked Superintendent Faber.

"A punch, a kick, a bottle—"

"What about a karate chop with the side of the hand?" Faber had been on Commando training in the war.

"That would do very well."

When I continued my examination in the mortuary I found blood in the main windpipe and bronchial passages and a few asphyxial haemorrhages on the surface of the heart. I saw no sign of any skull or other fracture, but the disintegrated liquid state of the brain made it impossible to discover whether unconscious-ness might have been caused by some other blow. In the absence of any other positive finding I attributed death to bleeding into the windpipe from the blunt injury to the throat. This would have disabled the victim so that he would have been likely to inhale the blood and die in a few minutes.

But was he the missing Peter Thomas? I put his age between forty and fifty: Thomas was forty-two. When stretched out, the body measured 5 feet 3 inches: Thomas was said to have been 5 feet 3 inches or 5 feet 4 inches. He had neglected attentions to his teeth so the dental data were no use. But it was said he had broken his left arm in youth, and X-rays showed an old fracture of the left forearm. He had a criminal record, so his fingerprints were on the files: the experts succeeded in getting some impressions of the skin peeling off his finger-pads which were identical with both the records and prints found in his home at Lydney. A tailor's tab in the jacket of the dead man's suit also led to Thomas. Beyond doubt Superintendent Faber had been right in his hunch – it could hardly have been more – that the man who had disappeared from Lydney had ended up dead in Bracknell Woods. How?

Peter Thomas had been living very simply in a tumble-down wooden bungalow outside this little Welsh border town, alone except for his dog. He pretended poverty and drew unemploy-ment pay although he had inherited about £5,000 from his father three years before. Letters found in his home revealed that he had recently lent £2,000 to William Brittle, a heating engineer sales-man of Hook, Hampshire, and the loan was due for repayment in the month Thomas had disappeared. It was a strictly business loan. Brittle had advertised in a Cardiff newspaper offering a "quick return" on a loan for an "agricultural prospect". Thomas, against the advice of both his solicitor and his bank manager, had lent him the money at $12\frac{1}{2}$ per cent interest (a moneylender's rate in those days) for six months.

Questioned by Faber, Brittle said he had motored to Lydney and repaid the debt on 16 June, the very day Thomas had disappeared. But there seemed to be no proof that the money had been received. Faber pressed Brittle to say how he got this large sum. Not from agriculture, he admitted.. "I got an accumulator on a roll-up system at the races," he said. Faber asked him for the names of the winning horses but he "could not remember them", nor could any of the bookmakers or betting shops in the district recognize his photograph. As evidence that he had been to Lydney on 16 June Brittle mentioned that he had given a hitch-hiker a lift on the way back home.

Brittle's car was "taken apart" at the Regional Forensic Science Laboratory without yielding anything more suspicious than a single beech leaf under the driver's mat. No beeches grew anywhere near Brittle's Hampshire home. A few scattered bloodstains were found on the sleeve of Brittle's coat: group O, the same as Peter Thomas's: but as it happened the same, too, as Brittle's. The police found out that while in the Army Brittle had attended a course in unarmed combat which would have included the use of "the chop". Although the blow required training rather than great strength, Brittle did not look like a man who could commit murder with one bare hand. "What, killed by *this* man?" his counsel, the redoubtable Quintin Hogg, asked scornfully at his trial. "Felled like an ox at one blow?"

Meanwhile Brittle's hitch-hiker had been found from his description. A golf caddy, he confirmed the truth of Brittle's story that he had gone to Lydney that day. To repay Thomas or to kill him? If Faber's suspicions were correct, Brittle had stopped to pick up the hitch-hiker on his way back when he had Thomas's body in the boot of his car. That would have been very cool; and, as Quintin Hogg was to point out, the most thorough and expert search of the vehicle had failed to produce a trace of the body. Wrapped in cloth or a sack or bag, of course, this might well be.

Faber had been working doggedly on the case for four months when a man named Dennis Roberts, a nylon spinner, came forward. to say he had seen Peter Thomas at Gloucester bus station, studying the timetable, on *20 June*. Roberts said they had exchanged greetings (they had once worked together in a sawmill) and he was sure of the date because it was the only day in his life when he had been on strike.

If Thomas had been alive on 20 June, the whole case against Brittle collapsed. His day of opportunity to kill Thomas was 16 June, and if Thomas was alive on 20 June, he had been dead only eight days at the most when I saw his body (and the tell-tale maggots) in Bracknell Woods.

"Is that possible, doctor?" asked the anxious Faber, who had brought Roberts's statement to my laboratory at Guy's.

"No, it isn't," I answered immediately. "And I am ready to stand up to severe cross-examination on the point if it comes to trial."

Faber looked as if I had taken a great load off his mind. If I had answered that one could never be absolutely sure about such a matter, the case would have crumbled and Scotland Yard would have lost confidence in me – with good reason. Why, if I had not been really sure, had I pin-pointed the time of death with confidence at the start?

Faber asked me for a written statement that he could attach to his report for the Director of Public Prosecutions, and I dictated one on the spot to my secretary Jean Scott-Dunn. It was as unequivocal as the estimate that I had given in my original autopsy report:

Guy's Hospital, 21 October 1964

I have today been shown by Detective Superintendent Faber a copy of a statement made by Dennis John Roberts to the effect that on Saturday 20 June he saw a man whom he recognized as Peter Thomas at a bus station. The condition of the body when examined in the wood suggested in the first instance, while still at the scene – "some nine or ten days, possibly more" – was a minimum period. Nothing in the post-mortem state of the body suggested any special conditions likely to have accelerated the ordinary process of maggot infestation and disintegration of the body.

And to put a final "nail in the coffin" I added:

> I have had considerable experience in the timing of death and would regard Dennis Roberts's statement as being wholly inconsistent with my findings.

To prosecute or not to prosecute? The question was for the Director of Public Prosecutions in London, and he considered it for several weeks. He took the opinion of Senior Counsel, and finally decided the case was not strong enough. He could not ignore Roberts's statement, and it might well deter a jury.

All Faber could do then was to refer the case to the coroner at Bracknell and let his jury hear the evidence; which they did, in an inquest lasting seven days. Nobody expected a coroner's jury to commit Brittle for murder after the DPP had declined to do so, but to everyone's astonishment the jury found Thomas had been murdered on or about 1-7 June and they named Brittle as the person responsible. The coroner committed him into custody, and he was tried at Gloucester at the Spring Assize of 1965.

His counsel, Quintin Hogg, QC – later Lord Hailsham, the Lord Chancellor – was making a trial return to the Bar after a distinguished career in the upper echelons of politics. Long before that he had been a very promising young barrister, and I expected a really testing cross-examination, especially when I heard he had taken the trouble to consult another Home Office pathologist, Dr David Bowen, and an entomologist, Professor McKenny-Hughes. It was a good thing I had decided to bottle a few maggots on that Sunday afternoon in the woods, for McKenny-Hughes wanted to see them and check if they really were the larvae of *C. erythrocephalus*, as I had said.

When I was examined by the Crown counsel, Ralph Cusack, I set out as clearly and briefly as I could the nature of the fat, third instar maggot, not yet pupated, yet plainly having passed the growing-up stages from the day the eggs hatched. I further set out the several periods of time that (it was accepted, I said) eggs took to hatch, and the three stages of maggot instar to develop before pupation. I added up the times and said, as deliberately and purposefully as I knew how:

"So, I had no doubt in my mind at the time" – I emphasized. that I had made up my mind at the outset – "that this man had been dead some ten days." Nine or ten was a minimum.

Cusack brought his examination to a quick finish. It was late in the afternoon, and he did not want to give the defence counsel the chance to discuss my evidence with his advisers before cross-examining me. But Quintin Hogg was an equally shrewd tactician.

"Doctor," he began, "may I assume" – counsel likes to use this phrase instead of "I am sure" – "that you made notes during the successive stages of uncovering that body in the woods?"

"Yes, I have them here in court." They were before me.

"My lord," he said, "I am going to ask that they be duplicated by photostat and handed to the members of the jury in the morning."

The judge agreed, and Quintin Hogg was able after all to consult his advisers before cross-examining me, and I expected them to supply him with an armful of questions, skilfully worded to probe any weaknesses in my evidence. Next morning I braced myself when he got to his feet and pulled at his gown.

"Doctor," he began, "I have only to say, of your notes, that the sketch which accompanies them is of more help to me in understanding the lie of the body than the police photographs!"

I was off the hook. He was not going to challenge me on my evidence.

But he still had Professor McKenny-Hughes, who was certainly more of an expert than I on the habits of the bluebottle and maggots. If anyone could pick holes in my evidence he was the man.

"Professor, you have heard the evidence given so far in this case," he began. "Will you kindly tell the court in what respects your views as to the times of egg-laying and hatching of the larvae differ from those of Professor Keith Simpson?"

The distinguished entomologist ran his fingers through his wispy hair and favoured me with a jovial beam. Was he going to enjoy himself cutting me up into little pieces?

"Well," he said, still smiling, "I'm not sure there's anything I really . . ."

"Professor," interrupted Quintin Hogg rather desperately, "can we agree about one thing?" His witness nodded and waited. "Let us suppose that the bluebottle lay its eggs on the dead body at midnight on the . . ."

"Oh, dear me, no!" exclaimed the entomologist. "No self-respecting bluebottle lays eggs at midnight. At midday, perhaps, but not at midnight."

There were stifled giggles in the public gallery, lawyers and reporters hid their smiles with their hands, and even the judge's face twitched. Poor Quintin Hogg tried again.

"At what period, then, Professor, would you expect the eggs to hatch?"

"Well, it all depends." The professor seemed oblivious of the effect he was creating. "You see, in warm weather—"

"Yes, Professor, we know it was June and quite warm," Counsel came in hastily. "How many hours would have elapsed before the first maggots were hatched?"

"Well, I agree with Dr Simpson," said McKenny-Hughes, looking as if he expected everyone to be pleased about that. "Say eight to fourteen hours for the first instar, and . . ."

"And these maggots would settle down on the dead tissues at once?"

"Well, maggots are curious little devils," the entomologist said engagingly. "Suppose this is a dead body." He had taken out a matchbox and placed it on the edge of the witness box. "And suppose you have a hundred maggots here." He indicated them with an expansive spread of his hands. "Ninety-nine will make their way towards the body, but the hundredth little devil" – the professor was back in the lecture hall, completely unmindful of his real surroundings – "he'll turn the other way."

Mr Justice Phillimore's face twitched again, the Crown lawyers hardly dared to exchange glances, the jury looked relaxed and almost happy, and Quintin Hogg's frown deepened into a furrow as he told the professor very frostily that he had no more questions for him.

But the defence had three more witnesses who were not at all as acceptable to the prosecution.

First, Dennis John Roberts told how he had seen and spoken to Peter Thomas at Gloucester bus station on 20 June. "Hello, Dennis," Thomas had greeted him, he said; and Ralph Cusack, QC, who led for the Crown, could not shake him in cross-examination.

Next Mrs Jane Charles, of Lydney, said she had seen Thomas walking along the road towards Blakeney village on 21 June. She knew the date because it was the longest day of the year. She had been a passenger in a car and could only have glimpsed him briefly, but she was sure it was Thomas whom she knew. Finally Mrs Gwendoline Padwick, of Blakeney Stores, also said she had seen Thomas on 21 June, in her shop, buying matches. He was a regular customer, and she knew the date because she had just made out a cheque for her mother, who was staying with her for the first time.

Cusack pressed both women hard in cross-examination. It was, as he pointed out, a long time ago – nearly nine months – and their memories could have played them false. He asked them what else they could remember of that day, and of the previous day. What else had happened? What had Thomas been wearing? And so on. All three witnesses seemed perfectly honest persons – they had been "found" by the defence but there was not a breath of suspicion about this – and the question was simply whether they had each made an honest mistake.

Quintin Hogg decided not to call Brittle, doubtless because he did not want his client exposed to cross-examination by the very skilful and penetrative Ralph Cusack. "He has already made three long statements," Hogg said, as if these rather contradictory accounts put his client in the clear. He went on to speak confidently of the three witnesses who said they had seen the dead man after 16 June; and since just one of them had been enough to raise sufficient doubt to stop the DPP from prosecuting, it seemed quite likely the jury would acquit Brittle. But, in the event, they decided my maggots were more reliable in their hatching habits than Quintin Hogg's three alibis, and found Brittle guilty of murder. He was given a life sentence.

The case was particularly satisfying to me. My insistence on the timing of death had become pretty well known, to the police, the Director of Public Prosecutions, the lawyers – and the Press, who would have scented a public disgrace for me if I'd been wrong.

A WELSH MUMMY

(Sarah Jane Harvey, UK 1960)

Robert Jackson

The best-known case in Britain involving mummified remains is that of Mrs Sarah Harvey, tried for the murder of her lodger, Mrs Frances Knight, but acquitted. Mrs Knight's doubled-up body, shrouded in the mouldering remnants of her night-dress and dressing gown, was discovered in a locked cupboard at Mrs Harvey's house in Rhyl, North Wales, in 1960. Mrs Harvey said that she'd put Mrs Knight there after finding her dead in her room in April 1940. The skin was shrunken and leathery, and the corpse had been mummified by the natural process of warm, dry air rising and circulating in the cupboard, slowly drying out the body tissues. But suspicion arose during a post-mortem examination, prompted by a groove on the neck associated with the disintegrating vestige of a knotted stocking. The pathologist concluded that Mrs Knight had been strangled, and Mrs Harvey was charged with murder. She denied the charge, and it was not supported by the physical evidence. Neither the hyoid bone nor thyroid cartilage was fractured, as would be expected in a case of strangulation. Cleared of murder, Mrs Harvey was nevertheless convicted of fraud, because for twenty years she had drawn a special pension to which her dead lodger had been entitled. Robert Jackson (1911–77), a Yorkshireman, was a journalist who worked as a foreign and war correspondent before turning to authorship with a series of biographies of twentieth century legal luminaries including the former Lord Chief Justice, Lord Hewart. Surprisingly, perhaps, he was also editor of Gardening Illustrated.

Of all the people who took part in the trial in October, 1960, of Mrs Sarah Jane Harvey, a sixty-five-year-old Rhyl, North Wales, landlady for murder, the most unremarkable was the woman in the dock.

The Solicitor-General, Sir Jocelyn Simon, QC, who prosecuted, was to become President of the Probate, Divorce and Admiralty Division of the High Court. Mr Elwyn Jones, QC his chief assistant, was picked by the Labour Prime Minister in 1964 to be Attorney-General. Professor Sir Sydney Smith, called the "patriarch" of all forensic experts, and Dr (later Professor) Francis E. Camps, one of the leading Home Office pathologists for a quarter of a century, attended to give advice to the defence on matters about which not more than a dozen men in the world could have spoken with authority. Sir Francis Walshe, the great neurological specialist was present, as was Lord Cohen of Birkenhead, the famous physician. Dr Edward Gerald Evans, Home Office pathologist for North Wales and West Midlands, was the chief prosecution witness and although the defence experts disagreed with his conclusions, they openly expressed admiration for his work. Not the least remarkable man in court was the defence counsel, Mr Andrew Rankin, a rugged figure, an expert in both Scottish and English law and a triple Blue (hockey, swimming and water-polo) of both Edinburgh and Cambridge universities who, at thirty-six, took on a formidable team of prosecutors.

Yet the frail, ailing, drab little woman in the court had done something which extraordinary and ordinary people could not think of without revulsion. For twenty years, she had kept the mummified body of Mrs Frances Alice Knight, her lodger, in a locked cupboard at the top of the bedroom stairs. She was suspected of murder, accused of it, and acquitted. As her counsel said, she must have gone through hell, knowing the body was there and that, having put it there, she could not turn back. With her secret always in danger of exploding, she walked the streets of the holiday town of Rhyl and except for her few friends nobody gave her a second look.

The case of the Mummy in the Cupboard, as it came to be called, was followed by the public for a number of reasons. To begin with, mummies are not found in cupboards every day of the week in Britain. The trial when it was held at Ruthin, the little assize town in Denbighshire, came to an end immediately after exhaustive cross-examination of the Crown's two principal witnesses, but particularly of the pathologist, Dr Evans. The two defence crime doctors, Sir Sydney Smith and Dr Camps, were present throughout. They did not give evidence but the knowledge that they were there – and what they would say if they were called – had a profound effect. There was another fact which made the trial interesting, although it was not revealed at the time. Barristers in murder trials have been experts on guns, poisons and other technical matters but the defence counsel, Mr Rankin, had an unusual qualification. For two years, he had studied medicine at Edinburgh University under one of his own forensic experts, Sir Sydney Smith.

To a large extent, Mrs Sarah Jane Harvey was responsible for her own predicament. Mrs Knight, the estranged wife of a Rhyl dentist who had gone in 1936 to live in Hove, Sussex, took a 30s. a week bed-sitting room in Mrs Harvey's house in West Kinmel Street early in 1940. The exact date she went there was not certain but a policeman handed her personally on February 27, 1940, the magistrates' order awarding her £2 a week for maintenance at the time she was living in another Rhyl boarding house. Mrs Knight found difficulty in walking from what was first thought to be rheumatism but turned out later to be disseminated sclerosis, a deadly crippling disease. She managed to get to the magistrates' office to collect the first payment. The second payment was made to Mrs Harvey, who showed the clerk's experienced assistant, Mr Albert Reveley, a chit signed by Mrs Knight authorizing her to collect the money. She continued to do so until she went into hospital herself with suspected cancer in April, 1960.

The death of Mrs Knight came to light in an unusual way, too. While Mrs Harvey was undergoing treatment in hospital her son Leslie, a taxi-driver, decided to do his mother a good turn. Mrs Harvey had no lodger but as she had given Leslie the key he began to redecorate the house. Leslie had lived in the house all his life until two years after he married, when he found a place of his own. It had often puzzled him why his mother had never allowed the cupboard built on to the wall at the top of the stairs to be opened but he accepted her story that it contained various articles belonging to a former lodger who one day would want them back. Leslie Harvey decided to make a good job of decorating the top landing and deal with the cupboard inside and out. He forced one of the doors with a screw-driver and peered through the dark, musty-smelling cobwebby interior with the aid of a torch. It was a severe shock when he saw what seemed to be a human foot. His wife was downstairs and he hurried her off to her father's house. The two men returned together to the house and immediately they had made certain that what was inside the cupboard was a body, they sensibly hurried to the police station for help.

A local doctor was called but realized that the task of examining a mummified body would have to be undertaken by a highly-skilled pathologist and within a few hours Dr Evans and Dr Alan Clift, a biologist from the Home Office Forensic Laboratory at Preston, had begun to unravel the mystery of the mummy in the cupboard.

Bodies do not become mummies in a day or two in cold, damp climates and the obvious person to question first was Mrs Harvey, who had lived in the house for over forty years. Mrs Harvey was naturally shocked to hear of the mummy in the cupboard. She was a respectable as well as a sick woman and the only blemish on her character was a conviction for the theft of £10 in 1942.

Her first reaction when the police called to see her was to feign surprise and say she knew nothing about the mummy. No doubt with thoughts of her own illness uppermost in her mind she forgot any prepared story – if in the course of twenty years living with the mummy she had ever had one clearly mapped out.

But Mrs Harvey was sharp and knew her way about. She must have realized quickly that the police would not shrug off the finding of the mummy as one of those inexplicable things that happen. They had already questioned Leslie about the lodgers he remembered and the name of Mrs Knight, a lodger in his boyhood days, had cropped up. Yes, Mrs Harvey told the police, she knew Mrs Knight, a crippled lady, who had lived with her until the end of the war. She now lived in Penymaes, Llandudno, with a Mrs Collins. Mrs Harvey said she was sure of that because every week, she still collected £2 due to Mrs Knight under a maintenance order and posted it on, either in cash or as a postal order.

The police made a note to look up Mrs Knight in Penymaes and asked her about other lodgers who might know something about the mummy in the cupboard. Mrs Harvey took her time to answer but eventually she said she did remember a couple, named White or Wright. They had come to Rhyl at the time the bombing started in the South of England. Mrs Harvey said they wanted to store "stuff and foodstuff" and she had let them use the landing cupboard. They had the key and went off with it about the end of the war. For two Christmases in succession she had had cards from the couple but they never returned to collect whatever it was they had left in the cupboard.

Mrs Harvey had furnished streets, places and names so that the police could trace Mrs Knight but they were unsuccessful. Mrs Harvey was being discharged from hospital temporarily but instead of going home she went, by invitation, to the police station.

She now decided that the time for fencing was over. The police had held her on a charge of obtaining one of Mrs Knight's weekly instalments of £2 by false pretences and in the cells she began to unburden herself. "Mrs Knight is in the cupboard," she informed Chief Inspector H. I. Williams. "I will tell you what happened. She died in the bedroom and I put her in the cupboard."

Bit by bit, the secret she had bottled up for twenty years came out. She said that soon after coming to lodge with her, Mrs Knight became very frail and weak and developed great pains in her knees. Four or five weeks after she arrived, Mrs Harvey was getting ready for bed in the back bedroom, when she heard Mrs Knight screaming in her own bedroom. "I went into the bedroom and saw her lying on the floor in her night-dress and coat. I asked her what had happened and she said 'I am in an awful lot of pain and would rather be dead'."

Mrs Harvey said she tried to pick her distressed lodger up but could not manage it. She dressed herself and went downstairs to make tea but when she returned, Mrs Knight was still lying on the floor and was dead. "I was on my own in the house and was scared stiff, so I pulled her along the landing and put her into the empty cupboard," she said. "I put fly-papers in the cupboard and then locked it. I didn't tell anyone she had died – but I kept trying to keep things covered up. I have gone through hell ever since. I have told you everything now and that is the truth."

The Rhyl detectives now had plenty of clues to follow up – apart from what the work of the pathologists would yield – since it was clear that Mrs Harvey's story would have to undergo the most stringent tests. Sudden death in a quiet house to a woman on her own can be a frightening experience but the question in the minds of the police and lawyers was simple: which was the more frightening thing to do – run into the house of a friendly neighbour and get help, or drag a freshly-dead body out on the landing, somehow – remembering that Mrs Harvey had said she could not lift Mrs Knight from the floor into bed – get her into the cupboard and wedge a bedspread between her thighs to prevent pollution.

A first thought was that Mrs Harvey, seeing Mrs Knight dead on the floor, suddenly realized that if only she could conceal the body she would in effect have inherited a pension of £2 a week. The prosecution at her trial went further and suggested that Mrs Harvey had done more than that – she had actually strangled Mrs Knight herself with a stocking so that she could continue to draw the money. The court did not accept the view but over the years, Mrs Harvey *did* collect £2,098 paid over by Mr Knight from Hove.

Mrs Harvey had also taken good care to see that the arrangement was not disturbed. The clerks in the magistrates' office showed an interest in their "clients" and often asked how Mrs Knight, whom they never saw, was getting on. Mrs Harvey's replies varied week by week, from "about the same" to "a little better" or "not too good". Occasionally at Christmas, Mrs Harvey negotiated for the money to be paid in advance and when it did not turn up, the clerks were surprised to hear that the invalid would be in a "bloody bad temper" or would "play hell" in consequence.

When the trial took place, Mr Reveley, one of the senior clerks, was questioned closely by Mr Rankin about the office system which had allowed Mrs Harvey to draw the money for so long. Mrs Harvey's signed authority could not be found in the files but Mr Reveley remembered that she had handed it over. It had never occurred to him to doubt her honesty. "I have known her forty or forty-five years and have always found her perfectly straightforward," he said.

In 1949, the dead woman in the cupboard must have been very much on Mrs Harvey's conscience because she sold a black trunk which had belonged to Mrs Knight and had her initials stamped on it. She remarked to the buyer that she did not think Mrs Knight would ever come back for it.

Mrs Harvey had undoubtedly taken trouble to keep inquisitive lodgers away from the cupboard. A miner who lodged with Mrs Harvey when he worked at a Rhyl colliery was traced to Newark. He said he and his wife were "a bit nosey" when they lived in the house for periods in 1950 and 1951 and had tried to open the cupboard. He lost interest in it when Mrs Harvey told him that it contained her best linen.

But the most significant discovery which the police thought cast great doubt on Mrs Harvey's story was a fly-paper found hanging from the roof of the cupboard. Mrs Harvey said that from the day Mrs Knight was put in the cupboard in the early spring of 1940, the door had remained locked. This could not have been true. The fly-paper bore a code number and the name of the manufacturer at Derby. That particular batch of fly-papers, the manager said, could not have been on sale before the early spring of 1942 – a whole year after Mrs Knight's death.

Some of these matters could be drowned or at least obscured by the vigorous cross-examination to which Mr Rankin subjected every witness. But in the end, the case against Mrs Harvey depended on the evidence given – or to be given – by the doctors who had treated Mrs Knight in life and those who had known her as what Dr Camps called "a shell of dried skin and bones".

Mrs Harvey, even twenty years before her trial, had not been particularly robust and part of the Crown case was that she was able to kill because Mrs Knight was "vulnerable". "You may think that the fact that Mrs Knight was a cripple is significant in considering whether she would not be an easy victim of attack," said the Solicitor-General, in opening the case.

Mrs Knight's friend, Mrs Phyllis Rogers, partially upset the idea that Mrs Knight was always miserable, complaining, and by inference, almost helpless. She produced a holiday snapshot which showed Mrs Knight looking quite happy, though admittedly she walked with a stick. "She was cheerful with a keen sense of humour," said Mrs Rogers. "She never complained of pain." Mrs Rogers maintained that though her condition was slowly deteriorating, Mrs Knight was chiefly worried because she was losing her sense of balance.

Mrs Rogers had taken Mrs Knight to Liverpool to see the famous consultant physician, Lord Cohen of Birkenhead, who had diagnosed disseminated sclerosis but anticipated that there would be some improvement in her condition. Mrs Knight's medical records showed that she was slightly overweight and there was nothing in them to suggest that she would die from natural causes within a short period.

But Sir Francis Walshe, the neurologist, advised the defence on a point in Mrs Harvey's favour. Her counsel took it up with Lord Cohen, who agreed that Mrs Knight had been suffering from a kidney infection which, in an acute form, might lead to death. He said anyone predisposed to the infection might fall dangerously ill suddenly and die within a fortnight. So, one of the most distinguished physicians went on the court record with the view that it was *possible* for Mrs Harvey's account of Mrs Knight's death to be correct.

The case reached the beginning of its crucial stage when crime doctor Gerald Evans stepped into the witness box to tell of the discovery and detailed examination of the mummy. There is a great deal of *camaraderie* among crime doctors, though they often speak in slighting terms of each other's work when talking privately. But there is no tendency for them to hang together and in most cases the cross-examination of counsel, usually based on the opinions of other crime doctors, are as a rule searching and prolonged. In the mummy case, Dr Evans was to be put to the fiercest test.

The mummy, it turned out, was not a "true" mummy, though the difference between "true" and "false" could be appreciated only by crime doctors. Mummification was drying until the moisture was removed from the tissues, said Dr Evans. The passage of a current of dry air over the body, day and night, led to mummification and the preservation of the features and contours of the body. It was well known in Egypt.

In the case of the Rhyl mummy, mummification might have occurred because of a freak of chance. For many weeks and months, warm, dry air had circulated up the stairs into the landing and cupboard where the body lay. A small trap door above the cupboard may have helped the draughts. Dr Camps said later that the explanation was over-simplified but he admitted that it seemed to satisfy the jury. Gruesome photographs of the body were handed up to Mr Justice Davies, who seemed to approve of them on the principle that one picture is worth a thousand words.

It had been late at night when Dr Evans climbed the carpeted stairs of Mrs Harvey's house and in the light of police torches began to make clinical observations on the contents of the cupboard. Laymen in the old courthouse at Ruthin listened in a kind of awed wonder.

The sight he saw was not pretty – the fly-paper saturated with flies, the thick cobwebs on the walls to which dead spiders clung in grotesque masses, and the object on the floor that had been a woman. Here the lacey cobwebs were several inches deep. He could also make out the shape of a mound of mould and literally many hundreds of pupa cases from which maggots had emerged as flies. They told their own story of what had happened when the natural putrefaction of the body set in.

A foot was visible, brown and skinny, as Leslie Harvey had seen it. Moving closer into the smell of decay, Dr Evans gently began to brush aside the cobwebs, mould and dust. He uncovered what had been a human face with nostrils dilated and lips stretched and distorted. But immediately he had had to retreat on to the landing to cough out the dust that rose in clouds and choked him.

The greatest care was obviously necessary in recovering the

mummy and Dr Evans examined the cupboard to see whether he could unscrew it to take it away. But the cupboard had been built on to the wall and it could not be done. So he began again to stir the dust as gently as possible and after a time he saw the outline of the mummy under a crumbling blue dressing gown and blanket. He had to remove two more types of material before the mummy was completely exposed – the bedspread, which had been packed between the legs, and a long-sleeved night-dress, the V-shaped neck of which could be traced.

The mummy under the touch of his fingers was rock hard – an absolute statue, Dr Evans said in court. It was lying on its back with the thighs bent backwards towards the abdomen and the legs bent or flexed at the knees. The left arm was extended down the side of the body and the right forearm, with a claw-like hand, lay across the chest. The whole of the skin from the neck to the feet was peppered with maggot holes.

Dr Evans's experience in removing the crumbling matter other than the body had made him apprehensive about what would happen when he attempted to take the mummy out of the cupboard but he need not have worried. Far from disintegrating, he could not budge the mummy. Finally, he saw only one solution. He would have to lever it from the cupboard floor. "Get me a spade," he said to the police.

In his own mortuary, Dr Evans made a detailed examination of the mummy before he put it in a bath containing a solution of glycerine to soften it. The mummy's head was turned to the right and when the dust had been brushed from the neck, he saw a distinct groove with a localized depression at the front. A great deal was to be heard at the trial about the groove. He tilted the mummy to see whether the groove ran all the way round the neck. It did, and what appeared to have caused the groove – a piece of tape-like material – fell away. A further piece of the same material was still embedded in the groove and when Dr Evans had eased it out he saw that it was part of a stocking. There was only a few inches of it altogether – the fragments were exhibited in a test-tube in court – but it contained an undoubted reef knot.

As Dr Evans said in court, the body was in a "deplorable" condition but the post-mortem on the mummy, and later the examination of the skeleton, produced a very adequate build-up of the sort of person the mummy had been in life. She was a European woman between forty and sixty, nearly 5 ft, 4 ins, tall with shapely ears. She was married – her ring finger was grooved but – another minor mystery – the ring was not in the cupboard.

She could not have had children without a Caesarian operation. She was right-handed and dragged her left foot when she walked. In her early teens, she had had an illness which had been cured by medicine containing arsenic, lead or iron. All her teeth had been extracted but her dentures were missing. Many of the internal organs had been eaten away over the years but the crime doctors did not think she had been poisoned. They had even been able to find her blood group. They compared it with blood groups of Mrs Knight's close relatives and, if they had been called to give an opinion in court, would have said that Mrs Knight's group might well have been that of the mummy's.

The defence discussed the possibility of trying to prove that the mummy in the cupboard was not that of Mrs Knight, relying on a legal objection to Mrs Harvey's own admission. The idea was quickly abandoned and the line they were to take became apparent soon after the cross-examination of Dr Evans began.

Dr Evans had been taken through his evidence-in-chief by the Solicitor-General and had told the court how he had seen the groove around the neck and retrieved the piece of stocking, with the tightly tied reef knot. When he put the stocking on the postmortem bench, it remained in a curve and this suggested that at one time it had encircled the neck. "If you tie a stocking tightly round a person and knot it and take the stocking off fairly soon after, you will get no depression. But if that stocking is left in contact with the skin over a period of time, then, especially after mummification starts, I think it is more than probable that an indentation would remain," he said.

There had been a depression on the side of the thyroid cartilage and he had found a knot in the stocking, but not where the depression was. Dr Evans found the groove on the left side difficult to associate with a natural fold of the neck and there was nothing in the cupboard which would account for the external pressure.

"Are you able on medical grounds, excluding the fact that you found a stocking, to state what was the cause of death?" asked Sir Jocelyn. "No," was the reply, "I am afraid I cannot do that to help the court."

"So that within your province as an expert, there is nothing to indicate what had happened?" The answer was "No".

Mr Rankin, impressive and confident, plunged into battle and Dr Evans told him that it was quite impossible to determine whether the stocking had been put round Mrs Knight's neck before or after death.

The judge intervened. "That is your opinion now?" "Yes."

"In your opinion now, was there or was there not a ligature?" pursued the judge. "Yes, there was a ligature."

Dr Evans explained that if there was a collar round the neck of a dead man and the skin became swollen, there would be a groove.

Said Mr Rankin: "Sir Sydney Smith and Dr Camps, whose experience is unrivalled, say that this was never a homicidal ligature." "I could well understand that," came the wry answer.

"They say that what you saw on the neck was caused by postmortem changes in the body, there having been before death what I have described as a natural ligature round the neck," said Mr Rankin. "That is an opinion I cannot agree with," answered Dr Evans.

"Could a groove made by a collar be mistaken for a homicidal groove?" "Not by a forensic pathologist."

Mr Rankin commented that, "We will see what another forensic expert will say" and Dr Evans thereupon amplified his answer. "If this body does not disrupt but goes on to a more drying process, I think this groove would disappear and the skin flatten out again."

"You think it disappears but leaves a mark?" queried Mr Rankin. "Yes."

Mr Rankin's comment that, "the difficulty you are labouring under is lack of experience of this kind of case" brought from Dr Evans the complaint: "I think you are putting it rather hardly."

It was, as Dr Evans had admitted, only the second case of a mummy he had dealt with but he had been in no way put out when Mr Rankin told him that every year Dr Camps, whose opinion differed from his on several aspects of the case, saw about four cases a year. "Four mummies twenty years old?" exclaimed Dr Evans, incredulously. "I am only sorry he has not written up his experiences."

Mr Rankin justifiably made all the capital he could from the fact that the thyroid cartilage had been accidentally fractured by an ear, nose and throat specialist to whom it had been sent for an opinion on possible abnormalities – Dr Evans had made it clear that when he first saw the cartilage, it was not fractured – and also because the neck skin had been cut up into many pieces during Dr Evans's investigation. Why had this been done, asked Mr Rankin.

"I thought it was necessary so as to identify any haemorrhages under the skin. But I found none. Laboriously I went on," said Dr Evans.

"You went on cutting it up into small pieces?" asked Mr Rankin. "You were doing away with what is regarded as a very important piece from the neck. This very important exhibit, which contains what is said to be a tightly-tied knot, was sent by registered post to the forensic laboratory, and in the post things could happen?" "I agree," said Dr Evans.

Mr Rankin returned later to the question of the skin collar. "My experts find it difficult to understand why in this case the skin collar does not show a groove running right round the neck." said Mr Rankin. Retorted Dr Evans: "Your experts – and I am sorry this has to be – have not seen the skin collar as a whole, but only a portion of it."

There was whispering between counsel and the defence pathologists. "I am informed by them that they saw a major part of the collar," said Mr Rankin. "Do you agree?" "No."

"If it had been preserved, there would have been some degree of certainty?" Countered Dr Evans: "Your experts could have had a much better chance of seeing what I saw."

"They have seen enough to be exceedingly puzzled why it is that some of the skin shows no groove marks at all," said Mr Rankin. "Would you agree that it would be reasonable to conclude from that, that there was post-mortem change with swelling which caused the mark you saw on the neck at the post-mortem?"

Dr Evans would not agree. "I would rather expect Sir Sydney Smith and Dr Camps to see the difficulty of this particular case, with glycerine as an additive," he said. A few questions later, he did not conceal his exasperation. "I am trying to be completely scientific and I am not prepared to be dogmatic, as apparently some are," he said.

There was little wonder that after nearly twelve hours in the witness box, Dr Evans became annoyed at the tone of some of the questions, in spite of honeyed words about his fairness. "You do twist things, don't you," he exclaimed to Mr Rankin at one point. "It's very difficult for me to put anything across."

The ligature had been put round Mrs Knight's neck either by Mrs Knight herself or by someone else and the defence developed an ingenious theory that Mrs Knight was wearing the stocking as a cure for a cold. It was no more than an idea which, according to some observers, made the court murmur in surprise. No doubt. Perhaps the surprise was felt at the idea of the wife of a professional man believing in such an old-fashioned remedy, quite apart from the fact that there was no evidence whatever that Mrs Knight had had a cold.

Dr Evans had not excluded the possibility that Mrs Knight had died naturally for the simple reason that he had very little tissue to work on. He was asked whether she could have died from a heart attack, lung infection like lobar pneumonia, bladder, kidney, or other infection. The answer in each case was "yes" because Dr Evans had already said that he did not know the cause of death. Why then, he was asked, was it suggested that Mrs Knight was strangled with a stocking? He replied that there were six reasons – the neck groove, the depression on the neck, the depression on the thyroid cartilage, the ligature itself, the tightness of the ligature and finally, the evidence as a whole.

After much sound, fury and wind, Dr Evans had conceded little at the end of his cross-examination and the only important point for the Solicitor-General to re-emphasize was how the distortion of the thyroid cartilage had occurred. "Is there any question of it taking place as a result of dissection?" he asked.

"In my opinion, no, or I would readily say so," affirmed Dr Evans.

The case for the prosecution was concluded with the evidence given by Dr Alan Clift, the biologist who had gone to Rhyl on the night of the discovery of the mummy. The fragments of stocking round Mrs Knight's neck were not much to go on but he said they showed that originally the stocking had been stretched tightly round her neck. Not only had the stocking been stretched but the fragment was the typical shape of a ligature. He was emphatic that the stretching had not occurred by the natural process of the swelling of the neck. He was asked whether the stretching of the stocking was of a homicidal character and his reply was "yes", with the surprise proviso that he could not rule out suicide.

Mr Rankin challenged the evidence of Dr Clift as vigorously as he had done that of Dr Evans. The late Lord Birkett in the Rouse case had confounded an engineering expert because he did not know the co-efficient of the expansion of brass and Mr Rankin attempted a similar manœuvre. He drew from Dr Clift an admission that he did not know how to distinguish between American, Egyptian and Indian cotton. Nevertheless Dr Clift answered firmly "I do", when he was asked whether he considered himself an expert on fabrics. Dr Clift agreed that he could find no other evidence on the stocking breaking under tension except that of insect attack.

At this point, Mr Justice Davies interrupted counsel's cross-examination. "The allegation here is that this stocking was used by the prisoner to strangle this woman. The vital question is 'Has it been unduly stretched?' That is the first question to my mind that should have been asked."

Mr Rankin bowed to the judge and asked Dr Clift whether he would be interested to learn that the defence had been to the Manchester Chamber of Commerce Commercial Testing House and their conclusion was that the stocking had not been abnormally stretched. "I don't agree," said Dr Clift.

It was clear that not only did the crime doctors disagree about the conclusions to be drawn from the marks on the body but that the fabric experts on both sides would be diametrically opposed.

Mr Eric Jones, director of the Testing House, had carried out a number of tests at the request of Mrs Harvey's advisers on how much tension would have been required to strangle Mrs Knight with a stocking. His conclusion, stripped of its technical terms, was that there was no evidence that the stocking round the mummy's neck had been under any abnormal tension, although the experts would not go as far as to say that the stocking had never been under an abnormal stretching force.

Dr Clift, before his evidence was complete, had fainted in the witness box and while the court waited for him to recover counsel for both sides talked the case over informally outside. The weakness of the prosecution case had been exposed and the Solicitor-General took the decision not to pursue it further.

The Judge was informed in his private room and later, in open court, Sir Jocelyn said that after considering his duty, the state of the case and the evidence so far, it would not be right to invite the jury to find a verdict of guilty.

For once in the case, the experts – this time on law – agreed. "There seemed to be manifold circumstances of suspicion in the case," said Mr Justice Davies. "But when one considers the evidence of Dr Evans, which was given with conspicuous skill, fairness and moderation, it comes to this: he cannot say whether the ligature was put on before or after death and he cannot say that the ligature caused death. If it cannot be proved that the stocking stretched, then the prosecution fails. Without saying any more; because we have not heard the defence evidence, it does appear that the prosecution are in no position to prove that the stocking was stretched."

The money to defend Mrs Harvey had been raised privately and Mr Graham Roberts, the young defence solicitor – like Mr Rankin, engaged on his first murder case – said that the considerable sum of £3,000 had been spent. When the jury had found Mrs Harvey not guilty of murder, Mr Rankin applied for costs. "I appreciate that it could be said that this lady left herself open to this kind of charge," observed Mr Rankin. "But whatever lies she may have told, or cold, cool, calculating woman she may have been, in the end the prosecution case came down to two witnesses, Dr Evans and Dr Clift." The heavy costs incurred by the defence, he said, had been in respect of those witnesses.

The Solicitor-General rose to his feet to resist the application but the judge stopped him. "I don't think I need trouble you, Mr

Solicitor," he said. "No, Mr Rankin," he added, dismissing the application.

Two token charges of fraud concerning Mr Knight's maintenance payments remained to be dealt with and Mr Justice Davies rejected Mr Rankin's suggestion that Mrs Harvey should be allowed to go free after her years of terrible strain. The judge said the medical evidence before him showed that Mrs Harvey was a very sick woman. But taking into account the frightful anxiety she had undergone, the fact that she had been on trial for murder and had been imprisoned for four months awaiting trial, it was still impossible to overlook the case. The sentence was fifteen months' imprisonment.

Sniffing smelling salts, supported by a nurse and a wardress, the inconspicuous figure of Mrs Harvey passed from the dock, without having said a word about her long and extraordinary ordeal. Nor were the comments of Mr Knight, the loser almost by chance of more than £2,000, ever made available.

A RAY OF SUNLIGHT UNMASKS A KILLER

(William Henry Podmore, UK 1930)

Tom Tullett

When the great pathologist Sir Bernard Spilsbury examined the hammer used to murder Vivian Messiter, he found a single hair adhering to the hammer head. It matched the hair from Messiter's eyebrows, proving that the hammer had indeed dealt the fatal blow. But Messiter's killer, William Podmore, was brought to book not by a single hair but a single piece of flimsy paper. It was, as one criminologist observed, a case of small clues and large inferences, which is why it remains of exceptional interest to the student of modern crime detection. Indentations were found on a page of a receipt book, produced by the pressure of the pencil through another sheet on which some figures and initials had been written. The initials – W. F. T. – were those of Podmore's alias, William F. Thomas. Photographs were taken of these tell-tale indentations using a strong light thrown on them from an oblique angle. This cast a shadow across the indentations, enabling the eye to read them quite clearly. Because this scrap of paper linked Podmore with his victim, and was a vital part of the evidence against him, the case is notable as a triumph for forensic photography. Tom Tullett (1915–91) was chief of the Daily Mirror's crime bureau and the only journalist to have been a member of the Criminal Investigation Department at Scotland Yard. With Douglas G. Browne, Tullett wrote the standard biography of Spilsbury in the early 1950s.

By the end of the 1920s, murder investigations had gained some sense of order, and the countrywide search for the killer of a man who had been dead for more than two months when his body was found shows how the use of technical aids and methods of record-keeping were paying off.

At 6.45 on the evening of 10 January 1929 a telegram from Mr McCormac, Chief Constable of Southampton, was received at Scotland Yard. It read: "A case of murder has occurred here. A man has been found shot dead in a room the door of which was padlocked. The body was found today and has probably been in the room for some eight or nine weeks. Will you please send an officer down to investigate the matter."

Detective Chief Inspector John Prothero was tall and commanding and his colleagues called him "Gentleman John". He was always immaculately dressed, and spoke in an accent thought then to be the mark of a university education. He wore spats and had his shirt cuffs showing, at that time a rich man's luxury. But he was not rich, nor had he been to university. He was a great detective, who decided he wanted to be better dressed than the rest of his colleagues. He never raised his voice, never appeared to be angry, but his quiet insistence got the facts he required.

Prothero took with him to Southampton Sergeant Hugh Young, a Scot from the Black Isle in Ross and Cromarty. Like others before him he was a country boy who rose to command the Squad, and the experience he gained on this particular case was a great stepping-stone in his distinguished career.

The detectives went first to the Southampton mortuary to see the body of the victim, Vivian Messiter. The local police surgeon said that the murder had taken place some weeks before, and Messiter had last been seen alive on 30 October 1928. The body was in a bad state of decomposition and the rats had been busy, so that the features of the dead man were unrecognizable.

Vivian Messiter had been found in a lock-up garage-cum-storeroom at 42 Grove Street, Southampton, where he carried on business as a local agent of the Wolf's Head Oil Company, whose head offices were in London. He had not been seen alive since he left his lodgings at 3 Carlton Road on the morning of 30 October. He was a quiet man of regular habits, and when he failed to return home as usual his landlord, Mr Parrott, an ex-police-man, informed the police he was missing.

An officer went to the garage, but on finding the place securely padlocked from the outside, concluded that wherever Messiter was, he was not in the garage.

Mr Parrott wrote to Messiter's employers, reporting his lod-ger's absence. They asked him to visit the garage and, by break-ing a window and peering through the aperture with the help of a candle, he could see that Messiter's car was safe and that nothing appeared to be amiss. It was concluded that Messiter had simply walked out of his job and had, perhaps, returned to the United States, where he had spent many years of his life. The subsequent lack of interest in his whereabouts was one of the striking features of the case.

Messiter was a member of an old Somersetshire family, edu-cated at a minor public school. As a young man he had gone to the States with his brother Edgar and together they started a horse-breeding ranch in New Mexico. When Edgar drifted into mining operations in Colorado, Vivian went into business in Denver. Later he went to New York City, where the new subway railroad under the Hudson River was in course of construction. Such was his energy and ability to handle men that he rose from a sub-ordinate position to the office of Chief Engineering Constructor. He became so well-known in this capacity that engineers from England were invited to meet him.

At the outbreak of the First World War he was wealthy and generally prosperous. He came home and enlisted, was commis-sioned in the Northumberland Fusiliers and went to fight in France. He was shot through both thighs and he remained slightly lame for the rest of his life. In 1928 he was fifty-seven, a reserved, solitary man, divorced from his wife, and he returned to England that year from another long absence in the United States and Mexico. Yet he had relatives in this country, and he had a job, and the fact that he was lost to sight and knowledge for more than two months without any serious efforts being made to discover what had become of him throws a curious light on the casual attitude of his friends and family and of the firm which not only employed him, but had recently made him a director.

Messiter's job was that of local agent for the Wolf's Head Oil Company and the garage in Grove Street was his headquarters. It was not until 10 January that this firm sent a Mr Passmore to take over the agency. With a friend Passmore gained access to the outer yard of the garage via the roof of the Royal Exchange public house next door. The garage was a long, narrow building with white-washed walls. Along the right-hand side was a double row of oil drums upon which boxes were piled. More boxes were stacked at the end, and in a recess was the body of Messiter lying face upwards.

After moving the body to the mortuary local police searched the garage. On the back seat of Messiter's car they found a duplicate order book and a memorandum book, from both of which a number of pages had been torn out. On one page of the memorandum book was a receipt signed by a Mr H. H. Galton for 2s 6d commission on the sale of five gallons of oil, dated 30 October, the last day Messiter was seen alive. The next page had been torn out, but on the following page were the words: "Cromer & Bartlett, 25 Bold Street, 5 gallons heavy". In the duplicate order book there was no writing of any kind, but, tucked away at the end of it, were two sheets of carbon paper on which could be just seen some names and addresses. The first was "Cromer & Bartlett" of Bold Street, Southampton. Then there was a note, "Sold to Ben Baskerfield, Clayton Farm, Bentley Road, near Winchester" and a third entry, "Ben Jervis, Crescent Bassett, 5 gallons number 8 at 5s 6d".

When the Yard men went to the garage they were given these items by the local police and then began their own search for any clues which might help. But first, since nothing had been moved apart from the body, they decided to reconstruct the crime. The local detective inspector persuaded Mr Hall, the licensee of the pub next door, to play the part of the corpse and he was placed in the same position as the body was found. A trilby hat had been found near Messiter's head, and to give a touch of realism for photographic purposes, Sergeant Young placed his own hat beside the recumbent figure of Mr Hall. The detectives noted the position of several bloodstained boxes in relation to the body, some of which had been splashed to a height of several feet, an almost sure indication of blows by a heavy weapon used as a club.

John Prothero then ordered all the boxes to be moved. "Search every nook and cranny," he commanded.. During this search three clues were found which played a vital part in the investigation.

The first was a rolled-up ball of paper, stained and begrimed with oil and dirt, lying between two oil drums near the garage door. It was a receipt for rent dated 20 October and bore the name "Horne" of Cranbury Avenue. On the back of this scrap of paper were some faint words which obviously referred to an order for "35 or 36 gals, Tuesday" and there was a signature – "W.F. Thomas" – the small "O" being crossed out.

A second piece of paper was found behind another oil drum and on that was a written message. It read: "Mr W.F. Thomas. I shall be at 42 Grove Street at 10 a.m. but not at noon. V. Messiter."

The third clue found in the garage was a hammer, lying at the back of more oil drums against the side wall. Both the shaft and the head of the hammer were stained with blood, and stuck in the blood there was a single eyebrow hair. This last discovery changed the whole complex of the killing, for the hammer was without doubt the murder weapon. Vivian Messiter had not been shot, as had at first been suspected, but battered to death, and the small wound in the dead man's forehead had not been caused by a bullet but by a ferocious blow from the pointed side of the hammer head.

The pathologist Sir Bernard Spilsbury was called in, and while the Yard men waited for him to arrive, they began to make inquiries about the other things they had found.

The landlady at Cranbury Avenue, Mrs Horne, established that she had recently had a quiet, well-behaved couple staying there for about two weeks. Their names were Mr and Mrs Thomas and they had left on 3 November, leaving an address care of Allied Transport Co., 38 High Road, Chiswick.

The Chiswick police checked and found there was no firm of that name and, moreover, there was no house in the High Road bearing that number. Further checks relating to names and addresses on the other scraps of paper found in the garage revealed there was no Bold Street in Southampton, nor any firm bearing the name Cromer & Bartlett. There was no such place as Clayton Farm anywhere near Winchester, while Ben Jervis had never been heard of at Crescent Bassett.

It began to look as though Mr W.F. Thomas was at least a liar and it did prove he had some connection with the murdered man. The only thing so far proved genuine was the signature of H.H. Galton, and it looked as though it had been deliberately left in the memorandum book to make him a suspect, for Mr Galton was traced and proved to be a genuine customer.

Messiter's lodgings were in Carlton Road, and among the papers he had left behind was a letter bearing the address of Cranbury Avenue and signed "W.F. Thomas". The writer was applying for an agency with Messiter in reply to an advertisement which the latter had inserted in the *Southern Daily Echo*. This was another link between Thomas and Messiter, but where was Thomas?

Prothero issued a full description of Thomas to the press, mentioning a small scar on his face. Newspapers always like a dramatic headline and so the hunt for Thomas became "Hunt for Man with a Scar".

Five days after the discovery of the crime Bernard Spilsbury went to Southampton and examined the body of the victim. He described his findings: "At least three blows on the head, any one producing immediate unconsciousness. The head of a large hammer, used with great violence, would account for injuries. Those across base and on right side produced when the head was on a hard surface. Position of injuries at back suggest that deceased was bending forwards. Puncture wounds on top of head – striking edge of tin box in fall."

The Yard men went over the information they had and came to the conclusion that the man they wanted was cunning enough to be no stranger to crime, as evinced by his inventing bogus orders to get commission; his flight from one place to another; the tearing out of what were probably incriminating pages from the books found in the garage; and the adroit way he had tried to cover his tracks. Sergeant Young suggested to his chief that the man might have a record.

"Send for Battley," Prothero said. A call to the Yard brought

Detective Inspector Harry Battley, then head of the Fingerprint Bureau, to Southampton and with him he brought all the files in the name of Thomas. There were eighty-three dossiers.

Battley examined the hammer and the shaft and all the other finds but there were no useful fingerprints. All the files holding photographs of men called Thomas were shown to the landlady, Mrs Horne, and to various other people who might have recognized him. But not one person was able to pair up a photograph and the missing man.

The investigation seemed to be running down when luck took a hand. The Wiltshire police, who had seen the circulated description of W.F. Thomas, sent a message that they were looking for a man with the same name. This man had worked for a building contractor named Mitchell at Downtown, near Salisbury. Thomas had entered the employ of Mr Mitchell on 3 November 1928 (the day Thomas had left his Cranbury Avenue lodgings) and had disappeared with more than £130 of his employer's money on 21 December. He had given as his previous employers the Allied Transport Road Association, Bold Street, Southampton.

A landlady in Downton told the police that a Mr and Mrs Thomas had lodged with her and, in a vase in the room they had occupied, was found yet another scrap of paper. It was a docket from an order book, headed: "A & R S".

Underneath was an address – 85 London Road, Manchester.

The piece of paper left at Downton was one piece of paper too many – it began to provide leads.

A swift inquiry was made to the Manchester police. They did not know a W.F. Thomas, but they did know Auto & Radio Services at London Road. A detective said, "We are looking for a man named Podmore who used to work for them. We want him for conversion of money he received for a car. His picture was in the *Police Gazette*."

Criminal Records now came into their own. William Henry Podmore had a file, and there was no question that he and Thomas were the same person. A check on his history was revealing and began to fill in the gaps. He was well known to the Staffordshire police, having been first arrested by them when he was only eleven. He was married but parted from his wife and

had been living with a young woman in various parts of the
country.

At one time he had lived with his parents at Greenly Road,
Abbey Milton, Stoke-on-Trent. Near his home was Bold Street,
the street name which kept cropping up in the Messiter case. He
had known a Mr Baskeyfield whom he always called Baskerfield,
the name of the person mentioned as living at the Clayton Farm
address, while a Mr Albert Machen, who actually lived at Clayton
Farm, Newcastle, Staffordshire, used to deliver milk to the
Podmore family. He also knew a Mrs Lucy Jervis, although
not personally.

, Podmore had made the mistake common to petty criminals,
that of mixing up familiar names and places in the faint hope of
appearing to be honest. It is an error that has helped to trap many
people. It began to look very much as though Podmore, alias
Thomas, was the man who had murdered Vivian Messiter. But
proof was still lacking. Prothero decided to concentrate his search
for the woman companion who was called "Lil".

Inquiries at Podmore's home revealed that he had stayed there
over Christmas and had left early in the New Year to take a job as
a garage hand at the Stonebridge Hotel, Solihull, near Birmingham. He had arrived there on 5 January 1929 with his "wife",
Lil, who was to work as a cook. Six days later, when the evening
papers printed the reports of the Southampton garage murder,
Podmore handed in his notice, saying he wanted to leave at once.
Next day Podmore and Lil departed without even asking for their
wages. Podmore obviously thought that Lil, called "Golden-
haired Lil" in the Press, was an embarrassment, and that it was
no longer safe for them to be seen together. The first signs of
panic had set in, and he sent her back to her home at Stoke-on-
Trent. There she was interviewed by the local detective inspector, Mr Diggle, who had been making all the inquiries in
Staffordshire. She told him she thought it likely that Podmore
would have gone to the Leicester Hotel in Vauxhall Bridge Road,
near Victoria in London.

Two telephone calls, one to Southampton and one from there
to the Yard, had Detective Charles Simmons with a sergeant
casually leaning against the reception desk of the Leicester Hotel

asking quietly for "Mr Thomas" or "Mr Podmore". He was in his room and agreed to accompany the officers to Southampton. Under the circumstances refusal would have been difficult although, in truth, there was little evidence of murder against him at the time.

On 18 January, just eight days after the finding of Messiter's body, Podmore met for the first time the two men who had been hunting him, Detective Chief Inspector John Prothero and Detective Sergeant Hugh Young. Podmore was nonchalant, almost cocksure. Prothero was his usual calm, gentlemanly self, and Young sat at a table, pen in hand and a pad of statement forms in front of him, the classic reception for all suspects.

It was clear that Podmore had been through this routine before and was fairly confident. It was also clear that he was not going to give in without a struggle. He admitted he was in trouble in Manchester and in Downton and that he had worked for Messiter. He had seen the report of the finding of Messiter's body. He was completely frank about using the names of Thomas and Podmore. He said he went to see Messiter on the morning of 30 October and that also there was an agent named Maxton or Baxton, a subtle suggestion that this was the man who had killed Messiter. He had only seen him once but he did not need pressing to give a description. Details of the man's height, build, hair, complexion and clothing rolled off his tongue in almost indecent haste.

Podmore said he had left Messiter's employ for a better job with Mr Mitchell at Salisbury. He admitted taking Messiter's car to go for the interview at Downton on 30 October, the last day on which Messiter was seen alive, and said that he had returned at 4.30 p.m. that day, parked the car in the garage and gone to his lodgings.

In its way this was a helpful admission. Unless someone else could be found who had seen Messiter later, Podmore was the last person to have seen him alive.

There was one obvious motive for the murder in Podmore's case – the bogus orders in equally bogus names and addresses – an easy way to get commission on non-existent sales of oil. And if Messiter had found out and challenged Podmore, what then?

Podmore was held in custody. This caused no problems to the Yard men, since he was already wanted for other offences. Meanwhile luck again turned in favour of the detectives. They had circulated a description of the hammer to the newspapers and a Mr Marsh came forward to say the hammer was his. He had bought it in France and was able to recognize it because it had been "touched up and filed down" by him. He remembered that at some time around 29 October a man with a scar on his face, who looked like a mechanic, had come to the motor works in Southampton where Marsh worked and asked to borrow a hammer. It was never returned.

Podmore blandly denied he had ever borrowed a hammer.

The case looked like breaking. Podmore was put up for identification with several other men of similar age, build and appearance and Mr Marsh walked quietly along the line. It is one of the nightmare moments in the life of a suspect. The parade was held in the yard of Bathgate police station with a uniformed inspector in charge. The Yard men stood well away. It was explained to Podmore, before the men formed themselves into line, that he could stand anywhere he chose.

It is a time for the mind to race. Which is the best place? Which of these men looks most like me? Which is wearing similar clothes? For the policemen it is slow, inexorable and ordinary. To the suspect it is mounting panic. "Will the expression on my face reveal my guilty knowledge?"

Mr Marsh tried hard. Three times he walked up and down the line and, in the end, shook his head.

"The man is not there," he said.

The volunteers departed and a relieved Podmore went back to the cells. Soon afterwards he was arrested by the Manchester police for theft of a car and he was sentenced to six months' imprisonment. For a while he was away from the attention of the Yard men, but he was not far away and not for long. Two months later he was brought from prison to attend the resumed inquest on Messiter, which had been formally opened and adjourned. He sat between two prison officers but was able to smile and wave at "Golden-haired Lil" who was also in court.

Only one red herring was trailed across the path of justice, when a man serving a sentence in Winchester prison was called as a witness. He had previously made a statement that a woman he knew had returned home at 2.30 p.m. on 30 October in South-ampton with blood all over her face. But before the coroner he admitted his story was pure invention.

During the inquest the exercise book containing the receipt from Mr Galton for 2s 6d was produced and handed to the jury, as were the two sheets of carbon paper found in the duplicate order book. The jury returned an open verdict, Podmore went back to prison to serve the rest of his sentence, and the Yard men took away the exhibits to carry on the investigation. They went back to the Murder Room at Scotland Yard and analyzed every bit of information they had collected. Prothero, Young and Battley debated the case for hours. Then Prothero picked up the exercise book and sauntered across to the window overlooking the Thames. They had nothing in mind but it was as though they were willing this tatty, torn book to yield up its secret. They looked again at the pages they had scrutinized so many times before. Then, as Prothero held the book up in the light, a ray of sunlight, striking the paper slantwise, threw up in relief the shadowy outline of some writing. It was not the actual writing itself, only the faint impression left on the page underneath the one which had been torn out, and on which the message had been written.

When photographed the shadowy words read: "October 28, 1928. Received from Wolf Head Oil Company commission on Cromer and Bartlett, 5 gals 5/6 commission 2/6. W.F.T."

Comparison handwriting tests proved that this message had been written by Thomas, alias Podmore.

This now proved, beyond doubt, that Podmore had been swindling his employer, Mr Messiter. And it proved that the page from the exercise book had been torn out with Podmore's own hand. If he was the murderer he would have had good reason to destroy every bit of written evidence which connected him with Messiter. If, on the other hand, somebody other than Podmore was the murderer, what possible motive could he have had in tearing out the pages showing details of the transaction between himself and Messiter?

Still the authorities hesitated to bring a charge of murder and still Podmore remained in prison. When he finished the first sentence for the Manchester offence he received another six months for stealing money from Downton. This rather Micawberish attitude may have been influenced by the verdict of the coroner's jury. What would have happened had not Podmore been safely in custody is an interesting conjecture. But something more did turn up; two of Podmore's fellow-prisoners in Wandsworth reported statements made by him, and one of these amounted to a confession. The man's name was Cummings and he gave a statement to Prothero and Young. That was in October, and on 17 December 1929, the Yard men were waiting outside the gates of Wandsworth Prison.

In accordance with regulations, a prisoner must first be released and the new arrest made outside the prison gates. Podmore walked out with his usual jaunty air. Perhaps he felt confident he had covered all his tracks and that he had nothing to fear. Then a handcuff was locked round one of his wrists. The other handcuff was already round the wrist of Sergeant Young and Podmore was taken back to Southampton to be charged with murder.

He was tried at Winchester Assizes in March 1930, fifteen months after the crime, before the Lord Chief Justice, Lord Hewart. He was convicted, and his appeal against conviction was dismissed. An attempt to take the case to the House of Lords failed and Podmore was hanged on 22 April.

There was some agitation by well-meaning people to alter the course of the law because of the delay in bringing to trial and because two convicted criminals had been called to give evidence. They shared the common misunderstanding of the value of circumstantial evidence. In the volume on the case in the *Famous Trials* series the authors, one of them a lawyer, pointed out that the case against Podmore rested not only on what was found, but on what was not found.

Had the books been unmutilated, had the missing invoice and the missing receipt been there, they would have established a case of swindling against the prisoner, but it is more than doubtful whether any jury would have held that they established more – it is a very long step from false pretence to wilful murder. But they were not there, and there could have been but one hand that removed them – the hand of the man who had fabricated the orders and signed the receipt. And that removal must have taken place after Messiter's death, for before it would have been useless. That was the evidence that really convicted Podmore.

There can be no doubt that Messiter discovered the swindle and taxed Podmore with it, threatening to call the police. If it had been Podmore's first offence he would have had no cause for undue concern. But he was already wanted by the police in Manchester. Podmore, who had never before used violence, lost his temper. The hammer was there, maybe in Podmore's pocket, certainly to hand, and Messiter was struck down. The worst feature of the attack was that while the unconscious man lay on the concrete floor his assailant rained more blows on him. That callous behaviour must have told on the jury, and so must his actions immediately afterwards. For Podmore admitted that he had locked the garage and taken Messiter's car to give his lady friend, "Golden-haired Lil", a drive and "some fresh air".

THE POISONER

(Kenneth Barlow, UK 1957)

Percy Hoskins

The first murder case in Britain in which the weapon was said to be insulin, the drug used to treat diabetes. Kenneth Barlow was a male nurse who claimed that insulin was the key to the perfect murder, since once it dissolved in the bloodstream it was untraceable. When his wife Elizabeth was found dead in her bath, a doctor noticed puncture marks on her skin. Samples from her body, tested on mice, led to the detection of insulin. In a groundbreaking experiment, a team of forensic scientists discovered that lactic acid which had formed in Mrs Barlow's muscles after death had prevented the breakdown of insulin. Barlow broke down while being interviewed by detectives. While he denied injecting his wife with insulin, he claimed he'd actually injected her with ergometrine in an effort to induce an abortion. In fact no abortifacient drugs were found in Mrs Barlow's body. Doctors, scientists and biochemists all gave conflicting evidence at Barlow's trial. The defence theory was that Mrs Barlow had fainted in the bath, causing a massive and fatal dose of insulin to be released into the bloodstream. But the jury was not persuaded, and Barlow was convicted and sentenced to life imprisonment. The legendary crime reporter Percy Hoskins (1904–89) joined the Daily Express *in 1928. He is best remembered for his work on the 1956 case of John Bodkin Adams, the Eastbourne doctor accused of killing rich, elderly patients in order to collect from their wills. Hoskins was the only Fleet Street journalist convinced of Adams' innocence, and reported accordingly to the* Express. *He also assisted in the doctor's defence. Adams was acquitted in 1957, the year in which the Barlow case occurred.*

Poison lends itself most conveniently to the dream of perfect murder. Use a gun, and the commotion will bring every copper for miles around, and the tell-tale mark of the firing pin is as damning as any fingerprint.

Strangle, and the pathologist will find you out, even if you fake murder to look like suicide by hanging *and* bury the body afterwards.

Chop the victim into pieces, dismember, drop the segments in tightly wrapped parcels into the sea and still the Murder Squad will triumph: witness the human wild animal called Hume caged in his Swiss prison.

Do what you will to escape detection: burn the body; suffocate; rain blows on the skull from behind; electrocute; knife; destroy the whole human frame, bones and all, in a tank full of acid; hide the corpse so well no man will ever set eyes on it again; push it through a ship's porthole and feed it to the sharks (as James Camb did to "Gay" Gibson) and even then stand trial for murder.

But poison: there you have a chance to get off scot-free. It is so easy to administer. The victim is hungry or thirsty and, in any case, unsuspecting.

And, if you do your homework sufficiently well, you may hit upon a poison that leaves no trace at all. I know of one, not too difficult to obtain, where the apparent effect is one of heart failure . . . with no trace of poison left in the system. That is the great attraction of poison to the murderer: the protection afforded by its worm-like stealth.

There are others. It is a weapon well suited to the weak, hence its popularity with women. And it is a joy to possess and use if you hate someone enough: of all methods of murder, here is the most painful, sly, and cruel. Poisons like arsenic, the commonest and easiest to obtain, guarantee a monstrously agonizing end.

For all these reasons, poison has been a popular method of

killing since the time of the Borgias. What is rare is to find
motiveless poisoning. It seems inconceivable that any man should
plan murder this way merely to see if it can pass undetected – or
does it?

Of all the cases that have come my way in this specialized field
of poison, the Barlow case rates a mention on two counts. He
committed the first known case of murder through injection of
insulin – his wife was a non-diabetic, so it led to her collapse and
drowning in the bath – and he did it for no reason anyone can
discover. The only conclusion I can draw from the known facts is
that he believed he could get away with murder by insulin and
experimented accordingly.

Kenneth Barlow, aged thirty-eight, lived with his wife Elizabeth in a terraced two-up and two-down in Thornbury Crescent,
Bradford, in Yorkshire. He was a male nurse and worked in St
Luke's Hospital in the West Riding town of Huddersfield. She
had a local job, in a laundry. They had been married less than a
year. They seemed to be ideally happy. The neighbours found
them a happy and apparently easy-going pair.

On the night of 3 May, 1957, between 11 p.m. and midnight,
Kenneth Barlow hammered on his neighbour's door and shouted
to them to call the doctor – *quickly*. He said his wife had passed
out in the bath, and he had found her with her head under water;
he had tried artificial respiration without success. Then he ran
back indoors, to continue artificial respiration, until the doctor
arrived.

Barlow had his story off pat when first the doctor and then an
observant Detective Sergeant called Naylor from Bradford CID
called round. His wife was tired that night, said Barlow, and had
gone to bed early. He put the child (from his previous marriage)
to bed himself, went round and locked up in the normal way, and
went upstairs some time later.

About 10 p.m. Mrs Barlow, who had complained of the heat,
said she now felt better and was going to take a bath. Right, said
Kenneth Barlow, and promptly dozed off: came to about 11 p.m.,
found his wife had not come back to bed, then noticed the light
still on in the bathroom. He went in to find her unconscious, with
her head well under water. He pulled the plug out at once and

began to administer first aid. Now he stood in the hallway, cool and composed although naturally sad, to greet doctor and detective as they arrived.

Both of them noticed how the pupils of her eyes were dilated, as though she were under the influence of some drug. Sergeant Naylor also spotted one curious thing: Barlow's pyjamas were bone dry, although – on his own admission – he was wearing them when he tried to revive poor Elizabeth Barlow. The alarm bells that ring to warn every good policeman things are not as straightforward as they seem sounded that night in the house in Thornbury Crescent, and Naylor called his superiors right away.

The Chief Constable of Bradford, Mr H. S. Price, went to the house. He looked at the body. He too was baffled by those dry pyjamas and another factor: lack of water on the walls and floor. Curious, when the bath was full enough to drown Mrs Barlow, that the attempts to lift her out and give artificial respiration had not even left one puddle on the bathroom floor.

He called in Dr David Price, the West Riding pathologist and the senior inspector from the Harrogate laboratories. Dilation of the pupils seemed a sure indication that Mrs Barlow was drugged when she died. The police found syringes in the house, but Barlow was a male nurse and his story that he had used one to give himself penicillin for a carbuncle on the neck seemed reasonable.

The body was taken to the mortuary for post mortem and extensive tests for poisons and drugs. More scientists were called in next day but immediate tests again showed nothing traceable in the system. What Dr Price did find, however, were four tiny red dots in the buttocks similar to marks left by hypodermic injection. He cut away the flesh around and below both sets of punctures and ascertained that they had been made shortly before her collapse and death in the bath.

More specialists were called in for consultation: Professor C. S. Russell, a gynaecologist from Sheffield (Mrs Barlow was found to be in the early stages of pregnancy); Professor Thompson, from Guy's Hospital in London; and a senior chemist from Boots' factory at Nottingham. They had to weigh the symptoms shown by Mrs Barlow before death – including her collapse before sliding under the level of the bathwater.

Insulin, of course, is not a poison in the sense that arsenic is. It is extensively used in the treatment of diabetics to reduce the sugar content of the blood. If it is injected into a non-diabetic, that person goes into a state of shock and collapse. So, if the bath should be full enough, such a fainting fit could well prove fatal.

Insulin? There was no known case of injection by insulin in the course of murder. Here was a completely virgin field of research for the combined Murder Squad – police backed by the scientists. While Dr Price and his colleagues concentrated on laboratory experiments, the police stepped up their inquiries into Barlow's background.

In the laboratory, samples taken from the flesh cut away from Mrs Barlow's body were injected into mice. Other mice were injected with insulin. The results were identical. The creatures went into a state of collapse and died. Guinea pigs were used in the same way with the same result. The human tissues were then injected with anti-insulin compounds and used again on the mice and guinea pigs, but this time, with the insulin destroyed deliberately, there were no ill effects. So it *was* insulin that was used to murder Mrs Barlow.

In the CID headquarters at Bradford every precaution was taken not to forewarn Barlow of their line of inquiry. Discreet checks were made at the hospital where he worked to see what medicines and drugs he had access to, and how much – if any – was unaccounted for. There was professional evidence aplenty that he often gave injections of insulin to patients.

Barlow was charged with the murder of his wife. All through the period of arrest and trial he protested his innocence.

Sir Harry Hylton-Foster, then Solicitor-General, led the prosecution. It is not the easiest of cases to take through the court, in spite of the magnificent backroom work by Dr Price and his associates.

Here you had a man and wife, known to be happy together, married less than a year. No shred of evidence as to any quarrel or bad feeling between them, no sudden blazing row that could have ended in a resolve to murder. What could the motive have been? There was no suggestion of gain. There was no hint of jealousy, no rumour of another man or woman in the marital background.

Barlow's story of how those two syringes came to be found in his house was still convincing enough. Traces of penicillin *had* been found on the one he said he used for the boil on his neck, and he said both he and his wife had used the other. She had given her father injections of morphia, he said, to ease the pain of cancer; and he had used it on her for injections of a drug called ergometrine, to end her pregnancy – at her own request.

He also said she had had fainting fits before: once in the bath, and he described how he had rescued her just in time on that occasion.

Sir Harry called on three witnesses who had heard Barlow refer to insulin in the past as one means to the "perfect murder". There was male nurse Harry Stork, who had worked with Barlow in a sanatorium in the middle fifties. He recalled Barlow saying it would be difficult to detect afterwards as it dissolved in the bloodstream.

A former patient at the same sanatorium remembered a conversation with Barlow who said of insulin: "Get a load of this, and it's the quickest way out." Then there was a woman nurse who had tended diabetics with Barlow, and remembered him saying: "You could kill somebody with insulin as it can't be found very easily – unless you use a very large dose."

There was, however, a significant weakness implicit in this line of prosecution argument. Barlow had been married to Elizabeth less than one year. Was the jury to believe he was already contemplating the murder of a wife he had yet to meet?

The defence, led by Mr Bernard Gillies QC, called as their expert witness Dr Hobson, from St Luke's Hospital in London. He told the court that in moments of stress (like anger, for instance, *or fear*) the human body automatically releases and pumps adrenalin into the bloodstream. This in turn raises the sugar level – which could produce an increase of insulin as a natural reaction.

"If [Mrs Barlow] knew she was slipping down and drowning in the bath," he said, "and that she could not get out, she would be terrified and I think that would produce all the symptoms the chemists have described."

Against this was the amount of insulin found below those hypodermic syringe marks in the woman's body. Insulin produced naturally in the way Dr Hobson described would be evenly distributed over the body – and it would need a fantastic amount to reach the overall level found round those puncture marks.

The judge told the jury: "If you are satisfied he injected insulin into his wife and knowingly injected it, you will probably find no difficulty in reaching the decision that he did so with intent to kill."

Mr Justice Diplock told them to make up their minds, saying "This is murder or nothing". The jury found for murder. Barlow was sentenced to life imprisonment, and a new page had been written in British criminal history.

Apart from my constant checks through Scotland Yard, I took no part in the police investigation before Barlow was finally charged. This was a matter for my associates in the northern offices of the *Daily Express*. What fascinated me, and took me to the trial, was the knowledge that this was to be the first trial for murder by insulin injection in any murder investigation.

I have discussed the case many times since with many an expert and always our talks have ended with the one question: why did he do it?

Barlow's first wife had died in 1956 at the early age of thirty-three. Even after the inquest, doubt existed over the precise cause of her death, although it was found to be from natural causes. If his protestations of innocence at the time of his trial for the murder of Elizabeth, his second wife, were genuine, then here was someone who had been dealt a doubly cruel blow by Fate.

But if the verdict was just – that he committed "a cold, cruel and carefully premeditated murder" as the judge said – even though he was happily married, we are left with only one possible conclusion. Here was a man who really believed he had found the way to commit the "perfect murder" and so carried it out as a cold-blooded and clinical experiment. On his new wife, who unfortunately happened to be the most convenient human guinea pig.

If his method of murder was unique, it shows Barlow held at least one trait in common with all poisoners: a callous disregard for suffering. He would have done well in any Nazi wartime concentration camp.

THE JEKYLL AND HYDE OF NEW YORK

(Dr Arthur Waite, USA 1916)

John Laurence

Even on trial for his life, accused of double murder, Dr Arthur Warren Waite laughed at the law. It was, he agreed, all true. He had indeed murdered his mother-in-law by mixing germs in her food. He had also killed his wealthy father-in-law, but when the germs failed, and arsenic too, Waite had used chloroform, suffocating the old man with a pillow to finish him off. Why? "For the money" said Waite. His trial was the New York sensation of its day. The debonair young dentist cheerfully explained how he had poisoned his mother-in-law mixing pneumonia, diphtheria and influenza germs into her meals. Waite's father-in-law had been a hardier soul, resisting tuberculosis bacteria sprayed up his nose, chlorine gas, and various attempts to give him pneumonia, including dampening his sheets. Science caught up with Dr Waite when arsenic he'd poured into the old man's soup was detected at the autopsy.

Doctor Arthur Warren Waite, dentist and crack tennis player, to all outward seeming was a child of fortune. He had everything the normal man wants and envies in others, good looks, charm of manner, athletic abilities, a charming wife, and a millionaire father-in-law.

Let us particularize. In appearance Doctor Waite was the

typical athletic American, clean-shaven, clear-eyed, regular-featured and frankly healthy. He was popular with men and women alike, and all with whom he came in contact trusted him. He was always perfectly groomed and had that *savoir faire* which comes from wide travel. A witty conversationalist, he could talk entertainingly on most subjects, and he was much in demand by the hostesses of New York.

His father-in-law was John E. Peck, a retired millionaire druggist of Grand Rapids, Michigan, of which town Waite himself was a native. Waite's parents were not well-to-do, but their son showed such brilliance and promise that he was encouraged in every possible way to obtain the best education which they could afford. He went to the University of Michigan and there took a dental course.

From there the brilliant student went to London and afterwards to South Africa, where he did a certain amount of practice in the profession for which he had been trained. Shortly after the outbreak of the Great War he returned to the United States and to his native town. There he met Miss Clara Peck. In spite of the wide gulf between their financial positions, a gulf which might almost have made people suspect he was a fortune hunter, no suggestion of the kind was made when it became known that the two were engaged. Everyone who met the good-looking dentist predicted such a successful career for him that he would never be in any financial difficulties.

Clara Peck and Arthur Warren Waite were married at Grand Rapids in September, 1915. To the surprise of many, however, he did not begin practising there, but moved at once to New York on the plea that the opportunities for advancement were much greater in that town, and his newly-married wife would have greater chances of amusement.

Waite was in no hurry to begin practising. He had always shown a great interest in medicine, and within a few days of arriving in New York he had got in touch with a number of doctors whom he deluded into believing he was a fully-qualified man himself, wealthy, and interested in scientific research, especially the study of bacteriology.

A certain amount of verisimilitude was given to Waite's story by the fact that he had a flat in the exclusive Riverside Drive Apartments, a flat which was richly furnished. The doctor was also well-known as a very good amateur tennis player who had only recently taken part in a number of tournaments at Palm Beach, Florida. He had, too, a considerable amount of medical knowledge, partly acquired through his study of dentistry, and partly learnt through an instinctive desire to acquire knowledge which might prove of use to him in later years.

Through various influences Waite got in touch with Dr Percival L. de Nyce, who was in charge of the bacteriological laboratory of the Flower Hospital, one of the best known institutions in New York. Dr Nyce was impressed with his new pupil, and the extraordinarily keen interest he took in all germ cultures. But it was only in the most virulent and deadly germs that his pupil was really interested, and he actually complained to Dr Nyce that the germs he was studying were not virulent enough for the experiments he had in mind!

Clara Waite firmly believed her husband was in practice as a doctor, and once or twice, in order to foster that belief and account for the necessary income to keep up their expensive style of living, he took her to the Flower Hospital and asked her to stay in the waiting room for a while. After keeping her there kicking her heels for half an hour or so, and reflecting on what he might be doing, he would return and announce that he had just finished an important operation. The deluded Clara, who understood not a single detail of the medical account her husband gave her, was full of pride that his abilities were being recognized in such an important institution.

It may well be asked at this stage, where was the comparatively poor student of a year or two ago getting the large sums of money which were necessary not only for his living expenses but for those in connection with the bacteriological experiments he was carrying out?

Waite had ingratiated himself so well with the Peck family that, with one exception, they were intensely proud of the brilliant addition to it. His wife's father helped financially so that his son-in-law should not be handicapped in any of his research work which he represented was necessary to advance in his profession.

He not only gave his daughter a very handsome dowry, out of which the Riverside apartments were so luxuriously furnished, but he allowed her £60 a month.

It must be admitted that Waite had an exceedingly great attraction for women, especially for women older than himself. Mrs Peck adored him. Nothing he could do was wrong, and her sister-in-law, Miss Catherine Peck, who had given her niece a cheque for nearly a thousand pounds as a wedding present, had even a higher opinion of him. So much did she value his advice, indeed, that she was easily persuaded to let him have £10,000 of her money to invest. It was on this money that Waite lived. Aunt Catherine was unwise enough to let it be known that on her death Waite would receive a very substantial legacy. It was also common knowledge in the family that Mr Peck's will left half his fortune to his daughter Clara. If Mr and Mrs Peck died, and Aunt Catherine died, and perhaps later on Clara Waite, Arthur Warren Waite would be a very rich and eligible widower!

A few weeks after their arrival in New York the devoted young husband – and there was not the slightest doubt that to all outward appearances he was infatuated with his young wife – suggested that her mother and father should be asked to stay with them for a while. Both parents were delighted to accept their son-in-law's invitation, but neither stayed very long on this first visit, for the air of New York did not seem to agree with Mr Peck. He felt run down almost as soon as he arrived. His son-in-law diagnosed a coming cold and sprayed his throat every evening. But that did not ward off the feeling of lassitude, any more than did the medicine which Waite had made up, and Mr Peck returned to Grand Rapids to be thoroughly overhauled there by his own doctors. They confessed themselves completely puzzled. However the air of Grand Rapids certainly suited old Mr Peck better than did that of New York and he was soon feeling as fit as ever.

Mrs Peck had found the visit to her beloved daughter and son-in-law all too short and as soon as she was satisfied that her husband was on the road to recovery and not likely to have a relapse, she paid them another visit – her last. Shortly after her arrival, she, too, began to feel ill, and a Doctor Porter was called in. He diagnosed that there was nothing very much the matter, though Dr Waite strongly disagreed, and asserted that he was sure his mother-in-law was seriously ill.

One night when Dr Waite was out ostensibly visiting his patients, a very remarkable incident occurred, though no one thought much about it at the time. Mrs Waite, who had gone to bed, detected a strong smell of gas and traced it as coming from her mother's room. When she entered it she found that the tap of the gas stove had been left on and if it had not been for the fact one of the windows was partly open there is no doubt her mother would have been asphyxiated.

From that day, however, Mrs Peck grew steadily worse, and on January 30th, 1916, she died. Doctor Porter, who had suspected nothing wrong, readily gave his certificate. Dr Waite, who seemed utterly grief-stricken by his mother-in-law's sudden death, accompanied her body to Grand Rapids, where he told various members of the family that her last dying wish was that she should be cremated. The ashes were buried in the family vault. The act of cremation had effectively destroyed all danger of anyone finding out the real cause of the old lady's death.

Mr Peck was overwhelmed by the loss of his wife and in February he accepted a second invitation to come to New York to visit his daughter. Both he and Clara had been very fond of Mrs Peck and both were eager to be together in their common sorrow. Old Mr Peck, too, liked his son-in-law, for the latter had been more sympathetic than even a devoted son-in-law might be expected to be. Waite was so charming, so anxious to make his father-in-law forget, so full of warmth on the old man's arrival, that for a few days Mr Peck really was cheered up and felt far less lonely than he had been feeling since his wife's death. There was a very strong bond of affection between his daughter and himself, for in her he saw again the mother as she was in the days when he first courted her and began his successful struggle for fortune.

During those early days of Mr Peck's second visit to the Riverside Apartment there occurred an incident which has a considerable bearing on the rest of the story. Dr Waite, as far as his devoted wife Clara knew, and her father knew, was an exceedingly busy man. He had to be out many evenings visiting his patients, and sometimes he was so hard-pressed that he did not return until the early hours of the morning. Actually Waite was very fond of wine, women and song. He had early discovered that he exercised a peculiar influence over women, and his life in New York was a continual round of gaiety. Although the delightful doctor distributed his favours on a fairly lavish scale, entertaining at the most expensive restaurants and dance cafés those whom he favoured, there was one lady in particular who proved more attractive than the rest, a Mrs Horton.

Margaret Horton, a beautiful young grass widow, had met Waite first at the Berlitz School of Languages. She was ambitious to become an opera singer. In a few days Waite had installed her in a suite of rooms at the Hotel Plaza. He himself was very fond of music and the two proved very congenial company for one another.

"Dr Waite had an extraordinary kind heart," she said some months after their first meeting. "He loved all the fine sentiments and the beautiful things of life. He used to say to me, 'Margaret, when you sing you make me weep, because you make me think of beautiful things'. He loved music. It was that love of music which drew us together."

It was while dining with Margaret Horton that Waite was seen by a Doctor Cornell, a relative of the Peck family, and a Miss Hardwicke. When Waite saw Cornell he made an excuse to his companion and walked across to the other table. He explained glibly that he had just completed an important operation.

"I have brought my own special nurse with me for dinner as I felt that she deserved something out of the ordinary for her skill and devotion to my work," he explained.

He told his story with easy confidence and all those at the table, with the exception of Miss Hardwicke, were inclined to believe it. But she had been watching Waite and Margaret Horton, and she was secretly convinced that there was a deeper relationship between the two than that of doctor and nurse. But she made no outward comment, though the time was soon to come when she was to crystallize her suspicions into such drastic action that Waite's name, in consequence, was to fill the front pages of the American newspapers for many a long day.

A few days after the incident in the restaurant Mr Peck was taken seriously ill and a Dr Moore was called in. He diagnosed digestive trouble and prescribed accordingly. Mr Peck's son-in-law was most attentive. The sick man did not like his medicine and Dr Waite soon found a way out of the difficulty. One evening Waite came into the kitchen and without any disguise poured some medicine into his father-in-law's soup. Later in the evening he came into the kitchen again when tea was being prepared for Mr Peck and poured some further medicine into the teapot.

"Dora," he explained to the servant, "father didn't like his soup, so I must put some more medicine in his tea."

Although Dr Moore had not considered the condition of his patient to be very serious, Dr Waite, as in the case of Mrs Peck, disagreed with him.

"He hasn't a very strong constitution," he declared, "and I should not be surprised if he did not live for long."

As with Mrs Peck, Waite's prophecy preved more accurate than had that of other doctors. On March 12th, but six weeks after his wife's death, Mr Peck died, and Clara Waite had lost both her parents. And as with the case of Mrs Peck, Waite declared that his father-in-law's last wish was that he should be cremated and his ashes placed beside those of his wife. Accordingly, the body, accompanied by the grief-stricken Clara and her sorrowing husband, was taken to Grand Rapids for that purpose. Before that journey, however, the body had been embalmed, a fact which should be borne in mind.

To Dr Waite's astonishment he found when he got to Grand Rapids that the family were not in favour of the old man being cremated. He was careful enough, however, not to raise any great objections, and after duly seeing his father-in-law buried he hurried back to New York – and Mrs Horton. Of late he had been spending money freely, too freely, but now, under his father-in-law's will, through Clara, he would have no cause to worry about money for some time. When he had, there was always Miss Catherine Peck, who had promised him a substantial legacy on her death.

There was one member of the Peck family who had never been very friendly with Dr Waite, who had always disliked him in fact, despite his great charm. That was Percival Peck, Clara's only brother. It was Percival Peck who had raised the greatest objections to his father being cremated. Just before the arrival of the body at Grand Rapids he had received a mysterious telegram from New York which read as follows: "Suspicions aroused. Demand autopsy. Keep telegram secret. – K. Adams."

The name of Adams was quite unknown to Percival Peck, but that fact did not influence him in the least. It transpired afterwards that K. Adams was the Miss Hardwicke who had seen Dr Waite and Mrs Horton dining together, and who had disbelieved the story the former told that the lady was his nurse. But the telegram, from whatever source it came, provided young Peck with an opportunity which he eagerly seized. He had a secret examination made of his father's body and at the same time employed private detectives to keep an eye on his brother-in-law and keep a record of his movements.

Clara, who had become seriously ill following upon the double shock of her mother's and father's deaths, had stayed behind at Grand Rapids, while her husband had hurried back to the gaieties of New York.

And then Waite received his first shock. He had left Grand Rapids fully satisfied that he had bluffed everyone, that he could now spend money just as freely as he wished, enjoy himself to the top of his bent. But a few days after his return Mr Peck's son-in-law received a shock. The undertaker who had arranged for the embalming of Mr Peck called upon him and asked that his bill should be paid.

"What's the hurry?" asked Waite. "You know the money is safe enough, don't you?"

He was surprised at the sudden demand for the bill, but he was more than surprised by the undertaker's reply. It worried him. It was the tiny black cloud on the edge of the horizon.

"It's really Mr Kane, sir, the embalmer," explained the undertaker. "He thinks he might not get his money."

"Why?" demanded Waite, struck by the uneasy look in the other's face.

"Well, there's some idea that arsenic had been used," explained the undertaker.

Waite was well aware that it was against the law for arsenic to be used in any embalming fluid, as he was also aware that arsenic would be found in Mr Peck's body if it were examined.

"I think I'd better see Mr Kane," he said evenly.

When the doctor saw Kane he did not beat about the bush.

"How much is it worth to you to say that you used arsenic?" he asked.

The embalmer named a sum, and after some haggling Waite agreed to pay him $9,000. But Kane's nerve broke at the last minute and he told a remarkable story to the police when questioned.

"Waite told me he was in a hole and asked me to put arsenic in the sample of embalming fluid I was to give the District Attorney. He said he would make me independent for life if I did what I was asked."

Waite by now suspected that his movements were being watched and he arranged for Kane to meet him casually in a cigar store.

"I met him there by a telephone booth," Kane related. "And he gave me a big roll of bills. I was so scared that I could hardly tell where I was. I stood there with the money in my hand.

"'For God's sake get that stuff out of sight,' Dr Waite said, 'and get the sample down to the District Attorney's office.'

"I went right home; I was so nervous that I couldn't count the money. I tried afterwards and couldn't do it. I put it in a bureau drawer. I was so nervous about the money that my wife noticed it. She got to worrying me and at last made me go to a doctor to find out if I was sick. I knew all right, but I didn't tell her. I shook like a leaf every now and then when I got to thinking about the money in the bureau drawer. Then I took it down to Greenport and buried it. I didn't put anything into the sample of my embalming fluid. I made up the sample just as I always make the fluid."

Kane's own record wasn't of the best. He had been suspected on more than one occasion of helping clients "who were in a hole" out of it on the payment of a reasonably large sum. But for the fact that Percival Peck had brought pressure to bear with the authorities and had had his own private detectives following his brother-in-law, the interview between Kane and Waite and the handing over of a large sum of money in the cigar store might not have been known until too late. But within a very short time of the meeting, it had been reported to the police, and Kane was asked for the sample of his fluid. Rumours were flying about, and it was these rumours coming to his ears which made him break down. He had embalmed the body of Mr Peck before it had been conveyed to Grand Rapids and he was now beginning to realize that there was trouble ahead. And this wouldn't be the first time he had been in trouble.

The District Attorney's suspicions had been aroused on receiving a report from Professor Vaughan, of the University of Michigan, who had made an examination of Mr Peck's body. He had sent in a report to the effect that the millionaire had died from arsemic poisoning. There was just a possibility that the arsenic had been in the embalming fluid, but when he heard Kane's story he immediately issued a warrant for the arrest of Waite.

The iron nerve of the suspected man was breaking fast under the strain of waiting, and it broke a few hours before the detectives called at his Riverside Apartments with the warrant for his arrest. He was found unconscious in the room adjoining that in which Mr and Mrs Peck had died.

But Waite was not to evade the law so easily. He was rushed to the hospital and strong emetics administered. In the hands of skilful physicians he made a rapid recovery. While he was getting over the effect of the drugs he had taken, however, he was thinking out what story to tell. He was now fully aware of the likely evidence against him and only a miracle could save him. He decided to play the part of Dr Jekyll and Mr Hyde.

When questioned by the District Attorney in hospital Waite at once admitted that he had given his father-in-law arsenic.

"Have you any accomplices?"

"Only this other fellow," replied the accused man with claborate carelessness.

"What other fellow?"

"The man from Egypt. He's always been inside me ever since I can remember. He has made me do things against my will. He made me take up the study of germs, as if I used them I wouldn't be detected. I was compelled against my will to put them in my father-in-law's food. Try as I would I could not get rid of my murderous other self. Often I have gone for long walks and fought against the evil one, and tried to run away from him. But he was so fleet of foot that he always caught me up."

So earnestly did Waite tell his story that it was partly believed.

"Did this Egyptian make you kill Mr Peck?" he was asked.

"When my father-in-law came to stay with us I wanted to help him all I could. Then the man from Egypt said Mr Peck was too old to live, that he ought to die, and if he did die I wouldn't have to worry about money. He brushed aside all my arguments. When Mr. Peck had first visited us the Egyptian made me spray his throat with germs, but though they made him ill they did not kill him. I was ordered this time to use arsenic as it was quicker. I was told to put it in his soup and tea and egg nog. I did my best, but the Egyptian was in control. Try as I could I found it impossible to get rid of him. But now that he has forced me to do these things he has left me, and for the first time I felt that my soul is free. He seemed to leave me last night and he hasn't returned again to-day to torture me with his evil suggestions."

The story told by Waite had exactly the effect he foresaw. It was so wild that it seemed as though only a madman could tell it. Some of the leading alienists in America were called in by the prosecution as well as by the defence.

Dr Jeliffe, the leading alienist for the prosecution, said at the trial, "In my opinion the prisoner was sane and knew the nature and quality of his act. He was fully aware of all the phases of his crime. In my opinion he is an average man, somewhat superficial, inclined to be snobbish and of no great intellectual attainments."

With that a number of other leading doctors agreed and ultimately their opinion prevailed.

While he was waiting his trial an amazing story came to light. Some of this has already been told. A search of Waite's flat resulted in the discovery of a number of books on poisons and a hundred and eighty slides containing germs of tetanus (lockjaw), typhoid, diphtheria, cholera and other deadly diseases with which he had been experimenting. He had spent large sums on women and amusement and had given Mrs Horton jewellery which had been entrusted to him by Miss Catherine Peck. Practically all the money the latter had given him to invest had gone in riotous living. Only the death of his father-in-law, indeed, could save him from exposure and ruin. So cunningly had he disguised his various amours that until he was arrested his wife had no knowledge of them.

"I was so shocked and amazed that I could not believe them true," she declared after her husband's arrest. "It seems impossible that a man who has been so uniformly gentle and kind to me and apparently so loyal could be guilty of the crime with which he is charged."

Dozens of people who knew Waite well were as puzzled. Many believed that he really was a Jekyll and Hyde, that he had been obsessed by the man from Egypt, as he asserted. Others asserted that the story was told deliberately in an attempt to evade the law. There was one man who never believed for one single moment that the doctor was insane. That was Percival Peck, the man who had received the mysterious telegram and acted on it so promptly, the man who at once employed private detectives to follow his brother-in-law's movements, who never ceased his efforts to unearth everything he could to prove Waite's guilt.

"I know that Arthur is guilty," he declared shortly after Waite's arrest. "The electric chair will be too good for him. Even if he were tortured his death would never bring back my beloved parents or pay for his horrible deeds. I will do all in my power to see that he is found guilty and executed.

"He is surely entitled to no consideration whatever. I am convinced that Dr Waite married my sister Clara with but one idea, and that was to get her money. Even before her mother died he predicted an untimely death for us all. We believed him to be a surgeon, and when mother died we suspected nothing. Even when the news of father's death came we did not suspect until I got that telegram. I am sure if it had not been for that my sister and my aunt would have died next."

Percival Peck was adamant to the last. He approached the prosecution shortly before the trial and said:

"I have only one favour to ask, and that is that I have a seat through every minute of the trial near that man, so that I can see the last gleam of hope gradually fade from his face."

In the witness box Waite was perfectly cool, and he made no
attempt to hide the appallingly evil personality of the man from
Egypt who had compelled him to commit and contemplate crimes
which shocked even New York. The more terrible his story, the
more coolly it was told, the greater the chance the jury would
believe that only a madman could do these things. His own
counsel, by clever questions, brought out details of the murder
of Mrs Peck and her husband which seemed to show that only a
madman could have acted the way Waite did.

"What did you do after you had given your mother-in-law the
fatal dose of poison?" asked his counsel.

"Why, I went to sleep, of course," answered the prisoner in the
witness box. He added that in the morning he went along to his
mother-in-law's bedroom and, finding her dead, quietly came out
of the room again and waited for his wife to make the discovery
her mother had died in the night. He told the jury of all the ways
he had afterwards tried to kill Mr Peck before he finally succeeded.

"I gave him a throat spray and a nasal spray containing germs,
and when that didn't work I got a lot of calomel which I
administered to him in order to weaken him so that he could
not resist the germs, but it failed. The man recovered every time.
I would get him to go out and expose himself to draughts in the
hope that he would catch cold, and I dampened his sheets for the
same reason. Once I got some hydrochloric acid and put in the
radiator in his room expecting the fumes would affect him.
Finally I gave him arsenic. I sat up with him that night, as
my wife was tired. He was in great pain, groaning. I gave him
some chloroform and when he was unconscious I placed a pillow
over his face and kept it there until he died."

Is that the evidence of a sane man or not?

"Waite has told you the truth. There is no part of his story that
is not true," said the counsel for the defence in his final speech.
"He has no moral sense whatever. What are we going to do with
such a man as this? You would not send to the electric chair an
idiot, a lunatic or a child. On the other hand we cannot permit
such a man as Waite to be at large. We must remove him from
society by placing him in an institution."

Mr Justice Shearn demolished the arguments of the counsel for the defence, in his address to the jury.

> You are not concerned at all with the question of the punishment of this man. The question raised by defendant's counsel of what to do with such a man is not the question at all. The law determines what shall be done. Your function is to determine the facts so that the law may operate.
>
> Don't get into your heads that you are called upon to determine anything but the facts. Juries have no right to set up standards of what constitutes right and wrong, and no right to discuss how the law shall deal with a man like this. You must not attempt to usurp the functions of the Legislature.
>
> In this case no claim is made that the defendant did it in the heat of passion. On the contrary he himself admits premeditation, intent and a motive. No matter what the defendant has confessed you must remember the burden still rests upon the prosecution to establish his guilt beyond a reasonable doubt. The defendant is entitled to have the case determined on the facts and not on what he says.

Part of the remainder of the judge's summing up is so phrased that a copy of it should be handed to every jury in a murder case where the defence is one of insanity.

> You might infer from arguments of counsel and some of the evidence that you are here to hold a medical clinic. That's not so at all. It would be absurd to ask twelve laymen to determine whether from the medical point of view a man is sane or insane, especially as men learned in the profession do not agree on the matter. The question is not whether he is sane but whether he was responsible under the tests prescribed by the law – that is, did he know the nature and quality of the act and know it was wrong. That's not a test for experts, but for men of commonsense. Moral indifference is not insanity.

The claim that the defendant was weak in will power and
that he was unable to resist suggestions like those from 'the
Man from Egypt' has also been passed on by the highest
courts, who have held that, no matter what medical authority there may be for such a claim, it cannot be assented to by
the courts. Indulgence in evil passions weakens the will
power and at the same time the sense of responsibility.

The trial was very much shorter than the great majority of
sensational murder trials in America, where money can hold
up justice for months. The trial only took five days and the jury
were only a little over an hour bringing in their verdict of
"Guilty."

To the last the condemned man showed that curious double
personality which puzzled all those with whom he came in
contact. He never wearied of talking about himself.

"My life consisted of lying, cheating, stealing and killing. My
personality was that of a gentleman and I went for music, art and
poetry."

He dedicated a long poem to himself, an address to his body by
his soul after death.

> And thou are dead, dear comrade,
> In whom I dwelt a time,
> With whom I strolled through star-kissed bowers
> Of fragrant jessamine.
> And thou wert weak, O comrade,
> Thyself in self did fail,
> And now the stars are turned to tears
> And sobs the nightingale.
> And though I now must leave you,
> The same old songs I'll sing,
> And o'er yon hill the same soft dew
> Will spread its silver wing.
> Across the fields, among the stars,
> I now must go alone,
> Your spirit now will roam afar,
> And leave you, friend, alone.

A few days before his execution, when he was reading the Bible, he remarked with his usual charming smile, "I was looking over the ten Commandments and found I had broken all but one – the one about profanity. I have never been profane."

He kept up his story about his two personalities until the last.

But it did not save him. He went to his death with that boyish smile and charming manner which had characterized him from the day he began his career.

THE TALKING SKULL

(Harry Dobkin, UK 1942)

Nigel Morland

A single female body unearthed amid the mass slaughter of the London Blitz was identified as a victim not of war but of a private, murderous act of mutilation – thanks to the evidence of the dead woman's dentist. Harry Dobkin, forty-nine, Russian by birth, bald, squat and bull-necked, killed his estranged wife Rachel who'd been pestering him to return to her. After crudely separating the head from the torso, Dobkin tried to remove all identifying marks, and concealed his wife's remains beneath the floor of a badly blitzed chapel. Finally, he set fire to the building under cover of enemy action, a singular deed for a man employed as a wartime fire-watcher. But the charred skeleton was discovered by chance more than a year later, and the Home Office pathologist Dr Keith Simpson reported that the unknown woman had been strangled. Her identity was established through the testimony of Mrs Dobkin's dentist, who recognized the curious shape of the upper jaw as well as other features of the teeth and gums. Dobkin was convicted of murdering her and duly hanged. Nigel Morland (1905–86), one of Britain's most prolific writers of crime fact and fiction, was a co-founder of the Crime Writers' Association. After a spell as a journalist in the Far East, he edited publications as diverse as Doctor *and the* Edgar Wallace Mystery Magazine. *He also ghosted a number of showbiz memoirs. Nigel Morland was the founder and editor of* The Criminologist *and other crime-related journals including* Forensic Photography, International Journal of Forensic Dentistry *and* Current Crime.

In the greater conflagration of war it is somehow remarkably incongruous that all the vast resources of detection and justice should be devoted to the seeking and condemnation of a civilian murderer with but a single victim notched to his credit.

While thousands die on the battlefields, there is a footnote to history in a nation's trivia of homicides, yet, clearly, it is the duty of the authorities to maintain law and detect transgressions of it even if the world is falling about their ears. The pen of the historian, then, had to turn aside from the horrors of World War I, in June 1915, to record the trial of that singularly revolting, utterly worthless creature, George Joseph Smith.

And in 1942, much in the same way, part of the country paused to watch the Baptist Church murderer stand his trial while Rommel was retreating in North Africa and the Germans receded like a spent wave from the rubble-fortress of Stalingrad.

Despite the chaos of World War II, Britain's aficionados of murder could still note with interest a trial that was indeed more distinguished for the medical work contributing to its solution than for its forensic colour.

The trial was a worthy occupant of the Central Criminal Court at Old Bailey, where so much legal drama has been played out, even if it failed to reach the heights of some of its predecessors.

Chance enabled me to be present at the hearing, though it was impossible to attend on the last day, for, and it may be of faintly ironic interest, I was receiving a reprimand for putting ideas into the heads of would-be murderers. It was a sound example of how officialdom sought to guard the innocent when, in a far larger way, the innocent were being slaughtered.

It happened I had written for a newspaper a short story involving an imaginary murder during an air raid. The plot concerned a man who slew his wife by means of a piece of flak, or anti-aircraft shell, fastened to a stick and used as an edged bludgeon. It contrived a death not attributable to himself but to the rain of shell fragments which were also London's protection. The scheme was foolproof except, like all fictional (and many real) murderers, he had made a mistake by leaving the fragment at his dead wife's side still bearing the string originally tying it to the bludgeon.

An over-conscientious features editor thought this just a bit too feasible and perhaps tempting; he mentioned it casually to a Ministry of Information official, who asked me to visit him, and suggested – and no more – that it was not the best of policies to make crime *too* easy. Could I not contrive something less likely to cause possible trouble for an over-worked detective force?

Thus it was I never heard Mr Justice Wrottesley's masterly summing-up on the final day of the Baptist Church murderer's trial, but the story of the case is a veritable marvel of the medical jurist excelling fiction by conjuring from little more than dust a recognizable human being whose gruesome end was finally avenged.

The July sunshine poured through the windows of the Gordon Museum at London's Guy's Hospital, making the room warm, a heat in no way improved by a tart chemical smell and the brittle, throat-catching aroma of ancient death.

There was a brown paper parcel containing remains for the attention of Dr (later professor) Cedric Keith Simpson, noted Home Office pathologist, a parcel already familiar to him.

Its contents were first seen on 17 July 1942, when a gang of demolition workers was clearing bombed premises at 302, Upper Kennington Lane, a short distance from south London's Kennington Oval cricket ground.

Raising a stone slab in what was the cellar of a now demolished Baptist church, human remains were revealed. According to the routine of such cases, the local coroner was informed. Dr Simpson, also according to routine, saw the remains in Southwark Mortuary the following morning and was not personally satisfied they were all that was left of an air-raid victim. He thought it wise to conduct a closer examination at Guy's Hospital because of the possibly long task of trying to get some sort of identification from an incomplete skeleton bearing decaying tissues. The poor fragments, the skull entirely separated from its trunk, were bundled into a prosaic paper parcel and transported for due attention on Monday morning.

The remains were transferred to a white dust sheet and these Dr Simpson pondered before commencing what was quite a considerable task in detective work at a time when his day was filled and his leisure almost non-existent.

The first thing was visual verification of his original surmise that death had taken place some twelve or eighteen months previously;* that the victim was female was easily discernable by the remains of the uterus being still present.

Using camel hair brushes and loosening the tissues, the doctor began slowly, and with extreme delicacy, gradually to clean the dirt from the almost mummified remains of the body. It was exacting and wearing, the adhering dirt being not easily removed; it required a combination of firmness and lightness, with special precautions to avoid damage to the soft tissues still remaining.

The following day saw progress add up to considerable results. It did not seem to Dr Simpson that this was an air-raid casualty. The skull had been severed cleanly from the trunk, the lower jaw was missing, and the skull also bore no scalp tissue other than a small fragment at the back – no bomb had the power to scalp and behead quite so selectively.

There were no lower portions to the arms or legs, which argued amputation. There were also marks of burning on the head, on the left side of the trunk and at the level of each knee – the left arm had been severed at the elbow joint and the right arm immediately above that joint, while the legs were separated on the left below the knee joint and at the joint on the right. The cut portions were all missing.

As a snap guess it was possible to wonder if the mutilation, and this included stripping the identifiable tissues, was the work of an unskilled person determined to hide a human identity by crude but effective methods even if, with careful disposal, she came to light some time after death.

It was without doubt a case of murder, for the small bones of the voice box bore an injury – with bruising showing it to have been sustained in life – which Dr Simpson knew was seen only when fingers had grasped the throat and strangulation had followed.

In the busy if pedestrian professional life of a great pathologist, it is only natural that the few real puzzles which stand out from the unhappily ordinary dead are challenges to his

* A deposit of yellowish powder over the whole was proved to be slaked lime.

ability and, after all, threads of colour in his more mundane daily round.

Dr Simpson knew he had before him a veritable mystery and wondered if his skill and knowledge would enable him to establish the identity of the victim, or at least sufficiently chart it for purposes of enquiry. He wanted science to give the police something sound to work on at the start of their enquiries.

The first thing to ascertain was the height of the dead woman in life. The weapon to be used was Pearson's formulae for the determination of stature, a process requiring the utmost knowledge and experience.

Reassembly of the body had revealed its stature to be about 5ft $0\frac{1}{4}$ in to 5ft $0\frac{3}{4}$ in, allowance being made for the missing lower legs, feet and soft tissue. Pearson's formulae, worked on the remaining long bone, the left humerus, gave height as 5ft $0\frac{1}{2}$ in to 5ft 1in.

The next step was to age the remains in life. This is done by checking the closure of the skull vault sutures (the zigzag markings or joints between the plates of bone in the skull vault). Here is an awkward gap from the anatomical point of view – till about twenty-five years of age the accuracy of age estimation can be achieved by several pointers in the human frame. Between that maximum and until roughly forty, there is little, except appearance, to help in closely estimating age.

But at about forty-years-old the skull vault sutures commence to close and other closures lend their aid to achieve reasonably accurate age estimates.

It was therefore possible from the skull sutures, and the closing of the palate suture (usual between 45 and 60), to settle on the approximate age of the corpse as 40 to 50; these bone fusions were remarkably helpful in Dr Simpson's reconstruction.

Colouring was proved by the fragment of scalp, to which some hairs were still attached; they were dark brown, ageing, and going grey.

There was a fibroid tumour of the uterus, a benign growth having nothing to do with death, but possibly of value in clinching identification. Finally, there were four teeth, and some roots, remaining in the upper jaw. These had received dental attention.

This initial data Dr Simpson gave to the police with his suggestion the remains might be those of a murdered person, a woman, aged 40 to 50; she was 5ft to 5ft 1in in height, with brown hair turning gray. She suffered from a fibroid tumour of the uterus, and had possibly received medical attention for it. She had met her death some twelve to eighteen months before and, if dental records could be found, there was an upper jaw with four teeth together with their details of dental repairs, fillings, and so on available for comparison or matching.

In the meantime police enquiries had followed *their* usual routine; Divisional Detective Inspector Frederick Hatton, of "M" Division, had caused to be checked the lists of women notified to the police as missing during the period in question, twelve or eighteen months previously.

A coincidence emerged and because detectives have frequently found that coincidences often lead to the discovery of important circumstantial evidence, Hatton's CID staff got a feeling they were on to something.

The coincidence was a missing woman named Dobkin, who had vanished some fifteen months before. Her husband had been a fire-watcher at 302, Upper Kennington Lane. He had looked after storage premises containing papers practically on the edge of the spot where the demolition workers had turned up the body. It was a pointer to a line of enquiry far too promising to be ignored.

Detective Inspector John Keeling, Hatton's second-in-command, obtained Dr Simpson's first findings and went to see Mrs Dobkin's sister (she had originally reported the disappearance to the police) in order to get a full description.

It was uncannily similar to the scientific reconstruction. The missing Mrs Rachel Dobkin had been 5ft 1in tall, with dark brown hair going gray. Her age had been forty-seven, and she had attended the London Hospital for a fibroid tumour of the uterus. Further enquiries began to turn up some very interesting facts.

The husband of the dead woman, Harry Dobkin, was a bald,

somewhat bull-like Jew of Russian birth* and just forty-nine years old. Before the war he worked as a ship's steward and cook, while, on shore, he managed to live by undertaking various jobs in the tailoring trade.

On 3 April 1941, a firm of solicitors engaged him as a fire-watcher to look after a small building belonging to them in which were stored quantities of papers and documents.

This building stood well back from the street in a yard containing the Vauxhall Baptist Church and its adjoining school, both places having been demolished by bombs. Two small houses fronting Upper Kennington Lane – between the Lane and the paper store – had also been bombed and were empty.

It was Dobkin's job to patrol round the paper store a prescribed number of times during the night in between which activities he made himself comfortable in a chair in one of the two small bombed houses. It would have been a pleasant life for a reflective man though, for certainty, Dobkin must have preferred to keep his mind strictly on the unforgiving minute and let the past bury itself.

A fortnight after his duties began, and, it was of interest to note, only very shortly after Mrs Dobkin's disappearance, there was a fire in the cellar under the site of the ruined church vestry. The fire brigade quickly put out the blaze, largely consisting of burning straw from a mattress lying within yards of the slab where later the scorched skeleton was to be found.

Dobkin at the time showed some agitation and made an odd, and uncalled-for, observation to a police constable that: "I didn't do it." The fire took place three days after Mrs Dobkin's sister reported the disappearance.

Police records revealed that as soon as news of the woman

* It may be of no possible sociological significance but of some interest that the origins of several people concerned in one way or another with notable British murder trials are remarkably varied; a casual handful picked haphazard from the headline names suggests the Island Race does not always lead: Florence Maybrick, American; Adelaide Bartlett, French; H. H. Crippen, American; George Chapman, Russian; Eugéne Marie Chantrelle, French; Buck Ruxton, Parsee; Jean Pierre Vaquier, French; Alma Rattenbury, Canadian; Oscar Slater, German, etc.

being missing was received, the husband was interviewed because, as I have mentioned before, police officers are inclined to go and talk lengthily to the husband when his wife vanishes – this is based on a simple, strictly sensible rule; frequently it pays dividends.

In this case Harry Dobkin made a statement which mentioned he had married a Rachel Dubinsky in 1920 at Bethnal Green Synagogue, a union that had failed from the beginning. A maintenance order for £1 weekly had been made against him a few months after the marriage, not that Mrs Dobkin ever succeeded in getting the stipulated amount from him. Becoming seriously in arrears over the payment landed Dobkin in jail for a brief term.

On 11 April 1941, Mrs Dobkin told her sister she was meeting her husband, apparently to try and coax some of the money due to her; as usual it was well behind. After lunch she set out and was seen in early evening by a waitress at a Dalston cafe having tea with Dobkin. That was the last of her so far as the world knew, though Dobkin was to swear he saw her off in an east-bound bus.

The following day her handbag, containing among other things an identity card and ration book, was found in a Guildford post office but never claimed. At five o'clock that afternoon Polly Dubinsky, the sister, gave information to the London police that Mrs Dobkin was missing. She bluntly accused the husband, who had physically attacked his wife in the past, of being the responsible party.

In the resulting police investigation it was suspected that Dobkin must have started the fire in the church himself. Searches were made there without any result, though detectives were within inches of the concealing flagstone; apropos, a trench – 6ft by 1½ ft – recently dug *was* found under the main church floor but there was no body in it.

Nothing ever came of this or of photographs published in the newspapers and gradually, through the enormous pressure of wartime work, the matter was dropped. Dobkin remained at his fire-watching job until May 1942, when his employers removed their documents and no longer required his services.

Having been a sort of custodian of the secret grave for all those months, Dobkin probably left his situation with some relief. It must have been galling for him to be told that within two months of quitting the post, demolition workers had retrieved the body and the problem of Mrs Dobkin had returned to the inquisitive world.

Dr Keith Simpson had already formed the private opinion that Dobkin must have murdered his wife by strangling in order to rid himself of an incubus, concealing the remains after mutilating the body and trying to destroy it by fire. The missing parts, never found, could easily have been disposed of in the Thames or in some similar way. But this was far from being a sound basis for a murder charge: identity had first to be transformed from a high probability into a complete certainty.

A technique was tried which Professor John Glaister and his colleagues initiated in the Ruxton murder case. The police had got hold of a portrait of Mrs Dobkin. It was enlarged for Dr Simpson to life size and a life size photograph of the jawless skull was taken. Superimposition of one on the other showed they corresponded exactly, the bony facial architecture forming a perfect foundation for the features in the portrait, the eye shape, set and angle aligning with the eye orifices in the skull and so on.

This was still by no means final. The next thing was the all-important dental data. Mrs Dobkin's dentist, on being found, supplied valuable evidence. This gentleman, Barnett A. Kopkin of North London, produced his dental treatment record card concerning this patient and was able to draw a diagram of Mrs Dobkin's upper jaw as he had last seen it together with fillings he had made.

The treatment given to the teeth in the skull was Kopkin's and later, seeing the actual teeth and their fillings, he immediately identified his work. He also stated that in extracting two teeth on the left side of the upper jaw in 1941, residual roots had been left, a not unusual occurrence. Sir William Kelsey Fry, a leading Guy's dental surgeon, made X-ray films of the skull and revealed those same roots. Identity was no longer in doubt.

Lastly, there was the question of how Mrs Dobkin had met her death.

The sprinkling of slaked lime on the body (the action of a layman in the belief that such lime destroys*) had preserved certain tissues round the neck. The hyoid and thyroid cartilages of the voice box were thus preserved, showing, on microscopical examination, clear traces of dried bruising. The upper horn of the right wing of the voice box was fractured, this part of the bone being driven inwards towards the windpipe, and since the bruising surrounding the bone could only occur in life, Dr Simpson's view was that death resulted from manual strangulation, the only likely cause of such a fracture.

There was also found a blood-clot on the back of the head indicating heavy bruising which could have been inflicted by a backwards fall or the result of the head being dashed more than once against the ground by the violence of the strangler.

It was not a comfortable thought, the processes of that grim murder, the stripping of the tissues, the partial dismemberment and disposal of material, all to hide identity. The murderer's tenacity must have been remarkable, backed by a sort of malignant determination to destroy.

Not only is it hard work for the unskilled to hack up a dead body, but to remove tissue requires a steel-strong nerve, and an absolute lack of pity. As a practising crime novelist, I know only too well how glibly dismemberment can be written about, and how fictional licence can excuse or strengthen the criminal. In real life it is subject to a hundred hazards, quite apart from the physical repulsion felt by the ordinary person who undertakes such a deed.

At last Dr Simpson was satisfied, as far as any scientist ever can be satisfied, with his work that he had properly identified Mrs Rachel Dobkin after three months' steady probing into the mystery. He had given all his results to the police and in October Divisional Detective Inspector Hatton moved. Harry Dobkin was arrested and charged with the murder of his wife.

* From the wild inaccuracy laid down by a medical witness at the Manning trial in 1849 (and the belief existed earlier) that lime destroyed bodies, murderer after murderer has shown a pathetic devotion to lime as a decomposition agent, using it recklessly and time and again causing the victim's corpse to be properly *preserved* for subsequent investigations.

The Press, quite unaware of this impressive drama of detection going on behind the scenes, awoke to the case with much excitement by the time Dobkin appeared in Lambeth court for the preliminary hearing. Any time lost was made up by an elaborate coverage achieved against the vaster claims of war: as always one locally slaughtered female body was worth, in news value, a thousand dead soldiers overseas.

The trial at the Central Criminal Court took place before Mr Justice Wrottesley on 17 November 1942. It contained little drama and an enormous amount of detail.

Harry Dobkin was an uneasy captive in the dock. He seemed to glare a great deal at various people concerned with the prosecution side, and frowned heavily at times with the concentration of an empty mind. He was extremely fortunate in having his defence in the capable hands of Mr F. H. Lawton, a youthful barrister who was so highly regarded by the accused's solicitors that they did not brief a K C to lead him even though he had never before handled the defence in a trial for murder.

Dr Simpson was the last witness on the second day of the trial; he was taken carefully through his evidence by Mr L. A. (later Mr Justice) Byrne, for the Prosecution. To reproduce a part of the court examination is to show how every point was elaborated. The book frequently referred to was a volume of photographs, containing notes, for the enlightenment of the court, every photograph having been taken and prepared for the support of Dr Simpson's findings by Miss Newman, in charge of the Photographic Department at Guy's Hospital.

Mr Byrne: As to the identification of the body, I want to deal with that. You told us first of all you were able to determine the sex. That was comparatively simple, was it not?

A. Yes.

Q. Then did you determine how tall the woman had been?

A. Yes.

Q. How did you arrive at that?

A. I did it by two methods, the first by reconstructing as far as was possible the body as shown in Plate 2 and making due allowance for the missing parts, the joints at the knee and for the flesh and the feet, and by those means I estimated the stature to be $59\frac{1}{4}$ inches – that is to say, three-quarters of an inch short of five feet. I estimated the height to be about five feet and a quarter of an inch to five feet and three quarters of an inch.

Dr Simpson went on to explain his tables in the book which showed how he had arrived at the height estimates:

. . . I did this by two methods: by using the Pearson's formulae I estimated the height to be five foot and half an inch to five foot one inch, using the left humerus, the left upper-arm-bone, and by using the Rollet's tables, which are not so accurate in my view, I estimated the height to be four foot ten and a half inches to four foot ten inches. The mean of those estimations from both methods give a height estimation of about five foot and half an inch.

The question of the superimposition of the photographs on the dead woman's skull was explained in Dr Simpson's answer:

. . . The general contour of the skull was the same, allowing for scalp thickness; the contour of the cheeks, allowing for flesh, was the same; the position and shape of the upper jaw fitted the photograph well, was the same; the position, the height, and the width of the nose space were the same, and fitted perfectly.

On the following day the examination was resumed. Dr Simpson taken detail by detail through his findings, while the prosecution tested every fact and, indeed, re-tested it, so there could not be the slightest possible doubt.

In the minds of the listeners it was clear how the medico-legal case proved contentions offered by Dr Simpson, but in spite of it, Mr Lawton made a brave showing for the defence.

He went through the facts with the same care as Mr Byrne but sought to disprove them or find a weakness in Dr Simpson's conclusions. The superimposed photograph received a great deal of attention, pointed by Mr Lawton's remark that:

Is not the difficulty exaggerated in this way, that when taking a photograph one is obviously taking something in two dimensions, but when you are taking a photograph of a skull you are taking a photograph of something in three dimensions, and does not that tend to lead to inaccuracy in the two photographs?

A. That is one of the objections. That is a difficulty we had in this case; we had no measured portrait or anything by which we could measure the portrait precisely.

Q. And in particular when dealing with the photograph of a skull which in its three dimensions . . .

Mr Justice Wrottesley: I want to make sure that I follow that. When you say "no means of measuring the portrait"; that means you have no means of reducing the portrait to three dimensions?

A. No, it means that we do not know the precise width of the head and the height of the head in life from a portrait; we have nothing, as was so in the Ruxton case, by which the portrait could be measured.

Mr Lawton then made use of references to *Gray's Anatomy*, the standard medical work on the subject. He asked Dr Simpson:

Q. See if you can follow this passage: "In comparing the shape of one skull with that of another it is necessary to adopt some definite position in which the skulls should be placed during the process of examination." Obviously, they have both got to be placed in exactly the same position, have they not?

A. Yes.

Q. In this case you have not got a skull, but a photograph, and you cannot be certain, can you, that you had them in the identical positions?

A. The answer to that is that it was possible to move the skull so as to place it in the same position as the photograph.

Q. And in the same plane?

A. That is in the same position.

Q. Not quite, is it? You could have it in the same horizontal position, but not necessarily in the same plane.

A. This was in the same vertical and the same horizontal position.

With item after item concerning the skull discussed, and not to the advantage of the defence, the cross-examination moved on to a check on the structure of the voice box and the question of manual strangulation. It was also the defence's last effort to try and discover holes in the expert findings.

It was established that Dr Simpson found the whole of the voice box in connection with the body.

Q. By voice box do you just mean the thyroid or the two bones that go top and bottom of the thyroid?

A. I mean the hyoid, which is the upper bone shown in this photograph on which the tongue is placed, and also the two wings shown below of the thyroid. Those two together compose the voice box.

Mr Justice Wrottesley: Those three together?

A. Yes; I am taking those two below as one; those three together, yes.

Mr Lawton: In addition to those three bones, the hyoid and the two branches of the thyroid, there are one or two tiny bones, besides, are there not?

A. Yes, there may be.

Q. Many tiny bones besides?

A. There may be, yes.

Q. In particular there are two rather important tiny bones called the arytenoids?

A. There may be.

Q. There are, are there not?

A. There may be; they are not always bony.

Q. If they are not bony, they are in the nature of cartilages, are they not?

A. Yes.

Q. In fact, I am right in saying, am I not, that it is not until late in life that those bones, the hyoid and the thyroid, become bony at all?

A. About in middle life.

Q. Did you find the arytenoid cartilages?

A. Yes.

Q. And just above the horns of the thyroid there are two tiny cartilages known as the triticia, or something like that?

A. Yes.

Q. Did you find those?

A. Yes.

Q. I want you to assume that this situation arises: somebody standing in the road, or on a piece of waste ground, with a lot of rubble about, parts of bricks, and so on, being thrown violently forward by blast from a high explosive bomb, and in falling catching the voice box on a kerb or a piece of brick or masonry, or something of that sort. Is not it possible – I do not put it any higher than that – that a fall under those circumstances might break the cornu of the right thyroid?

A. I have seen injuries under those circumstances on many occasions, and the injuries have never been confined to a fracture of the cornu, as is present here.

Q. That may be, but have you seen injuries under those circumstances which have in fact broken a wing of the thyroid?

A. Yes, but not broken the cornu; broken the thyroid wing, yes. That is not what I described here.

Q. No, I know that, Doctor. I confused the two. Have you seen injuries in the street which have broken a wing of the thyroid and a horn of the thyroid?

A. I have seen both broken together.

Mr Justice Wrottesley: The broken wing being, of course, the lower part?

A. Yes; I have seen the whole thyroid crushed, with both cornu and both wings crushed.

Q. Is your evidence "I have seen such injuries as are described by the throat hitting something"?

A. Yes.

Q. But they never occurred as here, that the thyroid was broken?

A. Yes. It is that which, in my view, is so significant.

Mr Lawton: Do you say it is impossible that a fall of the type I have described to you would break only the cornu of the thyroid?

A. I say that in fifteen years I have personally examined over 11,000 cases, and I have never seen this injury except in manual strangulation.

The defence had worked superbly against heavy odds. "Mr Lawton," one commentator rightly said, "did everything except the impossible" which was to get his client free. The patient medical evidence was too careful and too precise to be argued away.

Dobkin was put in the witness box. If the case against him was strong before he got there, the task was made much easier for the prosecution when Dobkin was to show himself a worse witness than anybody would have believed – it is ironic to think that the Criminal Evidence Act was meant as a privilege, and has often turned out to be the cause of many accused being convicted who, but for their showing in the box, might have got away with it.

Dobkin's eyes seemed to move sharply from point to point while his broad nostrils dilated continually during his destructive cross-examination by Mr Byrne. Most of the good work put in by pertinacious Mr Lawton was destroyed through Dobkin's reactions to certain questions.

In the end he was a sorry picture of panic and fear – I have seldom seen quite so grim a portrayal of a man betraying absolute guilt by a sort of gradual disintegration in which the shrivelled little soul was finally stripped bare of all pretence.

The steady hammering of the circumstantial evidence and Dr Simpson's work bore Dobkin down at every turn until he was accusing all the prosecution's witnesses of lying.

At some trials there always remains a feeling of doubt in the minds of certain of the expert spectators but Dobkin's prosecution was notable for the steady piling of fact on fact until the resulting edifice was as solid as the skills of science and detection could make it; the conclusions could not be gainsaid. There never was any question of Dobkin's guilt, and his protestations of innocence were futile. The defence tried to show the head bruising might have been a result of a fall by Mrs Dobkin after a bomb blast, and that, as a last surmise, the horn fracture was caused by a "tiny bomb splinter passing into the neck from the rear and getting into the throat". Dr Simpson thought this possible, but accepted it only as a remote chance. Granting such an event, there still remained the ancillary medical evidence, damning in itself.

For some there was the thought that perhaps, for all his brutality, Dobkin might not have premeditated his crime, that it was the result of overwhelming rage. Though he did what he did to get rid of the body, and he was a large man and she a small woman, it still might have been manslaughter. Yet, as he admitted nothing and flatly denied everything, the verdict of guilty was reached by the jury after only twenty minutes of consideration. It was by no means unexpected except, it would seem, by Dobkin. His features changed from white to red and back again, and he made a brief, rambling protest signifying nothing.

For Dr Keith Simpson, whose medical work had made the case into a modern classic,* there was to be one more meeting with Harry Dobkin.

It was on a foggy morning at Wandsworth Prison when, with the coroner and police officials, he made the customary postmortem always held on the body of a hanged person. It is said that Dobkin looked peaceful.

What Dr Simpson thought at the completion of this full circle

---

* The case has come to be quoted and written of in the standard textbooks on medico-legal subjects, as a classic example of the rewards of patient application of simple principles in identity reconstruction – comparing with, even exceeding in detail, the cases of Dr Parkman and Dr Ruxton. It happened also that it contained enough colour to achieve a place in the literature of crime detection.

cannot be guessed, but at least he had the knowledge given to few men that his own reconstruction from poor fragments of a dead and dismembered woman had given her back an identity, with the result her murderer was caught and hanged, a just and rightful conclusion with which no fair man can possibly quarrel.

THE JIGSAW MURDER CASE

(Dr Buck Ruxton, UK 1935)

Jonathan Goodman

The problem facing investigators in the gruesome Ruxton case was how to identify the human remains which had been wrapped in a newspaper like so much butcher's offal and thrown into a Scottish stream. Two heads were found, but the killer had been at pains to mutilate all the recognizable features: in one, the eyes had been removed, in the other, not just the eyes but the nose, lips and ears. The police believed they knew the identity of the two victims, and brought in two experts to help them prove it. Their brief, unprecedented in medico-legal history at the time, was to show conclusively that the remains were those of two women who had gone missing from home 100 miles away in Lancaster. The great forensic achievement was to show the astonished jury at Ruxton's trial life-sized photographs of the women in life and pictures of the skulls found in Scotland. Superimposed one on top of the other, they fitted exactly. The tale is told by Britain's leading crime historian, Jonathan Goodman (b.1931). After a successful career in theatre and television production, in 1969 he published his classic re-examination of the Wallace murder case, the first of a series of true-crime books which established him as the pre-eminent investigator of past crimes. He has also written crime novels, verse, plays, television scripts, short stories and articles. Jonathan Goodman has most recently written and presented the Discovery Channel's series on historical crime, Tales from the Black Museum.

If you are old enough to remember the first croonings of a romantic song, *Red Sails in the Sunset* – which, had there been such a thing as a pop chart in the mid-1930s, would have been top of it for a good many weeks – you may also recall an illicit version of the lyric which went like this:

> Red stains on the carpet,
> Red stains on your knife,
> Oh, Dr Buck Ruxton, you cut up your wife;
> The nursemaid, she saw you, and threatened to tell—
> So, Dr Buck Ruxton, you killed her as well.

The fact that this anonymous rhyme was recited and sung on innumerable occasions gives an idea of the interest and excitement caused by a double murder in a small northern county town.

So far as public awareness is concerned, the case began on the bright but chilly afternoon of Sunday, 29 September 1935, when Susan Johnson, a young Edinburgh woman holidaying with her brother at Moffatt, a picturesque village thirty-five or so miles across the Scottish border from Carlisle, took a stroll to the bridge over Gardenholme Linn, a stream running into the River Annan.

Glancing over the rough stone parapet, she saw . . .

No, it couldn't possibly be.

She looked again. Her heart was thumping by now.

The second look convinced her that she was staring at a human arm, protruding from some wrapping at the side of the ravine.

Susan Johnson rushed back to the hotel. When she told her brother Alfred why she was in such a state, he asked the landlord to give her some medicinal whisky, then raced to the bridge. Clambering down the heather-strewn embankment, he saw not only an arm just above the waterline, some ten yards from the bridge, but an oddly-shaped bundle wrapped in bed-sheeting and newspaper.

He timorously pulled apart the wrapping and saw that the parcel contained chunks of flesh and bone.

Deciding that he had seen enough – more than enough – Alfred went in search of the village policeman and told him how the beauty of Gardenholme Linn had been marred.

After confirming that this was no false alarm, Constable James Fairweather telephoned the headquarters of the Dumfriesshire Constabulary, then went back to the bridge. And waited.

Not for long. Dumfries is no more than twenty miles from Moffatt, and Sergeant Robert Sloan rarely needed to slow down on the gently curving road that Sunday afternoon.

One wonders what went through his mind as he drove. Did he perhaps think about the Brighton Trunk crimes that had caused such a stir the year before? Did he fear that something similar – parcelled remains rather than bodies as luggage – would create as much work, as many problems, for himself and his colleagues?

He parked near the bridge, and had a few words with Constable Fairweather and Alfred Johnson; then treading carefully so as not to disturb the ground, he lowered himself down the side of the gully.

Within a few minutes, he had observed four parcels. After an hour, he had carefully parted the paper and sheeting and made a rough inventory of the respective contents, which included parts of legs, hands (with the tips of fingers and thumbs lopped off), thigh-bones, miscellaneous pieces of flesh, the chest portion of a human trunk, and two heads, hideously mutilated so as to be unrecognizable.

By the time Sloan had completed his notes and marked the positions of the parcels, other policemen had arrived from Dumfries. It was starting to get dark. Constable Fairweather unlocked the diminutive mortuary in Moffatt Cemetery, and the parcels were transported there.

During the next few days, forensic experts from Edinburgh and Glasgow visited the mortuary and made preliminary examinations of the decomposing, maggoty remains. One of the experts was John Glaister, who had been appointed Professor of Forensic Medicine at the University of Glasgow four years before, following the retirement of his famous father.

Then the "bits and pieces," as John Glaister referred to the remains, were taken to the anatomy department at Edinburgh University. Between the time of their arrival there and 4 November, they were augmented by the contents of other parcels found by the police and the public close to Gardenholme Linn and along the River Annan. The parcel farthest removed from those that had started the investigation was discovered at Johnson Bridge, on the main Edinburgh–Carlisle road, nine miles from Moffatt.

The malformed, "Cyclops" eye of an animal was found among the remains. It was better preserved than the human flesh and tissues, suggesting that it had been immersed in formaldehyde, perhaps by someone interested in ophthalmology.

While the pathologists, an anatomist and a dentist tried to solve the two "jigsaw puzzles", and to find distinguishing marks to assist in identifying the victims, the police made inquiries about persons reported missing before 19 September, when there had been torrential rain in the area around Moffatt, filling streams and rivers; it seemed clear that the parcels had been left behind on the banks as the level of the water had fallen.

The police had one apparently important clue. A piece of newspaper that had helped to wrap one of the packages was recognized as being part of the *Sunday Graphic* of 15 September 1935: part of a special "slip" edition of 3,700 copies, carrying a report and pictures of the crowning of the Morecambe Carnival Queen, that had been distributed only around Morecambe and the nearby county town of Lancaster.

On the very same day that the Chief Constable of Dumfries got in touch with the Lancaster police, he happened to notice a report in the *Glasgow Daily Record*. Briefly tucked away on an inside page, the report referred to the disappearance, in mid-September, of Mary Jane Rogerson, the twenty-year-old nursemaid to the children of an Indian doctor named Buck Ruxton, who ministered to the sick at his home at 2 Dalton Square, Lancaster, 105 miles south of the bridge over Gardenholme Linn.

Struck by the Lancasterian coincidence, the Chief Constable initiated inquiries in that town. He soon learned that the disappearance of Mary Rogerson had been notified to the local police – also that there was a rumour that Dr Ruxton's wife had left him at about the time the nursemaid was last seen.

A detective was sent to get a detailed description of the missing girl from her stepmother, who lived in Morecambe, and as a result of the visit two further pieces of information came to light.

The human remains found at and near Moffatt had been wrapped mainly in newspaper and bed-linen – but a blouse and a child's romper suit had also been used. When the blouse was shown to Mrs Rogerson, she at once recognized it, saying that she had bought it at a jumble sale and given it to Mary just before Christmas 1934; she had no doubt that it was the same blouse, for she had sewn a patch under one of the arms.

Mrs Rogerson told the police that, during the summer, her stepdaughter and two of the Ruxtons' three children had spent a fortnight in a guesthouse at Grange-over-Sands, and that the landlady had given Mary some secondhand clothes.

A detective visited the landlady, Mrs Edith Holme, who instantly identified the romper suit as one of the things she had given the nursemaid: her own child had outgrown the suit; before parting with it, she had put new elastic in the waistband, tying the ends in a knot of her invention.

So far, the control and conduct of the investigation had been emphatically Scottish; but now, although the scientific work of piecing together the assortment of human remains continued in Edinburgh, overall responsibility for the case was passed to Captain Henry Vann, the Chief Constable of Lancaster.

Captain Vann and his subordinates already knew quite a lot about Dr Buck Ruxton – and in a few days, without having to put themselves out to any great extent, they learned much more.

When Ruxton was born in Bombay, in 1899, he was called Bukhtar Rustomji Ratanji Hakim, or Buck Hakim for short, but some thirty years later he anglicised his name by deed poll.

He was touchy about being referred to simply as an Indian, and would insist on the more specific designation of Parsee, pointing out that he was a descendant of the Zoroastrians who migrated from Persia to India in the eighth century.

He held three medical degrees, two from the University of Bombay and one (MB) from the University of London.

After gaining the first of those degrees, he served for about three years in the Indian Medical Corps and then travelled to Britain, where he lived first of all in London, working as a locum while pursuing his studies, and then in Edinburgh, preparing for the examinations for Fellowship of the Royal College of Surgeons of that city.

His failure in that examination may been due, at least in part, to the fact that his dedication to his studies was diminished by his infatuation for Isabella Van Ess, a woman two years younger than himself who, following her estrangement from her Dutch husband, was working as a waitress in a restaurant in Princes Street, Edinburgh.

Sharp-nosed, wide-mouthed, and with legs that did not narrow towards the ankles, Isabella was far less lovely than her name; but still, Ruxton was smitten from the moment she first took an order from him for tea and scones.

Presumably because he decided that Isabella would consider him more dashing if she thought he was an army officer, decently reticent about his many decorations for gallantry, he led her to believe that he was Captain Hakim.

He returned to London at the beginning of 1928, and Isabella joined him soon afterwards. Though she was now divorced, and though between 1929 and 1933 she gave birth to three children, she never married Ruxton.

In 1930, Dr and "Mrs" Ruxton, with their first child, Elizabeth, moved to 2 Dalton Square, a grey-stone terrace house of three storeys and a basement that stood next to a picture palace in the centre of Lancaster. Of the four rooms on the ground floor, two each side of a hall, Ruxton used three for his general medical practice, one as a waiting room, one for consultations, the third as a surgery; the fourth room, at the back, was a kitchen.

There were two living rooms and a dining room on the first floor, and at some time since the house had been built, towards the end of the nineteenth century, a bathroom had been squeezed in as a sort of addition to the first-floor landing. There was a master bedroom and three smaller ones on the top floor.

Ruxton soon had a large panel of patients. This was partly due to an insufficiency of doctors in the town, partly because his practice was very general indeed, including even dentistry and ophthalmology, and partly because he seemed invariably affable, worthy of the locals' descriptions of him as "that nice, obliging, young foreign doctor".

But Isabella did not consider him altogether nice. As the months, the years, went by, the couple quarrelled with increasing frequency and vehemence.

Sometimes the rows were over what Ruxton called "Belle's temporary sillinesses". Sometimes the cause was jealousy: Ruxton was particularly suspicious of a friend of Isabella's, a young man called Bobby Edmondson who worked in the solicitor's department at the town hall, just across the square from the doctor's house. And sometimes there was a sexual motive for the arguments, for both Ruxton and Isabella experienced enhanced pleasure from intimacy when it was part of "making-up".

By April 1935, Isabella was either tired of Ruxton's tantrums or terrified by his bad temper. As the result of a statement she made to a detective, Ruxton was invited to the police station. When he saw his "wife" there, he (in the detective's words) "flew into a violent passion and said, 'My wife has been unfaithful. I would be justified in murdering her'."

The detective pacified Ruxton (or thought so), reassured Isabella (or believed that he had), and put the incident out of his mind – until a month or so later, when he was called to 2 Dalton Square, again to act as peace-maker.

It would have been better for Isabella – and for the young nursemaid, Mary Rogerson – if, instead of seeking help from the police, she had waited until Buck Ruxton was answering a house-call and then escaped to a place where he might not find her or could not harm her.

Following the press reports of the gruesome discoveries at Moffatt – and long before the police suspected Ruxton of murder – a good many people in Lancaster, including the doctor's several charwomen and some of his patients and neighbours, wondered whether there was a connection between what they had read in the papers and the disappearance of Mrs Ruxton and the nurse-maid.

Both before and after the mutilated remains were found, Ruxton contended on various occasions and to various people that the two women had gone to Blackpool . . . that they were taking a holiday in Scotland . . . that the nursemaid was pregnant, so Isabella might have taken her away for an abortion . . . that Isabella had gone off with a lover . . . that she had returned to London.

When early newspaper accounts stated (wrongly, as it turned out) that some of the remains found at Moffatt were of a man, Ruxton was joyful. After giving one of the charwomen a rest from her chores while he read aloud a report of the "Ravine Murder," he chortled, "So you see, Mrs Oxley, it is a man and a woman – not our two," then burst into helpless laughter at Mrs Oxley's response that she sincerely hoped not.

But within a week of that incident he was distinctly unhappy about what the papers were saying. He turned up at the police station at half-past nine on the night of Friday, 11 October, and, waving a copy of the *Daily Express* in one hand and furiously gesticulating with the other, screamed at the Chief Constable that such publicity was ruining his practice.

While Captain Vann tried to get a word in edgeways, Ruxton sat on the desk, perched his feet on a visitor's chair, and banged the back of it with his free hand.

Abruptly changing the subject – and crying now – Ruxton accused a man of being Isabella's lover, claimed that he had tapped telephone conversations between them, and implored Captain Vann to intercept the alleged lover's mail.

Then, reverting to the press, he asked the Chief Constable to issue a statement that the remains found in and around Moffatt were not those of Isabella and Mary Rogerson: Captain Vann was still uming and ahing about that when the doctor stalked out.

Uming and ahing . . .? Well, yes. If only because Ruxton's arrival had interrupted a discussion between Captain Vann and a senior detective as to whether the time was ripe to charge the doctor with double murder.

Ever since the responsibility for the investigation had been passed to Lancaster from Dumfriesshire, the Lancaster Borough Police Force had been just as busy as the scientists gathered in the anatomy department at Edinburgh University, piecing together the incomplete jigsaws of flesh and bone, and drawing conclusions from what they found – and could not find.

The police knew, among many other things, that on Saturday, 14 September, Mrs Ruxton had driven to Blackpool in the doctor's Hillman car, registration number CP 8415, to see the illuminations with her two sisters, and that she had started the return journey just before midnight. Though she was never seen alive again, the presence of the car in Lancaster the next day indicated that she had arrived home.

Some of the strongest evidence against Ruxton came from his charwomen. At half-past six on the morning of Sunday, 15 September, Mrs Agnes Oxley was getting ready to go to the doctor's house when Ruxton drove up in his car and told her that she could have the day off as "Mrs Ruxton and Mary have gone away on a holiday to Edinburgh".

That afternoon, however, the doctor visited one of his patients, Mrs Mary Hampshire, and asked if she wanted to earn seven shillings and sixpence by scrubbing his staircase. He explained that he needed her help because Isabella was in Blackpool and Mary Rogerson in Edinburgh, and he had cut his hand badly in trying to open a tin of peaches for the children's breakfast. (He certainly had a severe wound on one of his fingers, and a subsequent remark to Mrs Hampshire that he had taken his children to stay with a dentist friend in Morecambe was true.)

When Mrs Hampshire arrived at 2 Dalton Square, she found that the place was far more messy and untidy than she had expected: the carpets had been taken from the stairs, which were scattered with straw; rolled-up carpets, stair-pads and a man's suit were lying in the waiting room, and in the back yard were other carpets, clothing and towels, all heavily stained with blood and showing signs that an attempt had been made to burn them.

Mrs Hampshire, a trusting soul, accepted the doctor's explanation that the carpets had been taken up because the house was to be decorated, and seems to have assumed that, though Ruxton did not look anaemic, the blood saturating the things in the yard had flowed from the cut on his finger.

She did not ask him to explain the straw protruding from beneath the doors to two of the bedrooms – or why those doors were locked and the keys removed.

Mrs Hampshire started tidying up, and, when her husband

came to the house a few hours later, got him to lend a hand. Ruxton gave the couple a load of soiled carpets and clothing, but presumably Mrs Hampshire was paid more than the promised seven shillings and sixpence for her labours, not only on the Sunday but on subsequent days, on some of which she was assisted by the doctor's regular chars.

The police had much more evidence against Ruxton, including the testimony of a cyclist who on Tuesday, 17 September, had been knocked over by the doctor's car on a road leading to Moffatt; Ruxton had not stopped but was caught by a policeman, who noted that he was as jumpy as a flea.

But all this evidence might be insufficient to convict Buck Ruxton if the scientists in Edinburgh were unable to establish that the bits and pieces of flesh and bone on their laboratory tables were the remains of Isabella Ruxton and Mary Rogerson.

It was vital that the separated, mutilated remains found in Dumfriesshire be identified as those of the doctor's common-law wife and his children's nursemaid. Admittedly, by the time of the Ruxton case there can have been few judges who wholly accepted Lord Halsbury's contention that "in the absence of evidence (that a body or part of a body has been found, which is proved to be that of the person alleged to have been killed) there is no onus upon the prisoner to account for the disappearance or non-production of the person."

Only the year before, a man named Davidson had been convicted of the murder of his small son though no body had been found, the presumption being that the body was consumed in a fire on a garbage tip.

But a clever defence lawyer might confuse less clever members of a jury about the meaning of "reasonable doubt" by speaking of ancient cases in which men had been hanged for the murder of people who had afterwards, like Mark Twain, complained of reports of their demise, and use any uncertainty concerning the fact of death to suggest uncertainty about the act of murder.

The team of experts at Edinburgh University not only used accepted methods but invented new techniques as they sorted out which of the remains belonged to one body, which to the other –

as they then searched for clues that might, singly or in relation to others, give more reality to the incomplete bodies than the original designations of "No 1" and "No 2" – as they sought indications of the cause, or causes of death.

Probably for the first time, an anatomist had been brought into a murder investigation. This was James Couper Brash, professor of anatomy at the University of Edinburgh – a city that, a hundred or so years before, had become associated, through the activities of Burke and Hare, with the unlawful aspects of the science.

Brash was able to get an exact fit between some of the dismembered remains and, using anatomical formulae and X-rays, classified other parts as belonging to one body or the other.

After weeks of work, two partially reconstructed bodies lay side by side on tables in the laboratory. "No 1" was less complete than "No 2", but Brash had gauged the living stature of the bodies as, respectively, five feet and five feet and three inches.

There was ample evidence that both bodies were female. If – a very large "if" at this stage – they were of the women from 2 Dalton Square Lancaster, then "No 1" was Mary Rogerson and "No 2" was Mrs Ruxton.

With help from an odontologist, Arthur Hutchinson, Brash estimated the age of "No 1" as 20 (as was the nursemaid) and that of "No 2" as being between 35 and 45 (Isabella Ruxton was 34).

Paradoxically, many of the mutilations of the remains assisted the pathologists in their search for evidence. The manner of dismemberment (without the use of a saw and with only slight damage to the separated parts), together with the fact that components that might have indicated cause of death had been removed, showed that the criminal was skilled in the use of surgical knives and that he had anatomical and medical knowledge.

The criminal had removed from both heads the eyes, ears, lips and nose – in all of which signs of asphyxia might be found – but so far as body "No 2" was concerned, there remained several indications that death was due to asphyxia by throttling.

The most iterated example of "negative evidence" comes from fiction – the dog that, as Sherlock Holmes noted, did not bark in the night. For a real-life example, it would be hard to better what the experts in the Ruxton investigation noted as being absent from the remains.

Virtually from the start, John Glaister and his colleagues supposed that the reason for many of the mutilations was to make identification more difficult, but it was not until the scientists knew some of the distinguishing features of the two missing women that they began to suspect answers to specific questions.

Perhaps the eyes of body "No 1" had been taken out because Mary Rogerson had a cast in one eye. Had the skin been removed from the upper part of the right forearm because Mary had a conspicuous birthmark there? Were the soft tissues shaved from the right thumb because the nursemaid had a scar there?

And had the nose of body "No 2" been cut off, and the teeth been extracted, because those were prominent features of Mrs Ruxton? Had the soft tissues of the legs been removed because Isabella's legs were the same thickness from the knees to the ankles? Were the toes lopped off because Isabella's were "humped"?

So many of the sites of the excisions and mutilations corresponded with those of distinguishing features of the missing women that there seemed only one answer. Added to the evidence already gathered, the "negative evidence" virtually proved that the bodies were those of Isabella Ruxton and Mary Rogerson.

But to make assurance double sure, James Brash did something that, so far as is known, had never been attempted in a criminal investigation. After obtaining photographs of the missing women, he arranged for the head and shoulders in each to be enlarged to life-size. He took immense care to ensure that the size of the enlargements was correct; for instance, a piece of jewellery worn by Mrs Ruxton in one of the photographs was located and measured to the nearest millimetre, so that the size could be used to establish the measurements of her head and features. The enlarged photographs were then superimposed on photographs, taken to the exact size, of the decapitated heads in the laboratory. The resulting "double exposures" showed a remarkable correspondence.

On Saturday, 12 October, after the evidence assembled by the
Scottish scientists had been added to that gathered by the police,
Chief Constable Vann invited Buck Ruxton to his office.

The doctor arrived at 9.30 in the evening and spent the next ten
hours answering questions. Then he was charged with the murder of Mary Rogerson.

He looked flabbergasted. "Most emphatically not," he splut-
tered. "Of course not. The farthest thing from my mind. What
motive and why? What are you talking about?"

Following Ruxton's arrest (on 5 November he was further
charged with the murder of Isabella), the investigators searched
the house in Dalton Square for more indications of his guilt.

They found a good many, of which the most important,
perhaps, was a sheet that had precisely the same peculiar fault
in the selvedge as did pieces of a sheet that had been used as
wrapping for the hideous bundles found at Moffatt.

By the start of the new year, the investigators believed that the
case against Buck Ruxton was complete, watertight.

But then they learned something that worried them greatly: the
doctor was to be defended at the trial by the velvet-voiced
Norman Birkett, who was thought of by some people as "the
courtroom magician", by others as "the murderer's best friend".

If anyone could persuade the jury in the Ruxton case to return
a nonsensical verdict, it was Birkett.

The trial started on Monday, 2 March 1936, at the old Manchester
Assize Court in Great Ducie Street, with Mr Justice Singleton, a
stickler for the niceties of courtroom behaviour, presiding.

J. C. Jackson, one of the best-known silks on the Northern
circuit, led for the Crown, assisted by two barristers who would
rise to high positions in government: one, a Socialist, was Hartley
Shawcross, and the other, a Tory, inspired the couplet:

> The closest thing to death in life
> Is David Patrick Maxwell Fyfe.

Buck Ruxton's defender, the tall, bespectacled Norman Birkett,
made few notes during the opening speech for the prosecution;

but right from the start, Ruxton, sitting in the dock behind Birkett, scribbled messages to his counsel.

According to Mr Jackson's view of what had happened in the house in Dalton Square, Lancaster, after Mrs Ruxton's trip to see the Blackpool illuminations: "When she went up to bed, a violent quarrel took place; Ruxton strangled his wife, and Mary Rogerson caught him in the act and had to die also."

There was, of course, much more to Mr Jackson's speech than that; he dealt with every aspect of the case, occasionally in greater detail than some observers thought necessary, starting with the discovery of the human remains at Moffatt and concluding with the arrest of the Indian doctor.

The speech went on till late in the afternoon, leaving only enough time for four prosecution witnesses to be called that day. Though the evidence of those witnesses was formal – to do with plans, photographs and the like – Norman Birkett cross-examined each of them in some depth.

And during the following seven days of the trial, hardly any of the prosecution witnesses – over a hundred of them – left the court without having been questioned by Birkett. At times, when there was a flurry of requests by counsel for the production of exhibits, the well of the court looked like an untidy jumble sale, with bottles, jewellery, books and kitchenware scattered over piles of clothing, carpets and bed-linen.

Mrs Mary Hampshire, one of the several women who had laboured to make the doctor's house presentable after the disappearance of Mrs Ruxton and the nursemaid, fainted in the witness box. Perhaps the sight of some bloodstained carpets, given to her by the generous doctor but taken from her by the police and now exhibits, made her feel queasy. As she was being carried from the court, the doctor peered from the dock at his former patient and gave his professional opinion that she would be all right. When she returned, he made a what-did-I-tell-you? gesture, then started scribbling again.

The last of the Crown's witnesses were the Scottish scientists who had made medico-legal history by their reconstruction and scrutiny of the bodies. They had done their work so thoroughly that Birkett scored few, and then only minor, successes in cross-examination.

Before the last of the scientists was called, Birkett wrote a memorandum for Ruxton's solicitor to show his client. It ended: "In my clear and very strong view, if Dr Ruxton desires to give evidence, we should confine our evidence to him, and exercise our right of the last word to the jury . . . Any other course, in my view, would be absolutely fatal."

Ruxton agreed, and on the morning of the eighth day of the trial was escorted from the dock to be the sole witness in his own defence.

His solicitor had warned him that he must remain calm, listen carefully to each question, and restrict his answers to what had been asked, but the flashily handsome doctor soon forgot – or, believing that he knew best, ignored – the advice.

After asking a few "tuning-up" questions, Birkett inquired about Ruxton's relations with Isabella – and was made most unhappy by the reply: "If I may be permitted to put it in appropriate English, I can honestly say we were the kind of people who could not live with each other and could not live without each other."

Not finished yet, Ruxton said something that his counsel didn't understand.

"You have added something else," Birkett muttered irritably.

"Forgive me the interruption," said Ruxton, "but I just used the French proverb, 'Who loves most chastises most.' My mentality thinks in French, and I have to translate into English everything you are asking me."

No doubt feeling that his task was hard enough without the imposition of a language barrier, Birkett from now on tried to leap in with a question as soon as Ruxton had delivered the first sentence of his answer to the previous one.

But Birkett was rarely fast enough, and eventually snapped, "Perhaps you will just deal only with the questions I put to you."

No use: the words continued to tumble out, and every so often Ruxton burst into tears.

His answers to two successive questions are often quoted to exemplify how witnesses should not respond.

Birkett asked, "It is suggested here by the Crown that on the morning of the Sunday after your wife had come back, you killed her?"

"That is an absolute and deliberate and fantastic story," the doctor screamed, waving his arms about. "You might just as well say the sun was rising in the west and setting in the east."

Next question: "It is suggested also by the Crown that, upon that morning, you killed Mary Rogerson?"

"That is absolute bunkum, with a capital B, if I may say it. Why should I kill my poor Mary?"

It may be that the jury never made up their minds about that – or about the motive for Isabella's murder – but after another couple of days, which included the cross-examination of Ruxton, the closing speeches, and the judge's summing-up, the jury returned a verdict of Guilty.

Asked if he had anything to say why sentence of death should not be passed, Ruxton raised his right hand, the palm towards the judge, in what could have been a salute or a blessing, and uttered some flowery but irrelevant remarks. He made the same gesture as the judge spoke the final words of the death sentence, then bowed before being escorted from the dock.

Six weeks later, after the doctor's appeal was dismissed, something rather odd happened. In towns from one end of the country to the other, masses of people, few of them certifiably insane, signed petitions for a reprieve; in Lancaster alone, there were six thousand signatories.

But the Home Secretary had the good sense to ignore the petitions, and Ruxton was hanged at Strangeways Prison, Manchester, on the fine morning of Tuesday, 12 May.

The following Sunday, anyone who had signed a petition and was also a reader of the *News of the World* should have been a trifle embarrassed. There on the front page was a facsimile of a confession to the two murders that the good doctor had written the day after he was arrested.

A CASE OF "HIDEOUS FEROCITY"

(Peter Griffiths, UK 1948)

Norman Lucas

Peter Griffiths, the killer of little June Devaney, was caught by his fingerprints. Griffiths had crept into a hospital ward in Blackburn where the child was sleeping and taken her from her cot. The child's body was found in the hospital grounds. She had been brutally raped. The murderer's fingerprints were found on a bottle by the child's cot. Three days after the killing, the baffled police took an unprecedented step. They decided to fingerprint the entire male population of Blackburn. Every one of the town's 35,000 homes was visited, and every man and boy aged sixteen or over asked for his prints. It was a long, laborious task, and early results were not encouraging. The breakthrough came after three months and more than 46,000 sets of prints. Peter Griffiths thought he'd slipped through the net because his name didn't appear on the local electoral roll. But he'd reckoned without the records of wartime ration books. After Griffiths' execution, the prints taken in the course of the inquiry were publicly burned. Norman Lucas (1920–98) was the Sunday Mirror's *chief crime reporter. He exposed the Kray mob in London's East End and broke the story of the first child's body being uncovered by Lancashire police in the Moors murders of the 1960s. Norman Lucas's experiences enabled him to write seventeen books on crime, two of which were reprinted in seven languages including Czech and Japanese.*

On the night of 14–15 May 1948, little June Anne Devaney was sleeping soundly in her cot in the babies' ward of Queen's Park Hospital, Blackburn, Lancashire. She had been suffering from pneumonia, but after ten days in hospital had been pronounced well enough to return to her parents, Mr and Mrs Albert Devaney, who lived in Princess Street, in the Waterfall district of the town.

It had been arranged that her aunt, Mrs Ann Whalley, would collect her the following day because Mrs Devaney, in addition to two other children at home, had had a new baby – born 5 May, the day June had been taken to hospital.

June, a big girl for her age – three years and eleven months although she looked about six years old – was very bright and intelligent. That evening she had been chattering happily to the nurses, and to her new black doll, about going home to Mummy and Daddy and seeing the new baby.

She was the eldest of the six children in the ward and the only one who could talk.

At 11.30 that night Nurse Gwendoline Humphreys took over duty in the babies' ward and the adjoining toddlers' ward, in which there were several more older children. She looked round both wards and the sun room and a side room, then went into the kitchen to start preparations for the children's breakfast. While she was seeing to the porridge she heard a child crying and found it was Michael Tattersall, a baby in the next bed to June Devaney. In her rubber-soled shoes she tiptoed to Michael's side and remained with him for about twenty minutes. She noticed that little June was fast asleep, and returned to the kitchen. Just before 12.30 she thought she heard a girl's voice from the direction of the porch door and went to investigate. She looked out into the moonlit grounds but could not see anyone, then a little girl in the toddlers' ward began to cry and she spent about fifteen minutes with her.

At 1.15 a.m. Nurse Humphreys returned to the babies' ward and immediately noticed that June Devaney's cot was empty. She looked around the ward and in the toilet, but there was no sign of the child. The nurse also noticed that a Winchester bottle of sterile water, which had been on a trolley in the ward, was lying beneath June's cot. Then, to her horror, she saw what looked like the prints of large bare feet running the whole length of the highly polished ward floor and more footprints beside June's cot. Nurse Humphreys raised the alarm and the police were called.

June's father, a thirty-three-year-old foundry worker, joined in a search of the hospital and grounds, and he was with the police when at 3.15 a.m. they found the body of his little girl. She was lying in the grass near a stone wall encircling the hospital grounds and it was plain that she had been raped and battered to death.

Within an hour of their gruesome discovery the local police had called in the country police and the country police sought the aid of Scotland Yard, so that by noon of the day of the murder the Chief Constable of Blackburn, Mr C. G. Looms, was conferring with Detective Chief Inspector Robert McCartney, of the Lancashire Constabulary, and Detective Superientendent Jack ("Charlie Artful") Capstick, of the Yard's Murder Squad.

Only the previous evening Capstick had arrived back in London after two months of intensive inquiries into the murder of Jack Quentin Smith, an eleven-year-old schoolboy who had been found stabbed and battered to death in Farnworth – barely thirteen miles from Blackburn. The police had a description of his killer – thin, tall and youngish, with deep-set eyes and a pimply face – given by another boy, David Lee, who had been attacked at the same time but had managed to escape. All possible leads to the boy's killer had proved abortive and Capstick returned to London for a conference at the Yard.

He was more than usually concerned at the failure to capture little Jack Smith's murderer because four years earlier a six-year-old girl, Sheila Fox, had disappeared on her way home from school in Farnworth, and within less than two years another child in the same town – nine-year-old Patricia McKeon – had been attacked near her home.

Not unnaturally, parents in that area of Lancashire were beginning to be really frightened and the murder of baby June added to the rapidly growing rumours that a "moon maniac" was at large.

It was four o'clock in the morning of 15 May when Jack Capstick, after only an hour or two in bed, was woken by the

phone and told by Chief Constable Looms about the murder of
June Devaney. By 6.20 a.m. Capstick and the late Detective
Sergeant John Stoneham were on their way back to Lancashire,
arriving in Blackburn by lunchtime.

In the meantime Detective Inspector Colin Campbell, chief of
the Lancashire County Constabulary Fingerprint Bureau, had
found an enormous number of confused fingerprints on the
Winchester bottle which had been found under June's bed,
and among them were seemingly fresh thumb, index finger
and palm prints. The footprints on the ward floor were photographed and were shown to have been made not by naked feet,
but by large feet enclosed in socks. The pattern of the weave was
clearly revealed and a few tiny fibres of wool from the socks were
found adhering to the wax polish on the floor.

The prints on the bottle showed that the killer had big hands;
those on the floor indicated large feet; the fact that there were no
hand prints on June's cot meant that the child had probably been
removed without the side of the cot being lowered – in other
words the police had a picture of a killer who was tall enough to
have leaned over the rail and lifted her out of her bed. They knew
they were looking for a man with big hands and feet who was
probably familiar with the layout of the hospital building and
grounds.

Everyone who might legitimately have handled the Winchester
bottle was fingerprinted – nurses, doctors, relief staff, patients'
visitors, ambulance drivers, electricians who had worked in the
ward, and tradesmen delivering goods. In three days 642 sets of
prints were taken from people who might have handled the bottle
in the preceding two years. This check eliminated many prints
but still left the fresh prints believed to have been made by the
killer.

Because the police were convinced that he was a local man
familiar with the hospital routine, the finger-printing was extended to all men who had been patients in the last two years, all
male visitors to the hospital, ex-members of the staff, husbands
and boyfriends of nurses – bringing the total prints to more than
2,000. But still the vital prints remained unidentified.

Then Detective Superintendent Capstick put forward an idea

which was at first regarded as impractical and impossible to implement – to fingerprint every male over the age of fourteen in the whole town of Blackburn. There had never been a mass fingerprinting of a town's population before and it was doubted if the people would co-operate. The Mayor gave the lead by volunteering to be first and the response of the town was very wholehearted. An undertaking was given that all fingerprints obtained in this great check-up would be destroyed when their purpose had been served, and the 50,000 prints were in fact ceremonially destroyed at a later date.

Every one of the 35,000 houses in the borough was visited, but the check had necessarily to go further afield because some men who had been in Blackburn on the night of the murder had moved. Some had been visitors, others seamen who had rejoined their ships or members of the armed forces who had returned to their units. Eventually prints were forwarded to Blackburn from places as far afield as South America, Sweden, Hong Kong, South Africa and Canada.

But still, none matched the vital prints on the Winchester bottle.

In the meantime the usual red herrings had been drawn across the path of detection. Two parties of nurses returning to the hospital on the night of the murder said they had been accosted by a man near the gates and had experienced difficulty in evading him while other nurses reported seeing a "Peeping Tom" peering into a bedroom window of the nurses' home. When this man was traced he was found to be the husband of a woman in the maternity ward. He was quickly eliminated from the inquiry.

A youth then came forward and confessed to the murder, and was found to be the same lad who had confessed to the murder of Jack Quentin Smith a few weeks previously. It was proved conclusively that he could have had nothing to do with either of the killings.

At this point in the inquiry the police had their first lucky break.

Food was still rationed in that post-war year of 1948 and in August a new issue of books was due. Inspector Bill Barton, of the Blackburn police, had the bright idea of checking the names on the enormous pile of fingerprints with the list of new ration books to be issued – and it was found that 200 men and youths had either deliberately or involuntarily slipped through the net.

So the final search began. Among the missing 200 was a twenty-two-year-old ex-Guardsman named Peter Griffiths living in Birley Street, Blackburn, who was seen by Police Constable Joseph Calvert on 11 August. Griffiths, then working as a flour mill packer, had somehow evaded the fingerprinting team when they had called at his house during the first big check, but raised no objection to having his prints taken when the second call was made.

The prints were sent for examination by the experts – and were found to match exactly those on the Winchester bottle.

At nine-thirty in the evening of 13 August Jack Capstick and Inspector Barton stopped Griffiths as he left 31 Birley Street, where he lived with his father Peter Griffiths senior, his mother, Mrs Elizabeth Griffiths, and his half-brother, James Brennan.

Told that he was to be arrested for the murder of June Devaney, he said: "What is it to do with me? I have never been near the place." Later he asked: "Is it my fingerprints why you came to see me?" He was told that it was.

He then said, "Well if they are my fingerprints on the bottle, I will tell you all about it". He made a statement in which he said that on the night of the murder he intended to spend a quiet evening on his own.

He had five pints of bitter at the Dun Horse public house, then went on to Yates Wine Lodge where he had two glasses of Guinness and two double rums. He returned to the Dun Horse and had about six more pints of bitter, leaving at closing time. In Jubilee Street a man in a car asked him if he would like a "spin" and took him to the front of Queen's Park Hospital.

"The next thing I remember was being outside the ward where there was some children," he said. "I left my shoes outside a door . . . it opened to my touch and I went in. I heard a nurse humming and banging things . . . so I came out again and waited a few minutes. Then I went back in again. I picked up a biggish bottle off a shelf . . . I overbalanced and fell against a bed. I remember a child woke up and started to cry and I hushed her. I picked the girl up out of the cot and took her outside. She put her arms round my neck and I walked with her down the hospital field. I put her down on the grass. She started crying again and I tried to stop her, but she wouldn't do like . . . I just lost my temper and you know what happened. I banged her head against the wall. I then went back to the veranda outside the ward and put my shoes on. I went back to where the child was, I just glanced at her but did not go right up to her but went straight on down the field."

Griffiths added that when he got home he slept on a couch downstairs. The following day he had his breakfast, went for a walk and then to a cinema and later returned home to tea.

"I looked at the papers and read about the murder," he said. "It didn't shake me so I just carried on normally after that. That is all I can say and I'm sorry for both parents' sake and I hope I get what I deserve."

On the day following Griffiths' arrest the police recovered from a local pawnbroker the suit the accused man had worn on the night of the murder. Bloodstains on the jacket and trousers were found to be of Group "A" – the same as the dead child's blood group – and fibres from the suit matched some found on her nightdress and body. Tests on a pair of Griffiths' socks showed that the colour, method of weave and number of twists to the inch tallied with the socks worn by the murderer as he walked through the ward. His footprints, too, matched those on the waxed floor.

A Miss Rene Edge told the police that on Sunday, 16 May – the day after the murder – she had gone for a walk with Griffiths and he had shown her a bloodstained Soldiers' Song Book. She asked how the blood had got there and he told her he cut his hand during a fight when he was in the Army.

Griffiths had been "walking out" with Miss Edge, a quiet, religious girl, for some time, but she did not approve of his drinking and in April that year had told him that their friendship must end. Four days before the murder she told him quite definitely that she would not change her mind that there could be no question of a marriage.

Griffiths' familiarity with the hospital buildings and grounds was also established when it was discovered that he had spent two years there as a patient between the ages of ten and twelve. His hospital record showed that he was suffering at that time from incontinence of urine.

When Griffiths stood before Mr Justice Oliver and a jury at Lancaster Assizes on 15 October 1948, there was really only one issue to be decided – not whether he killed June Devaney but whether or not he was sane at the time.

Mr W. Gorman, KC, and Mr D. Brabin appeared for the Crown and Griffiths was defended by Mr Basil Nield, KC and Mr J. di V. Nahum.

Dr Gilbert Bailey, police surgeon for Blackburn, giving evidence for the prosecution, described the child's injuries and was cross-examined by Mr Nield.

"In the course of your thirty-four years in medical practice you have from time to time dealt with cases of violent death?" – "Yes, many."

"In your experience have you ever seen any injuries more consistent than those in this case with the outburst of a lunatic?" – "I certainly consider the man who did this act must have been in a state of maniacal frenzy."

"Does that mean in a condition of complete ferocity?" asked Mr Justice Oliver. Dr Bailey replied: "Yes".

The judge: "A man is not necessarily mad because he acts in a ferocious manner?" – "Not at all."

"All you can say is that this was done by someone acting in a ferocious manner?" – "At that time."

Further questioned by Mr Nield, Dr Bailey said that the man who had murdered the child would be, in normal life, quite a normal man, but would have sudden outbursts of frenzy or mania. He had the impression that the man might be a schizophrenic. The motive in this case was an uncontrollable sexual impulse.

Mr Justice Oliver commented: "There was a sexual motive here; whether sane or insane, the jury will decide".

Mr Gorman, further examining Dr Bailey: "You have been asked a number of theoretical considerations in this case; is it necessary before you can arrive at a proper view as to the condition of this man that you should have him for some time under observation?" – "Yes. In this particular case, I would like to say now that I have not had this man under observation.

"I am not prepared to say what his true mentality is. All I am prepared to say is that the act of murder and rape on this child could have been the act of a man with a 'split' mind."

Opening the case for the defence, Mr Nield said it was his submission that Griffiths, at the time of the murder, was mad and he added: "I say to you frankly at this early stage that I cannot ask for this man's liberty, but I do ask for his life."

There were, he said, six categories of evidence which would help the jury to decide whether Griffiths was sane or insane.

Firstly, there was his family history. In 1918, for a period of about nine months, his father had been in a mental hospital suffering from what was described at the time as "delusional insanity" – a condition which in the more technical term of modern times was described as "paranoid schizophrenia".

Secondly, Peter Griffiths' own personal history had to be considered. When he was six years old he fell from a milk-float upon his head, but a doctor was not called. Later he spent two years in hospital suffering from something about which there was little real information – incontinence of urine. Might there not have been some neurotic foundation for that long stay in hospital?

"Even at the age of seventeen this young man was childish in his habits," continued Mr Nield. "He would shut himself up in a room and play with corks, pretending they were trains. So noticeable was this that his mother rebuked him and said he was going mental. Thereafter there is a long history of solitary habits, always alone, depressed, and a typical picture of an incipient schizophrenic who might at any time fall under the blow of this disease in which, in a moment of maniacal frenzy, this sort of hideous happening can occur."

Griffiths had left job after job, never remaining for more than a short time; as a boy he was unstable and stole things; his Army category was bad or indifferent and he deserted twice.

The third category of evidence, said Mr Nield, related to

events immediately preceding the act – and one of these was the meeting with Miss Rene Edge, whom the young man wished to marry, when she told him for the second time that she was not prepared to go on with the friendship.

"You may have in the case of a schizophrenic a precipitating factor which may produce one of these frenzies," he added, "and an unhappy love affair is typical of such a disturbance."

It was also quite plain that the accused had had a great deal too much to drink on 14 May, and medical testimony was that excessive alcohol might induce the mental disturbance.

The fourth consideration related to the act itself. It was recognized that an act of gross and hideous ferocity might well be an indication of mental disorder. "Can you think of a case of more hideous ferocity than this?"

The events immediately after the act were to be considered in the fifth category.

"This man went away from that hospital, slept that night as if nothing had happened, and then went out with this young lady," continued counsel. "There was no effort to wash away any stains from his suit and there was that unnatural calm which goes with one who has had a mental breakdown of the nature I have suggested."

The sixth category of evidence was that of the medical experts, said Mr Nield, who then called Dr Alistair Grant, of Whittingham Mental Hospital and Dr Geoffrey Talbot, Medical Superintendent of Prestwich Hospital.

Dr Grant said that he had twice examined Griffiths and had formed the opinion that he was suffering from schizophrenia. One of his reasons for that belief was the question of heredity. The man's father had suffered from what was probably paranoid schizophrenia and in sixty per cent of schizophrenics heredity was given as a cause.

In reply to questions put by Mr Nield, Dr Grant said that solitary habits and childish behaviour were the sort of symptoms found in early schizophrenia. Constant changing of jobs was very typical. An unhappy or frustrated love affair could precipitate the condition and it was a well-known fact that schizophrenics reacted badly to alcohol.

Cross-examined by Mr Gorman about the statement Griffiths made after his arrest, Dr Grant said the man might not have recalled raping the child because he did not mention it.

Mr Justice Oliver: "Why should he forget that if he remembered every other detail?"

Dr Grant: "In a case of ordinary schizophrenia, I would be rather surprised to find that a man had remembered so much and yet forgotten such an important thing, but that is the sort of partial amnesia you would get in a drunk."

Mr Gorman: "Is it not quite clear that the whole of that statement, with its details, with its lies, with its concealments, is the statement of an active mind appreciating what was being done at the time?" – "Most of the points you have made I am in complete agreement with, but I do differ about the material time, the time when he murdered the child."

"Will you tell me what there is in this statement that enables you to take a portion of time and say that within that portion of time this man was in this mental state?" – "I am judging by my direct experience in these cases, and I again repeat that, in my opinion, it is quite possible for a man, having schizophrenia, to have a maniacal attack lasting a short time and to recover himself fairly quickly afterwards."

Mr Justice Oliver: "I want to ask you one thing. Do you regard the raping of even small children as evidence of insanity?" – "No."

"Is there anything mad in what he did – on the part of a man who had been brutal enough to ravish her – is there anything mad in beating her brains out to stop her screaming?" – "I think so, for this reason, that she was a child, she would have no evidence against him, and he could have got away."

Dr Talbot gave evidence relating to the detention of Peter Griffiths senior in Prestwich Hospital and said that he was sent there by the Army as a dangerous lunatic soldier. The medical note entered on the record was a very good description of the condition now known as paranoid schizophrenia, which was known to be hereditary. Griffiths Senior had been discharged in 1919, after nine months, but that did not mean that he had been completely cured.

"My conclusion was that the type of mental illness from which he, the father, was suffering may have been regarded as hereditary and likely to appear in any or other of subsequent generations." he concluded.

The fourth medical witness, Dr Francis Brisby, Principal Medical Officer at Liverpool Prison and former Assistant Medical Officer at a Lancaster county mental hospital appeared for the prosecution. He said that from observation and examination of the accused man he had found no evidence of any disease of the mind which would prevent him from either knowing what he was doing or that what he was doing was wrong. Cross-examined by Mr Nield, he said he did not think the evidence suggested a complete picture of schizophrenia. He would expect some alteration of character, some change in the man's personality occurring before the event, some history of conduct alien to his nature.

In his lengthy and detailed summing up to the jury, Mr Justice Oliver said it would seem to him a most amazing disease when the man could be perfectly sane right up to the moment he laid the child on the ground, then a schizophrenic maniac during the time he was raping her and beating her brains out, then perfectly sane afterwards and remain sane ever since.

"It does indeed seem to be a very odd sort of disease," he said. "We are only laymen, we have not got the knowledge of the experts. I do not know whether you find it difficult to envisage a man quite sane and knowing what he is doing when taking the child out of the hospital ward and walking with it into the grounds, and then suddenly becoming bereft of his senses and raping and killing, and then getting his senses back again. I do not know whether it seems to you to be more likely, if that is really true, that the man would have a blank and would say, 'All I remember is picking the child up and taking her out, and I cannot tell you what happened until I found myself at home.' That may, at any rate, seem more consistent with the facts here, but you are the judges, not I."

The jury of nine men and three women were out only twenty-five minutes before giving their verdict of Guilty.

Passing sentence of death, Mr Justice Oliver said to Griffiths: "The jury has found you guilty of a crime of the most brutal ferocity and I entirely agree with that verdict." June Devaney's murderer was hanged in Walton Prison, Liverpool, on 19 November 1948. On the day before the execution he was interviewed by Superintendent Capstick and Detective Superintendent Lindsay, of Lancashire CID, who asked him if he had also killed Jack Quentin Smith.

Griffiths replied, "No", but Capstick remained convinced that the ex-Guardsman was the "moon maniac" of Lancashire and had been guilty of more than the one murder of which he was convicted.

DR PARKMAN TAKES A WALK

(Professor John Webster, USA 1849)

Cleveland Amory

This cautionary tale demonstrates that not only can scientists themselves stoop to murder, but that they can also be caught out by a simple scientific oversight. John White Webster was professor of chemistry and mineralogy at Massachusetts Medical College. He was a well-respected academic but he lived beyond his means, and borrowed money to fund his extravagant lifestyle. Webster became indebted to Dr George Parkman, who had given up a medical career to make a fortune in real estate dealings, and who was pressing Webster for his money. In a rage, Professor Webster murdered the miserly Parkman and burned the body in his assay oven. Webster was caught because the flames failed to consume Parkman's false teeth, which were found in the ashes. Cleveland Amory (1917–98) was a social historian who began his career as a newspaper reporter, becoming associate editor of the Saturday Evening Post. *A self-proclaimed curmudgeon, he hosted a hugely-popular radio show* Curmudgeon at Large. *This account of the Webster–Parkman case comes from his 1947 book* The Proper Bostonians *which scrutinized the wealthier and better-connected of Boston's residents.*

To the student of American Society the year 1849 will always remain a red-letter one. In that year two events occurred at opposite ends of the country, both of which, in their own way, made social history. At one end, in Sutter's Creek, California, gold was discovered. At the other, in Boston, Massachusetts, Dr George Parkman walked off the face of the earth.

The discovery of gold ushered in a new social era. It marked the first great rise of the Western *nouveau riche*, the beginning of that wonderful time when a gentleman arriving in San Francisco and offering a boy fifty cents to carry his suitcase could receive the reply, "Here's a dollar, man – carry it yourself," and when a poor Irish prospector suddenly striking it rich in a vein near Central City, Colorado, could fling down his pick and exclaim, "Thank God, now my wife can be a lady!"

Dr Parkman's little walk did no such thing as this. It must be remembered, however, that it occurred some 3,000 miles away. Boston is not Sutter's Creek or Central City or even San Francisco. There has never been a "new" social era in the Western sense in Boston's rock-ribbed Society, and it remains very doubtful if there ever will be one. The best that could be expected of any one event in Boston would be to shake up the old. Dr Parkman's walk did this; it shook Boston Society to the very bottom of its First Family foundations. Viewed almost a hundred years later it thus seems, in its restricted way, almost as wonderful as the Gold Rush and not undeserving of the accidental fact that it happened, in the great march of social history, in exactly the same year.

The date was Friday, November 23rd. It was warm for a Boston November, and Dr Parkman needed no overcoat as he left his Beacon Hill home at 8 Walnut Street. He wore in the fashion of the day a black morning coat, purple silk vest, dark trousers, a dark-figured black tie, and a black silk top hat. He had breakfasted as usual, and he left his home to head down town toward the Merchants Bank on State Street. Dr Parkman was quite a figure as he moved along. His high hat and angular physique made him seem far taller than his actual five feet nine and a half inches. He was sixty years old and his head was almost bald, but his hat hid this fact also. To all outward appearances he was remarkably well-preserved, his most striking feature being a conspicuously protruding chin. Boston Parkmans have been noted for their chins the way Boston Adamses are noted for their foreheads or Boston Saltonstalls are noted for their noses, and the chin of old Dr Parkman was especially formidable. His lower jaw jutted out so far it had made the fitting of a set of false teeth for him a very difficult job. The dentist who had had that job had never forgotten it. He was proud of the china-white teeth he had installed. He had even kept the mould to prove to people that he, little Dr Nathan Keep, had made the teeth of the great Dr George Parkman.

Although he had studied to be a physician and received his degree Dr Parkman had rarely practised medicine in his life. He was a merchant at heart, one of Boston's wealthiest men, and he spent his time in the Boston manner keeping sharp account of his money – and a sharp eye on his debtors. He had many of the traits of character peculiar to the Proper Bostonian breed. He was shrewd and hard, but he was Boston-honest, Boston-direct and Boston-dependable. Like so many other First Family men before his time and after Dr Parkman was not popular but he was highly respected. It was hard to like a man like Dr Parkman because his manners were curt and he had a way of glaring at people that made them uncomfortable. Without liking him, however, it was possible to look up to him. People knew him as a great philanthropist and it was said he had given away a hundred thousand dollars in his time. The phrase "wholesale charity and retail penury" as descriptive of the Proper Bostonian breed had not yet come into the Boston lingo, though the day was coming when Dr Parkman might be regarded as the very personification of it. Certainly he had given away large sums of money with wholesale generosity – even anonymously – yet with small sums, with money on a retail basis, he was penny-punctilious. "The same rule," a biographer records, "governed Dr Parkman in settling an account involving the balance of a cent as in transactions of thousands of dollars."

Children in the Boston streets pointed out Dr Parkman to other children. "There goes Dr Parkman," they would say. People always seemed to point him out after he had passed them. There was no use speaking to Dr Parkman before he went by. If you weren't his friend, Dr George Shattuck, or his brother-in-law,

Robert Gould Shaw, Esq, or a Cabot or a Lowell, or perhaps a
man who owed him money – and then, as someone said, God help
you – the doctor would ignore you. Dr Parkman had no need to
court favor from anybody. The Parkmans cut a sizeable chunk of
Boston's social ice in 1849, and they still do today. Like other
merchant-blooded First Families they were of course economic-
ally self-sufficient. They hadn't yet made much of an intellectual
mark on their city, but a nephew of the doctor, Francis Parkman,
had just published his first book and was on his way to becoming
what Van Wyck Brooks has called "the climax and crown" of the
Boston historical school. The Parkmans were in the Boston
fashion well-connected by marriages. Dr Parkman's sister's marriage with Robert Gould Shaw, Boston's wealthiest merchant,
was a typical First Family alliance. As for Dr Parkman's own
wealth, some idea of its extent may be gathered from the fact that
his son, who never worked a day in his life, was able to leave a will
which bequeathed, among other things, the sum of five million
dollars for the care and improvement of the Boston Common.

On the morning of that Friday, November 23rd, Dr Parkman
was hurrying. He walked with the characteristic gait of the Proper
Bostonian merchant – a gait still practised by such notable
present-day First Family footmen as Charles Francis Adams
and Godfrey Lowell Cabot – measuring off distances with long,
ground-consuming strides. Dr Parkman always hurried. Once
when riding a horse up Beacon Hill and unable to speed the
animal to his satisfaction he had left the horse in the middle of the
street and hurried ahead on foot. On that occasion he had been
after money, a matter of debt collection.

This morning, too, Dr Parkman was after money. He left the
Merchants Bank and after making several other calls dropped
into a grocery store at the corner of Blossom and Vine Streets.
This stop, the only non-financial mission of his morning, was to
buy a head of lettuce for his invalid sister. He left it in the store
and said he would return for it on his way home. The time was
half past one and Dr Parkman presumably intended to be home at
2.30, then the fashionable hour for one's midday meal. Ten
minutes later, at 1.40, Elias Fuller, a merchant standing outside
his counting room at Fuller's Iron Foundry at the corner of Vine

and North Grove Streets, observed Dr Parkman passing him headed north on North Grove Street. Fuller was later to remember that the doctor seemed particularly annoyed about something and recalled that his cane beat a brisk tattoo on the pavement as he hurried along. What the merchant observed at 1.40 that day is of more than passing importance, for Elias Fuller was the last man who ever saw the doctor alive on the streets of Boston. Somewhere, last seen going north on North Grove Street, Dr George Parkman walked off the face of the earth.

At 8 Walnut Street Mrs Parkman, her daughter Harriet and Dr Parkman's invalid sister sat down to their two-thirty dinner long after three o'clock. Their dinner was ruined and there was no lettuce, but Mrs Parkman and the others did not mind. They were all worried about the master of the house. Dr Parkman was not the sort of man who was ever late for anything. Right after dinner they got in touch with Dr Parkman's agent, Charles Kingsley. Kingsley was the man who looked after the doctor's business affairs, usually some time after the doctor had thoroughly looked after them himself. Almost at once Kingsley began to search for his employer. First Family men of the prominence of Dr Parkman did not disappear in Boston – and they do not today – even for an afternoon. By night-fall Kingsley was ready to inform Robert Gould Shaw. Shaw, acting with the customary dispatch of the Proper Bostonian merchant, went at once to Boston's City Marshal, Mr Tukey. Marshal Tukey did of course what Shaw told him to do, which was to instigate an all-night search.

The next morning the merchant Shaw placed advertisements in all the papers and had 28,000 handbills distributed. The advertisements and the handbills announced a reward of $3,000 for his brother-in-law alive and $1,000 for his brother-in-law dead. The prices, considering the times, were sky-high but Shaw knew what he was doing in Yankee Boston. Before long virtually every able-bodied man, woman and child in the city was looking for Dr Parkman. They beat the bushes and they combed the streets. Slum areas were ransacked. All suspicious characters, all persons with known criminal records, were rounded up and held for questioning. Strangers in Boston were given a summary one-two treatment. An Irishman, it is recorded, attempting to change a twenty-dollar bill, was brought in to the police headquarters apparently solely on the assumption that no son of Erin, in the Boston of 1849, had any business with a bill of this size in his possession.

Every one of Dr Parkman's actions on the previous day, up to 1.40, were checked. At that time, on North Grove Street, the trail always ended. Police had to sift all manner of wild reports. One had the doctor "beguiled to East Cambridge and done in." Another had him riding in a hansom cab, his head covered with blood, being driven at "breakneck speed" over a Charles River bridge. Of the papers only the Boston *Transcript* seems to have kept its head. Its reporter managed to learn from a servant in the Parkman home that the doctor had received a caller at 9.30 Friday reminding him of a 1.30 appointment later in the day. The servant could not remember what the man looked like, but the *Transcript* printed the story in its Saturday night edition along with the reward advertisements. Most people took the caller to be some sort of front man who had appeared to lead Dr Parkman to a dastardly death. By Monday foul play was so thoroughly suspected that the shrewd merchant Shaw saw no reason to mention a sum as high as $1,000 for the body. Three thousand dollars was still the price for Dr Parkman alive but only "a suitable reward" was mentioned in Shaw's Monday handbills for Dr Parkman dead. Monday's handbills also noted the possibility of amnesia but the theory of a First Family man's mind wandering to this extent was regarded as highly doubtful. Dr Parkman, it was stated, was "perfectly well" when he left his house.

All that the Parkman case now needed to make it a complete panorama of Boston's First Family Society was the active entry of Harvard College into the picture. This occurred on Sunday morning in the person of a caller to the home of Rev. Francis Parkman, the missing doctor's brother, where the entire Family Parkman in all its ramifications had gathered. The caller was a man named John White Webster, Harvard graduate and professor of chemistry at the Harvard Medical School. He was a short squat man, fifty-six years old, who had a mass of unruly black hair and always wore thick spectacles. He had had a most distinguished career. He had studied at Guy's Hospital, London, back in 1815, where among his fellow students had been the poet John Keats. He was a member of the London Geological Society, the American Academy of Arts and Sciences, and during his twenty-five years as a Harvard professor had published numerous nationally noted scientific works. His wife, a Hickling and aunt of the soon-to-be-recognized historian William Hickling Prescott, was "well-connected" with several of Boston's First Families.

The Rev. Parkman was glad to see Professor Webster and ushered him toward the parlour expecting that his desire would be to offer sympathy to the assorted Parkmans there assembled. But Webster, it seemed, did not want to go into the parlour. Instead he spoke abruptly to the minister. "I have come to tell you," he said, "that I saw your brother at half past one o'clock on Friday." The minister was glad to have this report. Since Webster also told him he had been the caller at the Parkman home earlier that day it cleared up the mystery of the strange appointment as recorded in the *Transcript*. Webster explained he should have come sooner but had been so busy he had not seen the notices of Dr Parkman's disappearance until the previous night. The minister was also satisfied with this. Webster further declared that, at the appointment shortly after 1.30 which took place in his laboratory at the Medical School, he had paid Dr Parkman the sum of $483.64 which he had owed him. This, of course, explained why the doctor had last been seen by the merchant Fuller in such a cane-tattooing hurry. It had indeed been a matter of a debt collection.

When Professor Webster had left, Robert Gould Shaw was advised of his visit. Shaw was intimate enough in his brother-in-law's affairs to know that Webster had been owing Dr Parkman money for some time. He did not, however, know the full extent of Webster's misery. Few men have ever suffered from the retail penury side of the Proper Bostonian character as acutely as John White Webster.

The professor received a salary from Harvard of $1,200 a year. This, augmented by income from extra lectures he was able to give, might have sufficed for the average Harvard professor in those days. But Webster was not the average. His wife, for all her connections with Boston's First Families, was still a socially aspirant woman, particularly for her two daughters of debutante age. Mrs Webster and the Misses Webster entertained lavishly at their charming home in Cambridge. Professor Webster went into debt. He borrowed money here and he borrowed money there. But mostly he borrowed from Dr George Parkman.

Who better to borrow from? Dr Parkman, man of wholesale charity, Proper Bostonian merchant philanthropist. He had given Harvard College the very ground on which at that time stood its Medical School. He had endowed the Parkman Chair of Anatomy, then being occupied by the great Dr Oliver Wendell Holmes. He had himself been responsible for Webster's appointment as chemistry professor. There were no two ways about it. When Webster needed money the doctor was his obvious choice. As early as 1842 he had borrowed $400. He had then borrowed more. In 1847 he had borrowed from a group headed by Dr Parkman the sum of $2,000. For the latter he had been forced to give a mortgage on all his personal property. He knew he had little chance to pay the debt but he was banking on the generosity of the "good Dr Parkman." A year later, in 1848, he even went to Dr Parkman's brother-in-law, the merchant Shaw, and prevailed upon him to buy a mineral collection for $1,200. This was most unfortunate. The mineral collection, like the rest of Webster's property, in hock to Dr Parkman and his group, was not Webster's to sell. By so doing he had made the doctor guilty of that cardinal sin of Yankeeism – the sin of being shown up as an easy mark. No longer was there for Webster any "good Dr Parkman." "From that moment onward," says author Stewart Holbrook, "poor Professor Webster knew what it was like to have a Yankee bloodhound on his trail. His creditor was a punctilious man who paid his own obligations when due and he expected the same of everybody else, even a Harvard professor."

Dr Parkman dogged Professor Webster in the streets, outside his home, even to the classrooms. He would come in and take a front-row seat at Webster's lectures. He would not say anything; he would just sit and glare in that remarkable way of his. He wrote the professor notes, not just plain insulting notes but the awful, superior, skin-biting notes of the Yankee gentleman. He spoke sternly of legal processes. Meeting Webster he would never shout at him but instead address him in clipped Proper Bostonian accents. It was always the same question. When would the professor be "ready" for him?

Dr Parkman even bearded Professor Webster in his den, in the inner recesses of the latter's laboratory at the Medical School. He had been there, in the professor's private back room – according to the janitor of the building – on Monday evening, November 19th, just four days before he had disappeared.

The janitor was a strange man, the grim New England village type, a small person with dark brooding eyes. His name was Ephraim Littlefield. He watched with growing interest the goings-on around him. Following Webster's call on Rev. Francis Parkman, which established the farthest link yet on the trail of Dr Parkman's walk, it had of course been necessary to search the Medical School. Littlefield wanted this done thoroughly, as thoroughly for example as they were dragging the Charles River outside. He personally led the investigators to Webster's laboratory. Everything was searched, all but the private back room and adjoining privy. One of the party of investigators, which also included Dr Parkman's agent Kingsley, was a police officer named Derastus Clapp. Littlefield prevailed upon this officer to go in to the back room, but just as Clapp opened the door Professor Webster solicitously called out for him to be careful. There were dangerous articles in there, he said. "Very well, then," said Officer Clapp, "I will not go in there and get blowed up." He backed out again.

The whole search was carried on to the satisfaction of even Robert Gould Shaw who, after all, knew at firsthand the story of Webster's duplicity via the mineral collection. And who was the little janitor Ephraim Littlefield to dispute the word of the great merchant Robert Shaw? As each day went by the theory of murder was becoming more and more generally accepted, but in a Boston Society eternally geared to the mesh of a Harvard A.B. degree the idea of pinning a homicide on a Harvard man – and a professor at that – was heresy itself. One might as well pry for the body of Dr Parkman among the prayer cushions of the First Family pews in Trinity Church.

But Littlefield was not, in the socially sacrosanct meaning of the words, a "Harvard man." He was a Harvard janitor. Furthermore he was stubborn. He wanted the Medical School searched again. When it was, he was once more prodding the investigators to greater efforts. He told them they should visit the cellar of the building, down in the section where the Charles River water flowed in and carried off waste matter from the dissecting rooms and privies above. The agent Kingsley took one gentlemanly sniff from the head of the stairs and refused to accompany the janitor and the other investigators any farther. The others, however, went on. As they passed the wall under Webster's back room the janitor volunteered the information that it was now the only place in the building that hadn't been searched. Why not, the men wanted to know. The janitor explained that to get there it would be necessary to dig through the wall. The men had little stomach left for this sort of operation and soon rejoined Kingsley upstairs.

Littlefield, however, had plenty of stomach. He determined to dig into the wall himself. Whether he was by this time, Monday, already suspicious of Professor Webster has never been made clear. He had, it is true, heard the Webster–Parkman meeting of Monday night the week before. He had distinctly overheard the doctor say to the professor in that ever-insinuating way, "Something, Sir, must be accomplished." Just yesterday, Sunday, he had seen Professor Webster enter the Medical School around noontime, apparently shortly after he had made his call on Rev. Francis Parkman. Webster had spoken to him and had acted "very queerly." Come to think of it, Littlefield brooded, Sunday was a queer day for the professor to be hanging around the School anyway. "Ephraim," writes Richard Dempewolff, one of the Parkman case's most avid devotees, "was one of those shrewd New England conclusion-jumpers who, unfortunately for the people they victimize, are usually right. By putting two and two together, Mr Littlefield achieved a nice round dozen."

The janitor's wife was a practical woman. She thought little of her husband's determination to search the filthy old place under the private rooms of the Harvard professor she had always regarded as a fine gentleman. Her husband would lose this job, that would be what would happen. Just you wait and see, Mr Littlefield.

Mr Littlefield deferred to Mrs Littlefield and did wait – until Tuesday, five days after Dr Parkman's disappearance. On Tuesday something extraordinary happened. At four o'clock in the afternoon he heard Professor Webster's bell jangle, a signal that the janitor was wanted. He went to Webster's laboratory. The professor asked him if he had bought his Thanksgiving turkey yet. Littlefield did not know what to say. He replied he had thought some about going out Thanksgiving.

"Here," said Webster, "go and get yourself one." With that he handed the janitor an order for a turkey at a near-by grocery store.

John White Webster had here made a fatal error. The call he had paid on Rev. Francis Parkman had been bad enough. It had aroused the searching of the Medical School and had brought Littlefield actively into the case. But as Webster later admitted he had been afraid that sooner or later someone would have found out about his 1.30 Friday rendezvous with Dr Parkman and felt that his best chance lay in making a clean breast of it. For this action in regard to the janitor's Thanksgiving turkey, however, there could be no such defence. If he hoped to win the janitor over to "his side," then he was a poor judge of human nature indeed. Harvard Janitor Ephraim Littlefield had worked for Harvard Professor John Webster for seven years – curiously the same length of time Professor John Webster had been borrowing from Dr Parkman – without ever receiving a present of any kind. And now, a Thanksgiving turkey. Even the deferentially dormant suspicions of Mrs Littlefield were thoroughly aroused.

Janitor Littlefield had no chance to begin his labours Wednesday. Professor Webster was in his laboratory most of the day. On Thanksgiving, however, while Mrs Littlefield kept her eyes peeled for the professor or any other intruder, the janitor began the task of crow-barring his way through the solid brick wall below the back room. It was slow work and even though the Littlefields took time off to enjoy their dinner – the janitor had characteristically not passed up the opportunity to procure a nine-pound bird – it was soon obvious he could not get through the wall in one day. That evening the Littlefields took time off again. They went to a dance given by the Sons of Temperance Division of the Boston Odd Fellows. They stayed until four o'clock in the morning. "There were twenty dances," Littlefield afterwards recalled, "and I danced eighteen out of the twenty."

Late Friday afternoon, after Professor Webster had left for the day, Littlefield was at his digging again. This time he had taken the precaution of advising two of the School's First Family doctors, Doctors Bigelow and Jackson, of what he was doing. They were surprised but told him since he had started he might as well continue. But they were against his idea of informing the dean of the School, Dr Holmes, of the matter. It would, they felt, disturb the dean unnecessarily.

Even a half-hearted First Family blessing has always counted for something in Boston, and Janitor Littlefield now went to work with renewed vigour. Again his wife stood watch. At five-thirty he broke through the fifth of the five courses of brick in the wall. "I held my light forward," he afterwards declared, "and the first thing which I saw was the pelvis of a man, and two parts of a leg . . . It was no place for these things."

It was not indeed. Within fifteen minutes Doctors Bigelow and Jackson were on the scene. Later Dr Holmes himself would view the remains. Meanwhile of course there was the matter of a little trip out to the Webster home in Cambridge.

To that same police officer who had been so loath to get himself "blowed up" in Webster's back room fell the honour of making the business trip to Cambridge and arresting the Harvard professor. Once bitten, Derastus Clapp was twice shy. There would be no more monkeyshines, Harvard or no Harvard. He had his cab halt some distance from the Webster home and approached on foot. Opening the outer gate he started up the walk just as Webster himself appeared on the steps of his house, apparently showing a visitor out. The professor attempted to duck back inside. Officer Clapp hailed him. "We are about to search the Medical School again," he called, moving forward rapidly as he spoke, "and we wish you to be present." Webster feigned the traditional Harvard indifference. It was a waste of time; the

School had already been searched twice. Clapp laid a stern hand on his shoulder. Webster, escorted outward and suddenly noting two other men in the waiting cab, wanted to go back for his keys. Officer Clapp was not unaware of the drama of the moment. "Professor Webster," he said, "we have keys enough to unlock the whole of Harvard College."

Boston was in an uproar. Dr Parkman had not walked off the face of the earth. He had been pushed off – and by the authoritative hands of a Harvard professor! Even the *Transcript*, calm when there was still a hope the Parkman case was merely a matter of disappearance, could restrain itself no longer. It threw its genteel caution to the winds. There were two exclamation marks after its headline, and its editor called on Shakespeare himself to ṣum up the situation:

> Since last evening, our whole population has been in a state of the greatest possible excitement in consequence of the astounding rumor that the body of Dr Parkman has been discovered, and that Dr John W. Webster, Professor of Chemistry in the Medical School of Harvard College, and a gentleman connected by marriage with some of our most distinguished families, has been arrested and imprisoned, on suspicion of being the murderer. Incredulity, then amazement, and then blank, unspeakable horror have been the emotions, which have agitated the public mind as the rumor has gone on, gathering countenance and confirmation. Never in the annals of crime in Massachusetts has such a sensation been produced.
>
> In the streets, in the market-place, at every turn, men greet each other with pale, eager looks and the inquiry, "Can it be true?" And then as the terrible reply, "the circumstances begin to gather weight against him," is wrung forth, the agitated listener can only vent his sickening sense of horror, in some expression as that of Hamlet,—
> "O, horrible! O, horrible! most horrible!"

There is irony in the fact that proud, staid Boston chose the time it did to provide American Society with the nineteenth century's outstanding social circus. Boston was at the height of its cultural attainments in 1849. In that year a scholarly but hardly earth-shaking book by a rather minor Boston author *The History of Spanish Literature* by George Ticknor, was the world literary event of the year and the only book recommended by Lord Macaulay to Queen Victoria. Yet just three months later, on March 19, 1850, Boston put on a show which for pure social artistry Barnum himself would have had difficulty matching. The Boston courtroom had everything. It had one of Boston's greatest jurists, Judge Lemuel Shaw, on its bench; it had the only Harvard professor ever to be tried for murder, John White Webster, as its defendant; it had promised witnesses of national renown, from Dr Oliver Wendell Holmes on down; and in the offing, so to speak, it had the shades of Dr George Parkman, perhaps the most socially distinguished victim in the annals of American crime.

Nobody wanted to miss such a sight. Trains and stages from all parts of the East brought people to Boston. They wanted tickets. Everybody in Boston wanted tickets, too. Consequences of re-volutionary proportions were feared if they could not be accom-modated. Yet what to do? There was only a small gallery to spare, it having been decreed in typical Boston fashion that the main part of the courtroom would be reserved on an invitation basis. Finally, Field Marshal Tukey hit on the only possible solution, which was to effect a complete change of audience in the gallery every ten minutes during the proceedings. It took elaborate street barricades and doorway defences to do the job, but in the eleven days of the trial, to that little gallery holding hardly more than a hundred souls, came a recorded total of 60,000 persons. Con-sidering that the constabulary of Boston assigned to the job numbered just fifteen men, this feat ranks as a monumental milestone in police annals.

From the suspense angle the trial, which has been called a landmark in the history of criminal law, must have been some-thing of a disappointment. By the time it began, despite Web-ster's protestations of innocence, there was little doubt in the minds of most of the spectators as to the guilt of the professor, A few days after his arrest a skeleton measuring $70\frac{1}{2}$ inches had finally been assembled from the grisly remains found lying about under the professor's back room, and while the sum total of this was an inch taller than Dr Parkman had been in happier days, there had been no question in the minds of the coroner's jury, of Dr Holmes, and of a lot of other people, but that Dr Parkman it was. The case against the professor was one of circumstantial evidence of course. No one had seen Webster and Parkman together at the time of the murder; indeed, during the trial the time of the murder was never satisfactorily established. But the strongest Webster adherents had to admit that it was evidence of a very powerful nature, as Chief Justice Shaw could not fail to point out in his famous charge to the jury, an address which lawyers today still consider one of the greatest expositions of the nature and use of circumstantial evidence ever delivered.

There were a number of pro-Websterites. Harvard professor though he may have been, he was still the underdog, up against the almighty forces of Boston's First Families. Many of the Websterites had undoubtedly had experiences of their own on the score of Proper Bostonian retail penury and were ready to recognize that Dr Parkman had been so importunate a creditor that he had quite possibly driven the little professor first to distraction and then to the deed. They went to Rufus Choate, Boston's great First Family lawyer, and asked him to undertake the defence. After reading up on the case Choate was apparently willing to do so on the condition that Webster would admit the killing and plead manslaughter. Another First Family lawyer, old Judge Fay, with whom the Webster family regularly played whist, thought a verdict of manslaughter could be reached.

But Webster would not plead guilty. From the beginning he had made his defence an all but impossible task. He talked when he shouldn't have talked and he kept quiet when, at least by the light of hindsight, he should have come clean. On his first trip to the jail he immediately asked the officers about the finding of the body. "Have they found the *whole* body?" he wanted to know. This while certainly a reasonable question in view of the wide area over which the remains were found was hardly the thing for a man in his position to be asking. Then, while vehemently protesting his innocence, he took a strychnine pill out of his waistcoat pocket and attempted to kill himself, an attempt which was foiled only by the fact that, though the dose was a large one, he was in such a nervous condition it failed to take fatal effect. At the trial Webster maintained through his lawyers that the body he was proved to be so vigorously dismembering during his spare moments in the week following November 23rd had been a Medical School cadaver brought to him for that purpose. This was sheer folly, and the prosecution had but to call upon the little dentist, Nathan Keep, to prove it so. Tooth by tooth, during what was called one of the "tumultuous moments" of the trial, Dr Keep fitted the fragments of the false teeth found in Webster's furnace into the mould he still had in his possession. Charred as they were there could be no doubt they had once been the china-white teeth of Dr Parkman.

The spectators were treated to other memorable scenes. The great Dr Holmes testified twice, once for the State on the matter, of the identity of the reconstructed skeleton and once for the defence as a character witness for the accused. Professor Webster's character witnesses were a howitzer battery of First Family notables, among them Doctors Bigelow and Jackson, a Codman and a Lovering, the New England historian John Gorham Palfrey and Nathaniel Bowditch, son of the famed mathematician – even Harvard's president Jared Sparks took the stand for his errant employee. All seemed to agree that Webster, if occasionally irritable, was basically a kindhearted man, and President Sparks was thoughtful enough to add one gratuitous comment. "Our professors," he said, "do not often commit murder."

Credit was due Webster for his ability as a cadaver carver. He had done the job on Dr Parkman, it was established, with no more formidable instrument than a jackknife. A Dr Woodbridge Strong was especially emphatic on this point. He had dissected a good many bodies in his time, he recalled, including a rush job on a decaying pirate, but never one with just a jack-knife. Ephraim Littlefield was of course star witness for the prosecution. The indefatigable little janitor talked for one whole day on the witness stand, a total of eight hours, five hours in the morning before recess for lunch and three hours in the afternoon. Only once did he falter and that on the occasion when, under cross-examination with the defence making a valiant attempt to throw suspicion on him, he was asked if he played "gambling cards" with friends in Webster's back room. Four times the defence had to ask the question and four times Littlefield refused to answer. Finally, his New England conscience stung to the quick, he replied in exasperation, "If you ask me if I played cards there *last winter*, I can truthfully say I did not."

In those days prisoners were not allowed to testify, but on the last day of the trial Professor Webster was asked if he wanted to say anything. Against the advice of his counsel he rose and spoke for fifteen minutes. He spent most of those precious moments denying the accusation that he had written the various anonymous notes which had been turning up from time to time in the City Marshal's office ever since the disappearance of Dr Parkman. One of these had been signed CIVIS and Webster's last sentence was a pathetic plea for CIVIS to come forward if he was in the courtroom. CIVIS did not, and at eight o'clock on the evening of March 30th the trial was over.

Even the jury seems to have been overcome with pity for the professor. Before filing out of the courtroom the foreman, pointing a trembling finger at Webster, asked: "is that all? Is that the end? Can nothing further be said in defence of the man?" Three hours later the foreman and his cohorts were back, having spent, it is recorded, the first two hours and fifty-five minutes in prayer "to put off the sorrowful duty." When the verdict was delivered, "an awful and unbroken silence ensued, in which the Court, the jury, the clerk, and the spectators seemed to be absorbed in their own reflections."

Webster's hanging, by the neck and until he was dead, proceeded without untoward incident in the courtyard of Boston's Leverett Street jail just five months to the day after he had been declared guilty. Before that time, however, the professor made a complete confession. He stated that Dr Parkman had come into his laboratory on that fatal Friday and that, when he had been unable to produce the money he owed, the doctor had shown him a sheaf of papers proving that he had been responsible for getting him his professorship. The doctor then added, "I got you into your office, Sir, and now I will get you out of it." This, said Webster, so infuriated him that he seized a stick of wood off his laboratory bench and struck Dr Parkman one blow on the head. Death was instantaneous and Webster declared, "I saw nothing but the alternative of a successful removal and concealment of the body, on the one hand, and of infamy and destruction on the other." He then related his week-long attempt to dismember and burn the body. Even the clergyman who regularly visited Webster in his cell during his last days was not able to extract from the professor the admission that the crime had been premeditated. He had done it in that one frenzy of rage. "I am irritable and passionate," the clergyman quoted Webster as saying, "and Dr Parkman was the most provoking of men."

The late Edmund Pearson, recognized authority on non-fictional homicide here and abroad, has called the Webster–Parkman case America's classic murder and the one which has lived longest in books of reminiscence. Certainly in Boston's First Family Society the aftermath of the case has been hardly less distinguished than its actual occurrence. To this day no Proper Bostonian grandfather autobiography is complete without some reference to the case. The Beacon Hill house at 8 Walnut Street from which Dr Parkman started out on his walk that Friday morning almost a hundred years ago is still standing, and its present occupant, a prominent Boston lawyer, is still on occasion plagued by the never-say-die curious.

Among Boston Parkmans the effect was a profound one. For years certain members of the Family shrank from Society altogether, embarrassed as they were by the grievous result of Dr Parkman's financial punctiliousness and all too aware of the sympathy extended Professor Webster in his budgetary plight, In the doctor's immediate family it is noteworthy that his widow headed the subscription list of a fund taken up to care for Webster's wife and children. Dr Parkman's son, George Francis Parkman, was five years out of Harvard in 1849. He had been, in contrast to his father, a rather gay blade as a youth and at college had taken part in Hasty Pudding Club theatricals; at the time of the murder he was enjoying himself in Paris. He returned to Boston a marred man. He moved his mother and sister from 8 Walnut Street and took a house at 33 Beacon Street. From the latter house he buried his mother and aunt, and there he and his sister lived on as Boston Society's most distinguished recluses. His solitary existence never included even the solace of a job. Describing him as he appeared a full fifty years after the crime a biographer records:

> Past the chain of the bolted door on Beacon Street no strangers, save those who came on easily recognised business, were ever allowed to enter. Here George Francis Parkman and his sister Harriet, neither of whom ever married, practised the utmost frugality, the master of the house going himself to the market every day to purchase their meager provisions, and invariably paying cash for the simple supplies he brought home.
>
> The windows of his house looked out upon the Common but he did not frequent it . . . He always walked slowly and alone, in a stately way, and attracted attention by his distinguished though retiring appearance . . . In cool weather he wore a heavy coat of dark cloth and his shoulders and neck were closely wrapped with a wide scarf, the ends of which were tucked into his coat or under folds. He sheltered himself against the east winds of Boston just as he seemed, by his manner, to shelter his inmost self from contact with the ordinary affairs of men.

Tremors of the Parkman earthquake continued to be felt by Boston Society often at times when they were least desired. Twenty years later, when Boston was privileged to play proud host to Charles Dickens, there was a particularly intense tremor. Dickens was asked which one of the city's historic landmarks he would like to visit first. "The room where Dr Parkman was murdered," he replied, and there being no doubt he meant what he said, nothing remained for a wry-faced group of Boston's best but to shepherd the distinguished novelist out to the chemistry laboratory of the Harvard Medical School.

A Webster–Parkman story, vintage of 1880, is still told today by Boston's distinguished author and teacher, Bliss Perry. He recalls that for a meeting of New England college officers at

Williamstown, Massachusetts, his mother had been asked to put up as a guest in her house Boston's First Family poet laureate, diplomat and first editor of the *Atlantic*, James Russell Lowell. Unfortunately Lowell was at that time teaching at Harvard and for all his other accomplishments Mrs Perry would have none of him. He had to be quartered elsewhere.

"I could not sleep," Mrs Perry said, "if one of those Harvard professors were in the house."

THE MURDERER WHO GOT AWAY WITH IT

(John Donald Merrett, UK 1926)

Macdonald Hastings

*This case presents one of the few occasions in which a human ear –
that of a murder victim – was produced in court as evidence. John
Donald Merrett was only eighteen when he was tried for the murder
of his mother. Mrs Merrett had been found in her sitting-room with a
bullet hole above her right ear. Her son, who inherited a fortune on
her death, claimed she had shot herself. At the young man's trial, the
Crown's ballistics experts claimed that the wound could not have
been self-inflicted. For one thing, Mrs Merrett could not have
mustered the strength needed to pull the trigger, and for another,
there were no powder burns around the bullet hole. The opinion of the
experts was that such burns would have been there if the gun had been
fired at close range by Mrs Merrett herself. The celebrated pathologist Sir Bernard Spilsbury, appearing for once for the defence,
disagreed. He testified that it was quite possible for the wound to have
been self-inflicted, explaining the absence of powder burns by pointing out that they would have been washed away by bleeding and in
the course of cleaning the wound. Although the case against young
Merrett was strong – he had also forged his mother's signature on
several hundred pounds'-worth of cheques – the jury felt unable to
disregard the sworn evidence of the great Spilsbury. Because the case
was tried in Scotland, they were able to return a verdict of Not
Proven on the murder charge. (Merrett was convicted of forgery and
was jailed for a year). Merrett resurfaced as Ronald Chesney more*

than a quarter of a century later, when he killed his wife and mother-
in-law and finally himself. The Merrett case was told by the writer
and broadcaster Macdonald Hastings (1909–82) in his biography of
Robert Churchill, the ballistics expert whose evidence featured in
many British murder trials in the 1920s and 1930s.

The newspaper headline, "NOW IT CAN BE TOLD," on February
17, 1954, announced that a controversy of the criminal courts
which had been the cause of debate, often bitter debate, for
twenty-eight years was at last resolved. Churchill and Spilsbury
were two of the central figures in the argument. The case was
essentially a conflict between experts, one which subsequently
lent weight to murmurings of doubt as to what value could be
reposed on the evidence of specialist witnesses. To make a cool
assessment of it, the story of the nefarious career of John Donald
Merrett is one which is best considered, not from its beginning,
but from its end.

On February 16, 1954, Ronald John Chesney, one of several
aliases which John Donald Merrett adopted during his life, was
found shot dead through the mouth in a wood on the outskirts of
Cologne. A Colt automatic, an ugly weapon which blew off the
top of his head, lay at his side. He had committed suicide; and
none too soon. He was wanted for the murder of his wife and
mother-in-law, who ran an Old Folks' Home in the normally safe
respectability of the London suburb of Ealing.

He killed his wife with the intention of obtaining a sum of
money he had settled on her many years before which he himself
had inherited from his mother after she too had had a violent end.
He killed his mother-in-law because she had the misfortune to
discover him when he was faking the appearance that his wife's
death was accidental.

It was a disappointing outcome for him, because he had put
himself to some trouble to prove that he could not have had any
part in the affair. He had previously made a visit to England from
Germany, a country where he had business interests and a
girlfriend, during which he stole a passport from a man he

met in a pub, and made a sufficient exhibition of himself at the port of departure to secure that he had an alibi. He subsequently returned on the stolen passport. His wife's murder – he sank her body in a bath – might possibly have passed as an accident if his mother-in-law hadn't interrupted him.

Thereafter it was only a matter of time before the police were on his trail. Merrett, alias Chesney, had a criminal record which identified him all over Europe. He shot himself because he recognized that his number was up.

At the age of seventeen and a half, on March 17, 1926, he had shot his mother through the side of the head. His reason was that he had been forging her signature on cheques, and was afraid that he was going to be found out. His history has become famous for the fact that, when he was tried in Edinburgh for matricide, the Scottish jury of ten men and five women brought in a majority verdict of "Not proven." He was merely sent to prison for twelve months for uttering forged cheques.

In his autobiography, Sir Sydney Smith, Emeritus Professor of Forensic Medicine at Edinburgh University, expresses the feeling that the verdict aroused among experts at the time:

> The slackness of the police and the credit given to the misleading evidence of Spilsbury and Churchill, who had made a mistake and were too stubborn to admit it, allowed Merrett to live – and to kill again. A worthless life was saved, and two innocent women were thereby condemned to die.

In retrospect, no one can fairly disagree with Sir Sydney's summing up of the case, except perhaps with the justice of his comment that Churchill and Spilsbury "made a mistake and were too stubborn to admit it." That opinion rests on what I believe to be a delicate and still unresolved point of professional conduct – the question as to how far the expert witness, especially when he appears for the defence, should volunteer evidence of value to the other side.

Churchill always insisted that he gave his evidence irrespective of whether it helped the prosecution or the defence. He refused

on principle to support Marshall Hall's plea in the Green Bicycle
Case. On several occasions, when he was called for the Crown, his
evidence destroyed the Crown's case. During the Merrett trial,
when a newspaper reporter asked him, "Do you think the prisoner is guilty?" he replied: "I don't know. I am only interested in
the firearms side of the case."

With the knowledge that Merrett was certainly guilty, it is
interesting to imagine oneself as a juryman in the trial before the
Lord Justice-Clerk (Lord Alness) which began at Edinburgh on
February 1, 1927, when what had previously passed as a suicide
case had been transformed into a charge of murder.

It is so perilously easy to be wise after the event that, on the facts
of the case, one wonders that the jury were ever in doubt. The
defence made scarcely an effort to clear Merrett of the charge that
he had forged his mother's signature on her cheques. The
evidence was overwhelming that, while he was supposed to be
a student at Edinburgh University, he was playing the Casanova
at cheap dance halls. He had purchased for £1 15s, after obtaining
a firearms' certificate from the police (on what grounds heaven
knows), a .25 automatic pistol of Spanish make with fifty rounds
of ammunition from Hardy Brothers in Princes Street. He was
alone in the room with his mother when she was shot. He had the
motive, the opportunity, and the means. The case rested on
whether it could be proved, without possibility of doubt, that
he did indeed shoot his mother, and that she didn't shoot herself.

Merrett had the inestimable advantage as a murderer that he
didn't run away. When he shot his mother, through the lobe of
her ear shortly after breakfast, he reported the event to the daily
maid. When the police came they never questioned that it was a
case of attempted suicide. Poor Mrs Merrett was detained at the
Royal Infirmary, Edinburgh, in a cell with barred windows in the
shadow that on her discharge arrangements would be made for
taking her into custody for attempted *felo de se*.

With a bullet in her head, she lived astonishingly for a fortnight. She told her nurses that she had heard "a kind of explo-
sion." She was surprised that a pistol was involved. "Did Donald
do it?" she asked. "He is such a naughty boy." Before he shot her

she remembered that she said: "Go away, Donald, and don't annoy me." Up to her death she never accused him. At the trial the judge described the failure of the police to take a dying deposition from her as "an almost criminal neglect of an obvious and imperative duty."

From the beginning the police and the doctors were at fault. The police, believing that it was a suicide case, failed to make a conclusive record of the position of the weapon and the body, and produced a witness in the daily maid who contradicted her story twice. Professor Harvey Littlejohn, the eminent pathologist of Edinburgh University, concluded from the post-mortem examination that the case was consistent with suicide. It was only later that it was discovered that Mrs Merrett's son had "uttered as genuine" twenty-nine cheques upon her bank account. Only then was he charged with murder and forgery.

Mrs Merrett believed that her husband, who had deserted her many years earlier, was dead. It emerged in the trial that he wasn't. There is reason to suppose that John Alfred Merrett had associations with the Secret Service.* Otherwise, it is difficult to understand how such a formidable, expensive, and determined defence was organised on his son's behalf. Mr Craigie M. Aitchison, KC, was briefed to represent him. Even more remarkable, Bernard Spilsbury, who had never appeared in any case except for the Crown, and Churchill, who himself normally gave evidence for the Director of Public Prosecutions, were called for Merrett's defence. It is one of those trials, like Mrs Barney's five years later, in which the circumstances are charged with question-marks.

Churchill himself said that he had never worked so hard on any case in which he had been called: "I took my wife with me to Edinburgh during the ten days I was there with the idea of making some visits to friends after Court hours, but counsel for the defence was indefatigable. We had conferences each evening

* Major Hugh B. C. Pollard writes: "Informed gossip at the time held that Merrett's father was a rather important figure in Intelligence in South America; not necessarily under the same name. Mrs Merrett was dead and 'reasons of State' are sometimes more important than the conviction of a horrible adolescent."

after dinner in which we went right through the transcript of the shorthand notes of the day's proceedings and prepared the next day's work as well."

The trial settled into a conflict between experts; and nine of them were called. The choice was to decide whether the shot which killed Mrs Merrett was sufficiently close to be self-inflicted or at a range sufficiently far to establish that the gun must have been fired by her son. It is important to remember that, at the time, the prejudice of the jury was in favour of suicide; and that the men and women on it were reluctant to convict a youth of the unnatural crime of murdering his own mother. Further, the evidence for the prosecution was inconclusive.

Professor Harvey Littlejohn, the chief medical witness for the Crown, had asserted after the post-mortem examination in April 1926 that:

> there is nothing to indicate the distance at which the discharge of the weapon took place, whether from a few inches or a greater distance. So far as the position of the wound is concerned, the case is consistent with suicide. There is some difficulty in attributing it to accident, although such a view cannot wholly be excluded.

When Sir Sydney Smith suggested to him that it was murder Professor Littlejohn, after various experiments, made a new report with a different conclusion, over a month after Merrett had been charged with the murder of his mother. Counsel for the defence didn't let him forget that he had changed his mind.

In fact, there wasn't a large difference in the factual evidence, although there was an important difference in conclusion, given by the experts on both sides. Merrett would have hanged if it could have been established that the bullet which killed his mother was fired at more than three inches' range. At a lesser range there was a reasonable doubt as between suicide and murder. It was that matter of inches which saved Merrett's neck.

Not the least difficulty of the nine experts on both sides was that there was no evidence of scorching or tattooing – or if there had been it had been swabbed away – round the wound through the lobe of Mrs Merrett's ear. If evidence of scorching from the powder in the cartridge could have been established it would have materially assisted the case for the defence because it would have shown that the pistol was fired from a range close enough to admit that the possibility of suicide couldn't be discounted.

The experts for the prosecution, led by Professor Harvey Littlejohn, waffled. Littlejohn, after reporting that the case was "consistent with suicide," changed his mind and made his second report that there was no indication of blackening or tattooing by ingrained particles of powder to suggest a near shot; "i.e. within 3″ of head." Professor Glaister said in evidence: "I am unable to exclude absolutely the production of such a wound as in this case by self-infliction." Mr McNaughten, the Edinburgh gunmaker, stated that the explosive in the pistol was "a modified form of cordite, called smokeless powder, which caused less discolouration than gunpowder."

By contrast, Churchill and Spilsbury commanded the court. Sir Sydney Smith, who had no love for either of them, makes in his autobiography a notable back-handed compliment:

> To counter Littlejohn's expert evidence they put up Sir Bernard Spilsbury, the Home Office pathologist, who was very brilliant and very famous, but fallible like the rest of us – and very, very obstinate. In England, where he always appeared for the Crown, many murderers were justly convicted on his evidence. Now he was making one of his rare appearances for the defence. With him was Robert Churchill, often described as the expert on ballistics. Robert Churchill was famous, too, and I am sure he was an excellent gunsmith. He also was stubborn and dogmatic. He and Spilsbury often appeared together in shooting cases, and they were indeed a formidable team – terrifying when they made a mistake, as they did here.

But did they? Merrett, as subsequent events proved, was guilty. But Spilsbury and Churchill were called to show that it was *possible*, on the existing evidence, that Mrs Merrett committed suicide. At the time nobody except Merrett himself knew any more. In that knowledge it is difficult to accept that Churchill's and Spilsbury's evidence was "mistaken." Churchill's own opinion was that the other side made a mess of the case. The prosecution insisted that it was impossible for Mrs Merrett's wound to have been self-inflicted, although their own expert witnesses were uncertain in the matter. Churchill and Spilsbury did no more than demonstrate that suicide was, in fact, a possibility.

Together they had worked hard on the case. Churchill maintained that the absence of scorching or blackening round Mrs Merrett's wound wasn't significant. "Smokeless powder will mark paper or cardboard but it will not indelibly mark skin. Experiments with animal skin are not satisfactory; it doesn't respond like live human flesh. Superficial powder blackening round a wound may be washed away by the flow of blood. This was especially true," Churchill added, "in the Merrett case where the weapon was a little .25 automatic pistol. The cartridge, with a two-grain charge of nitrocellulose powder, consumed itself within an inch of leaving the barrel. Our London experiments with a similar pistol confirmed this view."

Bernard Spilsbury insisted on the experiment. When Churchill told him that shooting at inanimate targets would prove nothing Spilsbury sent the word round the London hospitals that he wanted a lump of human flesh. In due course the amputated leg of an elderly woman patient was provided. Wrapped in a brown-paper parcel, the two experts took the macabre object in the train to Churchill's shooting grounds in Kent. They hadn't got the pistol in the case, but they used a weapon of the same calibre and ammunition from the same shop that Merrett had bought his own gun. At varying distances, firing at the amputated leg, they established that there was no trace of a powder-mark on the skin.

Churchill himself wasn't entirely happy with the experiment. He said to me years later that, if it had been any other than Spilsbury, counsel would have challenged his evidence by pointing out that the reaction of dead flesh is quite different from living flesh. But Churchill himself was in no doubt that the evidence of the experiment, such as it was, was of no significance.

Curiously enough, Professor Harvey Littlejohn, for the prosecution, had been experimenting with shots into human flesh himself.

Littlejohn, using Merrett's pistol, found that at three inches the automatic "left very definite powder and burning marks round the wound in the skin area. Further, the discoloration on the skin couldn't be readily washed off." Later Churchill and Spilsbury attended a demonstration in Edinburgh of test shots at white cardboard with the same pistol with similar results. Churchill believed that neither the results on cardboard on that occasion nor the dead flesh in his experiments with Spilsbury in London were conclusive.

He knew that Hugh Pollard, behind the scenes, had constructed ear membranes of a glycerine and gelatine substance which he had tested to see if any confidence could be reposed in the absence, or otherwise, of blackening. There was no decisive information to be drawn from that experiment either.

In his evidence Churchill described the scorching effect that a small automatic at close range would have on live human skin. But he advanced an explanation of Mrs Merrett's death, subsequently supported by Spilsbury, and the judge too, which transformed the case. Examining him, Mr Craigie Aitchison asked:

"Have you in your experience had a case of a suicidal wound behind the right ear?"

"Yes."

"Was that the case of a man or woman?"

"The case of a woman."

"Who shot herself behind the right ear?"

"Yes."

"Was the weapon directed forwards or backwards?"

"Forwards."

"Did it roughly correspond to the direction of the wound in this case?"

"Yes, roughly."

"And was that an undoubted case of suicide?"

"It was brought in as suicide."

"It has been suggested, but I do not think persisted in, that, in order to get the weapon into such a position as to produce a wound of the kind we have here, the hand would need to be put into a strained position. What do you say to that?"

"I say that it is quite possible to reproduce that wound without any movement of the arm at all – just a movement of the head. I teach shooting, and I find that women flinch from the discharge at first, by closing their eyes and by turning the head away from the discharge instinctively."

"Does it come to this, that supposing the weapon were pointed at the side of the temple, an instinctive movement of the head, without any movement of the arm, might get the pistol into the position that would give you the direction we have in this case?"

"You could reproduce this wound exactly by doing that."

"In your view, can the angle be easily accounted for on the view that the pistol was pointed at the temple, but there was an instinctive aversion of the head at the moment the trigger was pulled?"

"It is possible to reproduce this wound in that way."

"And, if this was a case of suicide, would you, from your experience of instinctive movements of the head when firearms are fired, think it a likely thing to occur?"

"Yes. I have also considered the wound from the point of view of accident."

"In your view, could a wound of this kind, having regard to all the facts, direction and so on, have been accidentally caused?"

"I could reproduce that wound by holding the pistol with the thumb on the trigger-guard and the fingers of the hand at the butt of the pistol."

"Assume that Mrs Merrett – she seeing the pistol in the bureau – had picked it up in that position, and assuming that she over-balanced and fell, is there any difficulty at all in getting an accidental discharge that would produce a wound in the head such as you find here?"

"No."

Churchill demonstrated his theory by putting his thumb on the trigger, with the butt of the pistol in the palm of the hand, and jarring the back of the hand on the ledge of the witness-box, the muzzle being pointed towards the head and the face averted from the pistol.

"Accordingly, are the facts in your view consistent with accident?"

"Accident is possible."

"Similarly, supposing that, having lost her balance at the moment the pistol was in her hand, she instinctively raised her hand to her head to protect her head in the fall, is there any difficulty in getting the pistol into a position that is consistent with accident?"

"There is no difficulty in getting the pistol into position, but I should not expect it to happen that way. I think I have given the two most likely ways that this could happen. I think the most likely way is to pick the pistol up with the thumb on the trigger guard and to fall on it."

"Which might happen if Mrs Merrett had her chair tilted up at the time?"

"It is possible to reproduce the wound in that way."

"Is it in accordance with your knowledge and experience of firearms that accidents occur which it is sometimes impossible to explain?"

"It is impossible to explain some of them."

"In the case of gunshot wounds where you are using a gun – I mean suicidal wounds where you are using a gun – where do you usually find them, or where do you often find them?"

"Usually in the mouth."

"Where you have a suicidal wounds from a long-barrelled revolver, where do you frequently find them?"

"Usually in the temple. I am saying usually, because sometimes they are in the mouth."

"But when you find a wound inflicted with a short-barrelled firearm, such as the automatic pistol you hold in your hand, where do you usually find them?"

"Usually in the side of the head. A shotgun, on account of its very long barrel, naturally can only be placed in the mouth. A long-barrelled revolver can be placed in the mouth, because there is something you can put in; and also it can be put, on account of its length, at the side of the head. But with an automatic pistol, such as I have in my hand, it is natural to do it at the side."

"Taking all the facts as you have them in this case, do you find anything in the position or the direction of the wound to exclude either suicide or accident?"

"No."

He was cross-examined by the Lord Advocate:

"Take first of all your suggested possible method, that of suicide, which you have demonstrated, are you assuming that this is a woman who is not skilled in firing pistols?"

"A woman who is nervous of firearms, and I find that every woman is nervous at first."

"Is it a very uncommon thing for a woman to commit suicide with a pistol?"

"I have had a few cases. Naturally, it is not common."

"And still more uncommon for women who are ignorant of the use of such weapons?"

"I would say that."

"Among these few cases, was there any one of a woman committing suicide with a pistol in the presence of a near relative, such as a son?"

"In one case a woman committed suicide for no apparent reason. The shot was behind the ear, and no action was taken against the husband, who was asleep in a chair alongside. That is the only case I can cite near to this."

"Assuming that sitting in the chair Mrs Merrett put her elbow at the angle you have suggested, it would come in contact, or risk coming into contact, with the bureau. Does not that exclude the possibility of your theory?"

"No."

"If it did come in contact, it would upset it. If there was a risk it would render it doubtful?"

"Yes."

"Come now to your suggestion of accident. The only suggestion you make, as I understand, is that the thumb goes into the trigger guard with the hand grasping the butt of the pistol?"

"Yes."

"But, surely, the person so grasping it must have known the pistol was there?"

"That is right."

"You could not put any papers between, or the thumb would not go into the trigger guard, would it?"

"No."

"Were you assuming that the pistol was picked up off the bureau?"

"I am simply assuming that the lady was sitting in the chair and was stretching out."

"You do not know whether she needed to tip the chair or not in order to reach the pigeon-holes?"

"No."

"Or whether it would be possible for her to tilt the chair?"

"I expect that in the case of accident she would have to tip the chair to fall."

"Are you assuming that she is sitting at an angle to the bureau, with her back half towards it?"

"Yes, falling back on the right hand against the bureau."

"The effect of that would be to jerk the pistol out of her hand, probably, would it not?"

"I am assuming that she falls on to the pistol."

"You are assuming that she stretched towards the pigeon-hole to get the pistol out of it?"

"Yes."

"Are you aware that there are some 20 inches between the pigeon-hole and the edge of the writing slab on the bureau?"

"No, I do not know."

"So that the pit of her arm would be touching the writing slab as she reached for the pistol?"

"I do not know that."

"That would rather affect the theory that you are putting forward?"

"It would, if the body were stopped by this bureau."

"You made certain experiments in London. It was you who actually did the firing?"

"Yes."

"Were those experiments made with a different pistol and different cartridges and gunpowder to those which we know were used in this case?"

"Yes, a pistol of similar make, of Spanish manufacture, and the ammunition supposedly of similar but of later make."

"It was a different maker, was it not?"

"It was Nobel's ammunition. They are all one combine."

"Do I understand that you experimented on both skin and cardboard in London and in Edinburgh?"

"Yes."

"Did the powder used in London produce more of a yellowish colour and not so black as in Edinburgh?"

"The powder used in London produced more tattooing."

"But was not the colour more of a yellowish tinge?"

"Slightly flame."

"You would agree, in view of your experience, that the advisable thing in every case is to carry out tests with the actual weapon, and with as identical powder and ammunition as you can get?"

"Yes."

"On the Sunday, 30th January, eight days ago, was it you who actually fired the pistol?"

"Yes."

"Was the pistol in good working order?"

"Yes."

He was re-examined by Mr Aitchison:

"You were asked whether you knew of any case in which a mother had shot herself in the presence of her son. You do recollect a case in which a wife shot herself in the presence of her husband?"

"Yes."

"And there was a Home Office investigation?"

"Yes."

"Was that established as a case of suicide?"

"Yes."

"And did the investigations reveal any motive of any kind?"

"No motive."

Churchill was followed into the box by Sir Bernard Spilsbury. Spilsbury added the opinion that women, through the lifelong habit of putting up their hair, had a great extension of the shoulder-joint and, as a consequence, it was possible to imagine that Mrs Merrett could hold a small pistol in a position to point it at the back of her skull. He insisted that her wound could not be considered as definitely inflicted by another person. Spilsbury said that he thought it was suicide.

The assuredness of the two expert witnesses for the defence undoubtedly carried the jury. The judge was equally impressed. In his summing up, in Scotland called "the charge to the jury," Lord Alness said that the chief objection suggested to the theory of suicide from the direction of the wound was that it would involve a constrained position of the arm on firing. "Well, you will consider whether that objection was not met, or invalidated, by the exceptionally simple suggestion made by the London gun expert, Mr Churchill, that a sudden and instinctive aversion of the head by the person who was going to fire the pistol would naturally account for the position of the wound, without any constrained position of the arm."

The jury brought in the middle verdict of "Not Proven" on the murder charge. While Scottish law is often criticised in England, it meant exactly what it said. Merrett wasn't proved guilty, but the jury thought he was. Further, it is unarguable that Spilsbury and Churchill between them saved his unworthy neck, although Churchill himself gave all the credit to the counsel for the defence.

"Mr Craigie Aitchison, afterwards Lord Aitchison, was in my opinion the best cross-examiner I ever heard. The way he used the Scottish phrase 'come awa' with it' to a witness until the witness did indeed 'come awa' with it' was wonderful. I was very tickled when, in examination, he waved his fingers prettily at Sir Bernard Spilsbury and said, more phonetically than I can write it: 'Now tell me, Saint Berr-nard!' In court, it passed unnoticed.

"The book of the case in the 'Notable British Trials' series does not reveal the skill with which Craigie Aitchison conducted his defence, how he threw quick-fire questions at one witness until he had conceded his point; how he played with another, not so intelligent, until he had got the evidence he wanted. Craigie Aitchison and his junior got Merrett off. In that case, counsel was the Scottish Marshall Hall, Muir and Norman Birkett rolled into one."

History has placed the blame for Merrett's acquittal firmly on the shoulders of Churchill and Spilsbury. It is undeniable that the evidence of the two best witnesses in the land influenced the judge and the jury. It is probably true that neither Spilsbury nor Churchill believed that Merrett was innocent. The heart of the affair is simply whether they thought, as they did, that Mrs Merrett's death could possibly have been caused by suicide or accident. It is a matter of conscience to decide whether it was right for Spilsbury and Churchill to advance the best argument that they could for the defence, or whether they should have refused to appear at all. Myself, I don't know the answer.

PICTURE A MURDERER

(Edwin Bush, UK 1961)

Richard Jackson

Identifying a suspect in a murder case can be a hazardous business. Witnesses are often confused, sometimes frightened, occasionally mistaken. But their ability to recall facial characteristics can be crucial. In the late 1950s, new techniques were developed to improve the likeness achieved by a combination of witness descriptions and artists' impressions. The first of these facial assembly techniques was known as "Identikit". Guided by an eye-witness, a skilled operator assembled transparencies of the suspect's key facial features into a two-dimensional composite. The picture could then be circulated by the police. In 1961, Edwin Bush became the first murder suspect in Britain to be brought to book by the Identikit method of compiling a picture of a suspect's face. Bush was arrested within four days of the Identikit's publication by a policeman on patrol. Richard Jackson (1902–75) was assistant commissioner (CID) at New Scotland Yard. But by training and temperament he was a criminal lawyer rather than a policeman, and an excellent raconteur, a trait that endeared him to the press. He held and expressed trenchant views of a range of subjects, including the need for tough sentences for violent criminals and a detestation of liberal reformers. When he retired in 1963, Richard Jackson received a knighthood and wrote his memoirs, in which he recalled how the new-fangled Identikit technique resulted in the arrest and conviction of a killer.

"If this paper remains blue," Sherlock Holmes told Watson, "all is well. If it turns red, it means a man's life." He dipped the litmus paper into a test tube and it flushed into a dull, dirty crimson . . .

Conan Doyle's stories may have had some influence in showing the police how science can be used as an aid to detection, and even more influence in leading the public to think of forensic science as a kind of magic. It is a very useful aid; it isn't a kind of magic. Criminals are caught by men, not by gadgets.

Forensic science has, of course, tremendously advanced since Sherlock Holmes's day, particularly in its ability to show, by matching minute particles of soil or dust or thread or cellulose, that a suspect must have been at the scene of the crime. As well as the laboratory techniques which support them, as it were, behind the lines, the police have acquired a number of gadgets to help both in their preventive and in their investigative work. Rapidly coming into use now are personal two-way radios carried by constables on the beat, hidden television cameras to keep a watch on vulnerable streets and markets and car parks, and an infra-red spotlight for use at night.

One device which we acquired during my period at the Yard caught the public imagination more than any other – the Identikit.

I first heard about it on July 30th, 1959. At a lunch that day in the Café Royal I met a huge genial giant of a man, called Pete Pitchess. He had been in the FBI and was now Sheriff of Los Angeles County. After lunch he came back to the Yard to see the Black Museum and the Information Room. When we were having a drink in my room afterwards, with a few senior officers whom I'd invited to meet him, he showed us a piece of equipment which had been invented by his Deputy, Hugh McDonald. It was a book of interchangeable transparent flaps, each with a drawing of some part of a face – eyes, eyebrows, hairline, nose, mouth, and so on; rather like those books in which children put the head of a giraffe on to the body of a lion and the legs of an ostrich. With this range of possible parts, Pitchess said, a useful picture of a wanted man could be built up from the selection made by a witness who had seen him.

There was nothing new, of course, about constructing pictures from eyewitnesses' descriptions. As long ago as 1935, when I was prosecuting in the Grierson case, I was struck by what a good likeness the police drawing had been of the man who eventually appeared in the dock; it was a profile, I remember, with a hooked nose and glasses. But in Britain (contrary to the practice in some other countries) the artist didn't normally work with the witness; he merely followed a description which was handed to him. And a witness who is shown a completed drawing is too apt to accept it, whereas an Identikit picture can be continually altered until the witness really does feel satisfied that it represents the face he saw.

I showed the Identikit to the Commissioner, and we both expressed interest in the possibility of acquiring it. A week or so later I received a letter from the American company which manufactured the equipment. (If the company had been British I dare say I should never have heard any more about it, not for months or years anyway.) Pitchess had told them of our interest, they said; they were willing to consider leasing it to us, and they invited us to send an officer to California for a course of training. I replied that I couldn't spare a man. There was further correspondence, during which they asked me, among other things, for a list of every police force in Britain with more than a hundred officers. I sent it to them. They pondered on the size of the potential market, and, the following spring, offered to send their representative to Scotland Yard, to run a course of instruction here.

After clearing this proposal with the Commissioner, the Receiver, and the Home Office I circulated it to all provincial forces through the Chief Officers Association and the Chief Constables of Scotland Association. The response was gratifying. We finally arranged a three-day course for the beginning of March 1961.

The class consisted of thirty-one officers – ten detective sergeants from the Metropolitan Police, twenty provincial officers, and one officer from the United States Air Force. Superintendent Du Rose of C1 was in charge, and the instruction was given by Deputy Sheriff Hugh McDonald himself, who proved to be extremely good.

The course ended on Friday, March 3rd. A detective sergeant

from "H" Division went back to his duties next day, and, using the Identikit, was immediately able to catch three men who had committed a robbery. But a more serious crime had been reported in "E" Division.

At 12.15 p.m. that Friday, before the Identikit course was even ended, I heard that a woman had been found stabbed to death in an antique shop in Cecil Court, off the Charing Cross Road. The body had been discovered by the proprietor, Louis Meier. A wireless car from Bow Street arrived, and the officers found the dead woman lying on her back with an antique dagger stuck in her breast and another in her neck.

She was Mrs Elsie May Batten, and she had been an assistant in the shop. The daggers, which had evidently been taken from the stock, still had their price tickets on them.

At 12.30 Detective Superintendent Pollard arrived. In those first few hours his chances of success seemed steadily to dwindle. There was no reason to suppose – and, since the weapons were clearly impromptu, it seemed unlikely – that Mrs Batten had been killed by a personal enemy; nor had she been sexually assaulted. Robbery was the likeliest motive, but her handbag and the box used as a till both appeared to be untouched; Mr Meier couldn't say if anything had been removed from his stock. Local inquiries elicited nothing. A hairdresser opposite had seen Mrs Batten open the shop at 9.15, but since then nobody had been observed going in or out. The only clue Pollard found was a piece of wood under the dead woman's legs, bearing the impression of a heel and faint sole marks.

When the pathologist, Dr Keith Simpson, arrived halfway through the afternoon he found a third dagger underneath the body and a third stab wound in the back. He said the woman had also been struck on the head with a heavy stone ornament, and he confirmed that there had been no sexual interference.

Then things began to move. A fifteen-year-old boy, an apprentice sign-writer, was brought to the police by his uncle. The boy had told his uncle, and now told us, that he had gone into Meier's shop at about half-past eleven that morning to buy a billiard cue, and had seen what he thought was a dummy lying on the floor at the back. When he realized it was a woman he assumed she had fainted – and promptly left the shop. Which doesn't seem a very chivalrous act. Perhaps he was a timid boy.

Meanwhile Meier recalled that a young man who said he was half-Indian and half-English had been in the shop during Mrs Batten's lunch hour on the previous day. This Eurasian had spent some time examining the antique daggers, but had left without buying anything. He had returned later, accompanied by a girl, and asked the price of a dress sword. Mrs Batten had remarked to Meier afterwards that it was odd for a man so poorly dressed to be interested in a sword costing £15. Meier gave us a description of the young man, and said he thought that he would be able to recognize him. All he could remember about the girl was that she looked somewhere between seventeen and twenty, and was fair-haired. There were several dress swords in the shop, and he couldn't say if any of them were missing.

A team of twenty detectives, under Superintendent Pollard, began working their way through all the other antique shops and jewellers. But they found what they wanted, next morning, only a few yards away.

Opposite Meier's shop was a gunmaker. His nineteen-year-old son had been alone there on the morning of the murder when, soon after 10 a.m., a young Indian walked in and tried to sell him a dress sword. The sword had been wrapped in a sheet of brown paper. When he was asked how much he wanted for it the Indian replied, "I paid fifteen pounds, but I'll take ten." The gunmaker's son rightly thought this a suspicious remark. He asked the Indian to come back at 11.15, when his father would be in. The Indian agreed and left the sword, but never returned.

The gunmaker himself now added a piece of information. A dark young man – he couldn't remember much else about his looks – had called at the shop on the previous afternoon, and asked, "Do you buy swords?" The gunmaker said he might, but he would need to see the article. The young man replied that this sword had an engraving on it, and he promised to bring it in.

So we now had the sword. It was immediately identified by another woman who worked part-time in Meier's shop, and who remembered having shown it to a customer the week before. The brown paper had gone, having been used to wrap up a pair of gun-barrels, but Pollard's men traced it to a customer in Kilburn, and sent it, together with the sword, to the fingerprint department at the Yard.

Meier and the gunmaker's son were each able to give a clear and detailed description of the young Eurasian; so, less than twenty-four hours after the course had ended, we had an ideal opportunity for giving Identikit a trial run. On March 4th one of the officers who had been on the course, Detective Sergeant Dagg, interviewed Meier and the gunmaker's son – separately – and built up pictures matching the descriptions they gave him. The two pictures proved strikingly similar, except for one detail: the hair style was quite different.

I was shown photographs of these two Identikit reconstructions. They looked good enough to be useful and close enough to one another not to cause confusion. I decided that not only should they both be circulated to all police forces, but they should also be published in the Press and shown on television. At the same time we released Meier's much vaguer description of the girl.

Four days later, at 1.40 p.m., a certain PC Cole was on duty in Old Compton Street, Soho, when he spotted a young man who seemed to match the picture. And the young man was accompanied by a girl of about seventeen with blonde hair. Cole stopped them, and told the man that he fitted the description of someone wanted for questioning in connection with the Cecil Court murder.

"Yes, I saw the photo in the paper," said the young man casually. "It did look a bit like me."

The accent – Cockney, not Peter Sellers-type Indian – also matched the police circulation. Cole asked them both to come with him to the police station.

"I'd rather not," said the man. "We're going to buy a ring."

Cole insisted, and, since this was a murder case, he took no chances. He searched the man, there and then. Finding no weapons, he marched the couple off towards a police telephone box in Cambridge Circus. An off-duty constable in civilian clothes saw what was happening and telephoned for a police car while Cole stood guard over his prisoners. Both the man and the girl repeatedly asked to be allowed to go; they were in a hurry, they said. Which merely intensified Cole's suspicions. Then a car arrived and whisked them away to Bow Street.

The young man was half-Indian, half-English, and gave his name as Edwin Bush. He was just twenty-one years old. As soon as he arrived at Bow Street impressions were taken of the soles and heels of his shoes. While these were being compared with the marks found under the body Pollard questioned the girl.

She was seventeen and had known Bush for about two months, and had come into the West End with him that day to choose an engagement ring. As it was also his twenty-first birthday, they were going to have a double celebration at an Indian restaurant.

She denied ever having been to the antique shop in Cecil Court, and, oddly enough, she was telling the truth. As we discovered later, the girl who had accompanied Bush was his sister, aged eighteen and not blonde at all but very dark. It was sheer luck that, because Meier wrongly thought she had been fair, the description happened to fit the couple whom Cole picked out from the crowd in Old Compton Street.

While Pollard questioned the girl, detectives called at Bush's home. His mother said he had left the house at 7.30 am on March 3rd, presumably for work. When in due course Pollard asked him about his movements on March 3rd he immediately said that he had spent the whole of that morning at home with his mother. The shoe-prints matched.

Pollard told the duty officer at Bow Street that he wanted to hold an identification parade. This was easier said than done, since it involved collecting nine men of similar age and colour who could speak English without a foreign accent. Eventually a group was assembled, and the parade was held at 10.25 p.m. Meier walked down the line first. He stood for some time in front of Bush, then said, "I'm not positive, but I think this is the man." The gunmaker's son was brought in. He picked Bush with no hesitation at all.

Pollard then charged Edwin Bush with the murder of Mrs Batten. After a moment's silence Bush said, "The girl is nothing to do with it. I did it alone." And he went on to make a statement admitting that he had killed Mrs Batten in order to steal the sword. Just to clinch matters, there was blood on some of his clothes, and his palm-print and two of his fingerprints were found on the brown paper in which the sword had been wrapped.

When he came up for trial at the Old Bailey in May he pleaded not guilty to capital murder. He now said that he killed Mrs Batten, not to get the sword, but after she had made an offensive remark about the colour of his skin. Cross-examined by Mervyn Griffith-Jones, Bush didn't deny that he had in fact stolen the sword.

"You admit that you went into the shop in order to steal it, and admit that having stolen it you killed the lady with these three daggers?"

"Yes, sir."

"You lost your temper simply because she passed the remark, 'You niggers are all the same, you come in and never buy anything'?"

"Yes, sir."

In his summing up the judge instructed the jury that, if they believed this was the true cause of Bush's attack on Mrs Batten, they ought not to convict him of capital murder. They didn't believe it. After two hours' deliberation they found him guilty – which, the judge said afterwards, was the only possible verdict. Bush was hanged.

The result was a great deal of publicity for Identikit. The newspapers hailed it as a marvellous new aid to criminal investigation; and, sure as a Pavlovian reflex, some people expressed alarm at this new danger to civil liberties. How risky it would be, they said, to use composite pictures as evidence against an accused man! No-one, of course, had ever suggested using them as evidence. If an arrest was made as a result of circulating an Identikit picture the witnesses would then have to identify the suspect in the ordinary way. "If hopes were dupes, fears may be liars" – and *vice versa*. The apprehensions about Identikit were wholly unjustified, and the enthusiasm too was exaggerated. Identikit is simply a way – one way among several – of fixing, illustrating, and making permanent a witness's recollection, so as to help in the hunt for a wanted man when no photograph is available.

Its spectacular success in the Batten case proved a considerable

embarrassment. Too much was then expected of it. As people saw
more Identikit pictures, enthusiasm turned to ridicule. How odd,
they said, that all wanted men should look just the same! But to
policemen they don't look just the same; Identikit puts into
visible form what a police description is supposed to provide –
a catalogue of the few distinguishing marks which divide the
wanted face from all the other human faces.

In his report to me after the course Superintendent Du Rose
pointed out that one of the advantages, if Identikit were widely
adopted, would be that a telephone call to a central index – the
Criminal Record Office, perhaps – could by using a code of
numbers and figures pass a likeness to other forces without any
need to transmit the actual picture. It could be useful internationally, he suggested; and he arranged a demonstration for the
Chief Superintendents of C1, which includes the Interpol Office,
C9, and the Criminal Record Office. Identikit requires trained
operators, and he recommended that a phased scheme for its
introduction should be adopted as soon as possible.

The arrangement we eventually made was that the apparatus
itself remained the property of the American company, which
would lease the sets to the forces which wanted them. The
Receiver of the Metropolitan Police District agreed to act as
the hiring agent for all British forces. Whereupon we immediately ran into a bureaucratic snag. We became liable for import
dues, assessed by the Customs at an exorbitant figure. Not
without difficulty, we obtained special exemption.

The possibility of using Identikit internationally was debated
at length during the Interpol General Assembly in 1962. I
realized then for the first time how many comparable systems
were already in use. The Canadians, for example, had been using
cut-up photographs of their own criminals for years; and there
were several rival systems in the States. Advocates of these other
systems objected to the use of the word "Identikit" as though it
were a generic, instead of a brand, name. The Assembly did not,
in the end, recommend its international adoption, chiefly because
it wasn't applicable at the moment to non-Caucasian faces.

That anyone could genuinely have objected, on principle, to
the use of Identikit remains, to me, a great puzzle – or, at least, an

example of the attitude of mind which is incorrigibly and irrationally suspicious of the police. British courts and our rules of evidence provide the most scrupulous protection for the accused. To extend this proper care and start complaining that the police weren't "sporting" in the way they acquired the evidence is to tilt the whole balance of the law in favour of criminals, who aren't "sporting" at all. In some ways the Americans have gone even further in this direction than we have, declaring inadmissible any evidence, however damning, which wasn't acquired in strict accordance with the rules – with the ludicrous result that confessed murderers have had to be released because their confessions weren't taken in quite the proper form.

Telephone-tapping is another example. On both sides of the Atlantic this aid to investigation has roused strongly hostile feelings and has now been forbidden except in very special circumstances. The Metropolitan Police are allowed to intercept telephone calls only on the signed authority of the Secretary of State after application has been made by the Assistant Commissioner. Such nice regard for privacy no doubt does us credit, but is it really necessary? Innocent people have much more to fear from the unimpeded activities of criminals than from the remote possibility that the privacy of their telephone calls might one day be unobtrusively infringed by the police – an infringement far less embarrassing to their domestic secrets than the crossed lines which our beloved telephone system is for ever mischievously providing.

THE BITER BIT

(Gordon Hay, 1968)

George Saunders

The case of teenager Gordon Hay was remarkable because he was convicted on the evidence of the teeth-marks found on the body of his victim. Expert medical evidence clearly showed that the characteristics of the bite-marks were consistent in every detail with a dental impression taken from Hay. The trial judge, Lord Grant, described forensic dentistry as a relatively new science, "but there must, of course, always be a first time." George Saunders (1923–95) reported Hay's trial for The Scotsman, *the newspaper on which he worked as law reporter for some thirty years. He included this account in a collection of Scottish cases published shortly after his retirement in 1991.*

The science of forensic odontology was still in its infancy in March 1968 when Scottish legal history was made by the conviction of an eighteen-year-old approved schoolboy, Gordon Hay, known as "Gags", for the murder of a fifteen-year-old Biggar schoolgirl, Linda Peacock. The successful use of odontology to identify Hay as the murderer by the bite mark he left on the young girl's breast was hailed as "a forensic triumph." Scottish courts had always been slow to accept the latest advances in science but, surprisingly, showed a new receptiveness on this occasion to careful scientific evidence in what became a classic case of circumstantial evidence.

Even the presiding judge, Lord Grant, the late Lord Justice Clerk of Scotland, described the case as "unique, difficult and puzzling."

The eminent pathologist, Professor Keith Simpson, then head of the Department of Forensic Medicine at Guy's Hospital, London, and leading expert on odontology, gave evidence at the trial. He had the highest praise for the Scottish team, who produced crucial evidence and showed infinite patience and attention to detail. They produced, he said, the finest "bite mark" photography and dentition-matching that had yet been brought to court.

Both the Scottish experts, Detective-Inspector Osborne Butler and Dr Warren Harvey, who later became honorary consultant Forensic Odontologist to the Glasgow Police, were aware that their work on the case was vital. The only proof of the murderer's identity, their evidence survived a most searching cross-examination at the trial.

Linda Peacock, who was only 5ft 1in tall, was the youngest of eight children. She was a bright and lively girl, interested in ponies, records and, naturally at her age, boys. She spent the afternoon of Sunday, 6 August 1967 at a farm busy with her favourite pastime, exercising ponies.

Linda then spent the evening in the Lanarkshire market town of Biggar. Normally, she would have gone to her sister's home in Main Street to wait for one of her brothers to take her home.

But, on that fateful evening, her sister was on holiday. Linda set off to walk more than a mile to her home at Swaire Cottage. She was last seen talking to friends in the town about 9.30 p.m. Next morning, she was found strangled under a yew tree in St Mary's Cemetery, only 269 yards away from where she was last seen alive. The police said there were sadistic touches to the murder and a massive manhunt began. The cemetery in unlit Carwood Road was screened from the narrow road by a 5-foot-high wall. It was not locked at night and was often used by courting couples.

The murder hunt was led by Detective Chief Superintendent William Muncie, the head of Lanarkshire CID who had successfully led investigations into fifty murders, including those committed by mass murderer, Peter Manuel. He later became Assistant Chief Constable of Strathclyde before his well-earned retirement. Muncie's patience, clever reasoning and dogged determination had made him a legend in the force.

More than 100 officers from the Lanarkshire force and the Regional Crime Squad began a house-to-house search in the vicinity immediately after Linda was found. Tracker dogs were used in the surrounding fields and every male over fourteen in the area was interviewed. A young couple had been seen on the road near the cemetery at about 10.15 p.m., just after Linda, on her own, was seen by two men who knew her and waved to her as they drove home. A woman told the police she heard a scream coming from the cemetery late on the Sunday evening.

Police began compiling reports on the movements of inmates and ex-inmates of nearby Loaningdale Approved School. The small town itself was in the grip of fear lest the killer would strike again. A petition calling for the return of capital punishment was signed by 20,000 people.

Nine days after the crime, the police returned to the scene of the murder to comb the area inch-by-inch. The bereaved parents, George Peacock, a retired electrician, and his wife, Mary, made an impassioned plea to the public for information.

But the investigation into their daughter's death would prove to be a slow and painstaking forensic exercise, and Hay would not be arrested and charged with the murder until 110 days after the crime. The police interviewed more than 300 people, drawing up a short list of 29 who could possibly have been involved. All of the short-listed individuals agreed to dental impressions being taken. After these were compared with transparencies of the bite marks on the girl's breast, the list was reduced to five.

Second impressions were then taken of these five. Six weeks after the murder, the team of four dental experts told the authorities they had eliminated everyone on the list except for No 11. It was only at this stage that it was revealed to them, in confidence, that No 11 was in fact Gordon Hay.

A further impression was still required in order for the dental experts to be absolutely certain. The Crown then took the unique step of applying to Sheriff-Substitute Gordon Gillies, QC at

Lanark for a warrant to authorise a third impression of Hay's teeth. The warrant was granted.

Hay, by then, was the principal suspect but had not yet been arrested. For this reason, the legality of taking a third impression of his teeth would be fiercely contested at his trial.

Largely on the strength of the odontological evidence, Hay was charged with the murder of Linda Peacock. Appearing at a pleading diet at Lanark, he lodged a special defence of alibi. When his trial opened in the High Court in Edinburgh on Monday, 26 February 1968, before a jury of six women and nine men, the Crown listed 105 witnesses, including Professor Simpson and other dental and medical experts.

Hay pleaded not guilty to murdering Linda by striking her on the head with an instrument, biting her on the breast, tying a ligature round her wrist and her neck and strangling her. His special defence of alibi claimed that between 9 p.m. and midnight, when the crime was alleged to have been committed, he was in the approved school.

Prosecuting for the Crown was Mr Ewan Stewart, QC, then Solicitor-General for Scotland who had already established a reputation as a terrier of a prosecutor – probably the best prosecutor in Scotland for many years. His patient and sometimes aggressive cross-examinations had proved the downfall of many criminals. He was assisted by Mr Hugh Morton (later Lord Morton of Shuna, a judge in the Court of Session). For the defence there was an equally tenacious Stewart, Mr Ian Stewart, QC (later Lord Allanbridge), who was assisted by Mr James Law. Their battle over the medical evidence was to prove the highlight of the trial.

Lord Grant immediately ruled that no witnesses under seventeen should be named, adding that inmates of the approved school who were over seventeen should be treated in the same way.

Five local girls, all aged 15 or 16, told the court that girls had dates with boys from the school and that a pre-arranged signal – an owl hoot – was used to attract the attention of the boys when they were not meant to be out of the school. The boys, they said, got out of the school through the gymnasium.

One girl said Linda had a boyfriend in the school but he had left. Another girl recalled Linda speaking to Hay and another boy on Saturday, 5 August 1967 – the day before she was murdered – at a fun fair at Biggar.

The girls all said the boys at the school could come and go as they pleased, especially at weekends. One girl said she met boys from the school at the pictures on Saturday nights and went to dances at the school.

A sixteen-year-old boy who was a pupil at the school at the time said he was with Hay when they met Linda at the fun fair. Linda spoke to the boy but he walked on. Hay stayed behind, but his schoolmate did not know if he said anything to Linda. Afterwards, however, Hay told him he would not mind a night with her. Hay's schoolmate also described how some of the boys from the school had attended a camp at Montrose. After a beach barbecue on Friday, 4 August, the night before they returned, he saw one of the boys pick up a metal hook on the beach. On the evening of Linda's murder, at about 9 p.m. he saw Hay wearing pyjamas, a dressing gown and boots in his dormitory. He did not see Hay again that night.

But a fifteen-year-old boy who was also a pupil at the time said that when, after the murder, the police arrived at the school, Hay told him something like, "We were in the dorm all last night". He understood that this was what he was to tell the police, although it was not true.

Mr Ewan Stewart asked, "Were you invited by Hay to tell a lie?" The boy replied, "That was what it sounded like but I wasn't sure."

The boy remembered Hay going to the toilet in his pyjamas. Afterwards he fell asleep and woke up with the wireless playing. He did not know how long he had been asleep.

Cross-examined by Mr Ian Stewart, the boy said he had tried to get a date with Linda but failed. He also had written letters to her. Because of this he was a little bit worried. The police took away his clothes as well as those of Hay.

Two separate witnesses recalled hearing a scream from the cemetery about 10 p.m. A farmer's wife testified that she saw a couple standing in the cemetery, and had remarked to her husband that she had heard of courting couples in many places but not in a churchyard. A local farmer who had known Linda all her life stated that while passing Carwood Road in his van he had seen Linda. He had dogs in the back of his van and could not offer anyone in good clothes a lift; otherwise, he would have picked her up and taken her home.

Linda's father testified that on the day before her murder his daughter went to Huntfield to help with exercising ponies, returning home at about 4 p.m. The following day, Linda again went to Huntfield. He and his wife spent the day in Carluke. When they returned they found that their daughter was not at home. Worried, they contacted the police and a full-scale search began. Two constables found their daughter's body in the cemetery at 6.40 a.m.

She was lying partly under a yew tree beside a grave. A purse was near her head. There were bloodstains on the grass and blood on her head and cheek. A piece of string was found hanging from a nearby tree. Linda was lying on her back and her clothing was displaced. There was a deep weal round her neck which had broken the skin. Her anorak was bunched up under her head.

Detective-Sgt John Paton, who photographed the body, said there was bruising on the girl's breast which looked like bite marks. A doctor who examined the body said she was fully clothed but her upper garments had been drawn up, exposing the upper part of her body. Her lower garments were also drawn up. It appeared that a cord or string had been tightly tied round her neck.

Bank manager, Thomas Aitken, testified that while driving home he saw a young couple in his headlights near the cemetery. At home, he put on the television and heard Dickie Henderson introducing Frank Sinatra, Jun. on the *Blackpool Show*. He was later taken to Scottish Television's Glasgow studio where he saw a re-run of the programme, using a stop-watch to indicate the precise moment he first saw the programme. It showed that he first saw the programme about 10.20 p.m. It took 20 minutes to drive from the point where he had seen the young couple.

On the second day of the trial, a fifteen-year-old boy from Fife said he saw Hay in pyjamas, dressing gown and boots on the night of the murder. Later he saw the dressing gown and pyjamas lying on Hay's bed in the dormitory they shared. He fell asleep and was awakened by the door slamming. Hay was there with all his clothes on. His face was dirty and there was dirt on the knees of his jeans. His hair was dishevelled.

Another boy, who slept in the same dormitory, recalled finding a metal fishhook on the beach at Montrose. He brought it back to the school and put it on top of a wardrobe. He showed the hook to Hay, who said something about using it for fighting in Biggar.

He saw Hay that night taking part in a whilst drive. Later, he watched *The Untouchables* on the television until about 9.55 p.m. He then went back to his dormitory but there was no one there. Because of something he had been told he looked for the hook but could not find it. The last time he saw it was the day before, when he had shown it to Hay.

He saw Hay's dressing gown and pyjamas on his bed. Feeling worried, and anxious to find the hook, he searched for Hay. He went through the dormitories, the games room, sitting room and dining room but Hay was not there.

Returning with another boy from his dormitory at about 10.15, he saw that Hay's dressing gown and pyjamas were still on his bed. Roughly ten minutes later, the two boys went to sleep.

The boy's most dramatic evidence described how he was woken up by the sound of the door slamming: "I saw Gordon was there. He had his clothing on, light-coloured jeans and a school jersey. He had nothing on his feet but his socks. I don't think he knew I was awake.

"His face was dirty. His hair was as if he had been out in the wind. It was blown all over the place. It was just like he had been out working in the garden and sweating and he drew his hand across his face. His knees were a bit dirty, just like he had been kneeling down."

Hay put on his pyjamas and washed at the sink. He was acting quite normally. Just as he was getting into bed a member of the staff turned out the lights and said "Goodnight". Hay said "Goodnight" back. Hay's room-mate awoke later when a car arrived bringing back their housemother. The three boys in the dormitory went to the window and spoke to her.

Hay's room-mate asked him where he had been; Hay denied he had been anywhere. The boy told Hay he had been looking for him; Hay asked him where he had looked and then said he had been in the bathroom. The next day, the boy found the metal hook in the bottom of the wardrobe and put it back on top.

When he was cross-examined, the boy admitted he had told lies to Hay's solicitor and to the police but said he was now telling the truth. Immediately after the murder he was not prepared to say anything that would implicate Hay but he later changed his mind.

A twenty-three-year-old student, William Bennett, who was acting as temporary housemaster at the school that night, had been in charge of Hay's dormitory. He told the court how Hay had won a prize that night at a whist drive. Not later than 10.35 p.m. Bennett went to the dormitory to turn out the lights. Hay had said "Goodnight". After 9.20 p.m. the staff were patrolling to see that the boys were getting ready for bed.

The deputy headmaster, Clifford Davies, who was in charge that night, said he saw Hay in his dressing gown about 9.45 p.m. There was usually a check on the boys at 10 p.m. but there was no check that night because of the whist drive.

Three days after the crime, Hay was transferred to Rossie Farm Approved School, Montrose where, four days later, the police arrived to interview him. The headmaster, Mr John Henderson, insisted on being present as the police questioned Hay from 10 p.m. until 3.30 a.m. He was prepared to intervene, he told the court, if Hay were treated unfairly.

Asked if he had occasion to intervene, Mr Henderson replied "The boot was on the other foot. The boy was impertinent to the police. He was truculent and aggressive."

The boy was later taken away to Lanark and was brought back to Rossie Farm, the following evening. Hay claimed his nose had been injured but Henderson saw no sign of an injury. It was not unusual for approved schoolboys to hint that they had been mishandled by the police. Henderson found nothing to merit investigation.

Dr James Imrie, a lecturer in forensic medicine at Glasgow University who examined Linda Peacock's body at the cemetery and also carried out the post-mortem, told the court there was a ligature mark round her neck as well as bruising and the mark of a ligature on the left wrist. There was an area of bruising over the left breast. He thought it was caused by a bite.

There were white spots in the centre of the bruising on the breast. Asked what form of tooth would cause such a mark, Dr Imrie replied, "A tooth with a hollow in its cutting edge."

In the doctor's opinion, Linda had died between 10 p.m. and midnight. She was a virgin. On her left wrist there was blackening due to scorching as well as a blister. There were also two lacerations and bruising on her head. The doctor had found bloodstains on a grey shirt and trousers belonging to Hay. He said he had seen many bites in connection with sexual assaults and had tested for saliva with varying results. No saliva test was taken in this case. Even if it had been taken it might not have helped. There was no sign of wetness on the skin.

He had not considered the possibility of identifying the assailant as a result of the bite. If he had seen obvious teeth marks he would have considered it possible to identify the assailant. At the time, he said, they did not have it in mind to use the bite as a means of identification. If he had thought of this, he would have sent for a dentist to look at the breast.

When he was shown a metal hook, he agreed it could have caused the girl's injuries, although there were many other blunt instruments which could have done so.

On the third day of the trial, Lord Grant was accompanied on the Bench by Lords Walker and Milligan. The proceedings were interrupted by a three-hour debate on the question of whether evidence arising from the warrant to take impressions of Hay's teeth for the third time was admissible or not. Retiring for only five minutes following the debate, the judges returned to announce that the evidence was indeed admissible.

A week after Hay's conviction, Lord Grant issued a written judgment on this important ruling, which depended upon the judges' finding that the warrant authorizing the Crown to take impressions of Hay's teeth was valid. It had been argued that, since Hay was not present at the hearing of the petition for the warrant before the sheriff, it had been incompetently granted.

Given that the Crown did not ask Hay's permission to take the third impression, the warrant would be illegal if it had not been competently granted. Had Hay been under arrest at the time, different considerations would have applied.

There was no doubt that a warrant to search premises was not illegal merely because the person concerned had not been apprehended or charged. The defence position, however, was that a search of premises was a very different matter from the possibly forcible invasion of the privacy of the person. Nor were there any reported cases of a warrant being granted to search the person.

Lord Grant said that although he was not persuaded that the difference was a matter of principle rather than degree a warrant to search the person should be granted only in very exceptional circumstances. Even if he was wrong in holding the warrant to be competent, he would have admitted the evidence, for in this case, by his committal to an approved school, Hay had largely ceased to be the master of his movements. In these very special circumstances, the Sheriff-Substitute was, in Lord Grant's opinion, justified in granting the warrant.

By the fourth day of the trial, the Crown had clearly shown that Hay was not around the school at the time of Linda Peacock's death. There was, however, little other evidence pointing to Hay as the assailant – until Professor Simpson electrified the court by confidently asserting that it was Hay's teeth which had caused the bite mark on the girl's breast.

Professor Simpson testified that he had thirty years' experience in forensic medicine and was consultant to New Scotland Yard. He had no dental qualifications but he had lectured all over the world on forensic odontology, had published articles on the subject, and was currently head of the Department of Forensic Medicine at London University: impressive credentials to support the crucial evidence he was about to give.

The marks on the girl's breast. Professor Simpson stated, were undoubtedly human bite marks. There were four marks which he regarded as quite characteristic of the points of pressure of teeth.

A firm hold had been made and the teeth had made a very distinct impression. There was some degree of suction; the bite must have been a painful one. In more than thirty years' practice the professor had seen many bite marks, both in his own cases and in others shown to him. He had never seen a bite mark with better defined detail than this.

It was accepted and orthodox practice to make transparencies and superimpose them over photographs of the injuries printed to the same scale in order to see to what extent exact matching took place. The methods in the Hay case followed the usual pattern. Professor Simpson was shown photographs taken from plaster casts of Hay's teeth as well as transparencies superimposed on photographs of the bite marks. He told the court: "I have looked at these with the greatest of care, as I commonly have to do with instruments of any kind in relation to marks on the skin.

"I see on this couple of superimposed transparencies a number of points of comparison, two of which, in my experience, are quite remarkable and quite unique.

"I would say that these two marks, in their position and in their character, and the other kind of mark which shows a scraping of the skin surface, for which I would require some explanation, are three quite exceptionally detailed marks.

"The presence of these three in this position and with those details would carry me a long way towards feeling that this was an exact comparison. I would be satisfied that this set of teeth-whichever it was – was the set that caused those marks".

He was satisfied that Hay's teeth caused the bite marks on the girl's breast. Under cross-examination the professor said a saliva test was another test that could be applied in such cases. Some people excreted blood in their saliva and it might be possible to group the blood.

Mr Stewart said it was agreed by experts that it was easier to prove that bite marks were *not* caused by a particular suspect than to prove that they *were*. Professor Simpson replied that less trouble was entailed in excluding certain teeth. Others had to be studied more closely.

The court was told that in fingerprints sixteen points of comparison were required to conclusively identify a particular suspect. Asked if a similar claim could be made for forensic odontology, Professor Simpson replied that the number of points of comparison was not as great as in fingerprinting. There had been, for example, eight to ten points in an English case.

Detective Inspector Osborne Butler, of the Identification Bureau of Glasgow City Police, told the court that he went through the twenty casts of impressions of teeth taken from pupils and staff at Loaningdale and found that only No 11, belonging to Hay, fitted the marks found on the girl's breast. When he superimposed transparencies of Hay's teeth on the bite mark he found "a demonstrable matching." Hollows on the upper and lower canines, he said, corresponded with the bite mark.

During cross-examination, Detective Inspector Butler stated that the teeth marks were "probably unique." Asked if there would be any other teeth in Great Britain which could have made the marks, he replied, "I would be surprised to find that." Mr Stewart asked, "Are you going as far as to say this is conclusive?" Inspector Butler indicated no doubt when he replied, "In my view, due to the characteristics in the teeth, this is conclusive."

Evidence was then given by other dental experts, who described how plaster casts had been taken from teeth impressions at Glasgow Dental Hospital. Hay's dental record card was produced, showing he required four fillings. Large diagrams of his teeth were used in court to ensure the jury understood the technical aspects of the evidence.

Two policemen who timed a run from the yew tree in the cemetery back to the school said it took one minute 43 seconds.

Detective Superintendent James Weir said that Hay's attitude was "one of resentment" when he saw him at Rossie School. When he was asked to account for his movements, Hay said he had watched television, had a game of cards and then went up to the dormitory at about 10.15 p.m. Two boys were in the "dorm" when he went in. Weir told Hay that his statement was in conflict with other statements. Later, when he asked Hay if he had left the school that night, the boy replied, "No, I never left the school. I can't change my story now, sir."

The most dramatic evidence in the case came to light on the fifth day of the trial when Dr John Warren Harvey, lecturer in dental surgery at Glasgow University, entered the witness box.

He told the court how he had examined the canine teeth of no fewer than 342 junior soldiers two months after the murder. He was trying to ascertain whether any of their teeth compared with the bite marks on the dead girl.

He looked at more than 1,000 canine teeth in the mouths of the soldiers. Only two had pitted eye teeth and none had pits in opposite canine teeth. He spent more than 200 painstaking hours studying the 29 teeth impressions taken. Only the canine teeth of Hay corresponded with the peculiarly-shaped bite marks on the girl's breast.

Using himself as a guinea pig, Dr Harvey demonstrated to the jury various bite marks. By pressing a copper impression of Hay's canine teeth against his finger he produced the peculiar pale-centred mark which was found on the girl's body. Using a small stick he produced from his pocket, he showed the jury the mark left by a solid object. Then, using a ball-point pen, he showed the court the mark left by a hollow-ended object.

Using Hay's upper right canine tooth, he showed that it left a mark on his finger which was pale in the centre and reddened round about.

When asked by the Solicitor-General if he could go any further than saying it was *possible* that Hay's mouth caused the bite marks, Dr Harvey said, "I find it extremely difficult to conceive that another mouth would have this number of extraordinary characteristics."

He said there was a broken edge on one tooth and a hook effect where part of a filling was missing. These were remarkable characteristics when taken together. The mark just below the nipple was quite unlike any mark he had ever seen described in forensic literature.

Dr Harvey described how he had been contacted by Inspector Butler while on holiday in Ireland. Returning to Scotland, he was given twenty-nine plaster models of teeth from impressions. They were identified by number only.

He was able to eliminate 24, leaving 5, including, as it was later revealed, the impression of Hay's teeth. A second set of impressions was taken. From these, Dr Harvey was able to exclude another four – leaving only No 11. The small pits he found in the tips of the upper and lower canines were "quite dramatic and extraordinary." He had never seen marks made by teeth which left a pale centre. It was something quite unusual.

Re-examining all twenty-nine of the impressions taken, Dr Harvey found one set which answered the problem of the gaps and the abrasions or tears in the skin. The set which made these extraordinary marks was No 11.

It was at this stage that he decided to make perfectly certain by using different materials and techniques to obtain a third, more finely-detailed impression. A warrant to take the final impression of Hay's teeth was subsequently granted.

Under cross-examination, Dr Harvey told the court that 80 per cent of the people in court might have hollows in their teeth but these were completely different from the strange pits in Hay's teeth. Asked if he could exclude the possibility of another mouth in Great Britain making the bite marks, he said he would find it extremely difficult to believe that such a mouth existed.

After more than five hours in the witness box, the doctor was unshaken in his conviction that the bite marks on Linda Peacock's body were made by Hay.

On the sixth day of the trial, Gordon Hay spent more than two hours in the witness box. Looking perfectly cool, calm and collected, he strongly denied that he was out of the school on the night Linda Peacock was murdered. He did agree, however, that he had left the school a few times to meet girls when he was not supposed to be out. He also agreed that he told lies in several of the statements he made to the police. He denied that his two room-mates were his alibi. The two boys he claimed, were telling lies and Mr Davies, the deputy headmaster, must be mistaken if he said he last saw him at 9.45 p.m. that night. Hay told the court he had been convicted of breaking and entering at Aberdeen Sheriff Court in December 1966 and arrived at Loaningdale Approved School in January 1967. He said he had never been convicted of assault.

He had seen Linda Peacock in Biggar a couple of times but had never spoken to her. The day before she was murdered, he went with two other boys and a master to the pictures in Biggar; that evening, they went to a fair. A girl came across and spoke to one of the boys. He did not know her at the time but he now knew it was Linda Peacock. He did not speak to her at all. Asked if he had said he would not mind going out with Linda, Hay replied, "Yes."

Hay said that he remembered another boy producing a metal hook and saying he was going to get someone with it. He told the boy he would only get into trouble and took the hook from him and threw it on top of a cupboard. The next time he saw the hook was in court.

He also denied saying to anyone that he intended going to Biggar, and claimed never to have left the school at all that evening. He had won a prize at a whist drive in the school and, before supper, changed into a white shirt with his pyjama bottoms. He did not think he had a dressing gown on. He was wearing his boots as he did not like the school sandals. After supper, he watched *The Untouchables* on television, which finished at 9.55 p.m. He then went to the dining room to watch a game of cards. At 10.02 p.m. he spoke to another boy and they checked their watches. He spoke to another boy for ten or fifteen minutes, returning to his dormitory between 10.15 and 10.30 p.m. One of his room-mates was already there; the second came in afterwards.

They got into bed and a member of the staff turned out the lights. Later the boys spoke to the housemother when she arrived back by car and then listened to the radio, which was switched off about midnight. Hay denied having had a conversation the next day with one of the boys about what they would tell the police concerning the murder.

Hay recalled being visited by detectives at Rossie School after he had been transferred there. They greeted him: "Hello, Gordon. You weren't expecting to see us again, were you?"

They said to him in the presence of the headmaster: "We know you did it, Gordon. Why not admit it?"

When the detectives went out, Hay was left alone with the headmaster, who told him: "They know you did it. I know you did it. Why not admit it?"

After being taken to Lanark, he was returned to Rossie, where he told the headmaster, "My nose was skinned." The headmaster asked him what had happened and he told him a detective had hit him. He also told the headmaster the police banged his head against a wall a couple of times and put him in a cell. They kept trying to get him to admit it.

Mr Ewan Stewart, cross-examining, said, "You are just lying to try to blacken everyone?" But Hay denied this.

Hay agreed he had sneaked out of the school and back again without the staff finding out. But he denied he had his eye on Linda. He admitted he had not always told the same story about his movements that night.

During the rigorous cross-examination, Hay remained completely unruffled, putting on an altogether calm and convincing performance. Re-examined by his own counsel, he again denied he was out of the school that night and denied killing Linda.

On the final day of the hearing of evidence, a dental expert called for the defence threw a small spanner in the works when he cast doubt on the significance of the bite marks. Professor George Beagrie, Professor of Restorative Dentistry at Edinburgh University, said he found it difficult to determine what the Crown experts meant by their statements that defects in canine teeth were rare.

He had carried out an experiment with fifty teeth impressions from his own department and found teeth with pits similar to those which the Crown said Hay's teeth showed. He accepted that the bite mark could have been made by Hay but he did not feel it was beyond reasonable doubt. The incidence of defective canine teeth was greater than the Crown experts said. He felt that there could be other mouths in Great Britain that could have caused the bite marks.

Addressing the jury, the Solicitor-General said the case had "some unusual features". A certain amount of evidence against Hay was dental and pathological evidence concerning the bite marks. It was clear from the dental evidence, he said, that the only set of teeth out of the twenty-nine that could have made the bite was Hay's.

He said there was no criticism of Linda Peacock of a sexual character. She was not sexually promiscuous. The jury might think it was highly unlikely that she would go voluntarily into the graveyard with some stray tramp who just chanced to meet her on the road. She would only have accompanied someone she knew to that place.

Hay, he said, must have "worn the cloak of invisibility" for he had not been seen after 9.50 p.m. by six of the masters at his school. His alibi should thus be rejected, root and branch.

When he came to deal with forensic odontology, Mr Stewart said: "We are not dabbling in some kind of experimental matter. There have been cases on the Continent and in England in which this form of identification has been used. But even supposing there were other people with this kind of mouth existing in the world or even in Britain, how many of these people had on August 5 been expressing a sexual interest in Linda Peacock? How many were living within two minutes of the cemetery? How many were sneaking back into their beds about ten minutes after the murder with their hair blown about and dirt on their faces and clothing? How many had in their possession an instrument such as a hook? How many of these people were next day trying to get their friends to tell lies? There is only one verdict here which an objective and just appraisal and evaluation of the evidence can lead to – a verdict of guilty."

Mr Ian Stewart, for the defence, said this was the first case of its kind in Scotland in which forensic odontology had been used. In Britain this science was in its infancy. Sixteen characteristics were required in fingerprints but that was not the case here. In Britain, he said, the experience of the dental profession was very limited in this type of case. Only one dentist had said it was beyond reasonable doubt that Hay's teeth caused the bite marks.

The fact that Hay had lied on occasion and may have lied in evidence did not make him the murderer, Mr Stewart argued. If the Crown broke Hay's alibi that still did not make him the murderer. The evidence for the Crown was circumstantial; the case was balanced "on a knife edge." The only evidence that connected Hay with the crime and, moreover, with the scene of the crime, was related to bite marks.

In his two-hour charge to the jury, gravel-voiced Lord Grant warned that circumstantial evidence was not enough to convict Hay. "For that reason," he said, "the dental and pathological evidence is of paramount importance. This forensic odontology, as it is called, is a relatively new science but there must, of course, always be a first time."

Lord Grant reminded the jury that scientific and medical knowledge advanced as the years went on. It was only comparatively recently that fingerprints had come to be accepted as infallible. It was only in 1945 that palm prints had been recognized. It was of importance that the law should keep pace with science.

Lord Grant said that the case was, as well as a grave one, in some ways unique, difficult and puzzling. But he thought it right to say that he and the jury had been assisted in their task by the way in which it had been prepared and also by the admirable presentation by the Solicitor-General, Mr Ewan Stewart and his colleague, Mr Ian Stewart, for the defence.

Lord Grant pointed out to the jury that even if Hay had told lies that was not sufficient to establish his guilt. They must therefore examine the evidence on the bite marks with care and in the light of their assessment of the expert witnesses. In assessing the evidence, he continued, the jury should keep in mind that the Crown experts had both made a special study of forensic odontology. The two experts for the defence, on the other hand, were being pushed rather beyond the field where their own expert knowledge lay.

The judge's dismissal of the defence experts' evidence was probably a crucial factor in the jury's deliberations and must have removed any doubts in their minds about the strength and weight of the scientific evidence for the Crown.

After an absence of two and a half hours, the jury returned a majority verdict of Guilty. The judge ordered Hay to be detained during Her Majesty's pleasure as he was under eighteen when he committed the crime.

Hay showed no emotion as he was led away. Sitting in court were his grey-haired mother, Mrs Hannah Hay, and the mother of his victim, Mrs Mary Peacock.

Mrs Hay said afterwards that her husband, Robert, a farm labourer, died on the day after Gordon's sixteenth birthday. "Up till then, Gordon was fairly happy and content but I think his dad's death had an effect on him. After that, I saw an awful change in my boy. He seemed to go completely off the rails."

Gordon wrote to his mother twice a week while he was awaiting trial. His mother said: "I always looked forward to his letters. He's my son and I can forgive him although I can never believe he did this terrible thing. I will stand by him."

Gordon Hay was a country-born boy who loved cars and often boasted about girlfriends. His love of cars got him into trouble and led to him being sent to an approved school. He danced well and was admired by the girls but friends said he was basically a loner.

Linda's parents, however, could never forget or forgive. Her father said afterwards the school should never have been in Biggar at all and that he would support any move to have it closed down.

Mrs Peacock spoke of her ordeal and her bitterness. "Linda was a lovely young girl whose life was cut short viciously by a boy from that school," she said.

It was the third time that tragedy had struck the Peacock family. Two years earlier, Linda's elder sister died after an illness and a year before that her uncle, a ship's cook, drowned in a dockside accident in England.

Hay's appeal two months later in the Court of Criminal Appeal in Edinburgh was heard by a bench of five judges because of the important legal question of whether the sheriff had the right to issue the warrant to take further teeth impressions from Hay before he was charged.

Lord Clyde, Lord Justice General, presided with Lords Guthrie, Migdale, Cameron and Johnston.

Mr Ian Stewart, in a strong argument, contended that the dental evidence obtained under the warrant was inadmissible and was prejudicial to Hay. The police were not entitled to search the person of a suspect before arrest, he claimed. His argument was particularly concerned with the search of a person as a means of identification rather than to find objects in his possession.

Police powers on identification were limited to such observation as was possible without interfering with the person. Interference with the person without consent and before the individual's arrest was technically as assault. It was a principle of Scottish criminal law that you could not search a person before arresting him.

Mr Stewart argued that there is always a conflict between the rights of an individual and the rights of the state. The right of the state to override the rights of the individual was a matter on which Parliament alone should legislate; it was not for the court to overrule a principle of personal liberty established for many years.

The Solicitor-General argued for the Crown that although the warrant in question was unique there was nothing unlawful about it. If the court could not accept that proposition, the circumstances in the case were such that an irregularity fell to be excused.

Moreover, there was a general power for magistrates to grant warrants for the advancement of the course of justice. In the present case, there had been insufficient evidence to put Hay on trial and the Crown wished to confirm further evidence. The warrant, the Solicitor-General argued, was perfectly valid in the special circumstances. There was no unfairness. Everything was done in the public interest and in the interests of the accused.

The five judges rejected the appeal and on 30 May 1968 gave their reasons. Lord Clyde said that although Hay was not present or legally represented at the hearing for the warrant, the presence of an independent judicial officer, such as the sheriff, afforded the basis for a fair reconciliation of the interests of the public in the suppression of crime and of the individual, who was entitled not to have the liberty of his person or premises unduly jeopardised.

The hearing before the sheriff was by no means a formality; the court had to be satisfied that the circumstances justified the unusual course that had been taken and that the warrant was not too wide or oppressive. The sheriff was the safeguard against the granting of too general a warrant. A warrant of this limited kind would, however, be granted only in special circumstances.

The judge held that the warrant was quite legal and the resulting evidence therefore admissible. Apart from anything else, there was in this case an element of urgency; a visit to the dentist or an injury to Hay's teeth could have destroyed the evidence.

After the conviction, there was a public outcry against the approved school. Biggar Town Council demanded it should be closed immediately or, at least, that the whole staff from the headmaster down should be changed. Provost James Telfer said that since 1963, when Loaningdale opened, the town had wanted a public inquiry into the running of the school. "We got it during the trial. The security there was terrible," he said.

In 1965, the Town Council, worried by a spate of petty crimes, demanded a meeting with the school's board of managers. It was an experimental school set up to rehabilitate young boys. A spokesman for the Scottish Education Department said at the time that it was not a penal institution to keep children permanently out of the community. Only boys who were thought capable of returning to society in a matter of months were to be admitted to the school.

Security at Loaningdale was tightened in January 1968, after the council met Mr Bruce Millan, the Under-Secretary of State responsible for education. A night alarm system was installed to alert staff to any break-out. If any boy left the school without permission he was immediately sent to a stricter establishment. But Councillor James Stephen summed up the feelings of local people when he said, "There is no doubt that this experiment has failed. You cannot cure a bad boy by permissiveness. And when prizes of cigarettes are given out at whist drives and thirteen-year-olds are allowed to smoke, the whole thing is ridiculous."

The headmaster, who was on holiday at the time of the murder, was in favour of trying to rehabilitate young offenders. He allowed smoking in the school and allowed the boys to call masters by their Christian names. He recommended Hay's transfer to another school because he did not think he was suitable for Loaningdale.

Provost Telfer, who joined the board of the school in 1965 after the first row, said, "If it was left to the people of Biggar, it would be closed immediately. There is a tremendous amount of ill-feeling in the town about it. Since the murder, there has been a fantastic amount of complaints by people who have not voiced them before."

Councillor Stephen, who canvassed more than 20,000 signatures for his petition calling for the return of the death penalty, said the Loaningdale experiment – it was the first "open" type of school in Scotland – had failed lamentably. The petty dictators of St Andrews House, he said, had decreed it would be sited at Biggar regardless of local feeling.

A spokesman for the Social Work Services Group at the Scottish Office said: "There have been, and always will be, enormous difficulties in rehabilitating young people who have been out of step with society. It is difficult to talk about success or failure in a social education context."

At the time, there were 36 boys in Loaningdale: 31 for theft, 3 for truancy and 2 for road traffic offences. This did not suggest the school was harbouring would-be killers.

After the meeting with Mr Millan, two more local people, a doctor and a minister, were added to the board of the school, of which Lord Birsay was chairman.

A Government spokesman summed up the difficulties of rehabilitation when he said: "Selection is a basic part of the experiment. A boy's record, IQ, family history and condition are all considered. In addition, great weight is given to an assessment of the willingness of a family to co-operate in treatment and of inter-family relationships."

Linda Peacock's parents at first considered suing the Scottish Education Department, who were responsible for selection of the boys sent to the school. Eventually, however, they accepted £2,000 compensation from the Criminal Injuries Board.

Mrs Peacock said:

The money is no compensation for Linda's life. We are more interested in punishment for all those responsible for the negligent system that led to her death. We had considered a civil action but have now dropped that as the only measure a civil court might take would be to award damages, which is little comfort to us.

Writing in the Glasgow Police magazine some time later, Dr Warren Harvey, in an article called "The Tooth, the Whole

Truth and the Police" revealed that twenty-five dentists were now linked with the police in Aberdeen, Dundee, Edinburgh and Glasgow to help in criminal cases. When a victim is bitten, Harvey wrote, the marks must be seen at the first possible moment by a dentist, a police photographer and a pathologist. He pointed out that the Biggar murder trial verdict was by a majority of 14 to 1 and that about one third of the 1,100 foolscap pages in the transcript of the evidence consisted of dental and medical evidence.

But, a few years later, allegations by an internationally known expert on forensic odontology, Dr Soren Keiser-Nielsen of the Department of Forensic Odontology at the Royal Dental College in Copenhagen, cast a slight shadow over the new science. He alleged that he came to Scotland before the trial but his evidence had been "hushed up" and he had been hurriedly got out of the way. In a letter to the Forensic Society's journal, he said he concluded there was nothing in the mark on the victim's breast to indicate it was a bite mark. Even if it were, he added, there were too few points of similarity to warrant a dental identification of the originator. He had explained his reasoning and conclusions, and asked whether the fact he had drawn conclusions adverse to the Crown case would come to the notice of the defence.

But the Crown revealed that the doctor had considered the evidence insufficient to justify a firm conclusion on identification and had declined to give evidence. Counsel for the defence had accordingly been informed by the Crown that Dr Keiser-Neilsen was not willing to give evidence.

The Crown also said the doctor's views expressed at the time did not match the views he expressed later. He had undoubtedly withdrawn, declining to give evidence. Mr Alistair R. Brownlie, Secretary of the Society of Solicitors in the Supreme Courts of Scotland, strongly denied the doctor's allegations. The doctor, Mr Brownlie maintained, had indicated he wanted nothing more to do with the case and was therefore not called as a witness. The police who drove him to the airport were merely exercising the customary courtesies. The doctor was not, as he later claimed, hurriedly got out of the way.

But the controversy still did not die down. Keiser-Nielsen

insisted in 1972 that the mark on Linda Peacock's breast was not a human bite mark. Hay's counsel, Mr Ian Stewart, recalled being told the doctor was not prepared to come and give evidence and that there was no point in calling him as a witness if he was unwilling to come.

 While there is little likelihood of compulsory dental examination becoming a standard feature of Scottish pre-trial criminal procedure, the courts clearly recognised the exceptional nature of the case in approving the warrant to take the vital third impression of Hay's teeth. The power given to the prosecution to secure that important evidence from the previously inviolable person of the suspect might well be used again if the course of justice demands it.

Had genetic fingerprinting, which has been hailed as the greatest breakthrough in forensic science this century, been available at that time, even more conclusive proof might well have been provided by the scientists.

ACKNOWLEDGMENTS AND SOURCES

The editor is grateful to Jonathan Goodman and Wilf Gregg for putting at his disposal their encyclopaedic collections of true-crime books containing many of the cases featured.

He would also like to thank the following people and organizations for their kind permission to reprint the following:

Albert Borowitz for *The Medea of Kew Gardens Hills* from *The Lady Killers*, ed. Jonathan Goodman (Piatkus, London 1990, © Albert Borowitz 1990). Reproduced by permission of the author;

Jonathan Goodman for *The Jigsaw Murder Case* from *Medical Murders* (Piatkus, London 1992, © Jonathan Goodman 1992). Reproduced by permission of the author;

Miss Lois Gribble for Leonard Gribble (writing as Leo Grex), *The Mystery of the Flying Blood* from *Mystery Stranger than Fiction* (Robert Hale Ltd., London 1979, © Leonard Gribble 1979);

Max Hastings for Macdonald Hastings, *The Murderer Who Got Away With It* from *The Other Mr Churchill* (Harrap, London 1963, © Macdonald Hastings 1963);

Sir Ludovic Kennedy for *The Birmingham Six* from *Truth To Tell* (Bantam Press, London 1991, © Sir Ludovic Kennedy 1991). Reproduced by permission of the author;

Clifford L. Linedecker for *The Vampire Rapist* from *Serial Thrill Killers* (Knightsbridge Publishing Company, New York 1990, © Clifford L. Linedecker 1990). Reproduced by permission of the author;

Mrs Shirley Lucas for Norman Lucas, *A Case of "Hideous Ferocity"*

Leslie Hale, *Physicians, Heal Yourselves* in *Hanged in Error* (Penguin Books, London 1961);

Percy Hoskins, *The Poisoner* in *The Sound Of Murder* (John Long, London 1973);

Sir Richard Jackson, *Picture a Murderer* in *Occupied With Crime* (Harrap, London 1967);

Robert Jackson, *A Welsh Mummy* in *The Crime Doctors* (Frederick Muller, London 1966);

John Laurence, *The Jekyll And Hyde Of New York* in *Extraordinary Crimes* (Sampson Low, Marston and Co. Ltd., London nd);

C. Ainsworth Mitchell, *Murder By Accident* in *A Scientist In The Criminal Courts* (Chapman & Hall Ltd., London 1945);

Edmund Pearson, *The Firm of Patrick & Jones* in *Five Murders* (The Crime Club, New York 1928);

David Rowan, *"Act of Mercy"* in *Famous American Crimes* (Panther, New York 1957);

Professor Keith Simpson, *A Riddle Of Maggots* in *Forty Years of Murder* (Harrap, London 1978);

Sir Sydney Smith, *The Case of Sidney Fox* in *Mostly Murder* (Harrap, London 1959);

Tom Tullett, *A Ray Of Sunlight Unmasks A Killer* in *Strictly Murder* (The Bodley Head, London 1979).